Managing the Built Environment in Hospitality Facilities

Thomas Jones
University of Nevada, Las Vegas

Dina Marie V. Zemke
Cornell University

Prentice Hall
Upper Saddle River, NJ 07458

Library of Congress Cataloging-in-Publication Data

Jones, Thomas J. A.
  Managing the built environment in hospitality facilities / Thomas Jones, Dina Zemke.
    p. cm.
  Includes bibliographical references and index.
  ISBN-13: 978-0-13-513574-7 (alk. paper)
  ISBN-10: 0-13-513574-5 (alk. paper)
  1. Hotels—Maintenance and repair. 2. Restaurants—Maintenance and repair. 3. Building management.
I. Zemke, Dina Marie V. II. Title.

TX928.Z46 2010
647.94—dc22   2008045458

Editor in Chief: Vernon Anthony
Acquisitions Editor: William Lawrensen
Editorial Assistant: Lara Dimmick
Project Manager: Renata Butera
Operations Specialist: Deidra Schwartz
Creative Director/Designer: Jayne Conte
Cover image/photo: Nigel Hicks/Dorling Kindersley Media Library
Director of Marketing: David Gesell
Marketing Manager: Leigh Ann Sims
Marketing Assistant: Les Roberts
Copyeditor: Christine E. Wilson

This book was set in 10 pt Palatino by GGS Higher Education Resources, A Division of Premedia Global, Inc. and was printed and bound by STP COMMAND WEB. The cover was printed by STP COMMAND WEB.

Pearson Education Ltd., London
Pearson Education Singapore Pte. Ltd.
Pearson Education Canada, Inc.
Pearson Education—Japan

Pearson Education Australia Pty. Limited
Pearson Education North Asia Ltd., Hong Kong
Pearson Educación de Mexico, S.A. de C.V.
Pearson Education Malaysia Pte. Ltd.

Prentice Hall
is an imprint of

www.pearsonhighered.com

10

ISBN-13: 978-0-13-513574-7
ISBN-10: 0-13-513574-5

Dedication

The authors wish to thank their families for their unwavering support during the writing of this work.

CONTENTS

  Incinerators 85

  Other Waste Transformation Systems 87

  Recycling 89

  Reuse 94

  Source Reduction 95

Hazardous Materials Handling and Disposal 96

  OSHA's Hazard Communication Standard 97

  Bloodborne Pathogen Standard 100

  *Summary 100 • Key Terms and Concepts 100 •
  Discussion and Review Questions 101*

Chapter 5 Water Systems 102

Introduction 102

Water Terms 103

Water Sources and Delivery Systems 103

  Water Supply—City or Well? 104

    CITY WATER 104

    WELL WATER 104

  Water Supply Distribution Systems 104

    CONSTANT PRESSURE SYSTEMS 104

    GRAVITY-FED, OR DOWNFEED, SYSTEMS 104

  **Removal of Wastewater: Storm Sewer and Sanitary
    Sewer Systems 107**

  Sanitary Sewer Systems 108

    CITY SEWERS 108

    SEPTIC SYSTEMS 108

    SEWER GASSES 110

    TOILETS 110

    SINKS 110

Water Quality 111

  What Do Guests Expect? 111

Heating Water 111

  Distributing Domestic Hot Water 115

  How Hot Should Domestic Hot Water Be? 115

    FIXTURES WITH ANTI-SCALD DEVICES 116

Swimming Pools, Spas, and Water Features 117

  Swimming Pools 117

    POOL CHEMISTRY 117

    CHEMICAL BREAKDOWN 117

    OZONE SYSTEMS 117

PREFACE

WHY HOSPITALITY FACILITIES MANAGEMENT?

Teaching facilities management in a hospitality program is challenging. Those of us who teach it face a classroom of students who have never considered the facility itself (other than on a cosmetic level) and who generally have no prior knowledge of how buildings work. Students are often confused about why they need to learn about "how stuff works" when they will most likely never hold the Chief Engineer's position.

Buildings and land comprise two of the largest assets on hospitality businesses' balance sheets. As for operating the building, a hotel generally spends about 10–12% of gross revenue to maintain the property and pay for utilities. An additional 3–7% (or more) is set aside each year to cover capital improvements to the building. While restaurants' expenses in this area are somewhat lower, the nearly 20% of gross revenue each year provides a compelling reason for any new manager in hospitality to be familiar with the asset that is consuming this money.

WHY THIS BOOK?

This textbook was written to serve an undergraduate hospitality management student audience in both two-year and four-year colleges. Graduate students with no previous experience in building management are also an appropriate audience. We undertook this project because we have both found that the texts available for this subject matter were either too technical for our students or the textbook was obsolete. The limited options available prompted us to respond to our own request: produce a textbook suitable for our audience.

Our combined experience in education and hospitality operations drives the format of this text. We have provided what we believe hospitality management students need at the beginning of their careers. The book will not teach any student how to perform repairs, install mechanical systems, or serve as the chief engineer in a hospitality property. The book will, however, provide the student with basic knowledge of how facilities form the core product of our industry, how systems work, and how to communicate with a good vocabulary with facilities management staff, asset manager, and vendors or contractors. This basic knowledge provides a foundation from which the student can expand his or her understanding of a particular facility. Most importantly, the student will be able to ask the right questions (using the correct technical terms) and take the right steps to control costs and contribute to the bottom line of any facilities-intensive business.

ORGANIZATION OF THE BOOK

This book is organized into three parts. The first part, "The Impact of Facilities Management," provides a broad overview of various perspectives on the facility's role in hospitality, information on how the facility is managed, and current issues and trends. The second part, "Building Systems," introduces the student to the building and mechanical systems that control the built environment of the property. The third part, "Building Planning and Design," provides an overview of building exterior systems.

Each chapter includes information on energy conservation and sustainable built environment practices. We also emphasize the importance of ensuring the safety of all building occupants and complying with the ever-changing codes and regulations. Ignoring or violating these important aspects of facilities management not only exposes a business to enormous liability, cost, and bad publicity, but also violates the basic spirit of hospitality. Our goal is to ensure that students go forth into the hospitality industry not only providing excellent products and service, but also providing them in the most ethical and cost-effective way possible.

ACKNOWLEDGMENTS

The authors would like to thank the following businesses, associations, and individuals for their cooperation and guidance. For without their assistance, this work would not have been possible. To Professor Ernest R. Weidhaas at The Pennsylvania State University for allowing us to reproduce his architectural renderings from *Reading Architectural Plans* published by Prentice Hall. To Mr. Scott Steinbach, Director of Facilities at Circus Circus, Las Vegas, Nevada, for allowing us to photograph his property and use his department's business forms. A special debt of gratitude goes to Dr. Arthur Weissman at Green Seal, Mr. Roger Frost at the International Organization for Standardization, Mr. John Polak at TerraChoice Environmental Services Inc., Carole Jakes at EcoLogo, Diane Dulmage at Scientific Certification Systems, and Jennifer Schill at the U.S. Green Building Council for providing figures for the book and also some much needed editorial advice. A debt is also owed to Tim King at Certified Fire Protection, Inc., Las Vegas, Nevada, and Amy Dougherty at Hobart Service in Las Vegas, Nevada, for providing photographs and technical advice. We are extremely grateful for the assistance of Jared Stinnett, Director of Facilities at the Las Vegas Hilton, for providing us with the opportunity to photograph his property at length. Thanks too, to Vic Nowak who allowed us onto his construction site to take photos. Thanks to Rebecca Borgony at American Metals Market for allowing us to use the recycled goods and composite prices that are in the text. Mr. Kim Kirkendall at MGM-Mirage was particularly instrumental in solving some last-minute problems associated with the work. Without his assistance, the work surely would have been delayed for weeks.

A sincere note of thanks goes out to Adrian Lark and Adam Blaskeslee for their significant contributions to this text. Thanks to the following publishing houses, Creative Publishing International, Inc./Black and Decker, Cengage Learning/Delmar Learning and John Wiley & Sons, Inc. for allowing us to use materials from their authors' works. Otis Elevator Company was extremely gracious in providing us with numerous photographs and rendering. Thanks to the Building Owners and Managers Institute (BOMI), the U.S. Environmental Protection Agency, and the Department of Energy for their resources and assistance.

Many thanks to our reviewers: Mike DiVecchio, Central Pennsylvania College; Bo Hu, San Francisco State University; and Terry Moran, Pennsylvania Culinary Institute—Le Cordon Bleu.

Finally, thanks to the University of New Hampshire, Cornell University, and the University of Nevada, Las Vegas, for their assistance with this textbook.

The Impact of Facilities Management

1

The Study of Facilities Management

"Once your consciousness has been raised it cannot be lowered."

—CHEERIOS BOX TOP

CHAPTER OBJECTIVES

After studying the chapter, the student should be able to:

- describe from memory the various rationales given for the study of facilities management.
- identify the concerns students have regarding the study of facilities management.
- identify impediments to understanding the role the building plays in the profitability and continued success of the hospitality organization.

STUDENT PERSPECTIVES

Traditionally, most hospitality students approach the study of the **building envelope** with mixed emotions. The facility management field is completely foreign to most. Even though students have spent their entire lives inside buildings, they are, for the most part, unaware of how buildings are constructed, how they operate, and their impact on occupants.

Many students also do not have a basic understanding of elementary physics. Every semester for over a decade, this instructor has asked college students questions (Figure 1.1) regarding basic scientific principles and every semester no more than a few come up with an appropriate response.

This is not to suggest that students are at fault. An emphasis on science-related curricula seems to be lacking in many elementary and secondary schools. Few students take a physics course in high school, and even fewer take one in college. In addition, most have never been exposed to

When you open the front door in the winter, does the heat rush out or does the cold rush in?
Why do people perspire?
How do we make electricity?
How does a refrigerator work?
Name three ways heat is transmitted?
What does "thermodynamics" mean?
In a fire is it hotter on the floor where the fire is, or near the ceiling?

FIGURE 1.1 Questions Posed to Facilities Management Students.

any aspect of building operations—in the classroom, on the job, or at home. The importance of the building as an asset to a company, its contribution to corporate profitability, and its role in human health, comfort, safety and security, has not crossed their radar screen—until they find themselves in this course.

So, as you begin the study of this rigorous and sometimes frustrating field, give it a chance. Do not commit one of the four common, but fatal, assumptions. (Figure 1.2). Rather, approach this subject with an inquiring and open mind. The study of facilities management has rewards for those who persevere, but those rewards may not be immediately self-evident. The payback comes when you are in management and the building and its operation directly impact you and your well-being.

1. This course does not pertain to me or what I do. I'm in (choose one: food & beverage, front desk, housekeeping, human resources, meetings and convention management, sales & marketing, etc.), and all of this is the responsibility of the engineering department.
2. I can't hope to understand this stuff. This is for people with a mechanical aptitude, and I'm a girl.
3. My forte is people—not things. I'm a people person and I will never understand any of these things.
4. All of this facilities stuff may be important, but it is so deadly boring I can't stand it.

See the following responses to the above objections.

1. The day of separate departmental "fiefdoms" in the modern hotel is long gone. Managers who insist on perpetuating the myth of separate and distinct operating responsibilities will find themselves "long gone" too. Today, interdepartmental task forces or process improvement teams, and the concept of shared responsibilities are the new status quo.
2. That excuse faded by the 1960s. There are no inherent sex biases in the comprehension of knowledge in this field. Have you been in "suspended animation" in a time capsule for the last 40 years?
3. Then get ready to spend your entire career on the front lines as a dining room host seating patrons for dinner. Being a good manager takes far more than a winning smile and a pleasant disposition.
4. So is wage and salary administration, but when it impacts your employees' paychecks, it becomes a critical issue to them and you. If you are bored, ask yourself why you are bored. Is it because you are still not convinced that this knowledge is important to you career? Perhaps, trying to find the answer to why you are bored will cause you not to be bored? Once you do find the answer, share it with your instructor and your fellow students. They may help you to change your attitude and conquer your boredom. And remember, bored people are typically boring people.

FIGURE 1.2 Four Fatal Assumptions.

However, your instructor and this textbook will attempt to demonstrate the importance of the material presented in this course, which will help you be successful as a manager. In fact, later in this chapter the focus of this book—its limitations and its objectives—will be outlined in detail in the section entitled, *A Balanced Approach*.

Finally, an overwhelming majority of hospitality students do not consider this department to be a suitable port-of-entry into the industry, and they're right. Ninety-nine percent of all of the students graduating from a school of hospitality management will never be a member of the engineering department, but this does not imply students are relinquished from their responsibilities to the engineering function. They will face engineering challenges throughout their career no matter what their area of expertise and the frequency of these challenges will only increase as they advance up their personal career ladder.

INDUSTRY PERSPECTIVES

The role of the facility in the continued profitability and well-being of the business is commonly, if not universally, recognized by those in the hospitality industry. This is demonstrated by the presence of the chief engineer on the general manager's "executive committee" and the existence of a vice president of facilities at the corporate level in many hotel organizations. Moreover, many large hotel companies have regional or district facility managers providing assistance to facility personnel at the unit level.

Unfortunately, the importance of the engineering function is not properly communicated to all employees in many firms, and there are still people who are "compartmentalized" in their approach to their jobs. They are compartmentalized in the sense that they believe engineering functions are, *not my job*. However, as Group Director of Engineering, Max Fankhanel of Shangri-La Hotels, said about the challenge of energy management, "The old school that considered energy conservation the responsibility of engineering is dead. It is everyone's responsibility, from the GMs on down." It has been said that the "boiler room" has a problem in getting their message across to the "board room." In other words, engineering is composed of "doers" not communicators. Engineers are often not conversant in *exec speak*. That is, they do not know how to explain their position in terms that executives (e.g., CEO's, COO's and CFO's) can relate to and appreciate.

Conversely, top management and others in the organization may not give due credit to engineering for their accomplishments. Engineering often falls prey to Frederick Hertzberg's infamous "hygiene" factor phenomenon. When they do everything right, it prompts no response and only when things go awry do others take notice. Water was Hertzberg's classic example. "When water is present, he stated, one's thoughts do not dwell on water—it does not motivate anyone—but when it is not present, or present in insufficient amounts, it becomes a demotivator." Engineering provides many hygiene factors such as upkeep, light, air, warmth, and, of course, water. Only when these are not present, or present in insufficient quantities, do employees and guests become upset.

Another factor is, frankly, ignorance—ignorance of the role of the chief engineer and the operation of the various engineering systems. Many employees and guests actually believe the primary duties of the department are to change light bulbs and unplug toilets. This ignorance of what the department does sometimes extends to the executive suite.

Some years ago, a chief engineer at a large Midwestern hotel boasted to this author's class that if he wanted, he could walk into his GM's office and ask for (and get) a check for a quarter of a million dollars. All he would have to do is tell the boss, "The chiller's kaput." He said his GM had no idea what a chiller was other than it had something to do with building cooling and furthermore, he really didn't want to know any more than that.

Unfortunately, far too many executives do not fully understand the role of engineering in the preservation of assets. Too many times, engineering (and housekeeping) find their budgets cut because they represent two of the largest budgets found in any hotel. Sometimes management does not or refuses to comprehend the ramifications when these departments' budgets are summarily reduced.

As traditional energy sources dwindle and the corresponding costs continue to rise, as water shortages increase and **potability** becomes an issue in many areas of the United States, and as landfill costs continue to increase, more and more operators will realize the importance of their engineering department's contribution to the bottom line and to the preservation of the company's assets. They should also begin to recognize engineering's substantial contribution to the health, comfort, and safety of the employees and customers.

EDUCATOR PERSPECTIVES

The study of facilities management in hospitality programs has a long and uneven history. In the biography of Ellsworth M. Statler, there is a passage that describes Mr. Statler's visit to the country's first hotel school at Cornell University, where he observed a facilities class in session. His initial reaction to the class and the program was less than auspicious (see Figure 1.3). Statler

FIGURE 1.3   Statler's Visit to Cornell.   *Source:* America's Extraordinary Hotelman: Statler.

When Professor Frank Randolph convened his class on stationary engineering and boiler firing that afternoon he faced not only his regular students but a half-dozen hotel men including the formidable E. M. Statler. . . .

With care and precision the professor launched into a discussion of the engineering problems of heating a hotel with a coal-fired boiler. As he continued his language became more and more scientific and he referred several times to the British measurement of thermal units. His students may well have understood what he was talking about, but it was far over the heads of his visitors.

After forty minutes he ended his lecture and make a graceful little speech of welcome to the visitors. He wondered if any of them would like to say anything to the students. Perhaps Mr. Statler had a few words?

Statler stood up and the young, eager faces all turned to him. He said, "Boys, you're wasting your time here. You don't have to learn this stuff to be a hotel man. When I have an engineering problem I hire an engineer. I don't know a damn thing about British thermal units, and there is no reason for you to, either. Go on home and get a job."

did not consider a formal education in hospitality management necessary, but he soon changed his opinion and subsequently donated much of his considerable fortune to the hotel program at Cornell and to scholarships for worthy hotel students wherever they attend school.

Facilities management is one of a series of courses in buildings and building operations often found in hospitality programs in the hotel and food-service industry. Other courses include lodging and foodservice architecture and design, energy management, equipment layout and design, and development courses. Housekeeping, security, and even portions of a front office course could also be lumped together under the building operations umbrella.

Most hospitality programs have at least one required buildings-related course in their curriculum (typically facilities management), but only the larger programs will have the ability to offer an extensive list of elective courses in this sphere. In the past decade, many schools of hospitality management have reduced their offering of operations courses in general—and buildings courses in particular—choosing to emphasize traditional business school offerings with a hospitality twist. Certainly the study of basic management theory, marketing, human resources, accounting, and finance are crucially important to the success of a hospitality program graduate. However, courses specific to the industry are what make hospitality programs unique. This argument was made with the founding of the Cornell School of Hotel Administration by Dean Howard Meek.

Ours is a unique industry that needs a specialized curriculum to properly prepare its future leaders, and a standard business school curriculum is inadequate to the task. The hotel and foodservice operator of tomorrow will see challenges in the buildings sphere increase—not decrease. To meet these challenges, managers must understand the engineering systems at work inside and outside the building.

WHAT THIS BOOK IS NOT

A common student complaint heard over the years is that they did not enroll in a hospitality program to learn how to fix air conditioners or repair refrigerators. That is certainly not the goal of this textbook. Students will not be able to fix an air conditioner, stop a leak, repair an escalator, or even unplug a toilet after reading this textbook. This is not a "how-to" or "do-it-yourself" book. This book is not as deeply grounded in basic mechanics as some of the other textbooks. A facility engineer once remarked to the author that another textbook was asking hospitality students to be able to do things even he, a facility engineer, was not asked to do. Most managers need to understand the larger issues, not the day-to-day processes involved in maintaining buildings. Those managers who are involved in the repair and maintenance of building systems would be best served by taking courses designed to enhance their mechanical skills and by reading some of the hundreds of texts focused on the development of these mechanical abilities.

However, it is true this book is filled with chapters devoted to equipment and systems found in a modern building. You will find chapters devoted to electricity, lighting, heating, ventilation, and other building-related topics, but everything is addressed from a manager's perspective. Everything focuses on what a manager who is not a building engineer should know.

A BALANCED APPROACH

You may well ask at this juncture, "What exactly will this book and course do for me as a manager?" Some of the reasons have already been hinted at, but the following enumerates five arguments for pursuing this course of study. In this industry the product is produced and the customer, or guest, is present in our "factory"; we do not conduct business in a vacuum. Consequently, we cannot ignore these influences upon our business and upon ourselves.

Lateral Management

The chief engineer is typically a member of the general manager's executive committee along with the food and beverage director, hotel manager, sales and marketing director, director of human resources, and the controller. No longer do these departments function independently. Interdepartmental co-operation is now the norm in any well-run organization. In hotels today where interdepartmental cooperation is practiced, everyone has a shared responsibility for the profitability of the enterprise. Everyone uses energy and water and everyone produces waste—some of it, hazardous. Since everyone contributes to these problems, should not everyone also contribute to their solution? Many hotels now have **Total Quality Management (TQM)** programs, or **Process Improvement Teams**, and will have employees from different departments working together on task forces to improve processes and procedures. Many of these processes involve the engineering department and may even feature issues related to energy, water, and waste management.

Travelers abroad often remark that when they speak the local language, the treatment they receive gets better. Speaking the native tongue, even a few phrases, is often considered to be a sign of respect. So it is for those who communicate with the engineering department. Learning the lexicon of the engineering department and having a basic understanding of what the department does can engender greater respect among colleagues. Every day, work order requests are submitted by members of other departments to engineering. If those requesting assistance can properly explain their situation and at the same time demonstrate an understanding of the nature of the problem and what needs to be done to rectify the issue, engineering may be even more responsive to their needs. Empathy and understanding breeds cooperation.

In the mid-seventies, there was a television sitcom titled *Chico and the Man*. One of Chico's (Freddy Prince) biggest laugh lines was, "not my job." This phrase permeated the business community during that time. Whenever employees were faced with a task that seemed to them to go beyond the scope of their employment, they would utter the phrase, "not my job." Thankfully, one seldom hears that phrase anymore, and for good reason.

Assuming the Role of the Building Engineer

In small lodging properties and restaurants, the business may not generate enough revenue to justify a maintenance person, let alone a department of specialists. In these circumstances either the hotel manager must perform these duties, or they must be **outsourced**. Typically, both happen. Management performs those duties they feel qualified to handle and the rest is done by outside contractors. The available cash flow usually does not give the hotel manager the luxury of outsourcing the entire engineering function.

Smaller operators are usually more "reactive" in their approach to building maintenance than their larger counterparts. They often lack the financial resources and expertise to adequately maintain the building environment. Industry associations, such as the **American Hotel & Lodging Association (AH&LA)**, strive to provide small operators with educational programs to expand their understanding of building maintenance and energy issues.

Although most hotel school graduates will end up working in a large corporate environment, some will gravitate to smaller independent properties. Others who have an entrepreneurial bent will buy bed and breakfasts, small inns, and free-standing restaurants. This textbook is intended to help prepare these entrepreneurs for the (sometimes truly unique) challenges they will face in the engineering area.

The Bottom Line

The building is the primary asset for the company. Protecting that asset and maximizing its profit potential is one of management's greatest responsibilities. If management either disregards or is ignorant of the role that the building plays in the day-to-day business operations, then management has abdicated one of its chief responsibilities, and those who occupy these seats of power are failures.

Hospitality buildings are maintained at a great cost to the business. Typically, the annual maintenance of a hotel will average 5% of the revenue generated by the property. In addition to the annual maintenance are the annual utility costs incurred by the hotel, which will average 4% of annual revenues. Global energy shortages will undoubtedly precipitate a continued growth of energy costs in the coming years.

The economic cost of the building does not end with the annual budgeted costs; there are also periodic remodeling costs and major capital expenditures at the end of the economic life of major equipment and systems. Even the structure of the edifice has its limits. When all costs are added together, total expenditures for the building may exceed 20% of annual revenues. Twenty percent of revenue is far more than an inconsequential sum.

A more in-depth analysis of costs will be presented in Chapter 2. The point being made here is that anyone who aspires to top management in the lodging or foodservice industries, either at the property level or beyond, must appreciate the costs involved in maintaining a facility and have an understanding of how to properly manage these costs.

President Harry Truman had a sign on his desk at the White House. It simply said, "The buck stops here," telling everyone he was ultimately responsible for whatever the government did. Compare this approach with many recent chief executives in the news who publicly disavow themselves of any personal wrongdoing when their companies are found to be engaged in criminal activity.

Legalities and Regulations

The engineering department and the human resources department have something in common. Of all of the departments in the hotel, these two have been impacted the most by a host of new laws and regulations governing their operation. In the last five decades, human resources has seen legislation enacted that has impacted how a firm hires, promotes, supervises, and terminates employees.

Likewise, the engineering department has witnessed a host of new laws that have affected its operation. Laws governing the use of energy, water, chemicals, fire safety, and the environment have impacted the engineering department. The trend is definitely toward more, not fewer, laws. Another prevailing trend has been the increase of lawsuits against hotels due to accidents caused by faulty equipment or hazardous conditions that have injured clientele.

Managers who ignore their responsibilities to the law and to their guests and employees, risk their careers. Responsibilities cannot be delegated; the "buck" stops at the manager's desk. Management does not have the luxury of transferring all of the liability to the shoulders of the engineering department.

A manager cannot plead ignorance either; for ignorance of the law is never an excuse. And for those who may mistakenly assume that a corporation limits individual liability, they are reminded that employees, particularly those in management, will probably be named as co-defendants in any lawsuit.

Personal Reasons

Contrary to the popular belief of many hotel students, there are also many personal reasons to study facilities management. To begin with, some of us may want to own a home someday. With home ownership comes considerable responsibility. Roofs leak, plumbing breaks, wiring becomes faulty, and utility costs continue to rise. This book is about buildings, commercial buildings to be sure, but whether the building is a skyscraper or a simple residence, there are similarities. So, much of the information presented in this book will benefit homeowners as well hospitality managers.

There is a saying in the environmental movement that rings true, "Think global, but act local." As free citizens we should all be concerned with what is happening to our planet, whether it is receding icecaps at the poles, changing weather patterns in the Gulf of Mexico, or drought in the Rockies. However, as individuals, we cannot bring much influence to bear on these negative trends. We cannot do much to save the depletion of the Amazon rainforest, but we can make monumental changes in our own backyard. If we altered the way we use energy and the way we create waste in our businesses and in our homes, and if all of us were willing to make these changes, we would start to see real, positive changes to these global problems.

Admittedly, some of these changes might be viewed as stopgap policies. They might not correct the underlying problems, but they might buy enough time to come up with permanent solutions to these problems. For example, **global warming** brought on by the introduction of too much carbon dioxide and other **greenhouse gases** as the result of burning fossil fuels may be the problem. But if we reduce the need for electricity in our homes by switching to fluorescent lighting which slows, but does not eliminate, the continued burning of fossil fuels, we might be able to slow the damage of global warming until the time when we can change the entire country over to **sustainable**, non-polluting energy sources. Another example is **recycling**; some call it **downcycling**, which means that we are still using up nonreplenishable materials. We have not created a truly sustainable practice with recycling, but we have slowed our prior pace of using up valuable materials and energy.

This concern might be viewed by some as a "tree hugger's" lament, but this is not about "Saving the Planet." The planet has proved over the eons that it can take care of itself. If man makes his environment so inhospitable that he destroys it himself, there is still an excellent chance that other life will survive and once again, another species will eventually dominate the planet.

No, this is about saving ourselves and not only saving ourselves, but also saving our prosperity, our commerce and, yes, even our luxuries, such as travel. William McDonough, author of *Cradle to Cradle,* envisions a day when we can enjoy the luxuries of life and not feel guilty about it by using renewable energy sources that do not pollute and by building our facilities out of materials that can be used over and over again, almost indefinitely, or building with renewable materials. It may someday be possible to lead sustainable existences without sacrificing the environment.

We need to start seeing ourselves as part of the solution, rather than as part of the problem, and we need to realize we do not own businesses, buildings, or homes permanently. We are only stewards occupying this planet for a brief instant before we pass everything onto the next generation. We must ask ourselves, have we made things better for that next generation, or have we made it worse than we found it? This is a question each of us must face.

Summary

It is hoped that by now the student reading this text has gained an understanding of and an appreciation for the study of buildings in the hospitality industry. We have seen how students typically react initially to this area and the reasons for that reaction. We have also seen how top and mid-level managers have also traditionally reacted to the engineering function. We have tried to explain that barriers to understanding may be caused by a breakdown in communications and an ignorance of the importance of the building to human health, comfort, and safety, and the profitability of the business.

We have also reviewed why hospitality schools have included facilities management and other operations-oriented courses in their curriculums, and we have attempted to explain what makes hospitality programs unique when compared to traditional business schools. Evidently, the need for schools of hospitality administration is evidenced by their growing number. In the United States alone, there are close to 200 baccalaureate programs in addition to dozens of graduate degree programs in the field.

Finally, we have examined in detail those reasons why a study of facilities management is important to the aspiring hospitality executive. We have examined the need for interdepartmental cooperation and understanding between the engineering department and all other departments in the modern hotel. We have also explored how management in smaller and simpler operations also need to have a firm grounding in the engineering function, because they may not have the luxury of having engineering personnel in their organization. We have briefly looked at the economic impact of the engineering function on the business organization and attempted to convey the importance of properly administering these building costs to top management in the organization. We have also reviewed the legal necessity of recognizing the impact of the building on people and the environment and the need for managers inside and outside of the engineering office to understand their responsibilities. In closing, we have looked at a personal and individual need for the study of facilities that embraces far more than just managers in the hospitality environment.

In the coming chapters we will explore in detail the engineering department, its primary responsibilities, and the strategies employed by those in the profession to meet these responsibilities. We will also explore in Part One, the key issues and trends facing the engineering department and the chief engineer.

Key Terms and Concepts

American Hotel & Lodging Association (AH&LA) *9*	downcycling *11*	potability *6*	sustainable *11*
	global warming *11*	process improvement teams *8*	total quality management (TQM) *8*
building envelope *3*	greenhouse gases *11*	recycling *11*	
	outsourced *9*		

Discussion and Review Questions

1. Imagine you are the new general manager of a full service hotel and you are about to have your first meeting with your chief engineer. Make a list of questions you would pose to the chief engineer at that meeting and explain why you have asked each question.
2. Interview a department manager in a hotel and ask what type of interdepartmental task forces they have served on in their career; report to the class on your findings.
3. In most facilities departments in nonhospitality buildings, the custodial function is part of the department's duties. However, in hotels it is a separate department. In fact, there may be two departments devoted to cleaning, a housekeeping department, and a public areas department that cleans offices, meeting and convention facilities, and lobbies. Why do you think this is the case? Support your opinion with examples.
4. Has this chapter convinced you of the need to know more about the engineering function regardless of your particular career path? If not, why not?

2

The Engineering Department

CHAPTER OBJECTIVES

After studying the chapter, the student should be able to:

- list the common titles used by hotels to describe the engineering department and its chief administrative officer.
- list and describe the expanding role of the chief engineer and the engineering department.
- list and define the various types of maintenance performed by the engineering department.
- describe the management processes that can be used by the engineering department, such as integrated resource management and reliability-centered maintenance, and its application to the engineering department.
- describe the use and value of certain accounting and financial tools to the engineering department, such as payback period, life-cycle accounting, and budgeting.
- define and describe the use of architect's renderings (blueprints), benchmarks, and forms by the engineering department.
- construct an argument against deferred maintenance, listing the reasons presented in the chapter.
- state the average annual costs of maintenance and utilities for a property as a ratio of the construction cost and as a percentage of the property's revenue, and also be able to state the money needed for the reserve for replacement as a percentage of the property's revenue.
- describe the purpose and value of computers and CMMS programs to the engineering department.
- construct arguments for and against the practice of outsourcing, using examples from the text.
- describe the average worker in the engineering department, including their educational background.
- describe the educational background of the chief engineer and the average chief engineer's salary level.
- list the organizations that offer educational opportunities to those who work in facility departments.

INTRODUCTION

Over time, titles will often change in business and other organizations. For example, what is now normally called the Human Resources department was for years the Personnel department and the Human Resource director's title was Director of Personnel. In the engineering department we have seen a trend away from the use of *engineering* to other titles. We now often see facilities department, facilities management department, property operations department, property management department, and others being used. For the executive in charge of the department, chief engineer has been replaced with director of facilities, director of property management, director of facility management, and in the larger properties, vice president of property operations, vice president of facility management, and vice president of property management. However, since there is still no consensus regarding an appropriate name for either the department or the manager in charge, all of the above titles will be used interchangeably throughout this textbook.

RESPONSIBILITIES AND ACTIVITIES—AN EXPANDING JOB DESCRIPTION

Of all of the departments in the hotel, the engineering department has experienced the greatest change in responsibilities during the last half of the twentieth century. In the 1960s, the major concerns of the department were keeping track of department expenses, coordinating activities with the housekeeping department, overseeing hotel safety issues, and providing traditional plant services (e.g., utilities and maintenance).

In the 1970s OPEC (Organization of the Petroleum Exporting Countries) held its first oil embargo. With that seminal event, the cost and scarcity of all utilities increased at an unprecedented rate. Energy management was then added to the chief engineer's list of responsibilities.

The establishment of the Environmental Protection Agency (EPA) in 1970 finally began to impact hotels during the 1980s. Requirements for proper solid waste disposal and air pollution from the EPA became the responsibility of the engineering department. There were also pronouncements from the Occupational Safety and Health Administration (OSHA) during that time that affected hotel chief engineers.

During the 1990s, the responsibilities of the department continued to grow as such diverse concerns as liquid and solid waste disposal, toxic waste disposal, hazardous materials handling, on-site waste treatment, air emission standards, indoor air quality, recycling programs, and a renewed interest in fire and life safety emerged. In addition, the economic downturn in the lodging industry at the beginning of the decade spurred an intensive program of cost reduction throughout the industry. Engineering departments were subject to intensive scrutiny in the ever expanding quest to shave costs. This focus on cost avoidance has generated a host of management tools and techniques designed to assist in tracking and evaluating all of the building's systems. The operation of these programs (many of them are computer-based) has become yet another responsibility of the chief engineer.

Since 2000, we have seen the role of the chief engineer continue to expand. All aspects of disaster control (including terrorism), and health issues, such as mitigating the transmission of contagious diseases, have become part of the chief engineer's growing list of responsibilities. As fossil fuels have continued to rise, there is an even greater focus now on energy management. The chief engineer is also viewed as the manager who is most responsible for *greening* the property, such as achieving **LEED** (*Leadership in Energy and Environmental Design*) certification from the U.S. Green Building Council.

The only other department that has experienced a similar increase in responsibilities during the past 50 years has been human resources. Federal and state legislation during this period, such as the Fair Labor Standards Act of 1938 and its subsequent amendments, the Civil Rights Act of 1964, the Pregnancy Discrimination Act of 1978, the Americans with Disabilities Act of 1990, and the Family and Medical Leave Act of 1993, along with new state legislation, significantly increased the duties and responsibilities of this department.

Unfortunately for the engineering department, there has not been a corresponding increase in capital or operating budgets to provide funding for either personnel or materials to meet these new demands. Chief engineers have had to devise new strategies and tactics to meet these challenges and in doing so, they have had to reorient their management philosophy. In the rest of this chapter we will look at how management has adapted to meet these challenges.

CATEGORIES OF MAINTENANCE—WHICH TO USE

There are many terms used to differentiate among the various maintenance strategies conducted on a hospitality property. Some of the common terms used are **routine**, **scheduled**, **preventive**, **predictive**, **run-to-failure**, **reactive**, **time-based**, **condition-based**, and **emergency**. Several of these terms are interchangeable and others are just variations of the major categories. In fact, there are really only three main maintenance strategies.

Time-Based Maintenance

One is time-based, or preventive, maintenance. Time-based maintenance implies that the maintenance is performed on a pre-determined schedule. Depending on the equipment, that maintenance schedule could be from once a day to several years. The concept is that if one performs maintenance on a regular schedule, the prospect of failure of that building component or equipment is reduced. Conventional thinking holds that most building components or equipment follow the *bathtub curve* failure pattern (See Figure 2.1). In the bathtub pattern, there is a high incidence of failure in the beginning (infant mortality). This is then followed by a steady, but much lower pattern of random failures. Then toward the end of the life of the component or equipment, the failure rate climbs as the unit wears out. By conducting preventive maintenance, it is expected the life of the equipment or building component will be extended. Routine maintenance is a form of time-based maintenance. It is simple maintenance (e.g., tightening a screw, oiling a gear, checking and adding

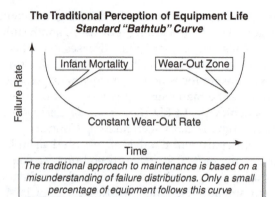

FIGURE 2.1 The Erroneous Bathtub Curve.

air if needed to a tire). It could even be something very simple like cutting the grass every Tuesday in the summer. Scheduled maintenance is maintenance that requires special preparation, the assembly of proper parts and supplies, and even special crews to perform this maintenance. Examples of this would be the annual inspection and repair of a roof, the draining and acid washing of a swimming pool, or the painting of the building's exterior.

Analogous to the practice of time-based maintenance is the function of **commissioning**. Commissioning is ascertaining that the building system and its components are functioning as they were intended to function. The American Society of Heating, Refrigeration and Air-Conditioning Engineers (**ASHRAE**) guideline *ASHRAE Guideline 0, The Commissioning Process*, defines commissioning as, "a quality-oriented process for achieving, verifying, and documenting that the performance of facilities, systems, and assemblies meets defined objectives and criteria." This practice is done once the building is constructed, but before it is occupied. It is often referred to as the practice of testing, adjusting, and balancing (**TAB**) systems. Instruments are used to evaluate and calibrate the equipment or system in question to ensure it is functioning as the equipment manufacturer, contractor, building engineers, and architect intended it to operate. Commissioning ensures energy savings and happy building occupants. One estimate held that for every dollar invested in building commissioning, there will be a return of four dollars in energy savings in the first five years of the building's operation.

Once considered to be a one-time practice, facility managers are now practicing **retrocommissioning** or *re-commissioning*. They have learned that systems and equipment can be compromised over time and their efficiencies will be diminished. This can be due to age and the natural wear and tear on the facility, or may be a result of a remodeling or renovation that compromises a building system. The system may continue to function, but it is no longer functioning at its original, optimal level. Human health and comfort may be compromised, and there may be an increase in energy costs associated with the malfunctioning system. The U.S. Green Building Council's *Leadership in Energy and Environmental Design* (LEED) program requires all building operators who want to achieve LEED status for their properties to undergo a complete building retrocommissioning.

Run-to-Failure Maintenance

Run-to-failure, reactive, or emergency maintenance is maintenance that is performed after equipment or a component fails. Traditionally considered to be a condition to be avoided because of increased costs or safety issues, there are times when it is an appropriate maintenance strategy. Sometimes it is far less expensive to practice emergency maintenance. In fact, equipment may be designed to run until catastrophic failure occurs. Then the broken part is replaced, not repaired. An example would be a hermetically sealed compressor on a walk-in cooler.

Condition-Based Maintenance

Condition-based maintenance, also known as predictive maintenance, employs the use of sensors and computers to monitor equipment and determine when maintenance should occur. An example of this type is found in new automobiles that notify owners when they need to change oil, rather than arbitrarily changing the oil based on mileage or the number of months since the last change. (These are time-based maintenance strategies.) Condition-based maintenance also enables the chief engineer to accumulate and analyze data on the operating performance of building components. This information can be used to make future purchase decisions on equipment.

Reliability-Centered Maintenance

For many years, the prevailing maintenance strategy has been preventive, or time-based. The *bathtub curve* has dominated the thinking of most building engineers. Chief engineers viewed time-based as the best way to prevent costly building-system interruptions. Then the United States military and the National Aeronautical and Space Administration (NASA) started questioning that logic and discovered that preventive maintenance is not always the best approach. According to a study conducted by NASA, over one-third of the $400 billion spent on preventive maintenance in the United States is wasted because the maintenance was unnecessary, redundant, and, at times, more detrimental than beneficial to the longevity of the system.

    Reliability-centered maintenance (RCM) is a way of viewing the performance of building systems in terms of the impact of a failure of those systems and then attempting to mitigate that failure by design, detection, or maintenance. It incorporates time-based, run-to-failure, and condition-based maintenance strategies and then applies the most appropriate strategy for a particular situation. RCM is a completely integrated approach. It is a process for determining the best maintenance to achieve design reliability at minimum cost. The benefit of RCM is that it promotes a proactive maintenance program instead of a typical reactive program. RCM forces the chief engineer to focus on the company's mission and goals. All RCM programs view safety and security followed by cost as major priorities.

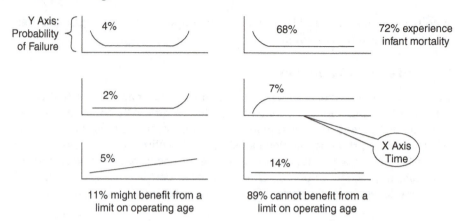

FIGURE 2.2 Failure Rates are Largely Random.

RCM begins with a thorough analysis of all equipment and building systems. If there are no consequences resulting from a building component's failure in terms of the business's mission, the environment, human safety and security, or life-cycle cost, maintenance should not be performed; that component should instead be run to failure and replaced. In those instances where abrasive, erosive, or corrosive wear takes place, material properties change due to fatigue, or a clear correlation between age and functional reliability exists, then time-based maintenance is the strategy to employ. Condition-based maintenance has become the maintenance strategy of choice since it has been discovered that many equipment failures are not wear or age related (see Figure 2.2). Computers and sensors used in condition-based maintenance can now be used to track many building systems, and have made it possible in many cases to identify the precursors of failure, quantify equipment condition, and schedule the appropriate repair with a higher degree of confidence than was possible with a time-based maintenance strategy. All of this makes condition-based maintenance the best maintenance strategy from a safety, security, and cost perspective for many building components. The chief engineer will then apply the appropriate maintenance strategy to all building components. RCM is an invaluable management strategy for the progressive chief engineer.

THE WHOLE IS GREATER THAN THE SUM OF ITS PARTS

Another extremely effective management tool for the chief engineer is **Integrated Resource Management** (IRM). IRM stems from a need to manage all resources available to the facility manager, in order to design and produce the desired results at the right time, in the right quantities, and right the first time. Using an IRM approach means that consideration is given to environmental, social, and economic issues, and finding ways for all of these issues to exist together with less conflict. How we manage or use one resource affects the management or use of other resources in an area. Managing each use or resource by itself is less effective than managing all of them in an integrated way. IRM is based upon, cooperation, communication, coordination, consideration of all values, and involvement of those potentially affected before an action is taken.

IRM considers how seemingly disparate problems may be linked and uses all available resources, not just one traditional approach, to solve problems and meet the needs of the building and its occupants.

Clearly a "new orientation" on how facility departments are managed is needed, because the department has not experienced a significant increase in personnel, materials, or money to meet the new demands placed on the department in the past 40 years. Using IRM makes the job of the chief engineer easier and, in turn, this helps to improve job satisfaction and reduce turnover in the department. The chief engineer is working smarter, not harder, to meet the challenges of the job.

One example of IRM in action would be in the area of pest control. Traditionally, there was only one solution, or so it was thought. That was to spray the strongest available insecticide on all of the insects on the property. That prescription had some drawbacks. To begin with, the pesticide may have had some nasty side effects. It might have killed beneficial insects in the area, too. It may have had an impact on other life forms, including birds, fish, pets, and people. The poison might have migrated to our water or food supplies.

Today, we may still employ an insecticide, but we might also employ other techniques, such as using good bugs to kill bad bugs. For example, praying mantises, lace wings, and ladybugs can be used in our landscaping to kill some of the bad bugs. We might use plants, such as marigolds, that deter insects. We might also use insecticides that are made from bio-degradable materials that are not harmful to people or other life forms. Finally, we might starve those critters to death by cleaning up our kitchens, storerooms, and offices, so they are not attracted to our buildings in the first place. This approach is known as **Integrated Pest Management** (IPM). IPM recognizes the different resources available to the plant engineer and also recognizes the impact of pest management on other aspects of the building's environment, making for a happier, healthier, and more productive and profitable enterprise. Other examples of the use of IRM will be presented throughout the textbook.

MAINTENANCE MYOPIA—TRYING TO DEFER THE INEVITABLE

Deferred maintenance is the postponement of maintenance, system upgrades, and repairs on buildings and equipment to future budget cycles, or when funds become available. It is a common practice in government and educational facilities and is also practiced in many commercial facilities, including hotels and restaurants. Deferred maintenance may be inevitable when the funds are simply not available, but many companies engage in the practice to "pump up" their bottom line on quarterly and annual reports by cutting budgets or by forcing chief engineers to live within their budgets even when unanticipated problems occur. Sometimes, the budgeted maintenance funds may be funneled to unexpected emergencies. However, these very same "emergencies" may be caused by equipment failures resulting from past decisions to defer maintenance.

There is an old axiom that states, "One must spend time and money to save time and money." This seemingly contradictive statement is an example of *net optimization*. We must invest resources from one area to maintain our resources in another area and without that investment, the assets of the firm will be reduced.

Other reasons for deferring maintenance are lack of sufficient manpower or expertise to make the repair. A scarcity of parts will also defer needed maintenance. If the maintenance would interrupt the operation of the business and result in an immediate loss of needed revenue (e.g., the shutdown of a hotel's chillers during the summer months leaving the property without air-conditioned rooms), the company may also decide to defer maintenance. If the maintenance can be done during a remodeling or refurbishment that is planned for the near future, then it may be deferred. Finally, there have been instances where the chief engineer may have deferred maintenance. This practice is often found in those companies where a bonus is given to those department managers who come in under budget. Where bonuses are given for this practice, the chief engineer's successor will often inherit a property in tatters.

When maintenance is deferred, little thought may be given to its true cost. In addition to the labor and parts when failure occurs, there are the factors of customer dissatisfaction, increased liability and safety hazards, employee productivity, and interruption of business. All of these factors carry an associated cost. Maintenance expert David Geaslin estimates that the average risk/reward ratio of deferred maintenance is more than fifteen to one. In other words, the cost of deferring maintenance and the resulting equipment failure will often cost more than 1500% of the initial maintenance. As Geaslin states, "No one would ever take those odds at a craps table." Those that control the final budget need to understand the old axiom, "Pay me now, or pay me (far more) later."

Chief engineers need to conduct facility audits to calculate the severity and extent of deferred maintenance in the facility. This audit will often require the services of several specialists (e.g., electrical engineers, mechanical engineers, fire protection engineers, etc.). Then an estimation of the risk needs to be calculated and a prediction of the costs incurred from the postponed maintenance must be done. Chief engineers should support their claims with examples of incurred costs from past examples of deferred maintenance.

However, traditional methods of assessment can be extremely time-consuming and expensive. Furthermore, the findings may not be able to be audited and they also lack reliability. (Repeated assessments may generate different findings.) The Washington, D.C.-based National Aeronautics and Space Administration (NASA) which has over 2,800 buildings with over 44 million square feet and a current replacement value of $21 billion dollars, discovered their traditional assessment methods to be prohibitively expensive and unreliable. Their new system, entitled *NASA Deferred Maintenance (DM) Parametric Estimating Method* has been found to be a low-cost, consistent, auditable method of evaluating the condition of their facilities and it provides a method to evaluate the relative condition of all of NASA's sites.

Chief engineers must convince top management to stop viewing the engineering department as a cost center and instead, view it as a profit center.

A cost-center approach is strictly concerned with adhering to the budget and decreasing expenses as much as possible. In contrast, the profit-center model realizes that investment and operating costs can be allocated to improve efficiency. This increased efficiency naturally results in higher profits. When the building and its contents are maintained in a timely manner, the profitability of the business should rise.

Finally, astute investors who are considering the purchase of a hospitality enterprise should always look at the annual maintenance and capital costs if the profit picture looks too good to be true. *Bleeding* a property (i.e., deferring maintenance) is an old trick that is used by unscrupulous sellers to increase the bottom line, and it still works on neophyte buyers.

THE COST OF DOING BUSINESS

Top management often focuses on revenues. Without sufficient revenues, the enterprise is doomed. As important as revenues are, attention should also be paid to the costs of doing business. When efficiencies are discovered and a nickel can be saved, that nickel flows directly to the bottom line. That nickel becomes a nickel of profit. However, short-term savings that generate larger long-term costs, as in deferred maintenance, should be avoided.

The Cost of Construction vs. the Cost of Maintenance and Utilities

When comparing building construction and maintenance costs, the widely held belief is that construction costs are approximately 25% of a building's total cost, and maintenance constitutes the other 75%. The significance of this ratio comes into play when constructing or modifying a structure. Management needs to consider the lifetime cost of an item versus its construction or modification costs. For example, if one model of a walk-in cooler for a restaurant is 5% higher than another model, but the more expensive cooler will cost 40% less to maintain over its estimated life, then the purchase of the more expensive model may be a very wise decision indeed. If the 5% difference between the two models is $600 and the estimated maintenance cost of the less expensive model is $350 per annum and the maintenance cost of the more expensive model is 40% less or $210 per year, that creates a savings of $140 each year. A calculation of the payback period shows a payback period of 4.29 years (see Figure 2.3).

If the more expensive model of chiller also happens to be more energy efficient than the less expensive model, then that savings should also be added into the formula. For example, let us assume that the annual energy savings is calculated to be $60 for the more expensive model of chiller. Then the net simple payback period becomes exactly three years (see Figure 2.4).

Difference in Purchase Price/Annual Maintenance Cost Savings
= Net Simple Payback Period

$600 ÷ $140 = 4.29 years

FIGURE 2.3   Net Simple Payback Period (First Example).

FIGURE 2.4 Net Simple Payback Period (Second Example).

Difference in Purchase Price/Annual Maintenance Cost Savings
+ Annual Energy Savings = Net Simple Payback Period

$600 ÷ $140 + $60 = 3 years

A simple payback period of three years or less on building modifications and equipment purchases has become a benchmark for many hospitality firms. This is anecdotal information, but many building engineers have expressed to this author that top management balks at any purchases or modifications that do not result in a three-year payback. Perhaps this trend is due to the realization that hotels are frequently bought and sold nowadays, and the pressure is now placed on publicly traded companies to provide a return to their investors in a timely manner.

Simple payback period is but one tool at the disposal of the chief engineer. In fact, there are far more sophisticated tools available, such as **Life Cycle Cost Analysis** (LCCA) which will be examined in the next section. However, simple payback does provide the chief engineer a relatively quick rule of thumb guide to the economic feasibility of a purchase decision. Some other commonly used measures are Net Savings (or Net Benefits), Net Present Value, Savings-to-Investment Ratio (or Savings Benefit-to-Cost Ratio), Internal Rate of Return, and in addition to the above-mentioned Payback Period, there is Discounted Payback Period.

Life Cycle Cost Analysis

LCCA is the most straightforward and easy-to-interpret measure of economic evaluation of buildings and building systems. It takes into account all costs of acquiring, owning, and disposing of a building or building system. LCCA is especially useful in comparing alternatives that meet the same performance requirements, but differ with respect to their initial costs, maintenance, and utility costs. It allows a comparison to be made in order to select the one that maximizes net savings over the life of the building or the equipment. For example, LCCA will help determine whether the purchase of a high-performance chiller which may have a higher initial cost, but has a reduced operating and maintenance costs compared to other units, is cost-effective or not.

There are numerous costs associated with acquiring, operating, maintaining, and disposing of a building or building system. Building-related costs usually fall into the following categories:

- Initial Costs—Purchase, Acquisition, Construction Costs
- Fuel or Utility Costs
- Operation, Maintenance, and Repair Costs
- Replacement Costs
- Residual Values—Resale or Salvage Values, or Disposal Costs
- Finance Charges—Loan Interest Payments
- Non-Monetary Benefits or Costs

Initial costs consist of the land, the building, and all of the fixtures, furnishings, and equipment necessary for the operation of the business. Land is included because there might be site alternatives available in the design phase. For example, a restaurant company might opt for either an existing building that can be converted into a restaurant or a vacant piece of land where a building can be erected from scratch. In the preliminary stages actual construction costs are not available, so the firm will use historical data from similar buildings or guidelines from the private or government sectors. Detailed cost estimates are calculated at the submittal phase of the building design and are usually made from proprietary cost databases, such as R.S. Means *CostWorks,* an online database.

Energy (fuel), water, and other utility costs are based on estimated consumption, current rates, and price projections in the design phase. In calculating energy usage, assumptions have to be made about occupancy rates in lodging, and number of estimated covers served in a restaurant. Operating schedules must also be factored in. For example, is the restaurant outlet open for 24 hours a day and seven days a week or just one meal period for five days a week? There are a number of computer programs on the market that will assist in the selection of HVAC (heating, ventilation, and air-conditioning) equipment for proper sizing.

Quotes of current energy prices from local utilities should take into account the proper rate category, rate structure, any seasonal or time-of-day rate differentials, and demand charges to obtain an estimate as close as possible to the actual energy cost.

One thing is for certain, utility rates have gone up considerably in the past decade, and are likely to continue to rise faster than inflation in the years ahead. Therefore, estimates of future rates must be obtained from local utility companies, or the firm can obtain a copy of estimated energy price escalation rates from the United States Department of Energy entitled, *Energy Price Indices and Discount Factors for Life-Cycle Cost Analysis.*

Of particular interest to the chief engineer are the *operations, maintenance, and repair (OMR)* costs. These costs can vary widely from facility to facility, even when the facilities are similar in age and type. Prevailing wage rates, union contracts, and historical costs of supplies and parts must be considered.

Replacement costs depend on the estimated life of the original building systems and the also the estimated period under study. Then the number and timing of replacements can be estimated. Usually, the same sources of the original systems and their costs are used as the base costs for replacements.

The *residual value* of a system (or component) is its remaining value at the end of the study period, or at the time it is replaced during the study period. Residual values can be based on value in place, resale value, salvage value, or scrap value, net of any selling, conversion, or disposal costs.

Finance charges and taxes also have to be added to the formula. Finally there are the *non-monetary benefits or costs.* The economic value of these items cannot be estimated; therefore they cannot be added in. An example of a non-monetary benefit would be the purchase of room *package terminal air conditioner (PTAC)* units that have very quiet compressors affording a guest a quiet night's rest and, it is hoped, return visits from that guest. Certainly, there would be an economic advantage for the property to buy these types of units,

	Pizza Oven "A"	Pizza Oven "B"
Initial Price	$4,380	$5,050
Installation Expense	$495	$675
Estimated Maintenance & Repair Expense	$2,950	$875
Operating Cost*	$8,350	$3,330
Depreciation**	10%	7.5%
Financing Expense	$1,400	$1,616
Insurance Cost	$395	$425
Salvage Value/Disposal Cost***	$295	−$210
Total Cost	$18,265	$11,761
Cost Per Annum****	$1,826.50	$904.69

*The operating cost of pizza oven *B* is less because of its design which includes substantially more insulation and a more sophisticated heating system which uses less energy. The cost of labor for operation is the same for both units.
** Pizza oven *A* estimated life is 10 years and pizza oven *B* which is made from more durable materials is estimated to last slightly longer than 13 years.
***Pizza oven *A* has a disposal cost of $295, but pizza oven *B* has a salvage value of $210 because of the materials used in its construction.
****Pizza oven *B* has an estimated 13 years of life versus 10 years for pizza oven *A*.

The comparison shows that even though pizza oven *A* has a better purchase price, pizza oven *B* will cost the operation less than half of pizza oven *A*. The time value of money should also be considered. A comparison should always be made between the investment of the capital in securities (e.g., a bank certificate of deposit) and the expected contribution the equipment would make. If there is more money to be made with a certificate of deposit than from the selling of pizza, then the investment should not be made.

FIGURE 2.5 Life Cycle Cost Example (All Costs are for the Estimated Life of the Equipment).

but it would be impossible to accurately measure their worth. Figure 2.5 is an example of an LCCA comparison.

Hospitality Industry Cost Averages

Maintenance and utilities were, for many years, insignificant expenses in lodging facilities. At one time, maintenance was less than 1% of the total revenue. That figure has changed. In 2004, **property operation and maintenance (POM)** costs for all properties were 5.1% of total revenues, or $2,026 per available room according to *Trends in the Hotel Industry*. In the same year, **utilities** costs were 4.2% of total revenues, or $1,691 per available room, again according to *Trends*. Table 2.1 demonstrates the average percentage of revenue by hotel type for utilities in 2004. Table 2.2 displays the annual property operation and maintenance costs expressed as a percentage of revenue, again by hotel type for 2004. As fossil fuel (oil, gas, etc.) production declines in the coming

TABLE 2.1   Hotel Utility Cost Percentage of Revenue by Hotel Category 2004

All Limited-Service Hotels	All Resort Hotels	All Full-Service Hotels	All Suite Hotels	Convention Hotels	All Hotels
5.3%	4.4%	4.4%	4.6%	3.9%	4.2%

TABLE 2.2   Hotel Property Operation and Maintenance Costs Percentage of Revenue by Hotel Category 2004

All Limited-Service Hotels	All Resort Hotels	All Full-Service Hotels	All Suite Hotels	Convention Hotels	All Hotels
5.8%	5.3%	5.1%	5.2%	4.7%	5.1%

years (several authorities believe we have already hit peak oil production), utility costs should rise significantly in dollars per available room, but may or may not rise as a percentage of total revenue.

When there is a softening of demand for rooms, hotel companies are reticent about raising their posted rates. When demand exceeds supply, hotels are more than happy to raise rates, driving down costs expressed as percentages of revenue. In 2000, utility rates skyrocketed around the United States and many hotel chains attempted to add a surcharge to their room rates rather than raise the advertised rates. This angered many group and transient markets, and culminated in lawsuits against several hotel chains. Consequently, most operators have long since dropped these hidden surcharges.

Engineering department costs are typically not allocated to the other hotel departments. Allocating utility and maintenance costs to the rooms division or the food and beverage area could be done if the hotel had sophisticated tracking systems, such as the **sub-metering** of utilities. Most properties do not.

In addition to the annual maintenance and utility costs are the periodic remodeling, refurbishment and restoration costs. Hotels and restaurants suffer from greater use and abuse than office buildings and even retail stores. These capital expenditure costs (**CapEx**), in comparison to the annual maintenance costs, can be ten times the annual POM cost. Top management should reserve sufficient funds for these expenditures from the business's revenue. An account should be established for these funds. This account is commonly known as the **reserve for replacement.** For the first two or three years after the hotel's opening, the reserve normally equals 3%–4% of the property's revenue stream. From that point the reserve should be increased and maintained at 7% of the total revenue.

Remodeling or *minor refurbishment* of a property implies that the hotel is repairing or changing out non-durable goods that show wear from guest and employee use. The first remodeling of the hotel may be as early as three to four years after opening for a luxury property, five to six years for a mid-scale property, and seven to eight years for a budget motel. Carpet may be replaced, as well as drapes and curtains, although not necessarily during the first remodeling. Hard furniture (**case goods**) may undergo refinishing to remove scratches and nicks. **Soft goods** (upholstered furniture) may be reupholstered during a remodeling. Mattresses which normally have a 12- to 15-year life may or may not be replaced. Wall coverings can be replaced and the interior is repainted. Bathroom countertops may be replaced or refinished, and fixtures such as worn faucets and tubs may be either replaced or refinished. Door knobs, door stops, electric switch plates, and locking mechanisms that show wear may be replaced. Televisions, lamps, and clock radios may be upgraded.

Around 10–15 years, *major renovation* is needed. This can entail replacement of lighting systems, all bathroom fixtures, all furnishings, all flooring, wall-coverings, and ceiling panels. Heating, ventilation, and air-conditioning (**HVAC**) systems may undergo major replacement. The property may be given an entirely new design.

When the property is 30 to 50 years old, it is probably due for an entire *restoration*. Mechanical, plumbing, and electrical systems will be completely redone. The building is often stripped down to its frame and non-supporting walls may even be rearranged. Many hotel and restaurant companies will tend to raze the building and build an entirely new facility rather than go through a complete restoration. The cost of building an entirely new facility may very well be more cost-effective than going through a restoration. Of course, buildings of historic importance or those that are architecturally significant will more likely be restored.

The reserve for replacement even at 7% of revenue is not likely to provide sufficient funds for restorations and may not even be enough for those major renovations. When this occurs, top management must seek out the necessary capital from lenders or stockholders.

LESS CAN BE MORE: COMPUTERS, TECHNOLOGY, AND RE-ENGINEERING

As alluded to earlier in the chapter, since the United States hotel industry suffered a $5.7 billion loss in 1990, there has been a continuing effort to reduce all unnecessary costs. Admittedly, prior to this economic downturn many companies were rife with "fat," particularly in the area of labor. The industry

It Pays to Pull a Permit

The Clark County Department of Development Services is the county government's building inspector for new construction and for remodeling, refurbishment, and renovation of existing structures. Whenever anything is done incorrectly and could result in a safety hazard, the building operator must obtain a permit from the county who will inspect the work and verify that it meets code. It was found that Roman Empire Development, a subsidiary of Harrah's, performed a number of remodeling jobs without securing (pulling) the requisite permits at the Rio Hotel & Casino, Harrah's, and the Flamingo. Some of the work performed compromised the hotels' life safety systems. Due to their neglect, Harrah's decided to eliminate the subsidiary, throwing 200 employees out of work. An internal employee memo, announcing the decision and authored by Harrah's Chairman and Chief Executive Officer Gary Loveman, was distributed late Wednesday to all employees of Harrah's Entertainment. "Many of you have no doubt heard recent reports about improper renovations at Rio, Harrah's Las Vegas, and Flamingo. These incidents have been the most disturbing issues I have faced in my five years as CEO. I am troubled that in Las Vegas, they may have jeopardized our most precious asset: the confidence and trust of our guests and employees," Loveman wrote. Cutting corners on safety can cost management far more than it saves.

discovered there were too many layers in their organizations, particularly in the ranks of management. In response, many of these organizations cut management positions rather than the front line, hourly-wage workers who were most responsible for seeing to the guest's needs. However, hourly-wage personnel did not escape completely unscathed. If any redundancies were discovered, positions were likely to be eliminated.

Although the engineering department is a fairly small department in terms of personnel, its workers are some of the highest paid in the hotel and the annual maintenance budget constitutes approximately 5% of total revenue. These very facts have made the engineering department a prospect for cost-cutting. At the very least, chief engineers have learned since 1990 that they no longer had a *blank check* with which to do business. This has created the need for them to be more creative in their approach to their responsibilities.

This approach was referred to as *re-engineering* in the workplace in the early 1990s. Re-engineering was the redesign of a business's processes to increase efficiencies. Proponents argued that a business should be organized around its processes instead of its functional areas. Establishing *cross-functional teams* in an organization designed around these processes was a common trait of re-engineering. For example, in addition to the engineering department personnel, members from other departments (e.g., marketing, housekeeping, front office, etc.) might be brought in to serve on a team designing a new work order process for the hotel engineering department.

Re-engineering has often resulted in downsizing. When personnel were found to be superfluous upon re-engineering an organization, they would either be reassigned or let go. On a number of occasions there was a wholesale reduction of personnel under the guise of re-engineering. This led one observer at the time to recommend that top management should not cut their staff by using a machete in a dark room. Regardless of the outcomes, chief engineers realized that they had to rely more on technology than additional labor to get the job done.

The expansion of technology has not been the sole domain of the computer, but the computer has been a major influence on how engineering departments approach their responsibilities. A **Computerized Maintenance Management System** (CMMS) is a software program designed to assist in the planning, management, and administrative functions that are required for effective maintenance. Most CMMS programs are not part of the hotel's **Property Management System** (PMS). Instead, they are stand-alone systems with their own servers and terminals. Typically, the only engineering function one might find on PMS programs is the generating and reporting of work orders because this function needs to be available to many personnel in many different departments in the hotel. The functions of a CMMS system can include creating work orders, **trend logging,** and other recordkeeping, monitoring of operating equipment, and the recording of parts transactions. The CMMS can be used to assure the high quality of both equipment condition and equipment output. Therefore, a CMMS is not just a means of controlling maintenance; it is one of the primary tools that can be used to improve the productivity of maintenance.

The benefits of a CMMS include increased equipment availability, longer equipment life, and—most significantly—increased labor productivity. If the system provides workers with a planned job, the procedures, and needed parts and tools, they will be able to work without delays or interruptions. Workers will also perform more safely, since job plans would include all safety procedures. Tangible benefits of a CMMS include reductions in overtime, outside contract work, maintenance backlogs, and costs per repair, as well as improved morale, better service, less paperwork, and reduced follow-up required by the supervisor. Two other factors, inventory control and environmental control, mean reduced inventory costs, less excess inventory, and a more consistent availability of parts. In terms of reduced inventory costs, experience shows that a reduction of 10% to 15% in parts stocked and consumed is possible. With respect to environmental control, safety and compliance issues are both important. Preventing accidents and injuries as a result of proper procedures (documented by CMMS programs) can save hotels a significant amount of money. Hotels also must comply with state and federal occupational safety and health agencies. By selecting a CMMS program that has similar provisions, engineering departments can be assured they are meeting regulatory standards, thereby minimizing fines for noncompliance.

ORGANIZATION

Organization of the department is predicated on the size of the facility (i.e., number of guest rooms). On average, there are approximately three employees in the engineering department for every 100 guest rooms. However, this ratio can vary widely. The class of the property (e.g., luxury, mid-level, budget, etc.) is a major determinant of the staff's size. The hotel's class can also influence the composition of the engineering staff. Higher quality hotels can afford more specialists as opposed to budget properties that tend to hire more generalists. Larger hotels (500+ rooms) may contain a number of tradesmen/specialists as well as multiple layers of management. There may be carpenters, electricians, painters, plumbers, draftsmen, boiler operators, refrigeration technicians, landscapers, as well as general tradespersons.

Mid-sized properties (100–500 rooms) may have one or two certified specialists on the staff in essential areas, such as, refrigeration repair, boiler operation, or perhaps a licensed electrician. Smaller properties (fewer than 100 rooms) will range from one or two employees in the department to none in small properties where the general manager assumes all maintenance responsibilities. The staff of smaller properties tends to be generalists. Needed expertise in the repair and maintenance of complex equipment is often contracted or **outsourced** to outside firms. Remodeling and refurbishment are also outsourced because there is an insufficient number of personnel in the department to meet normal obligations and to refurbish guest rooms and public areas at the same time. However, some of the full-time staff can and will be called upon to assist in remodeling efforts.

The engineering department is a **staff** department. Staff departments (e.g., marketing, HR, accounting, purchasing, and engineering) assist **line** departments (e.g., hotel, and food and beverage departments). Staff departments, along with the rooms and food and beverage divisions, make up the **executive committee** and as such, report directly to the **general manager**.

One existing stereotype of the engineering department is that chief engineers and other personnel in the department are not great communicators and consequently do not **manage upward** or laterally (i.e., other departments) very well. There may be more than a few grains of truth in this stereotype. Another possible explanation is that many top managers may have no concept about what this department does, as mentioned in chapter one. When the manufacture of chlorofluorocarbon refrigerants were banned in the United States, the Nevada Professional Facility Managers Association (NPFMA) considered the possibility of making a video for viewing by top management in the hotels in Las Vegas. Its purpose was to introduce this subject to these executive and prepare them for the substantial costs they would soon incur when the engineering department retrofitted their refrigeration equipment. Many chief engineers did not believe they alone could convey the enormity of the problem to their boss's.

The following two figures (Figure 2.6 and Figure 2.7) show the placement of the engineering department within the hotel and the organization of the engineering department in a large (500+ room) hotel.

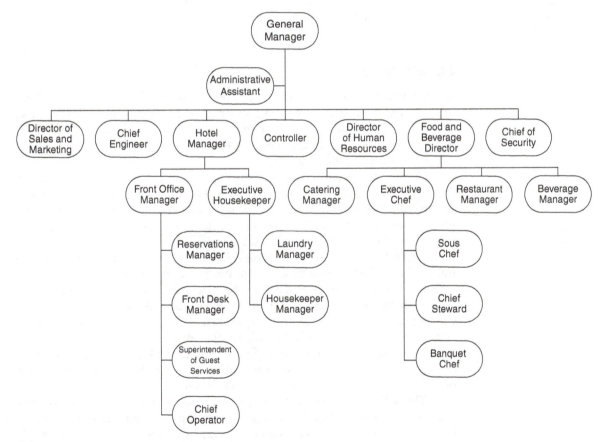

FIGURE 2.6   Organizational Chart for a 500-Room Hotel.

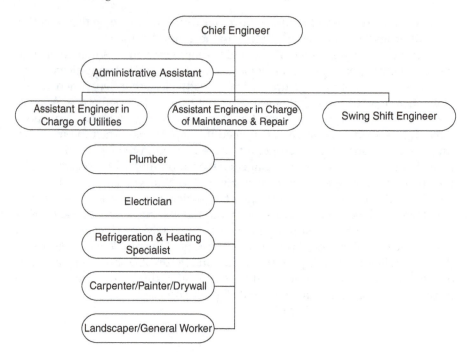

FIGURE 2.7
Organizational Chart
for the Engineering
Department in a
500-Room Hotel.

OUTSOURCING

As mentioned earlier, outsourcing, or contracting out tasks and responsibilities to outside entities, is a common practice among hotels of every size, shape, and description. Even the largest hotels have traditionally outsourced certain activities, such as the repair of elevators and computerized systems. The reasons for this are multifold.

First, specialized maintenance is expensive. Individuals who perform this work are often highly compensated and their benefits are often commensurate with their salary. To retain such a person on the staff full-time may not make economic sense to the business, particularly if that person's skills are not needed 40 hours a week, 52 weeks a year.

Second, if a person is not needed full-time, even if that person is cross-trained in another craft, a business cannot pay a person at two different pay scales and expect to retain that employee for any length of time. The employee will in all likelihood seek out a full-time position at the higher pay scale. Cross-training of personnel in multiple crafts is an excellent strategy, but the crafts should be within the same wage scale. For instance, a landscaper might be cross-trained as a painter, or a painter might be also trained as carpenter, but you would not have an elevator repair person also be trained as a painter, or a computer technician who also mows the lawn.

Third, the risk associated with certain areas, as in elevator repair, may be shared between the hotel and the contracting company. If Otis Elevator Company performs repairs on a hotel's elevators and an elevator malfunctions, causing harm to a guest, then the liability would be borne by both parties.

Risk, other than financial risk, can also be equally spread between both parties. For example, if a hotel's computer server crashes unexpectedly, a contracted computer repair service may be obligated to immediately respond regardless of the day or time.

Fourth, certain scheduled maintenance activities that may range from the pool winterization, roof inspection and repair, and boiler cleaning, to the remodeling of guestrooms may require special equipment, and more maintenance personnel, than the hotel has on its full-time staff. Hiring an outside contractor who has the personnel and the equipment may save the hotel thousands of dollars in equipment purchases and staffing.

When hiring outside firms, several precautions should be taken. The contract should clearly state that it cannot be assigned to another person or firm without the written agreement of the hotel. It should also allow either party to terminate the contract at any time, for any reason, with a stated period of notice (typically 30 days) without penalty. That way if the work performed is substandard, the hotel can terminate the contract without risk, and if the contractor wants out of the contract, it is in the best interest of the hotel to terminate the agreement. Unhappy contractors usually mean substandard performance, which means unhappy hoteliers.

Care should be taken to hire extra security and take extra precautions when large numbers of contracted workers are on the premises. Even a single, contracted maintenance person should be under surveillance when on the property, and contracted employees should never be allowed to wear hotel uniforms or hotel badges. Contracted employees have not been screened by the hotel and some of these people may take advantage of their situation and commit theft or worse while on the premises. When the hotel places these contracted workers in a hotel uniform or gives them a hotel badge, the guest is lulled into complacency when a contracted worker presents himself at a guest's door asking to gain admission to the room. There have been several cases where this has happened; the guest was beaten, robbed or raped, and the hotel has been sued successfully due to its negligence.

Some hotels have elected to outsource the entire engineering department. This is usually only found in large properties where the economies of scale are large enough to make the outsourcing of the department profitable for the contracting firm. Las Vegas hotels such as the Aladdin and the Venetian have outsourced the entire facilities department to outside contractors. Arguments in favor of such a practice include fewer staff on the payroll and a resulting cost savings in employee benefits. The claim is made that the skill levels of the contracted employees are higher than the old in-house staff, and that results in increased savings for the property. Innovative approaches to maintenance and energy management by these highly skilled contracted employees can produce substantial cost savings that will be passed on to the hotel. Another assertion is that the hotel's top management no longer has to focus their attention on the property, and instead, can direct their attention to serving and satisfying the guest.

Those opposed to outsourcing the department argue that there is no cost savings to outsourcing, and that ultimately, it will cost the hotel more than if they did it themselves. Another argument made is that quality levels will go down when work is being performed by contracted employees whose loyalty lies with an outside firm, and not the hotel. Finally, the hotel runs a substantial risk if ever there is a falling out with the contracted firm. Replacing a contractor who is responsible for the entire engineering function is far more difficult than replacing a contractor who is responsible for only a single area.

BUDGETS, BLUEPRINTS, BENCHMARKS, AND FORMS

Budgets, blueprints (architect's renderings), benchmarks, and forms are four tools used by the chief engineer to carry out the department's assigned responsibilities. Budgets are an integral part of the planning process. Architect's renderings have a multitude of uses, from safety and security planning and remodeling projects to making simple one-time repairs to the facility. Benchmarks facilitate comparison of the facility to other properties, industry averages, and to itself. Forms convey information and are essential to the management activity of delegation.

One of the chief engineer's primary responsibilities every year is to prepare annual budgets. There are several different types of budgets and accounts used by the engineering department. In the following passages each of these different budgets and accounts will be examined.

Better Check the Blueprints

Years ago, when one of your authors was a graduate student at UNLV's hotel school, the Del Webb corporation contacted the college for assistance with the training of approximately 200 new employees at the Mint Hotel & Casino. Del Webb had decided to get rid of a lackluster bingo parlor and coffee shop on their second floor and completely renovate the space into a vast food court with over a dozen outlets similar to what one finds in a shopping mall. Del Webb's attorneys and the human resources staff at the Mint had negotiated with the culinary union and won the right to create a host of entirely new union positions. Architects and designers were hired to design employee uniforms and the food outlets. Over a dozen of the UNLV hotel faculty were hired to write training manuals for the new positions and train the new hires. Construction crews were assembled and demolition began. When the construction crew went into the coffee shop to demolish a wall that separated the dining room into two parts, they discovered a massive steel beam. Upon further inspection, it was discovered that the beam literally held up the entire high-rise building. It could not be removed. The beam ran the length of what was to be the center of the food court. That effectively ended the entire project. No one had bothered to check the blueprints. It was a massive oversight that probably cost the company over a million dollars. Before Del Webb became a casino company, it was a construction company that built several of the hotels on the strip, including the Flamingo. For a construction company to be guilty of such an oversight was simply unbelievable! And it cost this newly married graduate student a great job for the summer.

The Pre-Opening Budget

Pre-opening budgets are a one-time affair. The purchase of all of the necessary tools and supplies for the engineering department prior to a property's opening can be an extraordinary sum. This expenditure, along with all of the property's other pre-opening expenditures (e.g., china and glass in the restaurants, sheets and towels in the hotel, grand opening parties, etc.) would skew the new property's performance profile if it were to be written off within the first accounting period or even the first year of operation. Therefore, these expenses are often **amortized** over a number of years (three to five) to reflect the **matching principal of accounting** which holds that expenses should be matched with revenue. In other words, expenses should be recognized when revenues occur so that a better evaluation can be made of the business's profitability and performance.

Annual Budgets

The engineering department has three annual budgets: property operation and maintenance (POM), utilities, and capital expenditures. The annual capital expenditure budget is for capital goods (e.g., flooring, equipment, plumbing, furniture, plumbing fixtures, etc.) that are intended to last from a year to several decades. Capital items are depreciated rather than expensed on the income statement. Preparation of these budgets is a major responsibility of the director of facilities.

Today, many companies insist that a technique known as **zero-based budgeting** be implemented rather than simply taking last year's budget and adding an inflation factor to next year's budget, or using a formula approach. Zero-based budgeting begins from *zero*, that is, every item in the budget requires a justification or an explanation why it is included in the budget. There are no assumptions when making a zero-based budget.

The annual maintenance budget has three major categories: 1) labor, which includes wages and benefits; 2) supplies, which can range from equipment parts and tools to chemicals used in the department; and 3) outside contractor fees (outsourcing), for maintenance performed by entities that are not employees of the property. Roughly half of the budget will be spent on labor. Supplies and outsourcing will each consume approximately a quarter of the budget. Maintenance budgets can vary widely from property to property. Unexpected and unplanned (emergency) maintenance can play havoc with the annual budget, particularly if needed capital goods (e.g., equipment) were not included in the property's annual capital budget. Then the engineering department is left with a choice. One option is to forgo purchasing equipment and material that were included in the capital budget and use the funds to purchase equipment that unexpectedly failed. Another option is to pay for the failed equipment with annual operating funds. This, of course, is not an option if the cost of the replaced equipment is significant for it might severely restrain the other maintenance activities. The third option is to appeal to top management to provide the funds to make the unanticipated repairs.

Although competent facilities directors may be able to analyze the state of their buildings and equipment most of the time, they are not infallible. Building systems and equipment cannot read budgets and calendars, so failure can and does occur at the most inopportune times (typically, at 4:00 A.M. on a holiday). When that unexpected failure does occur, its repair is most likely not in the budget. Given that a facility manager is expected to keep his or her costs in line; there is an expectation by top management that any variance in a cost from the budgeted amount is within established guidelines. When those guidelines are exceeded in either direction, either above or below the budgeted figure, the facility manager will be expected to explain the reason behind the variance to top management.

The seasoned facility manager fully expects to see a *surprise* or two over the fiscal year. Astute facility managers might budget for the unforeseen, but the budget does not have a category for unanticipated expenses. Nevertheless, facility managers may creatively pad their capital expenditure and annual maintenance budgets in anticipation of emergency maintenance.

Famed facilities expert Dr. Frank Borsenik was of the opinion that in a well-run engineering department, roughly 70% of the money and time should be appropriated for preventive maintenance, 25% should be appropriated for the improvement of the property (i.e., making it better than the day it opened), and only 5% should be needed for emergency maintenance. Borsenik's estimates should be viewed as goals that every professional chief engineer should aspire to meet, but even in the best-run facilities, the unexpected can happen. How well these emergencies are mitigated to protect the health, safety, and comfort of the building's occupants, and at the same time, protect the assets of the company is the mark of a true facility manager.

The annual utility budget will have a category for each type of energy used by the property. It will also contain categories for water and sewer charges and for solid waste disposal fees. The largest category (70%–80% of the total budget) by far for most properties will be electricity. The utility budget can vary widely. Two major variables impacting the budget are property location and construction. In different regions of the United States, utility rates may vary by as much as 35% or more due to available supply and demand.

Construction of the property, including the type of building systems and equipment used will also impact the utility budget. When energy management was not a major consideration in building construction, outside temperatures and weather conditions were more of a factor in building utility usage than occupancy. Now, with more energy-efficient buildings, occupancy is a greater factor in utility usage than outside temperatures and weather conditions. It is easier to predict utility usage than it is to predict utility costs, because costs will vary based on fuel supply, and the utility's propensity and ability to raise its rates.

CapEx budgets will vary widely from year to year. In some years when no remodeling, renovation, or restoration is anticipated, the budget will be minimal. It may contain only those individual items that typically fail during the year. For example, according to the property's repair history, it is estimated that six television sets will completely fail during the coming year; money will be budgeted for the purchase of six televisions in the annual capital expenditure budget.

When a complete restoration is anticipated in the coming year, that budget may swell to millions of dollars depending on the size and type of property. In addition to capital goods, labor costs associated with a remodeling, renovation, or restoration will appear on the capital expenditure budget.

Budget preparation often begins in the last quarter of the current fiscal year and may take the facility director months to complete the budget and have it approved. Top management may reject a submitted budget and request the facility director to revise and resubmit. This process may be repeated several times before the budgets are finally approved.

Blueprints

The craft of technical drawing, also known as drafting, enables architects and engineers to create accurate representations of three-dimensional objects (e.g., buildings, equipment) on a two-dimensional plane. These drawings, commonly referred to as blueprints, are no longer blue. The cyanotype printing process which makes white lines on blue paper was invented in the 19th century. It became a favorite method of printing large architectural and engineering renderings, primarily because it was a cheap method of printing. Today, building renderings and equipment schematics are often produced through the aid of computer programs (i.e., computer assisted design and drafting, or **CADD**) and, when printed, the paper is no long blue with white lines.

The blueprint **floor plan**, or bird's eye view, is an overhead perspective of a building's floor drawn to scale (typically ¼" = 1'). It shows permanent objects such as the location of walls, doors, and windows. Figure 2.8 is a relatively simple example of a floor plan.

Another blueprint is the **elevation plan** (Figure 2.9). There are typically four elevation plans for a building showing the front, rear, and two sides of the exterior of the building. It resembles a photograph of a building taken from a head-on (two-dimensional) perspective and is also drawn to scale.

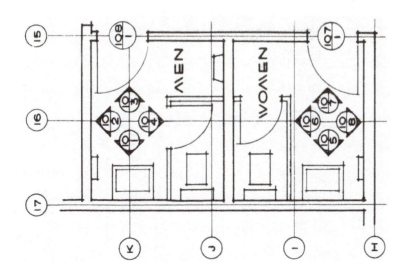

FIGURE 2.8 Floor Plan. *Source*: Reading Architectural Plans for Residential and Commercial Construction—by Ernest Weidhaas, Prentice Hall 1989.

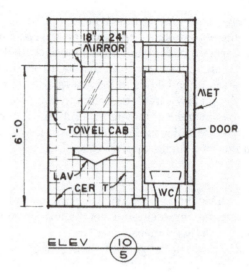

FIGURE 2.9 Elevation Plan. *Source:* Reading Architectural Plans for Residential and Commercial Construction—by Ernest Weidhaas, Prentice Hall 1989.

A third type of building blueprint is the **mechanical plan** (Figure 2.10). Mechanical plans show plumbing fixtures and water flow in a building, as well as HVAC equipment and ductwork drawn to scale. A counterpart to the mechanical plan is the **electrical plan** (Figure 2.11) or layout which shows the location of wiring, outlets, electrical equipment, and permanent lighting fixtures.

Another common blueprint is the **perspective projection** (Figure 2.12) which renders a three-dimensional image on a two-dimensional plane.

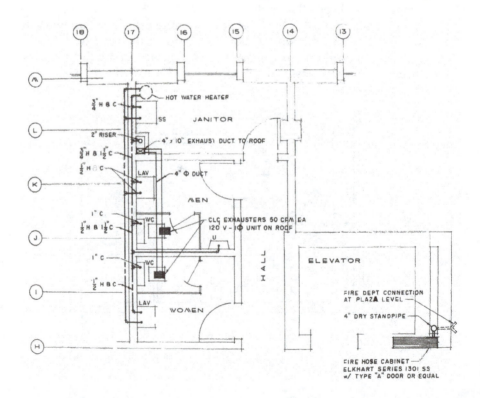

FIGURE 2.10 Mechanical Plan (Plumbing). *Source:* Reading Architectural Plans for Residential and Commercial Construction—by Ernest Weidhaas, Prentice Hall 1989.

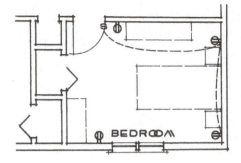

INTERPRETATION:

CONVENTIONAL NUMBER OF OUTLETS,
2 CONTROLLED BY SWITCH

BEDROOM

FIGURE 2.11   Electrical Plan. *Source:* Reading Architectural Plans for Residential and Commercial Construction—by Ernest Weidhaas, Prentice Hall 1989.

Perspective projections enable building owners and operators to visualize what a completed building will actually look like. **Detail views** (Figure 2.13) show construction details that cannot be shown clearly enough in a floor plan. Detail views can be referenced in a floor plan that will show contractors exactly what needs to be done in the construction of an element. **Section plans** (Figure 2.14) show cutaways of walls, floors, ceilings, and foundations. The cutaways may be either vertical or horizontal. Section plans are essential in visualizing what is contained within the structure, such as the placement of insulation in a wall. **Plot** or **survey plans** (Figure 2.15) are a bird's eye view of both the facility and the property. The difference between these two categories is the survey plan is done by a certified or licensed surveyor and can serve as a legal description of the property. **Contour lines** show the elevation above or below **benchmarks** on plot or survey plans. A benchmark is a point whose position is known to a high degree of accuracy and is normally marked in some way. They are used by land surveyors, builders and engineers, map makers, and other professionals who need an accurate answer to the question, "Where?" Many of these markers are part of the geodetic control network (technically known as the National Spatial Reference System, or NSRS) created and maintained by the National Geodetic Survey (NGS).

Finally, there are **equipment schematics** that show the wiring, fuses, switches, solenoids, and relays on a piece of equipment. These drawings are

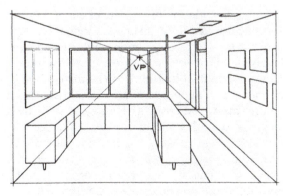

One-point interior perspective.

FIGURE 2.12 Perspective Projection. *Source:* Reading Architectural Plans for Residential and Commercial Construction—by Ernest Weidhaas, Prentice Hall 1989.

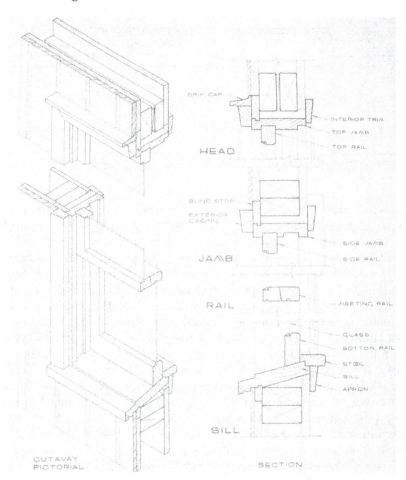

FIGURE 2.13 Detail
View. *Source:* Reading
Architectural Plans
for Residential
and Commercial
Construction—by
Ernest Weidhaas,
Prentice Hall 1989.

invaluable when performing preventive maintenance, or when a malfunction occurs and a technician attempts to **troubleshoot** the problem.

The original intention of these architectural renderings is to enable contractors to build the facility, but they also serve many other important purposes. The property's blueprints are also essential to remodeling and renovation. One example would be the installation of new furnishings in guest rooms. If the dimensions of the new furnishings were known, then the designer could determine if the new furniture will fit in the room with the aid of a floor plan, and without literally having to try out the new furniture in a room.

There are times when the blueprints can be misleading if they do not reflect subsequent changes to the property from the original construction. This can cause delays and may even create safety issues. For example, a remodeling crew may begin to demolish an interior wall that contains a gas line installed after the building was constructed, but the plans were never updated to reflect the installation.

Blueprints are also often lost or damaged over the years through improper storage and handling. This too can cause potentially costly and hazardous

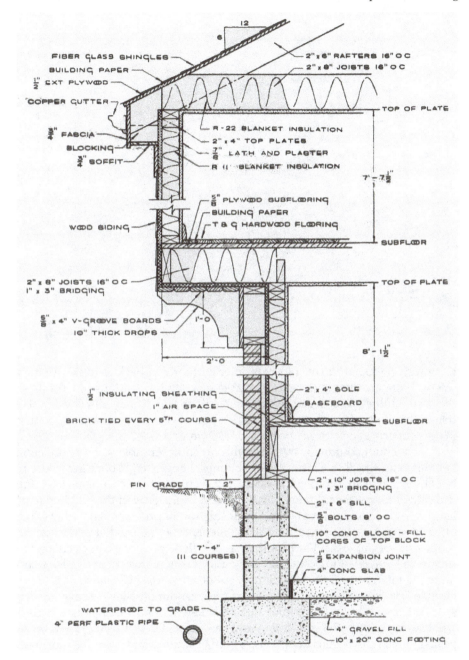

FIBER GLASS SHINGLES
BUILDING PAPER
½" EXT PLYWOOD
COPPER GUTTER
12
6
2" x 6" RAFTERS 16" O C
2" x 8" JOISTS 16" O C
TOP OF PLATE
¾" FASCIA
BLOCKING
¾" SOFFIT
R - 22 BLANKET INSULATION
2" x 4" TOP PLATES
⅞" LATH AND PLASTER
R II BLANKET INSULATION
7' - 7½"
WOOD SIDING
⅝" PLYWOOD SUBFLOORING
BUILDING PAPER
T & G HARDWOOD FLOORING
SUBFLOOR
2" x 8" JOISTS 16" O C
1" x 3" BRIDGING
TOP OF PLATE
⅝" x 4" V-GROOVE BOARDS
10" THICK DROPS
1'-0
2'-0
8' - 1½"
½" INSULATING SHEATHING
1" AIR SPACE
BRICK TIED EVERY 5TH COURSE
2" x 4" SOLE
BASEBOARD
SUBFLOOR
FIN GRADE
2"
2" x 10" JOISTS 16" O C
1" x 3" BRIDGING
2" x 6" SILL
⅝" BOLTS 8' OC
10" CONC BLOCK - FILL CORES OF TOP BLOCK
7'-4"
(11 COURSES)
½" EXPANSION JOINT
4" CONC SLAB
WATERPROOF TO GRADE
4" PERF PLASTIC PIPE
4" GRAVEL FILL
10" x 20" CONC FOOTING

FIGURE 2.14 Section Plan. *Source:* Reading Architectural Plans for Residential and Commercial Construction—by Ernest Weidhaas, Prentice Hall 1989.

conditions. A plan to ensure the proper handling of all building documents including blueprints should be instituted at the property. Building documents are as great an asset to the enterprise as the building's bricks and mortar. The intelligent facility manager will spend the time and money to have the building's blueprints scanned and digitized. The electronic version can then

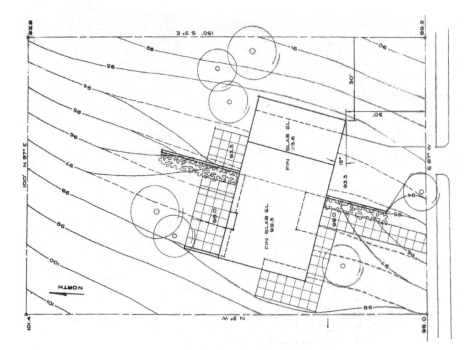

FIGURE 2.15 Plot Plan.
Source: Reading
Architectural Plans
for Residential
and Commercial
Construction—by
Ernest Weidhaas,
Prentice Hall 1989.

be stored on the hard drive of a computer with proper backup to ensure their safety. There are even programs available that can link various blueprints so that a computer operator can switch from a floor plan to a detail view of a section of that floor plan. Changes to existing plans reflecting a recent renovation in the property can be done through CADD programs.

As mentioned previously, blueprints are indispensable when remodeling or renovating a facility. This includes not only changes to the building's design, but also changes to improve the safety and security of the occupants (e.g., fire and other life safety equipment) and the energy efficiency of the building (e.g., lamp retrofits, window replacements, insulation improvements). Other blueprint uses include the scheduling of maintenance and custodial personnel for routine or special tasks. For example, from a floor plan one can calculate the square feet that need to be vacuumed in a convention area. Then a quick referral to the International Sanitary Supply Association's *447 Cleaning Times* to determine how many square feet a person can vacuum on a level surface with a specified size and type of vacuum and a calculation of how many man-hours it will take to vacuum the convention area can be made. This scenario can be repeated for literally dozens upon dozens of maintenance and custodial functions.

Benchmarks

Benchmarks are another set of tools used by the chief engineer to manage the facility. They allow comparisons to be made on the building's performance such as utility usage or efficiency, staffing levels, and maintenance efficiencies. The hotel's performance can be compared to industry averages, sister properties within a corporation, or even internal benchmarks when the property

> Maintenance Costs as % of Revenue
> Annual Maintenance Costs per Guest Room
> Annual Maintenance Costs per Sq. Ft.
> Annual Utility Costs as % of Revenue
> Annual Utility Costs per Sq. Ft.
> BTUs Used per Sq. Ft.
> Engineering Employees per Guest Room

FIGURE 2.16   Common Engineering Benchmarks.

compares its current performance to prior levels of performance. When done over a period of time, this is referred to as a *longitudinal comparison*. The benchmark may be stated in dollars, percentages, or a host of different measures, such as square feet, **kilowatts**, or **British Thermal Units** (BTU). The proper measure must be carefully selected, because certain measures may not be truly reflective of the building's performance. For example, in the case of energy usage, using a measure of dollars spent per square foot of property on energy over the past year may not be an accurate measure of energy conservation efforts. Utility rate increases would cause the benchmark to be an inaccurate portrayal of the engineering department's attempt to conserve energy. A more accurate portrayal of the hotel's energy usage would be the number of BTU's of energy consumed per square foot over the past year. Common benchmarks for hotel engineering are given in Figure 2.16.

Environmental benchmarks are among the newest types of benchmarks for hotels. According to the Environmental Protection Agency (EPA) the energy costs for United States hotels is approximately $5 billion per annum. In order to inspire hotel companies to conserve our nation's energy resources, the EPA has created a special category for hotels under their *Energy Star* program. Hotels can benchmark their energy usage against their competitors and if they are in the upper quartile of properties, they will achieve the designation of an *Energy Star Leader*. This certification can be used in the marketing of a property as an environmentally responsible organization. Thus, it provides a double benefit to the firm, because there is a reduction in energy costs to the hotel and the hotel is the recipient of some great public relations.

Forms and the Processes they Represent

There are a number of forms that are specific to the facility department, but none is more ubiquitous than the **work order,** also known as the *work request*. The work order is really more than just a simple form. It is a communications system that makes the facility department aware of maintenance problems so that action can be taken to rectify the situation in a timely manner. Since the facility department is a relatively small department (averaging three employees per 100 rooms) members of the department can't be everywhere every day. Other departments must serve as the eyes and ears of the facility department. Housekeeping, which has more employees than any other department in the hotel, often serves as the facility department's primary set of eyes and ears. Housekeeping also has the responsibility of entering every room in the hotel every day so they are often the first on the scene when a maintenance problem occurs. Some exceptional properties even establish work order quotas for the housekeeping department, forcing the housekeeping staff to look for and report maintenance problems.

In addition to housekeeping, any department in the hotel may have an occasion to submit a work request. The front desk is generally a major generator of work orders initiated by guests. Guests themselves may also directly generate work orders to the facility department through the telephone. There may even be forms in the guest room for guests who discover a problem. These work requests can then be left at or phoned in to the front desk. In Figure 2.17 there is an example of a work order in two parts; one of the sections is returned to the guests informing them of action taken on the request.

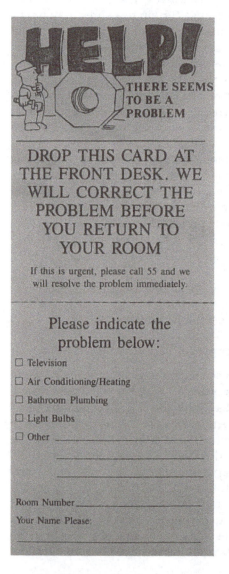

FIGURE 2.17   Two Part Work Order.

Figure 2.18 is an example of a computerized work order for a hotel. Evidently, a guest has reported problems with the door hinge. Once the problem is fixed the maintenance technician then enters an update on the work order that is filed into the computer's memory, where it can then be accessed by the individual who filed the request in the first place. There are even computerized versions of work requests that show a room's layout on the screen. The person who is entering the work order can merely point and click to specific areas of the room where the problem is located. Then the software program allows the operator to click on the exact problem from an array of possibilities, or enter the information if the problem is not listed.

All effective communication systems must contain a sender of the message, a recipient of the message, the message itself, and feedback so that the sender of a message understands that the message was received and understood. Since the sender and the recipient of a work order are often separated by time and space, there must also be a way to preserve the message

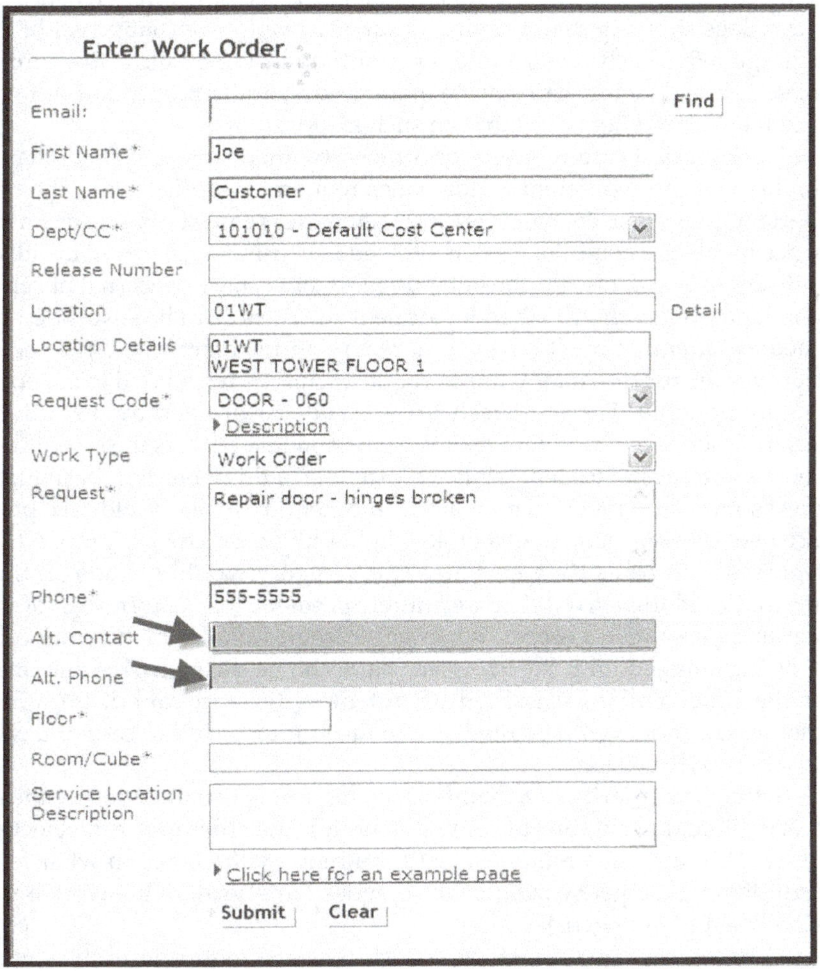

FIGURE 2.18
Computerized Work Order.

and the feedback. Consequently, most modern work order systems are computer-automated.

This also allows the department to create an electronic **maintenance log.** A maintenance log can identify trends (trend logging) that can point to maintenance issues and concerns. If the data can be queried, these concerns can "pop out" of the stored data. For example, it may be revealed that over 200 television remote controls in a 250-room hotel were replaced in one year due their being "appropriated" by guests. This information may prompt management to lock the remotes on the guest nightstand to reduce their loss.

Maintenance logs and work orders can also be used to track labor productivity, as well. Figure 2.19 is an example of a maintenance log on preventive maintenance tasks that would be filled out by a maintenance technician so that management can evaluate the technician's productivity.

Maintenance logs can even be used in court cases. A Las Vegas hotel was being sued for punitive and medical damages resulting from a guest who allegedly cut her leg on a bed frame. The hotel produced their maintenance and security logs showing that a similar occurrence had never happened before. The judge reduced the award to the plaintiff and did not allow the punitive damages since the hotel had never experienced a similar problem prior to this incident and could not have foreseen such an occurrence.

Work requests are typically prioritized by their urgency. There may be two, three, or more different maintenance request categories used. The most important category is the **emergency maintenance request**. Emergency maintenance involves a condition that, if allowed to continue, will result in either a significant financial loss for the hotel or guest, or a safety concern that can result in injury or death. All other department activities must be suspended and immediate attention must be given to rectifying the emergency. The second category is the **routine maintenance request** which is responded to as soon as humanly possible. These requests are typically prioritized by the order in which they are received. There may be an option that enables the submitter to request a faster response if possible. An example of this would be the failure of a guest's room air conditioner on a hot summer day which could take precedence over the replacement of a broken light bulb in a credenza lamp. A third category would be **as time permits.** This category would include all those items that need to be fixed that are entirely cosmetic (e.g., a torn strip of wall paper in an executive's office). When parts are not available, the work order will be **backlogged** until the necessary parts can be secured. This may mean that the room will be classified as **out of order** and cannot be rented. Sometimes, a room can be rented at a reduced rate, as in the case of a room with a broken television.

Setting the priority of a maintenance request is usually done by the engineering department, but in some properties, the submitter can select the priority. This approach requires careful training by the hotel on what really constitutes an emergency maintenance request, or else all of the work orders are likely to be "emergencies."

Most work orders are fairly straightforward requiring nothing more than the dispatching of the appropriate employee to fix the problem (e.g., a

PREVENTIVE MAINTENANCE WORK LOG

Work Order No : 0000010579   WorkTrade : **Hotel - Engineer**

Work Order Status : **Open**   Assigned to : **Yates, Dan**

PM Date : **01/11/2008**

Work Description : **Daily Work Log - Dan Yates - Friday**

Start Date: _____   Start Time: _____

Completion Date: _____   Completion Time: _____

Certification of Work Completion

Name and Signature of Employee			Name and Signature of Supervisor		
....	....	....	....	....	....
Print Name	Employee No.	Signature	Print Name	Employee No.	Signature

Estimated Labour Hours :   6

Daily Work Order Log

Location	Problem	Dispatch Time	Complete Time	Closed Time	Comments
_____	_____	_____	_____	_____	_____
_____	_____	_____	_____	_____	_____
_____	_____	_____	_____	_____	_____
_____	_____	_____	_____	_____	_____
_____	_____	_____	_____	_____	_____
_____	_____	_____	_____	_____	_____
_____	_____	_____	_____	_____	_____
_____	_____	_____	_____	_____	_____
_____	_____	_____	_____	_____	_____
_____	_____	_____	_____	_____	_____
_____	_____	_____	_____	_____	_____
_____	_____	_____	_____	_____	_____

TAKE
PRIDE
keep our property safe & clean

FIGURE 2.19
Maintenance Log.
Source: Courtesy of Circus
Circus, Las Vegas, NV.

plugged toilet requires the assistance of a plumber). However, the situation can be more complex. Sometimes a manager from the department must first be dispatched to ascertain the problem and determine which department employees are needed and in what priority to fix the problem. A problem such as an electrical short in a wall sconce may first require a carpenter, followed by an electrician, followed by another carpenter, and finally a painter to fix the problem. By sending a manager first, valuable time and money can be saved.

Other department forms, in addition to work orders and maintenance logs, include **inventory records, energy records, schedules, equipment data cards, room data cards,** assorted **flow charts, checklists/punchlists, standard operating procedures** for maintenance, and **material safety data sheets** (MSDS).

In a large hotel the facility department inventory storeroom can resemble a small hardware store. Everything from tools and furniture to light bulbs can be found in them. Maintaining the inventory (e.g., ordering, receiving, cataloging, and requisitioning items) may require several full-time personnel. Inventory records assure that prescribed levels are maintained and there is a complete accounting for every item that passes through the engineering storeroom.

Many properties do not rely exclusively on the utility's records of a property's energy usage. Mistakes can and do happen in billing, and are more often in favor of the utility than the hotel. Many hotels maintain their own metering system (either digital or analog) and their own records. This allows the property to respond more quickly to problems rather than waiting until the end of the billing period to discover that there is a problem.

A facility department will have employees' **work schedules** indicating when each employee in the department is scheduled to work. The department will also use **maintenance schedules** that are nothing more than a calendar indicating on what days specific time-based maintenance activities will take place.

Equipment and room data forms are standardized forms that contain critical information on specific rooms or pieces of equipment. One example is given in Figure 2.20.

A flowchart is defined as a pictorial representation describing a process being studied or even used to plan stages of a project. Flowcharts tend to provide people with a common language or reference point when dealing with a project or process. A flowchart with a lighthearted look at problem solving is pictured in Figure 2.21.

Checklists or punchlists are commonly used to inspect guest rooms and equipment. By following a checklist such as the one in Figure 2.22, the engineer inspecting the room is less likely to overlook any of the room or equipment components. Checklists are based on the hotel's established **performance standards** and are a method of delegation. A subordinate can take the checklist, and determine whether or not the guest room or equipment in question meets the company's standards without the presence of management.

Standard operating procedures are another one of the ways management can effectively delegate tasks to subordinates with a reasonable degree of assurance that a task will be done according to the company's standard. They are certainly far better than merely stating to the employee what is to be done and the expected results. SOPs can be used for most maintenance activities. A copy can be given to the technician to refer to when performing the maintenance activity. One is featured in Figure 2.23.

Building Number C East			Room Number 1214		
Area	Length	Width	Ceiling Height	Total Sq. Ft.	Sq. Yards
Bedroom Area	18'	14'	8'	252	28
Bathroom Area	8'	12'	8'	96	10.66
Carpet Texture	Carpet Fiber	Sq. Yards	Manufacturer	Cost per Yd.	Date Installed
Cut Loop	Nylon	28	Shaw Indust.	$14.00	07/2004
Drape Fabric	Length	Width	Manufacturer	Cost per Yd.	Date Installed
Rayon	7'	9'	Miller	$12.00	06/2006
Mattress Size	Manufacturer	Model	Special Features	Cost	Date Installed
Queen	Sealy	PosturePedic	Pillow Top	$1,245	08/2006
Bedroom Furnishings	Description/ Number	Bedroom Furnishings	Description/ Number	Bathroom Fixtures	Description/ Number
Mirror	1– 6' × 2"	Television	42" Panasonic LED w/remote	Counter	Corian Healing Colors
Dresser	1 Walnut Broyhill	Alarm/Radio	G.E. LED	Tile	Armstrong Earth Tones "Rust" rectified
Lounge Chair	1 Recliner – Lazy Boy	Cable Box	LodgeTech	Wall Color	Gliden "Forest" 124A
Occasional Chair	1 desk chair	Refrigerator	None	Ceiling Color	Gliden "Spring" 166AC
Night Stands	2 Broyhill	Pictures	2 Litho	Lighting	Makeup Bar 60 65 watt incandescent Ceiling 4/T-8 luminaire panel
Sofa	None	Wall Color	Gliden "Forest" 124A	Mechanical Data	Description/ Number
Lamps	2 End Table 1 Swag 1 Dresser	Ceiling Color	Gliden "Spring" 166AC	Heat Pump	Carrier – Model 52M
Desk	1 Broyhill	Bathroom Fixtures	Description/ Number	Pendant Sprinklers	1 Bath & 1 Bedroom
Headboard	1 Walnut Broyhill	Toilet	American Standard – Cadet	Sidewall Sprinklers	1 Bedroom
Telephone	2 Desk and Nightstand	Tub/Shower	Kohler Terracina	Locks	Schlage CM5100
Safe	None	Basin	Kohler Archer	Smoke Detector	2 - Cerberus Elite

FIGURE 2.20   Room Data Form.

Flowchart for Problem Resolution

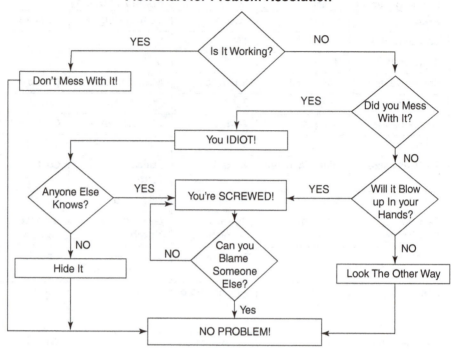

FIGURE 2.21 "Yes—it's a Flow Chart and it's also a Joke!"

An MSDS is created by a chemical manufacturer and explains the chemical's characteristics, recommended handling, use and storage, information on flammability, ingredients, health hazards, first-aid procedures, and what to do in case of a fire or explosion. This information must be disseminated to all employees who might come in contact with a chemical and should be available to them at all times. An example of a MSDS appears in Chapter Four.

WORKING IN THE DEPARTMENT

Employees in the facilities department are either specialists or generalists. Larger properties tend to have far more specialists, and the smaller hotels will tend toward fewer specialists and more generalists. Many of the employees in the department have received their education from local vocational/technical schools or community colleges. Some of the personnel may be retired military who have received their building operations training during their military service. Traditionally, the department has been male-dominated, but that trend is slowly changing and more women can be found in the facility department.

Many of the department's generalists have come directly from secondary education programs and have received all of their training in-house. The typical employee is paid at a higher rate than the employees in many other hotel departments. The average hourly wage rate for an engineering department employee is approximately $15.00/hr, not including benefits. Positions at union properties in large urban areas can be even more. Some positions require

PREVENTIVE MAINTENANCE CHECKLIST

Work Order No : 0000011588   WorkTrade : **Life Safety**

Work Order Status : **Open**   Assigned to : **Harmony**

PM Date : **01/14/2008**

Work Description : **Weekly Skyrise Electric Fire Pump**
Asset Name : **Skyrise Electric Fire Pump**
Location Name : **Skyrise**

Start Date: _____   Start Time: _____

Completion Date: _____   Completion Time: _____   % Complete

Certification of Work Completion

Name and Signature of Employee	Name and Signature of Supervisor
Print Name Employee No. Signature	Print Name Employee No. Signature

Estimated Labour Hours :   1

Weekly Skyrise Electric Fire Pump Inspection
10 Minute Load on Electric Pump

Pump rating: _____ gpm @ _____ psi @ _____rpm

                                                        Yes   No

1. Is fire pump controller on "automatic"?   ____ ____
2. Is jockey pump controller on "automatic"?   ____ ____
3. Are all jockey pump and fire pump control valves open? ____ ____
4. Is jockey pump running frequency normal?   ____ ____
5. Is pump room adequately heated?   ____ ____
6. Did fire pump start automatically by a drop in water pressure? ____ ____
Record the following: Pump start pressure   _____ psi
                           Pump discharge pressure _____ psi
                           Pump suction pressure   _____ psi
7. Are pump bearings operating at normal temperature?   ____ ____
8. Are pump packing glands leaking sufficient water?   ____ ____
9. Is pump free of unusual noises and vibrations?   ____ ____
10. Is pump circulating relief valve operating?   ____ ____
11. Is the pump test header drained to prevent freezing?   ____ ____
12. Is a charged fire extinguisher in the pump room?   ____ ____
13. Is pump room clean and free of combustion materials?   ____ ____
14. Is pump controller's "Power Available" light on?   ____ ____
15. Did all remote pump alarms function properly?   ____ ____
(i.e. running, controller not on "automatic", etc.)
16. Was water trank overfilled to verify it's full, or is reservoir at normal level? ____ ____
17. Was pump run for at least 10 minutes?   ____ ____
18. Were both the jockey pump and fire pump controllers left on "automatic"? ____ ____

TAKE
PRIDE
keep our property safe & clean

FIGURE 2.22   Fire Pump PM Checklist.   *Source:* Courtesy of Circus Circus, Las Vegas, NV.

Hotel Excelsior

Engineering Services—PM Standard Operating Procedure

Fire Alarm System

INSPECTION AND SERVICE OF FIRE PUMPS AND CONTROLLERS—QUARTERLY
NOTE: Instructions available at electrical supervisor's office.

1. Coordinate this routine with mechanical section for availability and shutdown.
2. Notify fire desk that fire pump will be taken out of service.
3. Only one fire pump can be removed from service for maintenance at any time.
4. Read Instructions before starting routine maintenance.
5. De-energize and tag out fire pump.
6. Inspect motor air cooling passage way, determine if clear and clean as needed.
7. Take megger readings of motor and record. Megger readings should be above 1 megohm.
8. If reading is below 1 megohm, disconnect motor at motor terminal box.
9. Inspect wiring at that point and megger motor again.
10. If Megohm readings are still low, report condition to foreman for further consideration.
11. Inspect the starter cabinet for signs of overheating, dampness, corrosion or signs of water entering cabinet.
12. Check interior for dirt and debris and clean as needed.
13. Inspect contacter contacts for excessive wear and replace as needed.
14. Check electrical connection, mechanic nuts and bolts and tighten as needed.
15. Re-energize fire pump circuits and remove tag.
16. Test run fire pump and use clamp-on Xer to record ampere load.
17. Record and report to foreman if any motor operates above name plate amperage.
18. Terminate fire pump test and return fire pump to mechanical section for operational use.
19. Notify the Fire Desk of end to fire pump servicing.
20. Report any problems or deficiencies to foreman, verbally and in writing on routine work order.

FIGURE 2.23 Standard Operating Procedure.

certification in some states, such as, boiler operation and maintenance, swimming pool maintenance, plumbing, and electrical.

Employees of the department may include but are not limited to:

- Secretaries/Dispatchers
- Electricians
- Plumbers
- Carpenters
- Refrigeration Technicians
- Boiler Operators
- Painters
- Landscaping and Grounds Personnel
- Fire Control and Security Systems Specialists
- Elevator Technicians
- Automotive Mechanics
- Computer Technicians

Whenever possible, employees of the department should be trained in multiple crafts that have the same pay scale. This flexibility will increase the department's productivity. However, this may not be an option in a unionized property.

MANAGING THE DEPARTMENT

The chief engineer or facility director of today is more at home in a suit behind a desk running a computer than walking around a property with a pipe wrench in his bib overhauls and a stogie in his mouth like his stereotypical predecessor. Even though the position of director of facilities is an executive position, it is not as highly paid as some of the other executive positions in the hotel. In fact, salary levels lag behind the almost all of the other managers who are members of the executive committee. Depending on the size and location of the property, the salary level will range from the mid-thirties to over $100,000 per annum with average of approximately $50,000 per annum.

In regard to the educational background, one might expect a chief engineer to have a degree in mechanical engineering, but that is rarely the case in the United States. Frankly, the pay scale for chief engineers in hospitality facilities is not high enough to attract those who possess an engineering degree. In Germany and Japan, salaries are competitive enough to attract individuals who possess an engineering degree.

In the United States, most chief engineers have risen through the ranks. Typically, they are individuals who are recognized by top management as having management aptitude. Some may have business degrees in their backgrounds, but far more receive their management training in-house. Another avenue open to a rank-and-file building engineer is to receive their education through associations serving building engineers. Organizations, such as the International Facilities Management Association (IFMA), the Building Owners and Managers Association (BOMA), and the American Hotel & Lodging Association, offer courses, educational materials, and certification programs to their members.

Summary

Managing the engineering department over the past half-century has not gotten any easier. To the contrary, the number and complexity of the responsibilities assigned to the department over the last 50 years have increased beyond anyone's expectations. Unfortunately, the chief engineer has not received a corresponding increase in either personnel or funding to meet these new responsibilities.

The chief engineer has had to rely on technology and the latest and most sophisticated management tools available to meet the department's obligations. The computer has proven to be an indispensable aid. The CMMS program helps the chief engineer to plan, manage, and administer almost every aspect of the maintenance function. Computers also help to mitigate the impact of the rising costs of all utilities through energy conversation programs.

Shrewd chief engineers have also employed many of the management strategies and tactics discussed in this chapter, from integrated resource management to zero-based budgeting. To remain competitive in the marketplace, the engineering department must continue to identify and employ the latest management tools and techniques, because the number and complexity of the department's responsibilities are certain to increase.

Key Terms and Concepts

Amortized *33*
as time permits *44*
ASHRAE *16*
backlogged *44*
benchmarks *37*
British Thermal Unit (BTU) *41*
CADD *35*
CapEx *25*
case goods *25*
checklists/punchlists *46*
chillers *20*
commissioning *16*
Computerized Maintenance Management System (CMMS) *27*
condition-based maintenance *17*
contour lines *37*
deferred maintenance *19*
detail views *37*
electrical plan *36*
elevation plan *35*
emergency maintenance *17*
emergency maintenance request *44*

energy records *46*
equipment data cards *46*
equipment schematics *37*
executive committee *29*
floor plan *35*
flow charts *46*
general manager *29*
HVAC *26*
Integrated Pest Management (IPM) *19*
Integrated Resource Management (IRM) *18*
inventory records *46*
kilowatts *41*
LEED *15*
Life Cycle Cost Analysis (LCCA) *22*
line *28*
maintenance log *44*
maintenance schedules *46*
manage upward *29*
matching principal of accounting *33*

material safety data sheets *46*
mechanical plan *36*
out of order *44*
outsourced *28*
performance standards *46*
perspective projection *36*
plot plans *37*
predictive maintenance *17*
pre-opening budgets *33*
preventive maintenance *17*
Property Management System (PMS) *27*
property operation and maintenance (POM) *24*
reactive maintenance *17*
reliability-centered maintenance *17*
reserve for replacement *25*
retro-commissioning *16*
room data cards *46*

routine maintenance *15*
routine maintenance request *44*
run-to-failure maintenance *15*
scheduled maintenance *16*
schedules *46*
section plans *37*
soft goods *25*
staff *28*
standard operating procedures *46*
submetering *25*
survey plan *37*
TAB *16*
time-based maintenance *15*
trend logging *27*
troubleshoot *38*
utilities *24*
work order *41*
work schedules *46*
zero-based budgeting *33*

Discussion and Review Questions

1. Write a job specification (list of requirements) for a director of facilities for a 100-room and a 500-room hotel. Compare and contrast the two specifications and discuss the differences with your fellow students.

2. Given the importance of the facility department and the responsibilities of the director of facilities, why do you think a facility director's average salary is lower than the rest of the hotel's executive committee (i.e., HR Director, Director of S&M, Hotel Mgr., Dir. of F&B, & Controller)? You should list as many possible reasons as you can, and compare your answers with other students.

3. Outsourcing is a common practice in many hotels. What are the potential pitfalls associated with the practice? What can be done to avoid problems with independent contractors?

4. Generate reasons why deferring maintenance is a particularly bad idea for hotels and restaurants? Discuss your reasons with the rest of the class.

3

Issues and Trends

CHAPTER OBJECTIVES

After studying the chapter, the student should be able to:

- describe the factors that influence global climate change.
- describe the impact of global climate change on the planet.
- describe the impact of global climate change on the hospitality industry.
- define "sustainability" and the "triple-bottom line."
- describe the process of green certification and the major third-party certification organizations.
- describe the five titles of the Americans with Disabilities Act.

INTRODUCTION

This chapter is devoted to those issues and trends impacting the United States hospitality industry in general, and the facility department in particular. Some of these issues are the result of recent legislation, such as the American with Disabilities Act that has continued to influence hospitality facilities since its passage in 1990. Others are the result of what man has done to his environment, such as global climate change, and the depletion of natural resources. We will begin with what has been called the greatest threat facing humanity today.

GLOBAL CLIMATE CHANGE

Earth's climate has never been constant and immutable. The Serbian astrophysicist Milutin Milankovitch (1879–1958) developed one of the world's most well-known and respected theories on the impact of the Earth's movement on long-term global climate change. Milankovitch theorized that there were three factors that impact climate change.

The first factor is the Earth's orbital eccentricity or shape. Over a period of roughly 100,000 years, the Earth will change from a relatively round orbit (low eccentric) to that of an elliptical (high eccentric) orbit. The high eccentric orbit brings Earth closer to the sun at its closest approach (perihelion) in this orbit. Thus, more solar radiation (i.e., insolation) is received by the Earth, which, in turn, makes it a warmer planet.

The second factor is the phenomenon of the Earth's change in its axial tilt (obliquity). This tilt varies between 22.1 and 24.5 degrees from the Earth's orbital plane around the sun. When the tilt is greater, the summers are warmer and the winters are colder. Currently, the Earth's obliquity is 23.5 degrees.

The third factor is the change in the orientation of the Earth's rotational axis (precession). If one hemisphere of the Earth is pointed toward the sun at perihelion and away from the sun when it is at its furthest point from the sun (aphelion), the seasons will be more extreme. This seasonal effect is reversed for the other hemisphere.

Studies of deep-sea sediment cores have supported Milankovitch's theory, and in the last two decades, it has been widely accepted by the scientific community. What is of particular interest is that, according to his theory, the Earth is in a relatively stable period with regard to global climate change.

Other factors influencing climate are volcanic eruptions, solar activity (sunspots), and greenhouse gases. Major greenhouse gases include water vapor, carbon dioxide, methane, and ozone. Increased solar activity contributes to higher temperatures on Earth as does an increased presence of major greenhouse gases. However, volcanic eruptions have the opposite effect. In fact, there have been times in history when global warming from sunspot activity has been reversed due to volcanic eruptions. *Greenhouse gases* are called that because they serve to trap solar heat much the same way as a greenhouse does, by allowing the solar heat in but preventing it from returning into space.

For the first time in history, man, not nature, is widely considered to be the cause of global warming. The burning of fossil fuels (e.g., oil, gasoline, coal, etc.) releases carbon dioxide into the atmosphere. As the National Oceanic and Atmospheric Administration (NOAA) measurements show, carbon dioxide has steadily risen throughout the latter half of the 20th century and into the 21st century, as well. This same conclusion has been reached by the Intergovernmental Panel on Climate Change (IPCC).

Founded in 1988 by the World Meteorological Organization (WMO) and the United Nations Environment Programme (UNEP), the IPCC does not conduct research on the climate. Rather, it provides decision makers with an objective source of information about climate change. It is composed of hundreds of scientists from around the world who contribute to the work of the IPCC as authors, contributors, and reviewers. The IPCC along with former Vice President Al Gore won the prestigious Nobel Peace Prize in December of 2007. The jury is in; man is drastically altering his environment and it is man who is most likely to suffer the consequences.

THE IMPACT OF GLOBAL WARMING ON THE HOSPITALITY INDUSTRY

A more appropriate term for global warming is probably global climate change. Ski slopes may receive more rain than snow in the winter and early spring. The ski industry is already reacting to this very real possibility by reducing their **carbon footprint**. Some are erecting wind generators to reduce their dependence on electricity generated with fossil fuels. Others are reducing their electric usage through the use of compact fluorescents (CFLs) in their buildings.

Coastal resorts may find themselves under water if the Greenland and Antarctic ice caps melt. It is expected that if the Greenland ice cap melts completely, it will raise the ocean levels by approximately 21 feet. This will put several major cities in the United States, such as, New Orleans, Miami, and New York under water. Entire countries, such as, Bangladesh and the Netherlands will be inundated and several island nations will be totally wiped off the planet.

Plants and animals, some of which are major tourist attractions, may become extinct. The rapid melting of the Artic sea ice has already placed the polar bear on the endangered species list.

It is expected that some areas will experience more rain than their historic amounts, while other areas will become drier. Drier areas of the Western United States, along with higher winter temperatures have led to the destruction of millions of acres of forests by increasing the number of forest fires and bark beetles. Cold winter temperatures have traditionally killed off these pests, thus reducing their impact, but in recent years the lack of a hard freeze in many Western forests along with drier temperatures has created an ideal environment for these tree killers. The lack of water stresses the tree, making it more susceptible to the beetles, and mild winters allows the beetle time to complete its full life cycle and thus increase its number. The result is wholesale forest destruction and a declining tourism industry for both winter and summer seasons.

Global climate change will also negatively impact agriculture and fishing, causing food prices to rise. This will lead to the likelihood of more global conflicts among nations and peoples competing for these decreasing sources of food. Rising prices will also channel more money into these necessities and away from discretionary items, such as travel. It is expected that countries and populaces of the world that are the poorest and most vulnerable (e.g., Africa, South America, and Asia) will be affected the most. Former Vice President Al Gore has called global warming the greatest challenge of our time.

SUSTAINABILITY

The World Commission on the Environment and Development (WCED), also known as the Brundtland Commission (named after its Chair, Gro Harlem Brundtland of Norway), is generally credited with defining the concept of sustainable development. In the commission's 1987 report, it defined sustainable development as, "meeting the needs of the present without compromising the ability of future generations to meet their own needs." This remains the most universally recognized definition of sustainability in use today.

Originally, sustainability applied to natural resources, but now it has broadened to include many more areas, including the environment and eco-systems, economic development, food production, energy use, and social organization. To be sure, no organization, society, or group of people has achieved complete sustainability to date. However, some have made greater progress than others. The new measure of success in this sphere has been through the employment of the **triple bottom line (TBL)**. These three bottom lines are *people*, *profit*, and *planet* (see Figure 3.1).

Every company and corporation since the beginning of human enterprise, has focused on the single bottom line of *profit*. Increasing the organization's profit was the obsession of every competent manager. However, within a sustainability framework, that focus has shifted to the economic benefit the business has brought to its host society. Obviously, businesses themselves still need to make profits, but the lasting economic benefit a business has on its immediate environment and all of society is more important.

People refers to the fair and equitable treatment of employees and people in the community and region where the business is located. A business should pay its employees a fair and decent wage, it should provide safe and healthy working conditions, and it should not employ child labor. Furthermore, a business should not in any way exploit the community or its labor force. This *bottom line* is often referred to as *social equity*.

Finally, we come to the third bottom line, the *planet*. This, of course, refers to sustainable environmental practices. A sustainable business would refrain from using up natural resources. In fact, it would either use those natural resources that can be regenerated indefinitely or those products that can be recycled indefinitely into new products. Even the materials used in the construction of the building would be selected on their sustainability. It would avoid the use of fossil fuels for its energy needs and would instead rely on renewable sources, such as, wind, solar, and geo-thermal. It would be careful to ensure that none of the byproducts of its services and products would eventually become toxic waste. It would also do everything in its power to minimize all products in its waste stream. The business would ensure that the building and its site have a minimal impact on the surrounding environment.

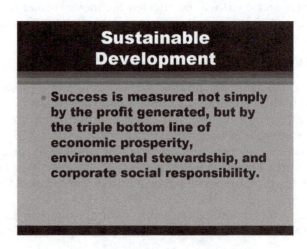

FIGURE 3.1 Sustainability and the Triple Bottom Line.

Measures would be taken by the business to conserve water and energy use in the facility. Cleaning and maintenance practices would reflect a concern for both the environment on the outside of the property and the facility's indoor environmental quality.

Besides making good, common sense, adopting the triple bottom line perspective can fulfill compelling business needs as well. It can help to reduce costs and liabilities, increase customer loyalty, stimulate growth, encourage innovation, enhance brand image and reputation, and strengthen relationships within the community where the business resides.

Sustainability is not a **zero-sum game.** To the contrary, in the long-run it should be viewed as a *win–win* proposition for all hospitality enterprises. To be sure, it will take considerable persuasion to convince existing companies employing the old single bottom line business model to join the sustainability movement. Unfortunately, some will never voluntarily make the switch. They will wait until the government mandates this change. These firms will find themselves *behind the curve* and they will assuredly suffer for it. In short, they will lose whatever competitive advantage they had.

So, where should hospitality facilities, in general, and engineering departments, in particular, begin? To answer that question will take the much of the rest of this textbook. In the chapters ahead, we will explore the changes that can be made to existing and new facilities. Every chapter that focuses on the engineering systems within a facility (e.g., heating, air-conditioning, plumbing, etc.) will use a sustainable framework or perspective. For now, let us turn our attention to the subject of establishing credibility as a sustainable organization.

CERTIFICATION AND SUSTAINABILITY

Any business that commits to do its part to the reduction of global warming and the practice of sustainable development will also aspire to communicate that commitment to its stakeholders. Unfortunately, **greenwashing** exists in abundance on the American commercial landscape. *Greenwashing* is the act of misleading consumers regarding the environmental practices of a company or the environmental benefits of a product or service, according to EcoLogo, the environmental certifying body. Any company can call itself *green,* or can use such terms as *natural,* or even *sustainable* on its products with impunity. Believability is enhanced when a company can show that its products are certified. The same holds true for hotel and restaurant operators that want their guests and customers to view them as a *green* property.

Professional certification has been around for many years for confirming an individual's expertise or skills. Architects, attorneys, doctors, and many other professions have certification programs for their members. There is even the Certified Facility Manager (CFM) program for chief engineers through the International Facility Management Association (IFMA). There are also product certification programs that aid the facility manager in selecting building materials, furniture, fixtures, and equipment. For many years, product certification has centered on durability, safety, and security. For example, the Underwriters Laboratories (UL) certification has been a long-standing assurance of safety on a multitude of electrical products, as NSF International's certification of water treatment products has been.

Product certification involves a three-step process (i.e., testing, validating, and auditing). *Testing* involves a controlled scientific analysis of a product against a pre-set standard. *Validating* refers to the recordkeeping process that is necessary to provide a written declaration of a product's compliance and the subsequent approval of the use of the certifying body's trademark. *Auditing* are those follow-up inspections that verify the product's continued conformity to the certifying body's standards.

Types of Certification

There are three categories of certification. The first category is referred to as first-party, or **self-certification**. It is the most basic type of certification. Sometimes the testing portion of the process might be conducted by an outside laboratory, but the other two steps are conducted in-house. At its worst, first-party certification is viewed as advertising hype, and at its best, it may offer ample assurance to consumers of a product's quality. However, lack of independent verification can raise serious concerns about the credibility of first-party certification, particularly when there are major safety and cost considerations.

Second-party, or **affiliated certification**, is when a trade association or an industry group certifies its members' products or services. Many believe that affiliated certification is sufficient particularly when the risk of using a particular product is low. The testing is usually conducted by an outside laboratory, but the validating and auditing function is done by the trade association. Second-party certification is the most common method of certification used in the United States.

Third-party certification is when the entire certification process is conducted by an independent entity that has no economic interest in the product or company being certified other than the fee the business pays to the certifying body for testing, validating, and auditing the product. Third-party certification is the most credible of the three types of certification for establishing product quality and performance. It is essential for those products with high-risk or liability potential. The trend in many fields is toward third-party certification even for low-risk/low-liability products. An increasing number of businesses are using third-party certification in order to differentiate and elevate their products and services from those of their competition.

Certification bodies may themselves undergo a type of certification called **accreditation**. *Accreditation* is performed by national or even international bodies that compare the standards of the certifying body to established international standards. One example is the ANSI-ASQ National Accreditation Board (ANAB) which is the United States accreditation body for management systems. The International Organization for Standardization (ISO) is the world's largest developer and publisher of international standards (**see** Figure 3.2), which began operations 60 years ago. The national standards bodies of 157 countries belong to this non-governmental organization. Fifty

FIGURE 3.2   The ISO logo can be found on more than 17,000 ISO International Standards, but it is not a certification mark or an environmental label. ISO prohibits the use of its logo to attest conformity to an ISO standard because ISO develops standards, but does not itself verify conformity to its standards.   *Source*: Logo reproduced with the permission of ISO Central Secretariat www.iso.org.

thousand experts from industry, government, researchers, scientists, engineers, and consumer representatives contribute to ISO standards. Business and industry, regulators, consumers, and accreditation, certification, and inspection bodies, as well as testing laboratories, are among those who rely on the more than 17,000 voluntary standards in ISO's current portfolio. ISO standards range from agriculture to construction and from mechanical engineering to medical instruments and information technology. Environmental concerns are addressed by several hundred standards for test methods such as for air, water, and soil quality, and for the environmental aspects of products, and by the family of ISO 14000 standards for environmental management. ISO 14001 (Environmental Management Systems) was launched in 1996 and has been implemented by public and private sector organizations in 140 countries. It specifies what environmental requirements an organization must meet, but does not specify how the requirements should be met. There are other standards in the ISO 14000 family, including greenhouse gas accounting and verification (ISO 14064), environmental labels (ISO 14020, ISO 14021, ISO 14024, ISO 14025), environmental performance evaluation (ISO 14031, ISO 14032), life cycle assessment (ISO 14040, ISO 14044, ISO 14049), and environmental communication (ISO 14063).

Of particular importance to the green labeling process are the ISO standards for environmental labels. ISO 14024 pertains to Type I labels, claims, assurances, and certifications from independent third parties. ISO 14021 is for Type II self-declared claims. ISO 14025 provides guidance on issuing quantified

ISO is not an Acronym

According to the International Organization for Standardization, ISO is not based on the initials of the organization. Because "International Organization for Standardization" would have different acronyms in different languages ("IOS" in English, "OIN" in French for *Organisation Internationale de Normalisation, etc.*), its founders decided to give it also a short, all-purpose name. They chose **"ISO"**, derived from the Greek *isos*, **meaning "equal."** Whatever the country or language, the short form of the organization's name is always ISO.

environmental information about products, based on life cycle data. This standard is not as well-known or understood as the first two types. The three standards are not themselves green labels, but provide requirements, guidance, and principles for such labels and associated claims.

There is also the Global Ecolabelling Network (GEN), a non-profit organization whose members are third-party environmental certifying, or are also known as performance labeling organizations (see Figure 3.3). GEN was founded in 1994 to improve, promote, and develop the *ecolabelling* of products and services. There are 25 ecolabelling practitioners, including Green Seal and EcoLogo that are members. GEN's membership requirements include reference to the ISO 14024 requirements.

Green Certification

For hospitality facilities, environmental certification (particularly third-party certification) of the equipment, furnishings, fixtures, supplies, and construction materials we use in our business is a major step forward in the *greening* of our properties. In the following section, we will examine the most important (and credible) third-party organizations that certify the products and services used by hotels and restaurants in the United States. But first, a note of caution on environmental certification and what it means.

A product, such as a cleaning supply, must be evaluated on several levels. Certainly, its impact on the environment and the health of those who may come into contact with it are of utmost importance. However, other factors are certainly as important. For example, a particular grease cleaner may have negligible impact on the environment, but the question then becomes, "Does it work?" Some green certification bodies may also examine and report on other aspects of a product, such as its efficacy and cost, and others may not. Therefore, it is always wise to either seek other respected third-party endorsements as to the durability, effectiveness, and cost of a product in addition to the product's *green* characteristics, or test the product under real world conditions (if possible) before making a commitment. Twenty years ago, many operators found green products to be more expensive and less effective than traditional products, giving the green movement a very negative, but well-earned, reputation. That is certainly not true today. The current generation of green products, on the whole, is very competitive with traditional products. Manufacturers seem to have learned their lesson. Claims of

FIGURE 3.3 Global Ecolabelling Network Logo. *Source*: Courtesy of the Global Ecolabelling Network.

FIGURE 3.4 Green Seal Logo. *Source*: Courtesy of Green Seal, Washington, D.C.

being green alone are not sufficient to offset other negative characteristics in the marketplace.

One of the most reputable environmental certification bodies in the United States is Green Seal (see Figure 3.4). Founded in 1989 as a 501(c)(3) nonprofit organization, Green Seal product tests more than 40 separate categories (e.g., paints, floor care products, and cleaning chemicals). Green Seal also has a lodging facility certification standard program (i.e., GS-33). The standard includes areas such as, purchasing policies, energy efficiency, water conservation, waste minimization, recycling, and reuse, hazardous waste, and waste water management. A full description of the program can be seen at the Green Seal website www.greenseal.org.

The United States federal government has two environmental partnership programs that include product certification. One is ENERGY STAR (see Figure 3.5), a co-sponsored program from the U.S. Environmental Protection Agency (EPA) and the U.S. Department of Energy (DOE). ENERGY STAR certifies a host of products for energy efficiency (e.g., appliances, lighting, office products, commercial foodservice equipment). Computers were the first products certified by ENERGY STAR. In 1999, ENERGY STAR expanded to include commercial buildings. Through their partnership program, ENERGY STAR provides guidance to commercial building contractors and operators to reduce energy usage. Buildings that can demonstrate their energy saving achievements can win the coveted ENERGY STAR certification. The energy performance of commercial and industrial facilities is scored on a 1–100 scale and those facilities that achieve a score of 75 or higher are eligible for the ENERGY STAR, indicating that they are among the top 25% of facilities in the

FIGURE 3.5 Energy Star Logo. *Source*: U.S. Environmental Protection Agency—U.S. Department of Energy.

country for energy performance. Commercial buildings that have earned the ENERGY STAR use on average 35% less energy than typical similar buildings and generate one-third less carbon dioxide. Increasing concern about the financial and environmental risks associated with climate change is driving more organizations to strive for the ENERGY STAR for their buildings, as it is seen as a symbol of an organization that is working to reduce global warming and its impacts. There are currently 247 hotels listed on the ENERGY STAR for Hospitality website. ENERGY STAR for Hospitality is a proven energy management program plus its *green* logo is one of the most recognized of all of the environmental logos.

Another environmental certification program is the EPA's *Design for the Environment (DfE)*. Like the ENERGY STAR program, DfE is a partnership program that works with manufacturers and distributors on a voluntary basis. Its mission is to reduce risks to people and the environment through the reduction of pollution. DfE, which focuses on the reduction of chemical risks and energy use, works with private companies, environmental groups, and state and local agencies. Its DfE label on a product means that the scientific review team at the DfE has screened the ingredients in a product for potential health and environmental effects and has found that the product contains only those ingredients that pose the least hazard. The consumer is assured that products that bear the logo are formulated with the safest possible ingredients.

The Canadian equivalent of Green Seal is EcoLogo (see Figure 3.6). It certifies a large number of products and services, including hotels. Many of their certified products are imported or made in the United States. EcoLogo is the oldest environmental certification organization in North America, and it is the only North American environmental certification organization that has been peer reviewed by the Global Ecolabelling Network against ISO standard 14024 for Type I (third-party certification) environmental labels.

The United States-based Scientific Certification Systems (SCS) provides neutral third-party product certification in a number of areas, including environmental performance, food safety and quality, and social responsibility in both the private and public sectors (see Figure 3.7). In their eco-products and green building sectors, SCS evaluates office furniture systems, components,

FIGURE 3.6   EcoLogo Logo.   *Source*: Courtesy of EcoLogo.

seating, and green building materials, carpets and rugs, hard surface flooring, paints, finishes, wood products, and cleaning products, among others. Certifications address issues such as indoor air quality, use of recycled and re-claimed materials, and broader "environmentally preferable product" and sustainability claims. In addition, SCS has pioneered the development of Environmental Performance Declarations, based on life-cycle assessment, which summarize the reductions in environmental and human health impacts attributable to products, groups of products, and buildings across the entire life-cycle. Finally, SCS evaluates power systems to help companies identify power options representing the lowest environmental impacts.

SCS is one of the leading providers of Forest Stewardship Council (FSC) forest management and chain-of-custody certification and has certified more than 1,000 clients in 31 countries. FSC promotes responsible management of the world's forests through the development of voluntary, internationally recog-nized forest management standards and has the most widely recognized forest certification program globally. The FSC requires that all manufacturers, distribu-tors, and retailers who purchase and sell FSC certified wood, and who wish to make a claim about the certified status of their product, undergo chain-of-custody certification by an accredited third party. SCS was among the first certifiers to become duly accredited to offer FSC-endorsed certification services.

Perhaps the most important environmental certifying organization to the lodging and foodservice industry is the U.S. Green Building Council (USGBC) and its Leadership in Energy and Environmental Design (LEED) certification system (see Figure 3.8). "The U.S. Green Building Council

(USGBC) is a 501(c)(3) non profit composed of leaders from every sector of the building industry working to promote buildings and communities that are environmentally responsible, profitable, and healthy places to live and work. The LEED® Green Building Certification System is the nationally accepted benchmark for the design, construction, and operation of high performance green buildings." A LEED certification may well be the highest environmental endorsement a hotel or restaurant could hope to achieve. There is a LEED rating system for many different types of buildings. There are presently nine categories in all. They include new construction, existing buildings, commercial interiors, core and shell, schools, retail, healthcare, homes, and neighborhood development (see Figure 3.9). There is no hospitality, hotel, or restaurant LEED rating system, nor is there likely to be a separate rating system for hospitality new construction. However, *new construction* would suitably fit all new hotels and restaurants. The USGBC has recently made changes to the *existing buildings* category. It is thought that these changes should make the program even more appealing to hotels. There are four levels of green certification (i.e., Certified, Silver, Gold, and Platinum). The level of a certification is based on points earned in several categories. For example, in the *Existing Buildings: Operation and Maintenance* rating system, there are six categories where points can be awarded (i.e., Sustainable Sites, Water Efficiency, Energy and Atmosphere, Materials and Resources, Indoor Environmental Quality, and Innovations in Operation & Upgrades). The total points scored determine a property's level of certification.

Admittedly, there are fees associated with the LEED certification process, but it is not the fees alone that have dissuaded hotel operators from pursuing the goal of certification. There is a widely held belief that either in new construction or in making changes to existing buildings, becoming *green* is too cost-prohibitive. Although it is true that building green will add some

LEED address the complete lifecycle of buildings:

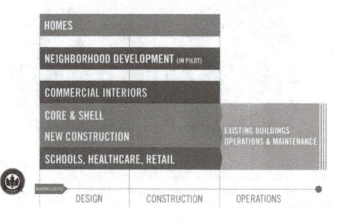

FIGURE 3.9   The LEED® Building Certification Categories.   *Source*: "LEED" and related logo is a trademark owned by the U.S. Green Building Council and is used by permission.

upfront costs to a building, according to Gregory Kats of Capital E, the cost of green buildings has fallen as the number has risen. He quotes one Seattle study where the construction cost of new LEED Silver buildings went down from a premium of 3%–4% to 1%–2%. In a related study, the average cost premium ranged from 6.5% for LEED Platinum down to .66% for basic LEED Certification status. When one considers the operating savings generated by buildings that are more energy and water efficient, in addition to the increase in employee productivity in a LEED building because of the attention paid to the indoor environmental quality, there is no question that building green is a wise financial decision. A LEED certified building saves 30%–50% in energy costs over the life of the building.

Certainly, one does not have to have LEED certification (or any other for that matter) to be an environmentally responsible facility, so the question might be asked, "Why bother with the added cost?" The answer is the traveling public is also becoming increasingly *green*. One study has even shown that the public will pay a slight premium to stay in a green hotel over a traditional property. In any case, pleasure, business, and convention travelers do appreciate properties that can demonstrate that they are environmentally responsible. In fact, some hotel chains, such as Kimpton Hotels, see environmentalism as a key tenet in their mission and goals and many hotel chains, such as, Fairmont, Intercontinental, Saunders Hotel Group, have been big proponents of the environment for many years. However, there are a number of other properties and chains that are environmental in name only (*greenwashing*).

What Needs to Happen

Every person and organization needs to immediately shrink their carbon footprint. That is to say, we must all reduce the use of fossil fuels and the release of more carbon dioxide into the air.

To date, the federal government has not taken a strong leadership role in this endeavor. The Kyoto Protocol was signed, but not ratified by the United States and Australia. The Australian Prime Minister who refused to sign it has since been voted out of office and his replacement has signed the accord, leaving only the United States as the last holdout among the developed nations. This should change with our next presidential administration.

In addition to energy conservation, hotels and restaurants might also think about purchasing carbon offsets. Carbon offsets allow a business or individual to offset their own carbon dioxide emissions that result from energy use by paying for carbon reductions that take place elsewhere. One common example is when a business pays for the planting of trees that absorb carbon dioxide. Another is paying for the development and production of renewable energy (e.g., wind, solar, etc.), when the business is using energy made from fossil fuels. For some time, this practice was loosely regulated and very informal. At the present time, however, more regulations are being developed; consequently, more safeguards are being put into place so that purchasers of carbon offsets can be assured that they are getting what they are paying for.

Sustainability at this juncture should be seen as a goal, rather than a realization. However, all of us need to work toward this goal. As mentioned earlier, this is not about saving the planet; the planet will probably survive no matter what we do to it. This is about saving ourselves and our children.

ACCESSIBILITY

It has been said that the quality of a society and a civilization is measured by the respect shown to the weakest of its members. For years, the disabled were often referred to as "shut-ins" because our society did nothing to accommodate them. They literally could not leave their homes. For those in a wheelchair, steps were an impenetrable barrier to entrance into both public and private facilities. Bathrooms were not designed to accommodate the physically disabled in most buildings. Loss of motion and other faculties (e.g., sight, hearing) prevented many people from traveling, eating, and sleeping in public accommodations. A disabled person may have had the desire and the money to travel, but could not because of barriers.

All of this changed on July 26, 1990 when President George H.W. Bush signed into law the American with Disabilities Act (ADA). The law required commercial and government buildings to change both their physical surroundings so that the disabled might be able to enter and use the facilities, and it also called for a change in behavior. Policies and procedures that effectively denied access to the disabled were also required to change.

The Titles

The act had five titles. Title I dealt with employment, and its intent was to prevent discrimination to qualified employees. In order not to create an undue hardship on small operators, Title I was implemented in stages. Businesses that had 25 or more employees were subject to the law on July 26, 1992. Smaller concerns (i.e., 15–24 employees) were not covered until July 26, 1994. Title II pertained to public services. It prevented discrimination in programs, services, or activities of public entities (e.g., state and local governments), including public transportation. This title was also phased into being to give these governmental agencies time to conform to the law.

Title III, public accommodations and commercial facilities, had the greatest impact on the hospitality industry. This title covers all existing and future construction of lodging establishments, restaurants, entertainment, and recreational facilities, to name but a few. Here again, the law was phased in to allow smaller establishments the time to make needed changes to their operation in the removal of barriers to the disabled. The title also required establishments to provide auxiliary aids to the disabled so they might fully enjoy the goods and services offered by the establishment. These auxiliary aids can range from amplified headsets for those who are hard-of-hearing in entertainment complexes to strobe lights on the back of guest-room doors to notify a hearing disabled guest that someone is knocking at the door. There are also bed shaker alarms for hearing impaired guests, for example.

Title IV addressed telecommunications for the disabled and Title V was a potpourri of miscellaneous issues including giving states and municipalities the right to establish regulations that are more stringent than the federal legislation. The entire act was enforced through the courts. There is no federal agency that inspects facilities and there are no ADA inspectors. When an instance of non-compliance is found, it is up to the plaintiff to seek redress through the federal courts. The Department of Justice (DOJ) may act as the plaintiff's attorney when the DOJ determines that the case is particularly egregious or the court's ruling will likely set a new precedent. Otherwise, plaintiffs must seek out their own legal counsel. Awards granted by the court were set by the federal statute to discourage a rash of nuisance lawsuits.

One important concept under the act was the matter of **readily achievable** modifications. Modification to a facility in anticipation of clients or guests who may have a disability was a requirement under the law. These modifications had to be made unless the modification caused much difficulty or expense to the enterprise—in other words, the modification had to be readily achievable. The court was given the authority to render a decision on whether or not a modification was readily achievable by the business or concern that had not made the modification. Figure 3.10 is an example of readily achievable priorities.

A second important concept was that of **reasonable accommodation**. Reasonable accommodations pertained to employees who are disabled. No modification needed to be made to the facility before a disabled employee was hired. However, if a qualified individual with a disability were hired, then proper modification had to be made, unless they posed a significant expense or difficulty to the operation. Again, it was up to the courts to determine if these modifications were *reasonable*.

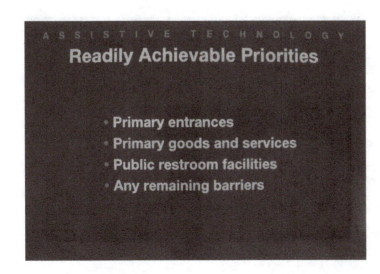

FIGURE 3.10 ADA Readily Achievable Priorities.

The Guidelines

Since the law came into being, a set of building standards has been developed called the American Disabilities Act Accessibility Guidelines (ADAAG). Architects, contractors, and, of course, building operators must comply with the ADAAG guidelines and other building codes (e.g., International Building Code [IBC]) and standards (e.g., American National Standards Institute [ANSI]) that pertain to the disabled and the removal of accessibility barriers. On July 23, 2004 the U.S. Access Board (*www.access-board.gov*) announced the release of new design guidelines that cover access for people with disabilities under the ADA of 1990. These guidelines update access requirements for a wide range of facilities in the public and private sectors. As part of this update, the board has made its guidelines more consistent with model building codes, such as the IBC and industry standards. It coordinated extensively with model code groups and standard-setting bodies throughout the process so that differences could be reconciled.

As a result, the historic level of harmonization that has been achieved has brought about improvements to the guidelines as well as to counterpart provisions in the IBC and other key industry standards, including those for accessible facilities issued through ANSI. The board believes that this will greatly facilitate compliance. However, these new guidelines are not enforceable standards until they are officially adopted by the United States Department of Justice, which has not done so as of this writing.

Figure 3.11 is an example of an ADA parking requirement. Sidewalks have to accommodate wheelchairs and the possibility that two people in wheelchairs may meet on the same sidewalk (see Figure 3.12). Standard disabled parking spaces must be at least eight feet wide and must have a five-foot access aisle. The aisle may be shared with an adjacent disabled parking space. Van-accessible spaces must also be at least eight feet wide. Their access

FIGURE 3.11   ADA Parking Construction Requirements.

FIGURE 3.12 ADA Sidewalk Construction Requirements.

aisle, however, must be eight feet in width. Here too, the access aisle may be shared with another parking space.

In the lobby of the hotel, accommodation should also be made for the lowering of a portion of the front desk to accommodate wheelchairs (see Figure 3.13). However, in the case of a small property where there is just one station at the front desk and a remodeling of the lobby would cause great difficulty and expense to the business, then alternate accommodations can be made. The agent could fill in the registration card for the disabled guest, or the guest could be given a clipboard to assist them in filling out the registration card. In the case of a sight-impaired guest, the front desk agent would be expected to fill out the registration card for the guest.

FIGURE 3.13 ADA Hotel Front Desk Specifications.

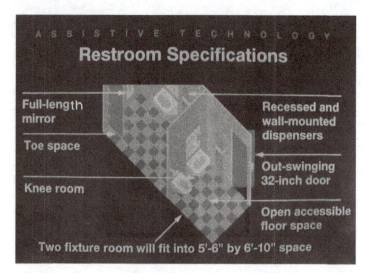

FIGURE 3.14 ADA Public Restroom Modifications.

In Figure 3.14 there are examples of some of the necessary modifications to public restrooms. Not shown are special easy-to-operate faucet handles for those who have limited use of their hands, cutaways at the sink counter that allow a person in a wheelchair access to a sink, and hot-water and drain pipes that are insulated so that a person in a wheelchair who has little feeling in his/her legs is not inadvertently scalded by the hot water.

Restaurants also have requirements for the accommodation of disabled guests, such as wheelchair accessible door width, wide aisles for access, and seating space for wheelchairs as shown in Figure 3.15. For those guests who are sight impaired, the restaurant should provide menus in Braille, on cassette tape, or servers should be prepared to read the menu to the customer. Lobbies, hallways, and foyers are also expected to have contrasting textures to help

FIGURE 3.15 ADA Restaurant Modifications.

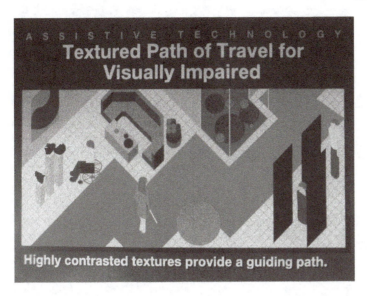

FIGURE 3.16 ADA Lobby and Hall Modifications.

provide the visually disabled assistance in negotiating their way through the property as shown in Figure 3.16.

In the guestroom, as seen in Figure 3.17, special accommodations include lowering peepholes in the doors, closet rods, drapery cords, door locks, and electrical switches so that someone in wheelchair can reach them without straining. Electrical switches on lamps should also be designed so that a person with limited hand motion can operate them. Televisions should have built-in closed caption decoders for the hearing impaired (see Figure 3.18). Hearing disabled guest rooms should also have visual alerts for fire notification systems,

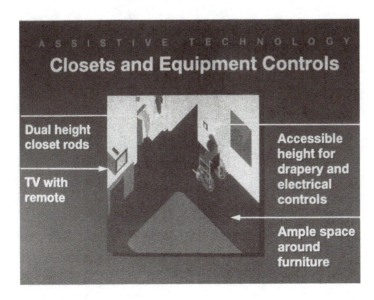

FIGURE 3.17 ADA Guestroom Modifications.

FIGURE 3.18 ADA
Television Requirement.

telephones, and special stroboscopic alerts when someone knocks on the guest's door (see Figure 3.19).

Disabled guest rooms should not be confined to one type or category, but should be available in all types of guest rooms (e.g., smoking and non-smoking rooms, suites, standard rooms, kitchenettes, rooms with preferred views, etc.). In new properties all entry doors should be a minimum of 32″ so that a disabled guest in a wheelchair can visit other rooms and public areas in the hotel, and can also be roomed in a non-disabled room if there are no disabled rooms available.

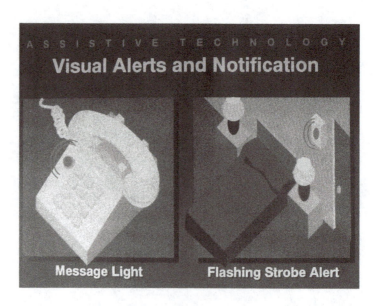

FIGURE 3.19 ADA
Visual Alerts for the
Hearing Disabled.

TABLE 3.1   Guestrooms with Communication Devices for the Disabled

Total Number of Guestrooms Provided	Minimum Number of Required Guestrooms with Communication Features
2 to 25	2
26 to 50	4
51 to 75	7
76 to 100	9
101 to 150	12
151 to 200	14
201 to 300	17
301 to 400	20
401 to 500	22
501 to 1000	5% of total
1001 and over	50, plus 3 for each 100 over 1000

There are two types of disabled guestrooms, hearing-impaired and wheelchair-accessible rooms. The ADA Accessibility Guidelines are very specific as to how many of each type is needed in a hotel. Table 3.1 lists the hearing-impaired guestrooms and Table 3.2 is a listing of the wheelchair-accessible rooms.

Stairways should be equipped with continuous handrails for those guests who are unsteady on their feet. Contrasting colors to distinguish the stair treads from the risers should also be provided for guests who have impaired vision as shown in Figure 3.20.

TABLE 3.2   Wheelchair Guestrooms Needed According to the Americans with Disabilities Act Accessibility Guidelines

Total Number of Guestrooms	Minimum # of Required Rooms Without Roll-in Showers	Minimum # of Required Rooms With Roll-in Showers	Total # of Required Rooms
1 to 25	1	0	1
26 to 50	2	0	2
51 to 75	3	1	4
76 to 100	4	1	5
101 to 150	5	2	7
151 to 200	6	2	8
201 to 300	7	3	10
301 to 400	8	4	12
401 to 500	9	4	13
501 to 1000	2% of total	1% of total	3% of total
1001 and over	20, plus 1 for each 100, or fraction thereof, over 1000	10, plus 1 for each 100, or fraction thereof over 1000	30, plus 2 for each 100, or fraction thereof, over 1000

ASSISTIVE TECHNOLOGY

Stairway with Handrail Extensions

Continuous handrails required

Contrasting color or texture for top of steps

Tread depth at least 11 inches

12-inch handrail extension beyond step

FIGURE 3.20   ADA Stairway Requirements.

Every property that has more than two stories must have at least one elevator serving each level of the facility. Signs by the elevator designating floors must not be higher than 60 inches and should not protrude more than four inches into the hallway. The elevator's command buttons should not be more than 42 inches above the floor.

Water fountains, signs, telephones, and fire extinguishers should be recessed into the wall, or protrude no more than four inches into a path of travel. The blind who use canes may not detect a wall mounted object, thus putting them at risk of injuring themselves on a protruding object.

For telephone communication for guests with hearing disabilities, the hotel must provide a teletypewriter (TTY), on request, for use in guest rooms. The hotel also will need to have a TTY (also known as a telephone device for the deaf [TDD]) at the front desk, and perhaps at other telephone stations, for handling billing inquiries, taking room service orders, or responding to other guest calls. Hotel desk staff should be trained in handling TTY equipment.

A fire in a multi-story building is a special concern for mobility-impaired guests. Elevators are programmed to cease functioning and a disabled guest may become trapped on an upper story. Although it is not an ADA requirement, a device called the Evac-Chair enables a disabled guest to be transported down a stairwell (see Figure 3.21) and out of a building to safety. Although it requires an able-bodied person to assist the disabled passenger, a lighter smaller person can effectively remove a much larger and heavier disabled person down several flights of stairs. The wheels retract and a friction belt slows the descent of the disabled person as he or she is being lowered down the stairs. In fact, a heavier person will descend much slower than a lighter person.

Although every department shares responsibility for meeting the needs of disabled guests and customers, it is the engineering department's responsibility to ensure that architectural barriers in the property are removed for the

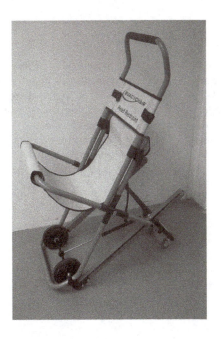

FIGURE 3.21 The Evac+Chair Model Mk3 *Source*: Reproduced with the permission of Evac+Chair North America LLC.

sake of their disabled guests. Even though there may be costs associated with these renovations, it makes good business sense to make these changes to help their disabled guests, and it also meets the legal requirements of the law. It is estimated that there are over 51 million Americans who are disabled. Wouldn't any astute manager want all of that business staying at his or her hotel?

Summary

The issues covered in this chapter are not the sole concerns of the hospitality industry and its facility managers. Other issues include the application of new technologies to hospitality facilities, the impact of the economy on building maintenance, the presence and transmission of pathogenic organisms in hospitality facilities, and the growing concern over the health of building occupants exposed to man-made pollutants. In fact, these and many other issues are addressed in many of the remaining chapters. However, this chapter's content is of paramount importance to our industry's continued survival and prosperity, and deserves our special attention.

Key Terms and Concepts

carbon footprint 55
accreditation 58
affiliated
    certification 58

greenwashing 57
readily achievable 67
reasonable
    accommodation 67

self-certification 58
third-party
    certification 58

triple bottom line
    (TBL) 56
zero-sum game 57

Discussion and Review Questions

1. Why do you think the lodging and foodservice industry has been reluctant to change from traditional modes of operation to *green* practices? What arguments would you make to a restaurant operator or a hotel manager to convince them to pursue a LEED rating? Then play devil's advocate and make an argument not to green your operation. The instructor should select students to role-play both sides and then have students vote on the winners.

2. Visit the websites of Energy Star, Design for the Environment, Green Seal, ISO, USGBC, and EcoLogo and report on impressions of these sites.

3. Visit a lodging property in your area. Tour the public areas (inside and outside) to see if there are any architectural barriers preventing the disabled from full access to the facility. Report your findings to the class.

PART
II

Building Systems

4

Solid and Hazardous Waste

CHAPTER OBJECTIVES

After studying the chapter, the student should be able to:

- identify municipal solid waste statistics.
- list the characteristics of hazardous waste.
- identify the composition of different classifications of solid waste.
- describe the cost of hauling charges and tipping fees for solid waste.
- describe the different types of modern landfills and how they are constructed.
- describe each of the options available in an integrated waste management program and the positive and negative aspects of these options.
- list the steps (in order) that need to be taken to set up a recycling program.
- describe OSHA's Hazard Communication Standard and the use of material safety data sheets.
- describe the purpose of OSHA's Bloodborne Pathogen Standard.

INTRODUCTION

Municipal solid waste (MSW) includes paper and paperboard, yard trimmings, glass, metals, plastics, wood, food scraps, rubber, leather, textiles, and miscellaneous waste. According to the EPA, in 2005, paper and paperboard constituted 34% of the total MSW. Yard trimmings were the second-largest component at 13%. Glass, metals, plastics, wood, and food scraps each constituted between 5% and 12% of the total MSW generated. Rubber, leather, and textiles combined made up about 7% of MSW, while other miscellaneous wastes made up approximately 3% of the MSW generated in 2005. The United States generated 245.7 million tons of MSW in 2005. That figure equates to an astounding 4.54 pounds per person, per day.

WE ARE ALL DOWNSTREAM

Make no mistake, there is no such thing as "away," as in, "I am going to throw this bottle away." That bottle is going somewhere; it doesn't disappear into the ether. It goes into the **waste stream** and probably ends up in the traditional **landfill** where it will probably sit for hundreds or even thousands of years in a best-case scenario. In a worst-case scenario, that waste may leach into the soil and end up polluting an underground aquifer, a possible source of drinking water for the community. One of the biggest fallacies around is the belief that a traditional landfill is a giant compost pile where everything eventually turns into dirt. Nothing could be further from the truth. Most modern landfills are designed to be *dry tombs.*

For thousands of years man used rivers and streams to carry waste and **human effluent** away from his community. That strategy worked fairly well as long as there wasn't anyone living upstream engaged in the same practice. Today, we are all *downstream,* so to speak. None of us on this planet can claim we live upstream or upwind from the dangers of pollution.

Waste has negative connotations. In fact, the definition of the word in the *Oxford American Dictionary* is as follows:

> *waste (wayst) v.* **(wast·ed), (wast·ing)** *1. to use extravagantly or needlessly; or without an adequate result;* he is wasted as a schoolmaster, *the job does not use his abilities fully;* advice is wasted on him, *has no effect when given. 2. to fail to use (an opportunity). 3. to make or become gradually weaker,* wasting away for lack of food; a wasting disease. *4. (slang) to kill*
>
> *waste adj. 1. left over or thrown away because not wanted;* waste products, *useless byproducts of manufacturer or of a bodily process. 2. (of land) not used or cultivated or built upon, unfit for use.*
>
> *waste n. 1. an act of wasting or using something ineffectively,* a waste of time. *2. waste material or food, waste products; wastes, excrement. 3. a stretch of waste land*

To this, one might add, "a cost." Yes, waste is a cost to any organization. It is a *sunk cost,* a cost that is irretrievable. It cannot be recouped and it is a cost that should be avoided whenever possible.

Waste Categories and Classifications

There are three main categories of waste: waste gases, liquid waste, and solid waste. All three waste categories can be **hazardous waste.** Hazardous waste is a waste with properties that make it dangerous or potentially harmful to human health or the environment. The universe of hazardous wastes is large and diverse. Hazardous wastes can be liquids, solids, contained gases, or sludge. They can be the by-products of manufacturing processes or simply discarded commercial products, like cleaning fluids or pesticides. Hazardous wastes are regulated by the EPA under the Resource Conservation and Recovery Act

E-waste—The Newest Waste Category

Here's another (and particularly horrific) new category of waste. E-waste is composed of computers, televisions (covered elsewhere), cell phones, fax machines, copiers, re-chargeable batteries, VCR's, stereos, etc. These products, which are fairly harmless when sitting on your desk, can be extremely dangerous under other conditions. Many of these devices contain lead, mercury, arsenic, and many other heavy metals. Most of these devices are made from composite materials including glass, metal, and plastic, which makes it difficult to separate their contents for recycling. More than 70% of the 3.2 million tons of e-waste generated in this country every year ends up in landfills. That accounts for an estimated 40% of all of the heavy metals found in municipal solid waste. What happens to the other 30% of the e-waste that is recycled? It often ends up in third-world countries where it pollutes the environment and sickens the people engaged in this trade. Even though China has laws against the importation of e-waste, it is said that a cargo container of e-waste can get through customs if a $100 bill is taped on it. For example, Guiyu, China is, by some observers' estimates, truly a hell on earth. There the recycling of computers and other e-waste is a cottage industry. People literally do it in their homes with small smelters to melt the plastics and metals. The lead content in Guiyu is 190 times the World Health Organization's safe level, chromium levels are 1338 times the level deemed safe in the United States, and tin levels are 152 times the United States threshold. These people have sacrificed their health and their children's health for a $1.50 a day in wages. Everyone who owns electronic equipment that is no longer usable should make sure that it gets recycled properly, the manufacturers should be made to set up proper recycling procedures for all of the equipment they sell, and the United States government should have signed the Basle Agreement of 1996, which forbade the exportation of e-waste to third-world countries.

(RCRA). The EPA has published lists of specific hazardous wastes, but a substance can be declared a hazardous waste even if it is not on the list.

If a substance exhibits one of the following characteristics, it is regarded as a hazardous waste.

- *Ignitability:* Ignitable wastes can create fires under certain conditions, are spontaneously combustible, or have a flash point less than 60°C (140°F). Examples include waste oils and used solvents.
- *Corrosivity:* Corrosive wastes are acids or bases (pH less than or equal to 2, or greater than or equal to 12.5) that are capable of corroding metal containers, such as storage tanks, drums, and barrels. Battery acid is an example.
- *Reactivity:* Reactive wastes are unstable under "normal" conditions. They can cause explosions, toxic fumes, gases, or vapors when heated, compressed, or mixed with water. Examples include lithium-sulfur batteries and explosives.
- *Toxicity:* Toxic wastes are harmful or fatal when ingested or absorbed (e.g., containing mercury, lead, etc.). When toxic wastes are land disposed, contaminated liquid may leach from the waste and pollute ground water.

Millions of Hotel TVs Enter the Waste Stream

Hotels at every level are switching out their cathode ray tube sets for flat screen televisions. Chains and independents alike perceive that their guests want the same viewing experience while traveling that many now have at home. Another factor at play is the switchover from analog to digital broadcasting on February 17, 2009 in the United States. This will make millions of older sets obsolete as well. It is estimated that over 80 million television sets will be thrown away in the next two years.

The hotel industry should do everything in its power to prevent these TVs from going to the landfill. Televisions contain many valuable materials, such as, gold, silver, plastics and glass. Sets that still work should be sold or given to charities and sets that are unusable should be recycled properly.

The hotel industry should work to ensure that the e-waste it generates is not sent to the landfill, but instead is either reused or recycled appropriately. Some computer companies, such as Dell and Hewlett-Packard, have recycling programs in place. In addition, California has passed laws banning the burying of anything that contains a cathode ray tube. Unfortunately, other states have not passed such bans. Clearly, more needs to be done in this area.

In the conventional hotel or restaurant, the prevailing attitude is that there are no hazardous wastes present, but that is simply not true. They can be found in paints, floor finishes, chemicals used in boiler operations, solvents, and cleaners to name but a few sources. Every effort should be made to substitute products that are not classified as hazardous, if at all possible. Not only is it better for the environment inside and outside the property, but the disposal costs are substantially less. All *waste should equal food*. Not that people should be able to convert waste to food, but waste should be food to someone or something, even if that something is a one-celled bacteria. When waste cannot be used by anything or anyone; that waste is truly *hazardous*. Radioactive waste that has a half-life of thousands of years comes to mind as an outstanding example.

We tend to lump the things we throw in the wastebasket together. We may call it waste, trash, or even garbage. However, there are nine very specific classifications for different types of waste. They are:

- *Type 0—Trash.* Primarily paper. After incineration there is less than 5% residual solid remaining.
- *Type 1—Rubbish.* 80% trash, 20% restaurant waste; 10% is incombustible. This term includes all non-putrefying refuse except ashes. There are two categories of rubbish: combustible and noncombustible.
  a. *Combustible:* This material is primarily inorganic—it includes items such as paper, plastics, cardboard, wood, rubber, and bedding.
  b. *Noncombustible:* This material is primarily inorganic and includes tin cans, metals, glass, ceramics, and other mineral refuse.
- *Type 2—Refuse.* 50% trash, 50% rubbish. Has a residual moisture content of 50%. Requires firing at a higher heat to burn. Leaves 10% solids after firing.

- *Type 3—Garbage.* All food waste—70% water. Designates putrefying wastes resulting from handling, preparing, cooking, and serving food.
- *Type 4—Residue.* Includes all solid wastes. In practice this category includes garbage, rubbish, ashes, and dead animals.
- *Type 5—Ashes.* Residue from fires used for cooking, heating, and on-site incineration.
- *Type 6—Biologic wastes.* (Includes human and animal remains.) Wastes resulting directly from patient diagnosis and treatment procedures; includes materials of medical, surgical, autopsy, and laboratory origin.
  a. *Medical wastes:* These wastes are usually produced in patient rooms, treatment rooms, and nursing stations. The operating room may also be a contributor. Items include soiled dressings, bandages, catheters, swabs, plaster casts, receptacles, and masks.
  b. *Surgical and autopsy wastes (pathologic wastes):* These wastes may be produced in surgical suites or autopsy rooms. Items that may be included are placentas, tissues and organs, amputated limbs, and similar material.
  c. *Laboratory wastes:* These wastes are produced in diagnostic or research laboratories. Items that may be included are cultures, spinal fluid samples, dead animals, and animal bedding. Eighty-five percent of this type of waste is released to morticians for incineration.
- *Type 7—Liquid by-product wastes.* Usually toxic and hazardous. Must be treated with germicidal/disinfectant prior to disposal in sanitary sewers.
- *Type 8—Solid by-product wastes.* Toxic, hazardous; capable of being sterilized, packaged, and discarded with normal trash.

A hotel would rarely have biological wastes on the premises, but it is wise to remember that anything that can happen in society can take place in a hotel. Any of the preceding categories can produce **infectious waste**. It is the method of handling, however, that allows for safe disposal. Each environmental service center will develop its own procedures for disposal of all types of waste.

Avoiding Waste at the Olive Garden

Everyone knows that the Olive Garden restaurant chain serves a bottomless bowl of salad and endless refills of their yummy breadsticks. However, if you ever order more salad or breadsticks, you will also notice that your second serving is decidedly less than the original serving. You will get roughly half the amount the second time and if you ask for another, (Don't ask how I know this!), your order will be half the size of the second order. The reason is, Olive Garden managers are taught to abhor waste. In fact, when the restaurants are inspected by corporate, they are evaluated on how much waste there is in their garbage cans at the end of the day. An empty garbage can is a sign of a well-run property and a happy store manager.

The Cost of Landfills

The **tipping fee** is a fee charged for the unloading or dumping of solid wastes at a landfill, transfer station, recycling center, waste-to-energy facility, and other types of facilities. The fee is usually expressed in dollars per ton. It is not the only charge associated with waste removal. The hotel must either transport the property's solid waste to the landfill or hire a waste hauling company. These costs are called **hauling charges**. The hauling charges are easily the most expensive aspect of waste removal. Hauling charges will vary considerably from municipality to municipality.

Tipping fees were a major concern in the United States during the 1980s and 1990s. According to the National Solid Waste Management Association, these fees were escalating at a rate of 7% per annum until 1998. Between 1985 and 1998 tipping fees increased by 300%. Since then, the fees have stabilized and the national average tipping fee from 1995 to 2005 has changed less than 7%. In 2004 the national average was $34.29 per ton, but it varied widely. Areas of the country that were more populated typically had higher tipping fees. The Northeastern area of the United States had the highest rates in 2004, at $70.53/ton. The lowest rates were found in the south central United States at $24.06/ton, almost one-third the cost of the highest region.

Las Vegas has a fairly unique fee structure for commercial accounts. Hotels are charged by the size of the dumpster and the number of *pulls*, or number of times the dumpster is removed from the property. Las Vegas is estimated to have over 100 years of landfill space left at the present generation of waste. This is not true in many other areas of the country.

Landfill Construction

Many landfills have turned into environmental disasters. Rain percolates through the top layer of the landfill and mixes with the landfill's contents creating **leachate.** Contents of the leachate can vary depending upon the landfill's

---

Perchlorates in your Lettuce

In Henderson, Nevada, a suburb of Las Vegas, there is a Kerr-McGee rocket fuel plant that had leaked perchlorates for many years and these perchlorates were flowing into Lake Mead on the Colorado River, which is Las Vegas' major source of drinking water. Perchlorates are thought to cause a health risk to children and pregnant mothers according to scientists. The city breathed a collectively sigh of relief because it was then reported that where they were entering the lake was downstream from the city's water intake pipes. Later a companion story appeared in the newspaper when it was discovered that these perchlorates were being absorbed by the lettuce being grown in the Imperial Valley, a major food production area in Southern California that gets its water from the Colorado River. So Las Vegans who had dodged one bullet were being hit by another every time they went to the grocery store and purchased lettuce grown in the Imperial Valley. None of us are *upstream*—we are all *downstream.* Luckily, the perchlorates were finally stopped from entering the Colorado River by improved cleanup procedures.

R.C. Farms—The other Las Vegas Buffet

Composting is extremely difficult in a desert climate. The lack of water severely compromises the process. So, what should be done with all of the waste food product generated by Las Vegas' gargantuan hotels? Enter R.C. Farms, a mammoth pig farm in North Las Vegas with 5,000 of the porcine creatures. Over 30 tons of waste food from the hotels ends up at R.C. Farms (named after the founder Robert Combs) daily. There the food is blended, cooked, and fed to the hogs. Former Harrah's Director of Facilities, and current professor at UNLV, Ken Teeters has called it a perfect example of recycling. "There," says Teeters, "waste food is fed to the hogs and returns to us in the form of bacon on tomorrow's breakfast." The operation is so famous that the Discovery Channel's show *Dirty Jobs* did an episode there.

contents, but it is typically highly acidic and may contain heavy metals and toxins, as well as other elements. This leachate has been known to flow out of the landfill and end up in groundwater supplies, poisoning aquifers that are the sole source of water for a community.

Modern landfills in the United States refuse the storage of hazardous waste, thus minimizing the toxicity of the leachate. They are also constructed with semi-impermeable clay on the top and bottom of the landfill and lined with plastics meant to contain the landfill's contents (see Figure 4.1). This construction may not entirely contain the leachate, but at least it will slow its migration down and thus protect the groundwater. Pipes are also installed in the landfill that allow for the controlled release of methane (a greenhouse gas) that can be used as an energy source for the generation of electricity.

A new, experimental landfill, called a *bioreactor landfill* (see Figure 4.2) may extend the life of a landfill by as much as 20 years. A bioreactor landfill operates to rapidly transform and degrade organic waste. The increase in waste degradation and stabilization of the landfill is accomplished through the addition of liquid and air to enhance the microbial process.

INTEGRATED WASTE MANAGEMENT

Although landfills in one form or another have been around for hundreds, perhaps thousands, of years, and will be with us for many years to come, but there are alternatives available. Not everything in the waste stream belongs in a landfill. The competent director of facilities needs to weigh the alternatives available to him and then determine the optimal mix of alternatives for the waste generated at the property.

Incinerators

In some areas of the country incinerators or waste-to-energy plants are available. Turning useless waste into needed energy sounds like a superb alternative to landfills, but is it? From a cost perspective, incineration is typically not a good alternative. The average tipping fee at incinerator plants in the United States is twice the expense of landfills.

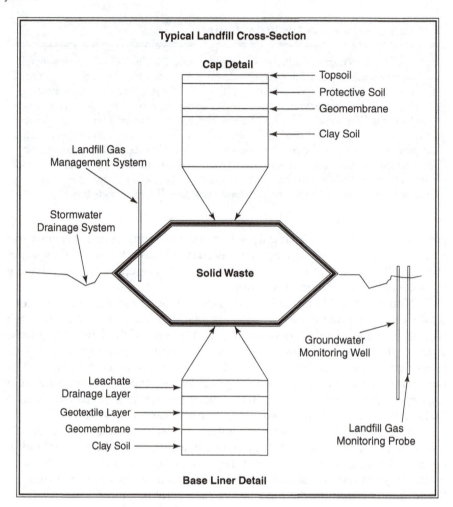

FIGURE 4.1 Traditional Landfill Design.

Traditional incineration is not a pollution free solution either. Unfortunately, the process is not flawless and some residues (e.g., dioxin) and gases may still escape into the environment, including carbon dioxide, a major greenhouse gas. In addition, the use of scrubber technology adds a substantial cost to the process. Most waste does not burn without assistance. Natural gas must be added to the process to generate enough heat to completely burn the waste that may have high moisture content. Finally, there is an aesthetic problem associated with these plants. They can smell incredibly bad; consequently, no one wants to live next to a waste incinerator. Many communities have banned them and this *not in my backyard* (NIMBY) attitude has made their availability relatively scarce. It is fairly unlikely that this attitude will change in the near future without the introduction of a more sophisticated technology. However, it should be noted that the EPA has identified incineration as the best method of destroying certain hazardous wastes.

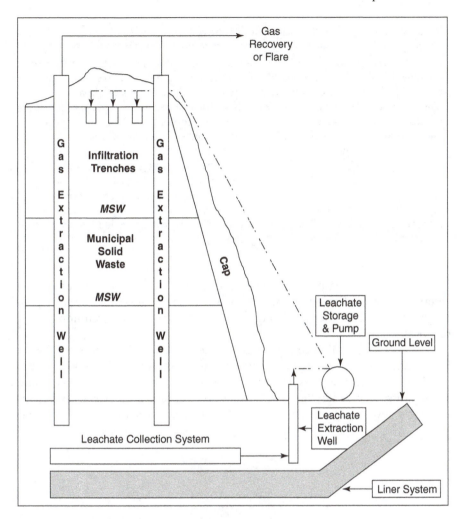

FIGURE 4.2 Bioreactor Landfill Design.

One variant is the plasma gasification method which burns waste at an incredible 8,000 degrees Fahrenheit. As of this writing, much controversy surrounds the process. Waste-to-energy systems may someday become a preferred method of waste disposal, but it is not ready yet.

Other Waste Transformation Systems

Incineration transforms solid waste into waste gases and energy. However, there are other systems that transform solid waste into liquid waste or may merely reduce the volume of waste so that it takes up less space in the dumpster and the landfill.

The **garbage disposal** found in many residential and commercial kitchens reduce solid waste to slurry that can then flow into the sewer line and on to the sanitation plant for processing. It accomplishes this feat through the use of rotating blades. Never insert a hand into a jammed garbage

Reduce, Reuse, Recycle, and now, Renew?

Contrary to conventional thinking, the waste stream does not start at the dumpster. It begins in the purchasing department. Traditionally, all goods were compared to certain specifications or *specs,* such as quality, cost, color, availability, and convenience. Eco-purchasing considers these traditional specifications, but also considers the item's hazardous characteristics, packaging content, recyclability, energy savings, and the materials content. The materials content is where the fourth *r* for *renew* comes into play. One example that has been given elsewhere is in the use of disposable eating utensils that can be composted rather than being made out of plastic that is not biodegradable. Other new and promising materials include bamboo floor coverings and furniture rather than slow growth hardwoods that cannot be easily replenished, and cloth made from hemp rather than cotton that uses more water, fertilizer, and pesticides. The idea is to choose products that are made from materials that are *renewable.*

disposal and or attempt to retrieve an object from inside the disposal. Make certain the unit is turned off and the power is cut at the circuit breaker panel before any repair is attempted. Figure 4.3 is an example of a common garbage disposal.

A **pulper** is similar to a garbage disposal, because it reduces solid waste to fine slurry, but the slurry is not discharged to the sewer. The water is separated from the ground waste and the waste is discharged to a waste container. These units, pictured in Figure 4.4, reduce the impact of the waste on the community's sewage treatment plant. Some communities have even banned

FIGURE 4.3   Hobart Foodwaste Disposer. *Source*: Courtesy of Hobart, Troy, Ohio.

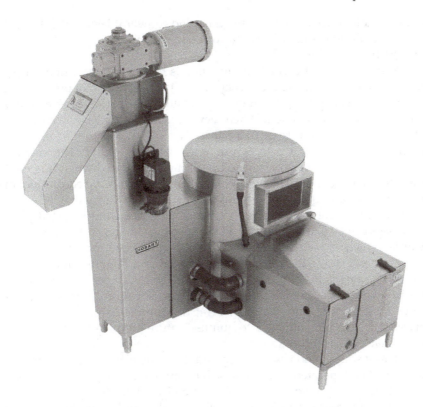

FIGURE 4.4 Hobart WastePro 1200. *Source*: Courtesy of Hobart, Troy, Ohio.

garbage disposals in favor of pulpers in commercial kitchens in order not to overwhelm the sewage treatment system. Las Vegas, at one time, was one of those cities.

Compactors of all sizes are common in many kitchens. They merely reduce the volume of the waste that will be sent to the landfill. Some haulers and landfills that charge by the cubic yard rather than by the ton, charge more for compacted waste.

Recycling

Recycling, the process of turning products back into their raw state so they may be made into another product is a less-than-perfect solution, too. There are costs associated with recycling programs, but those costs can be offset by the reduction in landfill expenses, the money generated from the sale of recycled goods, and the money saved from the recovery of **unintended throwaways.** Hotel and restaurant operators have seen almost everything of value end up in the trash from silverware and perfectly good china and glasses to linens, cleaning products and more. One major Las Vegas Strip hotel found that they were generating $5,000 a month in savings from their recycling program and another $5,000 a month from the recovery of hotel property (unintended throwaways) that had found its way into the trash. Obviously, sometimes those items that are thrown away are not *unintended.* One traditional method of smuggling hotel property out of the hotel is to place it into the trash and recover it later at the dumpster. One of your authors found five perfectly good gallons of ice cream (still frozen) in the garbage one time.

Another major drawback to recycling is that many items don't recycle, but instead are downcycled. Downcycling is the recycling of a product into a product of lesser quality. High quality white paper comes back as a lesser quality paper when recycled. When recycled again, it may come back as paperboard and then as a tissue or a paper towel. Then it cannot be used again and must be landfilled. Plastic is also a downcycled product. The long polymer chains of molecules that make up plastic are sheared when it is melted down and reformed into a new product. The resulting recycled product may only have one or two generations before it becomes so flimsy that it cannot be recycled. A sterling example is a garbage bag made from recycled plastic. These bags can be extremely flimsy. Downcycling is not a problem with some materials, such as metals, yard waste, and food waste. Aluminum *universal beverage containers* (UBC) can be recycled again and again—almost indefinitely. The same is true for most other metals and even for some varieties of plastic. In addition, there is a considerable cost saving from recycling metal rather than mining and manufacturing it. Yard and food waste can be **composted**, turning them back to humus. Nature ultimately recycles all biological materials, including us.

Before some goods can be recycled, they must be separated by types. Metal must be separated. Paper is worth far more if it is separated (e.g., white bonded stationery, colored, newsprint, etc.) by type. Most plastics used in packaging are imprinted with a recycling symbol and a number. The seven major categories of plastics are listed in Figure 4.5. When plastics are recycled, they must be separated by type; if they are not, an entire batch of recycled plastic containers will be unusable and will end up in the landfill. In some cases, even one container mixed in with 9,999 others will result in a contaminated batch. In order to recoup the maximum value from recycled paper, it

---

The Plastic Glut

Some would argue that it's impossible, but we need to learn to just say "no" to single-use plastic packaging and materials. Others would argue that plastic knives, forks, spoons, and those ubiquitous Styrofoam clamshell to-go containers are essential for take-out foodservice, but are they? Enter compostable packaging made out of plant materials, such as corn. There are literally dozens of companies on the market making these products out of plants, not plastic. Some of the companies include Genpak's Harvest Collection, Vegware, and Biodegradable Food Service. The products are made from potato starch, corn starch, bamboo, and sugarcane. Some of these products (not all) are microwavable and dishwasher safe, and all are biodegradable. Prices vary, but the argument can be made that even if they cost more than their plastic counterparts, it is a very small percentage of an operation's total operating costs and they do present a positive public relations opportunity to the foodservice operation that adopts them. Some cities, such as San Francisco, have begun to implement plastic packaging bans.

Recycling No.	Abbreviation	Polymer Name	Uses Once Recycled & Health Hazards
(1)	PETE or PET	Polyethylene terephthalate	Polyester fibers, thermoformed sheet, strapping, soft drink bottles. No known hazards.
(2)	HDPE	High density polyethylene	Bottles, grocery bags, recycling bins, agricultural pipe, base cups, car stops, playground equipment, and plastic lumber. No known hazards.
(3)	PVC or V	Polyvinyl chloride	Pipe, fencing, and non-food bottles. Contains Bisphenol A (PBA), an endocrine disrupter. Also, flexible PVC may contain Phthalates which in turn may be linked to damages to the liver and the testes and other health issues. Burning PVC may produce dioxin which is a known carcinogen.
(4)	LDPE	Low density polyethylene	Plastic bags, various containers, dispensing bottles, wash bottles, tubing, and various molded laboratory equipment. No known hazards.
(5)	PP	Polypropylene	Auto parts, industrial fibers, food containers. No known hazards.
(6)	PS	Polystyrene	Desk accessories, cafeteria trays, toys, video cassettes and cases, insulation board and expanded polystyrene products (e.g., Styrofoam). Some believe carcinogens may leach into liquids and food contained in polystyrene and Styrofoam.
(7)	OTHER	Other plastics, including acrylonitrile butadiene styrene acrylic, polycarbonate, polylactic acid, nylon and fiberglass.	Polycarbonate contains Bisphenol A (PBA), an endocrine disruptor.

FIGURE 4.5 Plastic Categories.

must be separated by type. Glass too has to be separated into clear, green, and brown glass or it is virtually worthless as a recycled commodity. Some recycled items are worth more if they are partially processed. For example, if recycled **PETE** bottles are shredded into flakes, they are worth more than bottles that have merely been pressed into bales.

Some recycled goods are expensive to transport to manufacturing plants where they are remanufactured into new products. Glass is heavy and is worth very little (from $29.00 to as little as $8.00 a ton depending on the color). Transportation costs make it prohibitively expensive to truck it for any distance, so it may well end up in local landfills. At least glass is inert and will not cause any leaching problems in a landfill. The good news is that glass is just starting to be used as a replacement for sand on some beaches that have been worn away from tidal action. The glass (which started out as sand) is finely ground so that it will not scratch anyone.

Hotels and restaurants should not expect to make anything from the sale of the recycled goods. The profit from the sale of the recycled goods usually ends up in the pocket of the recycling firm contracted by the hotel. Instead of paying the recycler, they receive the recycled goods from the property. The property's reward is the reduction in the hauling charges and tipping fees to the landfill plus the money saved from the return of those unintended throwaways.

The value of recycled goods can and have varied widely. Average national prices for recycled goods can be seen in Figure 4.6. Note that some have risen over the years, but some have fallen and others have stayed the same.

Although recycling is a less than a perfect solution, one should not for a moment believe that recycling is not worth the effort. In fact, recycling is truly a win–win situation. Recycling will generate significant savings for most hospitality firms and it is good for the environment. It is hoped that some of the shortcomings of recycling will be overcome in time.

When establishing a recycling program in a company, the first question generally asked is, "How?" What follows are some general guidelines that can be of immense help to any company who is grappling with the task of setting up a recycling program.

- First find a champion—someone who is impassioned about setting up a recycling program—and put them in charge. Next, put together a committee under your champion. Make sure every department in the enterprise is represented, if at all possible.
- Next, do an assessment. (You can also call it an audit, but that's a scary word.) Determine what potentially recyclable products are in your waste stream and also determine how many of these products are used on the property. This requires representative or random samples to be taken, products to be weighed, counted, and measured.
- Once you know what is in your waste stream, start identifying recyclers and the goods they recycle in your area. You may discover there are no local markets for some potentially recyclable goods in your waste stream. If there aren't, then look outside your locale. Check out all of the possibilities.
- Make appointments with the recyclers, describe the recyclables in your waste stream, and give them estimates on the amount of recyclables you are generating weekly. The volume of recycled goods you are generating will have an impact on the recyclers' bids. In a small operation, such as a restaurant, you may have to pay a recycler to pick up the recycled

American MetalMarket

May 16, 2008
COMPOSITES

METAL		This Issue	Last Issue	Year Ago 5/16/2007
Ferrous ($/ton)	Used steel cans	335	335	170
	No. 2 bundles	297	297	147
	Municipal shredded	357	357	181
	Shredded auto scrap	410	410	223
Nonferrous (¢/lb.)	Aluminum UBCs	87	85	83
	Auto batteries	4	4	4
PLASTIC				
Baled (¢/lb.)	Clear PET	19	19	18
	Green PET	18	18	17
	Natural HDPE	31	31	27
	Mixed HDPE	19	19	18
	Mixed PET	16	16	16
	Mixed HDPE & PET	9	9	8
Flaked (¢/lb.)	Clear PET	34	34	34
	Green PET	30	30	31
	Natural HDPE	37	37	37
PAPER				
Post consumer ($/ton)	Corrugated	101	110	91
	Newspaper #6	81	81	67
	Newspaper #8	107	107	97
	High-grade office (h)	167	167	146
	Colored ledger	142	142	125
	White ledger	251	251	215
	Computer laser	232	232	199
	Computer laser-free	232	232	202
Pre-consumer ($/ton)	White ledger	234	234	209
	Colored ledger	161	161	144
GLASS				
($/ton)	Clear	29	29	29
	Green	8	8	8
	Brown	17	17	17

National averages based on the average of prices in covered cities. Published biweekly.

FIGURE 4.6 Recycled Goods Composite Prices. *Source*: Courtesy of American Metal Market, Pittsburg, Pennsylvania.

goods. In a large operation, the recycler may provide equipment and even personnel to run the recycling center, and may even split the proceeds from the recycled goods.

- As recycling companies are chosen and contracts are drawn up, purchase the needed equipment for the program including recycling containers, shredders, balers, dumpsters, etc.
- Train all personnel in what to recycle and how to recycle. Work with the purchasing department to purchase recycled goods. You are not recycling unless you are *closing the loop* (i.e., purchasing recycled goods).

Create recycling goals for your property. Remember, there is no arbitrary percentage of the waste stream that can or should be recycled. There is always room for creativity and improvement.
- Monitor and review the program to see if you are meeting your goals. If not, investigate why and then retune and refine your goals.

Like anything else in life, recycling programs are subject to inertia. They need stimulation from time to time. As one executive remarked, "They are like spinning plates. Once you get them all spinning, you have to go back and give them another spin to keep them going."

One final thought on recycling: an effective recycling program should be in place even before the property opens. There should be a plan to recycle all of the construction waste generated at the building site. The USGBC's LEED program requires all new construction projects seeking certification to have a recycling program for their construction waste.

Reuse

Reusing material is a better choice than recycling, incineration, or landfilling. Reusing differs from recycling in that recycling breaks an item down to its elemental parts and makes a new product out of it, but reusing an item keeps the material in its original form and uses the item over and over for the same or different purposes.

Examples of **reuse** in the hospitality industry are numerous and are often applicable to most hotels and restaurants regardless of their type or location. Here are a few examples of material reuse in action:

- Instead of dispensing bottled beer that generates all of those empty beer bottles, there is draft beer in kegs. The keg is returned to the brewery through the distributor. Beer aficionados will tell you that draft beer tastes better glass for glass than bottled beers. Also, the cost per ounce is less than bottled beers, on average. Not only do you eliminate the bottles from your waste stream, but the packaging of those bottles is eliminated as well. The taps and lines do take some maintenance, but your distributor will usually do that for you.
- Soda can be purchased in cans or bottles, or your operation can purchase just the syrup mix and then add water and carbonation through a dispensing system on site. Sometimes the syrup comes in 20 liter bag-in-boxes that eliminate a considerable amount of packaging over individual containers, but the cardboard box cannot be reused, nor can the inside bag. Alternatives include aluminum containers, and now Coca-Cola has developed a series of new containers for their European operations called *Intermediated Bulk Containers* that can be reused repeatedly. These containers hold up to 250 liters of syrup, so fewer deliveries have to be made. These units are not yet available in the United States, but they will substantially reduce waste when they do become obtainable.
- Used office computer paper can be made into notepads for the hotel's employees and guests. The Saunder's Hotel Chain in Boston reuses all

of their paper in this way, getting a second *life* out of it before it is finally sent to the recyclers. Other hotels have donated their used office paper to elementary schools to use for art projects before it is recycled.

- Packaging can be reused. Bread and milk companies have done that for years with steel or plastic containers that are returned to the bakeries and dairies to be used again and again. Other examples include everything from ice cream cone packaging to pallets.
- Using that coffee mug over that Styrofoam cup that has a useful life of 30 minutes, but does not biodegrade and will be with us for literally thousands of years is a no-brainer, but there are other areas of reuse in foodservice. One place to look is in the employee's cafeteria where single-use utensils seem to predominate in some properties. Styrofoam cups, plates, and plastic knives, forks, and spoons are often found. Switching to reusable items just makes good common sense for both the environment and for the property's bottom line.

Reuse is not always a viable option, but when it is, it is the most environmentally responsible approach to the waste problem next to this final alternative in an Integrated Waste Management program.

Source Reduction

Source reduction, also known as waste prevention, keeps waste from entering the *stream* in the first place. It is the most cost-effective approach of all of the processes. Effective source reduction takes planning and the cooperation of the purchasing department, or all of those managers who have purchasing responsibilities.

One strategy is to minimize packaging whenever possible. Some manufacturers serve multiple markets and their packaging may be different for each market. Hospitality companies should explain to the supplier their packaging needs and request the packaging that adequately protects the product during transportation and storage. For example, beer is sold by grocery stores, liquor stores, restaurants, and on-sale bars. It is packaged in bottles, cans, and kegs. Retail outlets, such as grocery stores, prefer that their bottled beer packaging consist of cardboard boxes with four additional paperboard cartons in each box so that the beer can be sold by the *six-pack*. For on-sale retail operations, such as restaurants and bars, the beer comes in cardboard boxes of 24 bottles with paperboard separators (i.e., *loose pack*).

On-sale operations have no need for the six-pack cartons. On-sale operators do not need to have their liquor bottles delivered with retail Christmas packaging. When this author was a bar manager in a hotel, his orders were delivered with fancy individual Christmas packages for each bottle. Upon inquiring about the excess packaging, he was told that all he needed to do was to request his shipments be sent in the loose pack configuration, which would eliminate the excess packaging. One would have thought that any bar or restaurant would not have even had to ask for the liquor to be delivered in a loose pack configuration!

Ken Teeters, former Director of Facilities at Harrah's Las Vegas, convinced the hotel's food and beverage department to purchase Perrier water in

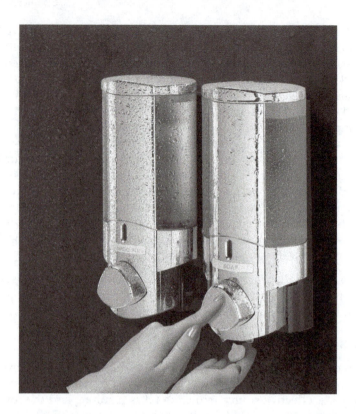

FIGURE 4.7 Guestroom Amenity Dispensers. *Source*: Photo courtesy of Dispenser Amenities, Inc. London, Ontario.

bulk (i.e., one-liter bottles) rather than the 220 ml individual bottles they were using, to reduce packaging waste.

Several hotels have installed soap and shampoo dispensers in their guest rooms, eliminating tens of thousands of those individually sized shampoo bottles and bars of soap. Buying items in bulk can generate considerable savings and reduce waste, which is truly a *win–win* proposition. Figure 4.7 is an example of these guest room amenity dispensers.

There are several strategies that can be employed in the executive offices as well. Using the duplex button on the copier and copying on both sides of the paper is one simple, but very effective, way to kill fewer trees. Eliminating hard copies whenever possible such as using e-mails instead of memos is another highly effective strategy. Encouraging all employees to bring their favorite coffee mug to work instead of using disposable Styrofoam cups, which is almost never recycled, is the very least that we can do to reduce waste in the workplace.

HAZARDOUS MATERIAL HANDLING AND DISPOSAL

We have already introduced the subject of hazardous waste, and in this section we will examine the proper procedures in the handling and disposal of these products. There are specific state and federal laws that govern the handling and disposal of these products and everyone in the hotel should know what to do if and when they come upon any of these products.

As stated earlier, ideally there should be no hazardous materials in the hospitality environment, but that is an ideal that cannot be achieved at this point in time. Some hazardous materials are essential to a facilities operation. For example, **disinfectants** that ward off disease and are an essential part of the cleaning process, are by the EPA's definition *pesticides* and are therefore hazardous materials. It stands to reason that anything that is intended to kill microorganisms might also negatively impact multi-celled organisms as well. As a result, disinfectants and **sanitizers** require special precautions and handling. Other examples of hazardous materials found in a hospitality environment would be certain types of solvents and cleaners used to remove rust, grease, and other contaminants from equipment. Then there are special chemicals used in closed loop water systems, such as boilers, that keep any minerals in the water in solution and other chemicals that reduce the oxygen content of the water to prevent the buildup of corrosion and rust. There may be a need for certain petrochemicals, such as oil and gasoline, in the building's operation. These too would be considered hazardous chemicals.

OSHA's Hazard Communication Standard

The Occupational Safety and Health Administration (OSHA) was established in 1971 to protect American workers from accidents and hazards in the work place. Since 1988, hotels have been required to comply with OSHA's Hazard Communication (HazComm) Standard (29CFR.1910.1200), which applies to the handling and storage of hazardous chemicals. Hazardous chemicals include, but are not limited to, aerosols, detergents, floor chemicals, carpet chemicals, flammable chemicals, cleaners, polishes, laundry chemicals, bathroom cleaners, and pesticides.

To be in full compliance, management should read the HazComm Standard. OSHA maintains a website, <http://www.osha.gov>, that provides extensive information on what an employer should know to be in compliance with the law. Visit this website and, using the search tools, you can find yourself at the guidelines for employers on how to set up a hazard communications program. For an excellent overview visit, http://www.osha.gov/dsg/hazcom/finalmsdsreport.html and read *Hazard Communication in the 21st Century Workplace.*

The hotel must inventory and list all hazardous chemicals on the property. The Hazard Communication Standard has three elements: training, labeling of chemicals (including chemicals transferred to sprayers and other containers), and, of course material safety data sheets (MSDSs) from the chemical manufacturers. These MSDSs should explain the chemicals' characteristics, recommended handling, use and, storage, information on flammability, ingredients, health hazards, first-aid procedures, and what to do in case of a fire or explosion. This information must be disseminated to employees and should be made available to them at all times. See Figure 4.8 for an actual Material Safety Data Sheet. The hotel must also formulate a HazComm program for the property and establish a training program for all employees who use or come in contact with hazardous chemicals. Finally, the property must provide all necessary protective equipment for its employees.

CORPORATE EXPRESS *1 Environmental Way* Broomfield, CO 80021 Business Phone: 1.888.203.5101 24-HR MEDICAL AND DOT EMERGENCIES: 1.888.322.0912	MSDS #: MSDS SEB6500		
	Hazard Rating	**HMIS**	**NFPA**
	Health	1	1
	Flammability	0	0
	Reactivity	0	0
	Special	None	None

MATERIAL SAFETY DATA SHEET
Complies with ANSI Z400.1 Format

SECTION 1: PRODUCT IDENTIFICATION

Product: HEAVY DUTY GENERAL PURPOSE CLEANER Sustainable Earth® 65   **MSDS CODE:** SEB6500.1007
This MSDS applies to Product Numbers: SEB6501, SEB6502QM, SEB6504HM, SEB6510 and SEB6520

GENERIC DESCRIPTION	DATE ISSUED	SUPERSEDES	PREPARED BY
Concentrated General Purpose Cleaner	10-1-07	6-1-07	Regulatory Specialist

SECTION 2: COMPOSITION AND INFORMATION ON INGREDIENTS

Components*	% by Wt.	CAS #	Exposure Limit	LC_{50}/LD_{50}
Hydrogen Peroxide	1-3	7722-84-1	**OSHA** TWA: 1.4 mg/m₃ **ACGIH** TWA: 1.4 mg/m₃	ORAL 1518 mg/kg (rat) DERMAL 4060 mg/kg (rat) VAPOR 2000 mg/m³ 4-hrs (rat)
Alcohol Ethoxylate	15-20	68439-46-3	Not Established	
Water	60-100	7732-18-5	Not Established	

SECTION 3: HAZARD IDENTIFICATION

Primary Entry Routes: Skin Contact   **Signs & Symptoms of Exposure:** Incidental skin contact is not expected to cause any significant irritation. **Effects of Overexposure:** Based on Corrositex *in vitro* testing this product is not corrosive and with prolonged skin contact or eye contact may cause slight reddening but will be non-irritating. This product has a low potential for skin absorption based upon review of the absorption information provided by individual ingredients manufacturers.

SECTION 4: FIRST AID MEASURES

Emergency First Aid Procedures: SKIN CONTACT: Rinse skin thoroughly with water. EYE CONTACT: Flush eyes with water for 15-20 minutes. If reddening occurs and persists then get prompt medical aid. INGESTION: Drink large amounts of water, consult a physician.
24-HR MEDICAL EMERGENCY PHONE: 1.888.322.0912

SECTION 5: FIRE FIGHTING MEASURES

Flash Point: None- This product is not considered a fire hazard, nor will it support combustion. **Extinguishing Media:** Use standard firefighting measures to extinguish fires involving this material (water spray, dry chemicals or foam).

SECTION 6: ACCIDENTAL RELEASE MEASURES

Release or Spill: Recover liquid with wet mop or wet/dry vacuum. Flush residue to sanitary sewer with water. Use care, floor may become slippery. All Federal, State and Local regulations should be carefully followed. Discarded product is not a hazardous waste according to RCRA, 40 CFR 261.

SECTION 7: HANDLING AND STORAGE

Keep out of reach of children. Avoid eye and prolonged skin contact.

SECTION 8: EXPOSURE CONTROLS AND PERSONAL PROTECTION

Respiratory Protection: No special requirements under normal use conditions. **Protective Gloves:** No special requirements for normal use conditions. **Eye Protection:** No special requirements for normal use conditions. **Other Protective Measures:** None

FIGURE 4.8   Material Safety Data Sheet. *Source:* Courtesy of Corporate Express U.S., Broomfield, Colorado.

Corporate Express
Material Safety Data Sheet
Page 2 – HEAVY DUTY GENERAL PURPOSE CLEANER Sustainable Earth® 65   SEB6500.1007

SECTION 9: PHYSICAL AND CHEMICAL PROPERTIES

Appearance/Odor: Clear, green liquid   **Boiling Point:** >212F   **Evap. Rate:** NA   **pH:** 6.5
Vapor Density: ND   **Vapor Pressure:** <1.0   **Specific Gravity:** 1.01   **Solubility in Water:** Complete   **%Volatile:** 100
V.O.C. Content (by weight): <1%

SECTION 10: STABILITY AND REACTIVITY

Heavy Duty General Purpose Cleaner is stable and non-reactive.

SECTION 11: TOXICOLOGICAL INFORMATION

Oral Toxicity: This product is non-toxic based upon current information available to Corporate Express and provided by all ingredient manufacturers. It exhibits acute oral LD_{50} values greater than 5g/kg for rats and acute dermal LD_{50} values greater than 2g/Kg for rabbits. **No PBTs**: This product contains none of the persistent, bioaccumulative and toxic chemicals **(PBT)** as listed by EPA: dioxins & furans, toxaphene, PCBs, Mirex, Mercury & compounds, Octachlorostyrene, alkyl-lead, DDT, Hexachlorobenzene, aldrin/dieldrin, benzo(a)pyrene and chlordane. **No Butyl:** Contains no 2-butoxyethanol (butyl). **No Endocrine Modifers:** Based upon information provided by manufacturers of all ingredients used to manufacture this product, none of the ingredients used in this product contain APE, OPE, NPE or dibutyl phthalate. **Ingredients:** All ingredients of this product are listed on TSCA 1985 Chemical Substance Inventory and 1990 Supplement. This product does not contain any chemical subject to the reporting requirements of CERCLA or SARA Section 302 or 313. No ingredient in this product is currently listed as a carcinogen, or reproductive toxins by NTP, IARC or OSHA.

SECTION 12: ECOLOGICAL INFORMATION

The organic ingredients are readily biodegradable based upon the Modified OECD screening tests. After this product's use, it will biodegrade in sewage systems and/or the environment. Contains no nonyl phenol ethoxylates or alkyphenol ethoxylates **(APE)**. No ingredients used to make this product are listed in the toxic release inventory **(TRI)** chemicals list under Superfund Amendments and Reauthorization Act (SARA) Title III, Section 313. This product contains no ozone-depleting chlorinated compounds as specified by the Montreal Protocol. This product contains no paradichlorobenzene 1,4-dioxane, sodium hypochlorite, NTA or sodium EDTA. Heavy Duty General Purpose Cleaner is packaged in recyclable Type 2 HDPE plastic gallon containers.

SECTION 13: DISPOSAL CONSIDERATIONS

Waste Disposal Information: Waste Disposal Information: No special method. Observe all applicable Federal, State and Local regulations, rules and/or ordinances regarding disposal of non-hazardous materials. Discarded product is not a hazardous waste according to RCRA, 40 CFR 261. This product is not considered a hazardous waste as defined in WAC 173-303-070 or as characterized in WAC 173-303-090. Observe all applicable Federal, State and Local regulations, rules and/or ordinances regarding disposal of non-hazardous materials.

SECTION 14: TRANSPORT INFORMATION

DOT EMERGENCY 24-HR: 1.888.322.0912   **U.S. DOT Class:** Not Regulated
DOT Shipping Name: Compound, Cleaning Liquid

SECTION 15: REGULATORY INFORMATION

SARA Title III Section 313 and 40 CFR Part 372 Notification: See section 2.
No ingredients in this product are currently listed as carcinogens by NTP, IARC or OSHA. All components of this product are listed or are excluded from listing on the U.S. Toxic Substances Control Act (TSCA) Chemical Substance Inventory.

SECTION 16: OTHER INFORMATION

Always follow label directions carefully when using this or any other chemical product. If information about this product is required, please contact CORPORATE EXPRESS at 1.888.203.5101 or visit our website at www.corporateexpress.com . Keep MSD Sheets filed and organized in an area accessible to workers according to the Hazard Communication Standards.

FIGURE 4.8   (*continued*)

Bloodborne Pathogen Standard

One other common hazard substance in the hospitality industry is the presence of pathogens in human tissue, blood, and other bodily wastes. OSHA has recognized this danger and in 1991 the Bloodborne Pathogen Standard (29CFR.1910.1030) was passed into law. All lodging facilities that have departments with a propensity for exposure (housekeeping departments through soiled linen), engineering departments (cuts and abrasions), food and beverage departments (more cuts and abrasions), and security departments are required by law to have an *exposure control program*. This program must address limiting/eliminating exposure through *universal precautions* (use of equipment and handling of contaminated waste), *personal work practices*, the use of *protective equipment*, and good housekeeping practices. The program must also deal with the use of warning labels or signs and exposure procedures, and must also establish an HBV vaccination program (which is free to employees). Finally, compliance with the law must be verified through good recordkeeping.

Summary

When it comes to waste management, there is room for improvement within almost every hospitality operation. The trouble has been that the industry has lacked the economic incentive to reduce, reuse, and recycle more, and instead has relied almost exclusively on the landfill. Establishing an integrated waste management program at a hospitality property is a *win–win* proposition. The morale of the staff will increase, because they will know that through their efforts they are having a positive effect on the environment. The property will save money and those savings will increase over time as the use of landfills continues to increase in cost. The environment and community certainly benefit as we reduce our need for landfills and make a greater effort to purchase renewable, reusable, recyclable, and less hazardous items.

Finally, it must be remembered that managing waste is not just the facility department's job. Waste management and the area of life safety and security share one thing in common. Everyone who works at the property is responsible and should be held accountable for both of these areas. We are all part of the problem because all of us produce waste. We are also part of the solution because individually and collectively we can make decisions that will help to eliminate the problem of waste.

Key Terms and Concepts

Compactors *89*
composted *90*
disinfectants *97*
garbage disposal *87*
hauling charges *84*
hazardous waste *80*

human effluent *80*
infectious waste *83*
landfill *80*
leachate *84*
municipal solid
   waste *79*

PETE *91*
pulper *88*
reuse *94*
sanitizers *97*
source reduction *95*
tipping fee *84*

unintended
   throwaways *89*
waste *80*
waste stream *80*

Discussion and Review Questions

1. Your property, a 200-room hotel does not have a recycling program. You have made an appointment to see the general manager. How are you going to persuade her that recycling is a good idea? Make a list of your talking points and compare your ideas with your fellow students. Discuss and then vote on what are the ten best ideas to present to the G.M.

2. What could the areas of Front Desk, Food & Beverage, Accounting, Housekeeping, Marketing, and Human Resources do to reduce the amount of a hotel's waste stream?

3. How would you build excitement and encourage buy-in among your fellow employees for a new recycling program at your hotel?

4. What are the benefits to the members of the EPA's WasteWise program? Would you recommend that your hotel or restaurant join this program?

5. The California Waste Recycling Act of 2003 has what many consider the most progressive set of laws regarding e-waste in the country. Visit http://www.ciwmb.ca.gov/ for more information and then discuss in class why other states have not passed similar legislation.

5

Water Systems

CHAPTER OBJECTIVES

After reading this chapter, you should be able to:

- define various technical terms related to plumbing systems.
- identify the major components of a building's water supply and wastewater removal systems.
- describe the components of water and how water is treated to address the needs of the people and equipment that use it.
- describe how domestic hot water systems work, including issues related to safety.
- discuss how to manage water used for swimming pools and spas.
- describe water conservation measures that the hospitality industry can use.

INTRODUCTION

The subjects of plumbing and water management do not usually come to a hospitality manager's mind when thinking about managerial issues. The manager will consider service quality, staffing levels, revenue management, and a number of other issues. However, let's consider it from the guest's viewpoint. If a guest checks into your hotel, what is he or she really purchasing? Many of you will think of beds, televisions, and a host of amenities such as wireless Internet service, room service, frequent guest programs, and many other services. But what is it that the guest actually does *in* the room? Without going into too much detail, a lot of it involves water—both supply and disposal. The guest may choose the hotel for the service and amenities but will have a miserable stay without water. Thus, water is a service that we need to provide, both in lodging facilities as well as in food and beverage facilities.

Proper management of water systems is becoming an increasingly important issue for hospitality properties. In the past, water was relatively inexpensive to purchase and manage. However, many areas now experience droughts, which may be severe. These water shortages have led water utility companies to examine supply; permanent water shortages are now a major concern. With shortages come increased expenses for the end-user. The hospitality industry operates on relatively thin profit margins, and increases in water costs can jeopardize the hotel's financial position. In this chapter, we will examine how to manage water costs through the proper management of water supply, disposal, use, and conservation.

WATER TERMS

This chapter will use several technical terms to discuss water and wastewater systems. You should know the following terms and concepts before continuing to read:

- *Fixture:* The term **fixture** is used in a variety of ways throughout the building to describe plumbing, electrical, and a number of other types of equipment. Plumbing fixtures are items such as sink faucets, bathtub faucets, showerheads, and toilets.
- *Flow pressure:* Flow pressure is measured in **pounds per square inch (psi)** in the United States. This **pressure** is the amount of pressure that is exerted inside the plumbing pipes near the fixture through which the water will emerge.
- *Flow volume:* The volume of water that flows through a fixture is measured in **gallons per minute (gpm)**.
- *Gravity:* Supplying water requires overcoming the effects of gravity to move water from a lower level to a higher level. However, water removal systems use gravity almost exclusively to remove water from sinks, toilets, and other water using fixtures and appliances.
- *Pressure drop:* As water travels, it experiences conditions that slow down the flow and reduce pressure. These conditions include moving water upwards and friction from the water pipes. A building's water supply will have water at a higher pressure (psi) than will be found at the fixtures, since water will lose pressure as it travels through the building. This concept is important because too much pressure drop will result in a weak flow from a faucet or showerhead which, in turn, will negatively impact guests and employees.

WATER SOURCES AND DELIVERY SYSTEMS

We must get water from somewhere, right? We will look at how we get water today shortly, but first, let us think about the past. Was there plumbing before the modern era? You may be surprised to hear that sophisticated plumbing systems have been around for over 2,000 years. You may be familiar with the aqueducts that were built around Europe by the ancient Romans to transport water throughout the Roman Empire. But did you know that many of the Romans' public and residential buildings had indoor plumbing? These systems brought water into the building and removed wastewater from the building through a separate system. Today's plumbing systems operate on the same principles and are much like the old Roman systems.

Water Supply—City or Well?

CITY WATER   Most restaurants and hotels that are located in or near cities will have access to a city water supply. The city's Department of Public Works will have a division dedicated to providing an adequate supply of **potable water** to the residents and businesses in the district. Potable is the term used in water management to indicate water that is safe for humans to drink.

The water authority may get its water from reservoirs that collect water from rain or from a river, or it may get the water from **aquifers**, large deposits of water that lay deep underground. The water is pumped into a water treatment plant where it is filtered, tested, and treated with chemicals or ultraviolet light to kill any impurities that would be harmful to humans. The water is then pumped out to customers. You will often see towns with a large water tower. This is an emergency supply of water in case of fire or other disasters.

WELL WATER   Hotels and restaurants that are located in places without access to a city water system will usually obtain water through wells that are located on the property. The hotel or restaurant must maintain the pump, storage, and testing equipment to ensure that the water will be there when it is needed and that it will be acceptable for human use.

Water Supply Distribution Systems

Once the water is in the building, we need to move it throughout the building. There are two major types of systems for accomplishing this: **constant pressure systems** and **gravity-fed systems**.

CONSTANT PRESSURE SYSTEMS   Constant pressure systems work by using a pump to provide a constant supply of water throughout the building (Figure 5.1a). When a person uses a faucet or toilet, the water is pushed through the faucet or refills the toilet by the pressure provided by the pump. This type of system is very economical for low-rise buildings (six floors or fewer) that have relatively low amounts of water usage. A typical restaurant or a low-rise hotel or motel will probably use a constant pressure system.

GRAVITY-FED, OR DOWNFEED, SYSTEMS   A building that uses a large quantity of water or that is higher than a few floors requires very large pumps and large amounts of energy to provide water on demand. Taller buildings also require a larger quantity of water available in the event of a fire. Fires often cause a power loss, which could shut down the constant pressure pumps. The systems used for higher-rise and/or higher volume buildings are called gravity-fed systems.

Gravity-fed systems, often called downfeed systems, consist of one or more water tanks located on top and/or intermediate floors of buildings. Pumps are used to pump water up through the building and into the tank (Figure 5.1b). When a person or a piece of equipment in the building uses water, the water is supplied from the tank. The pump only operates to refill the tank when a **float valve** in the tank tells it to send more water up.

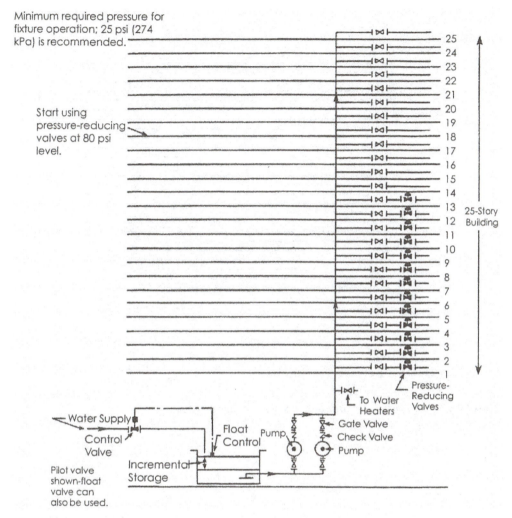

Minimum required pressure for fixture operation; 25 psi (274 kPa) is recommended.

Start using pressure-reducing valves at 80 psi level.

Water Supply

Control Valve

Pilot valve shown-float valve can also be used.

Incremental Storage

Float Control

Pump

To Water Heaters

Gate Valve
Check Valve
Pump

Pressure-Reducing Valves

25-Story Building

FIGURE 5.1a Constant Pressure System. *Source:* BOMA.

What is a float valve? A float valve is the type of device that you will find in your toilet's tank at home. If you open the lid, you will see something that looks like a metal or plastic balloon on an arm (Figure 5.2). When you flush the toilet, the water level in the tank drops and the float goes down too. When the level gets low enough, the float tells the fill valve to open, which adds water to the tank. As the water level rises, the float rises as well; once it reaches a high enough level, the water shuts off.

The gravity-fed water supply system works the same way. The supply tank on the roof is full of water that is used when building occupants turn on a faucet or use a toilet. If the water level in the roof tank is higher than the pre-set low level, the pump does not refill the tank. Once the water level is low enough, the float valve turns on the pumps, which then fill the tank to its high

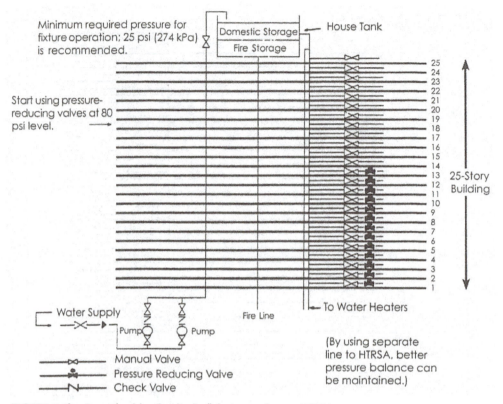

Minimum required pressure for fixture operation; 25 psi (274 kPa) is recommended.

Start using pressure-reducing valves at 80 psi level.

Domestic Storage
Fire Storage

House Tank

25
24
23
22
21
20
19
18
17
16
15
14
13
12
11
10
9
8
7
6
5
4
3
2
1

25-Story Building

Water Supply

Pump   Pump

Fire Line

To Water Heaters

(By using separate line to HTRSA, better pressure balance can be maintained.)

Manual Valve
Pressure Reducing Valve
Check Valve

FIGURE 5.1b   Downfeed (or Gravity-Fed) System.   *Source*: BOMA.

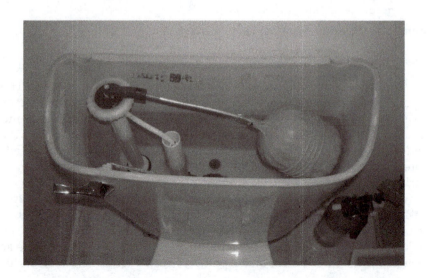

FIGURE 5.2   Float Valve.   *Source*: Dina Zemke.

level. The result is a constant supply of water without requiring extremely large, powerful pumps that are expensive to operate. Gravity does most of the water supply work for the building.

Removal of Wastewater: Storm Sewer and Sanitary Sewer Systems

Now that we have water in our building, we need to consider what happens to it once it is used. The building will have a system of drains to remove the water from the building, called the **sanitary sewer system**. While the water supply to the building usually requires pumps to get it into the building, the wastewater removal system operates almost entirely through the force of gravity. The drain pipes are installed with just enough downward slope to ensure that there is enough velocity to make the water and waste flow downwards and out of the building. The water then travels to a location where it is rendered safe for human consumption once again.

We must also consider water that occurs naturally. This water, including rain, landscape watering runoff, and snowmelt, also needs to be carried away from the property. Water that occurs naturally is not inside the building and does not utilize the sanitary wastewater removal system mentioned above. Instead, this water flows into a **storm sewer system**, where the water is never treated for impurities and often flows directly into lakes, rivers, reservoirs, or other natural bodies of water (Figure 5.3).

Would we want the untreated water from inside the building to flow into our local lakes and rivers? The answer is a resounding "NO!" While the water from rain, landscape watering, and other natural sources is disposed of through the storm sewer system, the water from inside the building will usually be transported to the city's water treatment facility through a sanitary sewer system.

FIGURE 5.3a Storm Sewer in a Las Vegas Street. *Source*: Dina Zemke.

FIGURE 5.3b Close-up of Environmental Warning. The Fish's Name is "Kip." *Source*: Dina Zemke.

Sanitary Sewer Systems

Liquid waste is called **effluence**. The term "sanitary" in this case does not indicate that the contents of the drain lines and sewer are clean and safe for human consumption. It is quite the opposite—the system is a closed system that prevents the water from coming into contact with the outside environment. There are two general types of sanitary systems for carrying waste away from a building: city sewer systems and septic systems.

CITY SEWERS   If a building has a city water supply, it is likely (although not guaranteed) to be connected to the **city sewer system**. The city's municipal water authority will be responsible for not only supplying water to the building, but also for disposing of the water once it has been used. This is convenient for the building owner because the task of waste disposal is performed by someone else.

Many buildings have wastewater pipes that are below ground, and below the city's main sewer line. Gravity does not work upwards—in this instance, one or more **ejector pumps** will be needed to pump the waste up and out of the building and into the sewer system. These pumps have large impellers (the pump parts that move the liquid) that can handle both liquid and semi-solid material without clogging. All managers should know where the ejector pumps are located in a hospitality facility. It always seems like these pumps break down during weekends or holidays! If the chief engineer is not on-site, the manager on duty is often responsible for managing the problem and should be able to describe the situation to a plumber who will fix the problem.

SEPTIC SYSTEMS   Just as not every hospitality facility's water is provided by a city water supply, the same situation exists for wastewater disposal. When a city sewer system is not available, the building owner needs to dispose of wastewater on-site, using a **septic system** (Figure 5.4). A septic system works in the following way:

1. The wastewater flows through the building's drain system into a **septic tank** located either beneath the building or just outside the building. The septic tank is lined with concrete or steel to prevent the wastewater from entering the environment immediately.
2. The wastewater collects in the tank and is relatively still (not moving).
3. The solids and heavier waste matter settle at the bottom of the tank and the water on top forms a scum layer. The water in the middle is relatively clear, although by no means clean. Microbes in the tank digest a lot of the harmful bacteria and other impurities in the water.
4. The water slowly flows into an area next to the septic tank called a **septic field**. The septic field is installed underground and consists of several perforated pipes. The pipes allow the water to seep slowly back into the ground, where nature returns it to its home in the earth. The soil naturally contains microbes that break down any impurities. By the time the water reaches the water table, an underground stream, or an aquifer, it is reasonably clean.

Does the idea of having toilet water enter the yard frighten you? The septic system is designed to address the impurities so that the water that seeps into the septic field is not harmful to the environment. However, the waste that settles at the bottom of the septic tank needs to be removed periodically by a septic tank cleaning service. The tank might also be treated with a septic tank cleaner,[1] such as Rid X™. Septic tank cleaners work by introducing bacteria and enzymes into the septic tank that feed on the impurities, rendering the water safe to reintroduce into the environment. Disposing of harmful chemicals, particularly drain openers, is bad for septic tanks, because the chemicals may kill the tank's microbes.

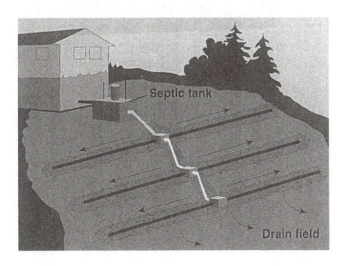

FIGURE 5.4 Septic System. *Source*: Black & Decker.

SEWER GASSES Wastewater pipes are rarely completely full of effluence, since they must be large enough to handle the maximum amount of water that exits the building at a single moment in time. Once the waste has exited, the empty pipes could permit sewer gasses from either the city sewer system or the septic system to rise and reenter the building. How do we prevent these gasses, which smell bad and may be flammable, from entering the building? Plumbing drain fixtures are designed to form a liquid seal that blocks sewer gasses from reentering the building. Here's how they work:

TOILETS The bottom of a toilet bowl has a pipe leaving it that is shaped like either the letter S or P (depending on your point of view). This part of the toilet is called the siphon. Water collects at the lowest point of the siphon and provides an automatic seal that prevents sewer gas from infiltrating the bathroom. For a fun demonstration of how a toilet works, go to www. howthingswork.com[2] and enter "toilet" in the search field.

SINKS Sinks, bathtubs, and showers also make use of an S-shaped or P-shaped structure in the drain pipes (Figure 5.5). These curves in the drains are called **P-traps** or **S-traps**, depending on which shape is used. They work in a similar manner to the siphon shape in a toilet. Water collects in the bottom of the curve directly below the drain opening in the sink and forms a seal that prevents sewer gas from rising into the room. These fixtures are called "traps" for a good reason—they often trap objects that fall down the drain, such as earrings, rings, and occasionally, partial dentures or removable dental bridgework. Your building engineers will occasionally go to a guest's room to open the trap to retrieve the fallen object.

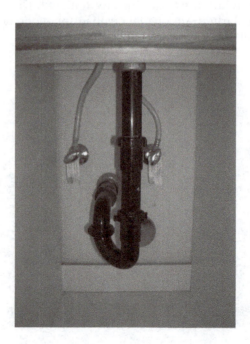

FIGURE 5.5 P-Trap Under a Hotel Sink. *Source*: Dina Zemke.

WATER QUALITY

Once we get our water into the building, what sorts of concerns might we have? The water that entered the building will be potable. But is that enough? Look around you the next time you are in class. Do you notice that many people are carrying bottled water around? If the water from the tap is drinkable, why do people buy water? Some people simply do not trust the water supply system. Others find the taste of the water objectionable—the water may have a chlorine taste (from the treatment plant), a metallic taste (if there is iron in the water), or may have other tastes that are not good. We need to examine our water to see if it meets our guests' requirements.

What Do Guests Expect?

Our guests and employees expect that the water that comes out of the tap will be potable, or safe to drink. Each one of the following conditions may be present in water that is perfectly safe to drink but which may cause concern for people:

- *Color:* Is the water colorless, or is it brown, gray, reddish, or another color?
- *Odor:* Does the water have an odor? Common odors include chlorine, sulfur, and a metallic smell caused by iron in the water.
- *Taste:* Is the water tasteless, or is there a taste of chlorine, salt, or metal?
- *Clarity:* Is the water crystal clear, or is there cloudiness or sediment floating in the water?
- *Mineral content:* Does the water have a high mineral content? Common minerals include iron and sulfur. Minerals can sometimes affect people's digestive systems negatively and can also be harmful for equipment on the property.
- *Acidity/alkalinity:* Is the water acidic or does the water have a high alkaline level? High alkaline water is quite common—we often refer to this condition as "hard" water. This is caused by a high mineral content, usually calcium-based, and causes problems with minerals building up in equipment and soap not lathering.

Some of the problems listed above can easily be treated with equipment installed at the main building supply. For example, "hard" water can be treated using a **water softener**, a system that replaces the calcium in the water with sodium or potassium salts to lower the alkalinity. Other problems are more difficult to correct and may indicate a serious problem with the water supply system. For example, a glass of water containing black granules that settle to the bottom and a sharp odor may indicate high levels of sulfur.

HEATING WATER

There are two major hot water systems in a building: domestic hot water and heating hot water. Hot water for heating systems will be discussed in Chapter 7.

Domestic hot water, usually abbreviated in building drawings and on hot water pipes as DHW, is the hot water that circulates through the building for human use. This includes hot water for showers and bathtubs, kitchen and guestroom sinks, laundry operations, dishwashing operations, and any other use that will result in human contact with the water.

How is water heated? There are three major ways to heat water: electric heaters, "indirect" heaters, and instantaneous heaters. The first type, the **electric water heater**, is similar to the type of hot water heater that you would find in your house or apartment building. The system consists of a large tank that is filled with water. An electric element with a thermostat is immersed in the tank. The water is then heated to a preset temperature. When the water temperature drops below a certain level, electricity is supplied to the heating element, heating the water surrounding it. The tank is also equipped with a float valve. When the water level in the tank reaches a particular low-level point, a valve opens and fresh (cold) water is supplied to the tank. When you take a shower and run out of hot water, the tank has been drained and the new water has not had time to heat up.

Electric heating elements are useful in smaller commercial buildings and single residential buildings. They are inexpensive to install and maintain, and they do an adequate job of providing domestic hot water throughout the building. However, heating large quantities of water with electricity is inefficient and is very expensive in the long run. Larger buildings or buildings that use a lot of water generally use another type of fossil fuel, either fuel oil or natural gas, to heat their water. These systems push water through a boiler and are exposed to heat that is supplied by burning natural gas, propane, oil, or by steam (Figure 5.6). One arrangement for heating water is a

FIGURE 5.6 Hot Water Boiler in a Hotel.
Source: Las Vegas Hilton.

fire-tube boiler, where water enters a very large tank and surrounds a series of tubes through which either fire or steam travel. The heat from the fire or steam transfers to the water, thus heating it. Another type of boiler is a **water-tube boiler**. This is similar to a fire-tube boiler, but the water passes through the tubes and the heat from fire or steam is in the tank through which the tubes pass, heating the water.

Instantaneous heaters have been common in Europe for many years and are now beginning to appear in the United States. These heaters may be heated using electricity, natural gas, or propane. The system overall is much more energy-efficient than traditional boilers because no storage tank is required in an instantaneous heater—it just heats exactly the amount of water that is needed, at the time it is needed. While they require more energy to actually heat the water, the savings occur because no energy is consumed keeping the water hot when there is no demand for it. Instantaneous heaters are used to heat both domestic hot water as well as heating hot water (Figures 5.7a–c).

One type of instantaneous heater that is already very common in the North American hospitality industry is a **booster heater** on a dishwashing machine. The booster heater takes the already heated water that is used in the cleaning cycle of the dish machine and increases the temperature to 180°F for the sanitizing cycle. The booster heater is often an electric heater, although steam and natural gas systems are available. Booster heaters may also be found in laundry systems to provide very hot water during certain cleaning cycles.

FIGURE 5.7a An Instantaneous Domestic Hot Water (DHW) Heater. *Source*: UNLV.

FIGURE 5.7b Several Instantaneous DHW Heaters In-line. *Source*: UNLV.

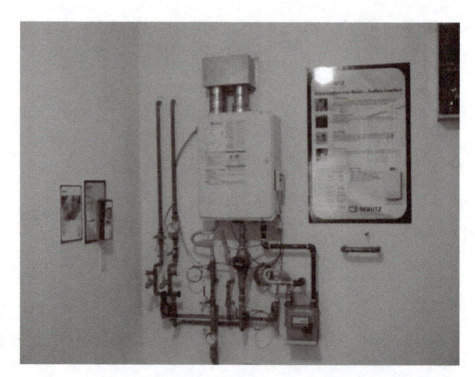

FIGURE 5.7c A Residential Version of an Instantaneous DHW Heater. *Source*: UNLV.

Distributing Domestic Hot Water

Once the water is heated, we must now send it throughout the building. Smaller buildings, particularly restaurants, will typically use only standard plumbing pipes to distribute water. This method is not desirable in hotels and motels. If domestic hot water is not in use, the water in the pipes stands still. Over time, the water cools and a guest who rises and wants to bathe or shower early in the morning may have to wait a few minutes to get hot water at the tap. This is poor service and will result in unhappy guests!

There is a two-step solution to this problem. First, the domestic hot water pipes should always be wrapped in insulation to prevent heat loss. This will increase service quality and will save money. The second step is to install a circulating pump in the domestic hot water system. This pump will circulate hot water constantly through the building and back to the boiler. A circulating pump will ensure that hot water is immediately available at all times—good service and happy guests!

How Hot Should Domestic Hot Water Be?

We would like to provide water that is hot enough to satisfy all guests. However, a fine line exists between hot enough to please guests and hot enough to scald people.

We know that keeping food temperatures in the "danger zone" between 40°F (4.4°C) and 140°F (60°C) can promote bacterial and other microbe growth. This is also true for water. In recent years, the U.S. government's Occupational Safety and Health Administration (OSHA) has issued guidelines to prevent microbial growth in domestic hot water systems. OSHA recommends that domestic hot water storage tanks be held at a minimum of 140°F, with water circulating through the system at a minimum of 122°F (50°C).

However, 140°F is far too hot for human exposure and will result in scalding. The most common instances of scalding occur in the shower, where the person is completely doused in hot water. You may ask yourself "Why don't people just test the water before they get in the tub or the shower? Can't they tell it's too hot?" This seems like common sense on the surface. However, many people cannot gauge the temperature of the water. For example, certain medications reduce our sensitivity to heat, and people taking these medications could be scalded without realizing it immediately. Just because the person cannot feel it does not mean that he or she will not be harmed. Scalding is often fatal. There have been tragic incidences involving a small child climbing into a tub of water that was too hot and being scalded. Aside from the tragic consequences for the victim and his or her family, hotel or restaurant bathroom hot water scalding results in bad publicity for the property, employees may be traumatized, and the victim will probably sue the property, causing significant damage to the property's financial position. The importance of water temperature safety cannot be stressed enough.

How do we protect our guests from the dangers of overheated water? There are several important methods that the property should implement. The water coming out of any tap on the property should **NEVER exceed 115°F**. The water may be warmer as it leaves the boiler, but it will lose heat as it travels through the building. You should have a policy of testing the hot water temperature at taps in the kitchen and/or guestrooms and bathrooms to ensure that the water is not dangerous for guests and employees. (This does not mean that the water has to be 115°F—it simply means that it should not exceed that temperature.) You may find that your employees and guests will be happy with lower temperatures, which will reduce the cost of heating water.

FIXTURES WITH ANTI-SCALD DEVICES If we need to store hot water at 140°F and provide water circulating through the system at 122°F, how do we ensure that the water coming out of the tap is only 115°F? There are a variety of plumbing fixtures available, such as faucets and showerheads, that contain a heat sensor. If the sensor finds that the water is too hot, cold water is automatically mixed in with the hot, providing hot water that is not dangerous (Figures 5.8a and 5.8b).

FIGURE 5.8a Anti-scald Device. *Source*: UNLV.

FIGURE 5.8b Inside an Anti-scald Device. *Source*: UNLV.

A study conducted in 2004 found that scalding water temperatures were discovered in nearly 90% of the hotel rooms surveyed.[3] This was the water temperature coming out of the faucet, not circulating through the system. While the study only included 142 rooms at 101 hotels, the investigators found that over 57% of the properties provided water for showers in excess of 125°F, while 16% of the properties provided water that was over 140°F. It only takes 3 seconds of exposure to water at 140°F to cause a first-degree burn on human flesh.

SWIMMING POOLS, SPAS, AND WATER FEATURES

Many lodging properties have recreational facilities that include swimming pools and spas (i.e., Jacuzzis or hot tubs). These amenities use water and have special needs for maintenance and operation.

Swimming Pools

Many lodging facilities provide indoor and/or outdoor swimming pools for guest use. Swimming pools are usually maintained, and sometimes managed, by the facilities management department, which may be responsible for the hiring and managing of lifeguards as well as ensuring the safety of the pool equipment.

POOL CHEMISTRY Providing a safe pool environment requires additional treatment of the water chemistry to ensure that microbes do not contaminate the pool. Swimming pool water needs to have the proper balance of not only chlorine or bromine, but also the correct pH and mineral levels. Chlorine and bromine are the two most common methods of sanitizing water in pools and spas. Both chemicals are effective at killing a variety of microbes, bacteria, viruses, and other types of contaminants that could make swimmers sick or discolor the water. The pH level and mineral levels will contribute to your guests' comfort while in the pool. A pool that has a high mineral content and a high pH level may cause skin and hair to "dry out." A pH level that is too low (i.e., acidic) will irritate swimmers' eyes and skin. A swimming pool supplies vendor can provide you and your staff with the proper testing equipment and chemicals to provide the right chemical balance for your property's water.

CHEMICAL BREAKDOWN Heated swimming pool water is usually held in the range of 78°F–82°F. Outdoor, unheated pool temperatures will vary, depending on climate and sunlight. Water that is heated and/or exposed to sunlight experiences a more rapid breakdown of chlorine or bromine than water held at cooler temperatures. This means that the water needs to be tested more frequently to ensure that the chemical levels are high enough to provide safe swimming water.

OZONE SYSTEMS One solution to the problems posed by pool chemicals is through the use of an ozone system. This type of system uses ozone gas (O_3) to sanitize the water. While you cannot avoid using chemicals altogether, an ozone system will reduce the amount of chemicals that will be required. Caution: ozone systems are not permitted in every jurisdiction. You will need to check with your local authorities to see if you will be allowed to use one of these systems for your pool and spa facilities.

Water Safety

The city or county where the property is located will have its own regulations for operating a pool that is open to the public, meaning your guests. You should become familiar with the local regulations and check frequently for changes in the laws. Laws often become stricter over time and you will be responsible for complying with them. Some typical operating requirements include:

- *Lifeguards:* You may or may not be required to provide a certified lifeguard while the pool is open. Guidelines for evacuating the pool during electrical storms should also be provided.
- *Signage:* The laws will tell the property the type, content, and presentation style of any pool safety signage and where it must be posted.
- *Pool markings:* The pool will be required to have the depths of water marked along the edge of the pool. Your local laws will outline the requirements for the size, presentation, and locations of the markings.
- *Pool safety equipment:* Your local laws will provide a list of required safety equipment and where it must be located. Equipment will include such items as life rings and tubes, grappling hooks, first aid kits, defibrillation equipment, and telephone equipment for emergency communication.
- *Fencing:* Your local jurisdiction will provide guidelines on the proper fencing and other barriers to prevent unauthorized people from accessing the pool area during hours when the pool is closed. The property must provide additional security to ensure that people—guests or non-guests—do not climb over the fence to gain access to the pool. Any injury that is suffered in this case will still be the responsibility of the lodging property, even if the property took all of the precautions required by law.

Winter Shut-Down

Many lodging properties with outdoor swimming pools close the pool for the cold-weather season. This involves draining the pool, since water that remains in the pool can attract debris, such as leaves and twigs, as well as animals. Preparing the pool for warm weather use is easier if a large quantity of dirty water does not have to be drained and the pool cleaned. However, many areas have a high water table, which freezes in cold weather. When water freezes, it expands. It is not unusual for an empty pool that is surrounded by groundwater to pop out of the ground—a very expensive problem to fix. Therefore, you will often see a closed pool that is approximately 25% full of water for the winter.

As previously mentioned, this water can get very dirty and be quite unsightly for your guests. Some jurisdictions will permit the installation of a cover

over the pool for the winter season. This, however, comes with some hazards. Animals often get trapped under the cover and cannot get out of the pool, which reveals an unpleasant surprise when the cover is removed in the spring. More importantly, there have been cases in the past where people, particularly children, have gained access to the pool area, fallen into the pool, and been trapped under the cover. This is a tragic circumstance, so using a pool cover should be approached with caution. In fact, many jurisdictions ban the use of covers on commercial pools for this reason, or require newer styles of safety covers that are seamless and gapless. Check your local codes for compliance requirements.

Spas

Spas are also a very common amenity for a lodging property to offer in the swimming pool area (Figure 5.9). The spas we refer to here are not full service spa facilities with massages and cosmetic treatments, but Jacuzzis or hot tubs. Maintaining and operating a spa is quite similar to maintaining and operating a swimming pool. However, there are a few special conditions that are present with spas.

HEAT EFFECTS   The water in a spa is usually held in the range of 102°F–105°F. We now know that as heat increases, the breakdown of the chemicals in the water increases as well. Heat also increases other types of activity. First, many types of microbes, such as bacteria, yeast, and viruses, will multiply and thrive in water at this temperature. It is therefore important to check the chlorine/bromine levels more often in the spa than you will for the swimming pool.

Heat increases other activity as well. For example, people in the spa are wearing bathing suits (we hope). The warm water in the spa will draw out any residual laundry detergent that is in the bathing suit. It will also draw out any residual soap, shampoo, lotion, sunscreen, and hair styling products that the

FIGURE 5.9   Spa.
Source: Dina Zemke.

people in the spa use. To go one step further, warm water also causes perspiration and draws out body oils. To say the least, the knowledgeable reader should infer that the water in a spa and the spa surfaces need to be cleaned frequently.

If you turn the water jets on in a Jacuzzi and a thick, rich foam appears, it is crucial that the spa be cleaned. This foam consists of laundry detergent, body soap, skin oils, lotions, sunscreen, and various other oil or fat-based substances that people carry with them into the spa. Under these circumstances, you need to follow five steps to clean the spa:

1. Shut it down.
2. Drain it.
3. Clean it, making sure that it is rinsed well so that cleaning products do not remain in the spa.
4. Refill it with fresh water.
5. Shock it with chemicals and wait for chemical levels to return to a safe zone before permitting guests to reenter the spa.

SPA SAFETY CONCERNS   The warm water of a spa also offers some hazards that require special attention from an operational perspective.

Temperature's effect on the body The relatively warm temperatures of the spa water can result in lowered blood pressure for many people. The effect is even more pronounced when the swimmer has consumed alcohol or is taking certain medications or drugs. A warm environment, particularly the one present in a spa, can cause vasodilation, or the dilation/widening of the arteries. This reduces blood pressure and can eventually lead to fainting in the water, obviously a potential drowning hazard. Security and monitoring of the spa is key in preventing this type of tragedy. Pregnant women should also not use spas or hot tubs.

Children in the spa Young children should not be permitted in the spa. The warm water effects described above may be more pronounced with children. In addition, very young children often wear diapers, which may leak into the surrounding warm water that provides a fertile environment for microbe growth. Do not permit small children in the spa.

Guests may complain about the above restrictions and monitoring, but they are in place for everyone's safety.

WATER USE AND CONSERVATION

The hottest issue in water management is conservation. Planet Earth is made up of 75% water, so why do we have to conserve it? Most of the water on the planet is sea water, which requires intensive treatment to render it fit for human consumption. The remaining fresh water is becoming increasingly scarce and expensive. Since any good conservation measure should not only reduce consumption of water but should also reduce costs, we will first review how we pay for water.

How Do We Pay for Water?

Hospitality properties that use a city water supply receive bills for the water on a monthly or quarterly basis. There are two basic charges on the bill: one for the water supply, the other for use of the sewer system to remove wastewater. The rates that customers pay for water are usually stated (in the United States) in terms of a rate per 100 cubic feet (ccf), which is equal to 748.05 gallons.

Water utility employees will read a building's water meter on either a monthly or quarterly basis. While there are several different types of rate structures for water, the two components that a property manager will be able to control are the **consumption charge** and the **sewer charge**. The consumption charge is based on the amount of water used in ccf's. The second charge, the sewer charge, is usually calculated based again on the number of ccf's that were consumed. The building essentially gets charged twice for water—once for water coming in and once as the water goes out (Figures 5.10a and 5.10b).

FIGURE 5.10a Water Meter. *Source*: Craft Construction Company.

FIGURE 5.10b Water Meter Dials. *Source*: Craft Construction Company.

The water utility will automatically assume that the sewer water volume will equal the amount of water supplied and it uses this as the basis for calculating the total water bill. However, does a hospitality property's outgoing water always equal the amount of water that comes in? The answer is a resounding no! The three major ways that water leaves the property without using the sanitary sewer system are:

1. *Swimming pools:* Water evaporates from the pool, reducing the amount of water that exits via the sewer. This is especially true for outdoor pools.
2. *Landscape watering and irrigation:* This water is either absorbed by the soil or runs off into the storm sewer system, for which the water utility does not charge based on consumption.
3. *Cooling tower operation:* The cooling tower is part of a centralized air-conditioning system. Condenser water is sent to the cooling tower, which is open to the outdoor environment. Some water is lost due to evaporation; this loss can be substantial during the cooling season.

Is it fair that we pay for sewer service that we do not use? Again, the answer is no. While all buildings have a meter for incoming water, the knowledgeable property manager will install a meter on the outgoing sewer line as well. This will provide a reading for the true amount of sewer outflow and will present opportunities to save money on the water bill.

Cost of Water

The cost of water in the United States, until the present time, has been relatively low and has not increased with the rate of inflation. However, many areas of the country experience periodic droughts, some of which last for several years and are severe. Many areas are also finding that the natural sources for the water supply, such as aquifers, are beginning to dry up. Some areas will reach a crisis level in the relatively near future unless good water management is implemented. The droughts and the rapid depletion of the aquifers are already forcing water utilities to raise rates at unprecedented levels. Careful management of water usage will not only help preserve the water resources, but will help protect the hotel or restaurant's bottom line by minimizing the water expenses.

Water Conservation Methods

We have two ways to approach reducing our water usage and costs: first, use less water and second, recycle water that we have already used. Hospitality properties have several areas that offer opportunities for reducing water consumption.

USING LESS WATER   The key to any good conservation measure in a hospitality property is to insure that water is saved without reducing guest comfort and satisfaction. The guest will usually only come into contact with water in public restrooms, guestrooms, and in the pool/spa areas. Public restrooms and guestroom bathrooms share two areas of water consumption—sinks and toilets.

SINKS Sink water use can be reduced by either installing an aerator on the sink spout or by using a low-flow sink faucet fixture. Aerators are small devices that simply screw onto the sink's spout. Aerators reduce the total amount of water that flows through the fixture, but the pressure of the water supply is often increased. This results in lower water usage without the guest noticing a reduction in water supply. The increased pressure makes up for the reduced volume.

Low-flow faucets are manufactured with water flow restrictors built in. Most new construction and building renovation projects require low-flow faucets to be installed, rather than the old, high-consumption fixtures.

The newest type of fixture for sinks is a fixture that is operated with infrared control. The base of the faucet has a small infrared light that detects when a person is close to the spout. Activation of the light starts the flow of water. When the light no longer detects the person, the water flow stops. This has been very effective in reducing the amount of water that is wasted when someone does not turn off the faucet. Infrared control faucets are common in public restrooms but have not been installed in many hotel rooms since the requirement to wave a hand in front of the faucet to keep it running would reduce guest convenience, comfort, and satisfaction.

TOILETS There are two primary ways to reduce the water consumed by toilets. The first way is to install low-flow toilets. These toilets use 1.6 gallons per flush—55% less water than an older toilet that would use 3.5 gallons per flush. Low-flow toilets can come in either the tank style of toilet (the kind that we have in our bathrooms at home) or in a **flushometer** style of toilet (Figure 5.11). A flushometer toilet is usually found in public buildings and back of the house areas of a hotel—and example of one is shown in Figure 5.11a. They are not as aesthetically pleasing as the tank style. If you cannot replace an older toilet with a low-flow toilet, you may want to install a tank restrictor in the tank. Tank restrictors come in a variety of shapes and styles, but they all essentially work by reducing the amount of water that the tank can hold. A classic type of

FIGURE 5.11a
"Flushometer"-style
Flush Valve.
Source: Dina Zemke.

FIGURE 5.11b
Pressurized Low-flow
Toilet. *Source*: Dina
Zemke.

restrictor that you may find in people's homes is a brick in the toilet. The brick takes up room, reducing the amount of water that the tank releases during each flush. As long as there's an adequate amount of water and pressure to provide a good, clean flush, a tank restrictor will offer a relatively low cost way to reduce water usage and expenses. We do not recommend putting a brick in a guestroom tank. Guests sometimes look in the tank and may not receive a favorable impression if they see a brick! Bricks also deteriorate over time, which can hurt the flushing mechanism in the tank.

Figure 5.11b shows an example of another type of water-conserving toilet: a high-pressure toilet. This toilet provides the appearance of a standard toilet with a tank, which is preferable in hotel guest rooms and mid- to upscale restaurants. However, rather than use the normal amount of water to flush the toilet, the high-pressure toilet uses a small amount of water. Some models use as little as one gallon per flush. The water is sent into the toilet bowl at a very high speed and pressure. This provides an efficient flush while saving 50% or more of the water used in a standard toilet. One drawback to these toilets is that the flush mechanism cannot be retrofitted into an older toilet. The bowl must be configured to work with the flush mechanism. Therefore, if you are responsible for renovating a bathroom and would like to use this type of flush technology, you will probably have to replace the entire toilet.

The guestroom also uses water in the bathtub and/or shower. Water savings can be found if a low-flow showerhead is used in the shower. The new low-flow showerheads use 2.5 gallons/minute—as much as 50% less water than the old style showerheads that would use five gallons/minute. We strongly recommend, though, that the lodging manager test a variety of showerheads at various locations throughout the hotel. Each showerhead will provide more or less flow, depending on the water pressure in the pipes. One of the authors worked at a major hotel in New York that ordered very expensive and elegant showerheads for several floors of guestrooms that were under renovation. Unfortunately, once the guests began to occupy the rooms, the hotel discovered that there was not enough water pressure to make the showerheads work, leaving the guest with a poor shower experience! We attempted to increase the water pressure in the system, but found that the system's piping was unable to support the higher pressure (many pipes began to fail, creating a lot of flooding). The hotel had to purchase new showerheads that did work with the existing water pressure—a very expensive move.

GUEST PARTICIPATION PROGRAMS   A final way that guests impact water use is through towels and linens. While the guest does not come into direct contact with the water in this situation, washing towels and linens requires a lot of water. A method to reduce the amount of water used to wash guestroom linens is to offer guests who will have a multi-night stay the option to not have the bed linens and/or towels changed. However, it is important that the guest has a choice in whether he or she wants to participate. We still need to provide the level of service that the guest expects.

There are many suppliers of the signage and notification cards that guests use to indicate what they would like to be changed. Two popular suppliers are the Green Hotel Association (www.greenhotels.com) and Project Planet (www.projectplanet.biz). These companies provide signage and door hanger tags that come in a variety of styles that will blend with the hotel's image. Project Planet has found that a 100-room hotel will save approximately 72,000 gallons of water per year and will reduce the disposal of laundry chemicals into the sewer system by 480 gallons. Ninety percent of guests approve of these programs and many hotels find that they experience a high percentage of multi-night stay guests who choose to participate in the program.

Kitchens

Many commercial kitchens waste a large quantity of water. The following are tips for reducing water waste in the kitchen:

Fix leaks and drips: This is the simplest and most obvious measure. However, many commercial kitchens in both hotels and restaurants have faucets that drip. Fix the leaks.

Cold food prep/thawing frozen food: You may find in some kitchens that frozen foods, especially meat, are thawed by running cold water over them in the sink. It may take several hours to thaw a large piece of meat, with the water running the entire time. The way to fix this is to work with the chef or kitchen manager to change the way that the operation is run—perhaps more advance planning where the frozen food that needs to be thawed is placed in the refrigerator to thaw. It will take longer to thaw, but water will not be wasted.

Dishwashing: Dish machines can use a lot of water. Run the dish machine only when needed, running full racks of dishes and flatware rather than partial racks. If you have the opportunity to purchase a new machine, be sure to purchase one that is EnergyStar® rated. EnergyStar® is a program through the U.S. Environmental Protection Agency that works with the industry to manufacture appliances and equipment that use less energy and, in the case of water-using appliances, less water.

Peddle-activated faucets: Not all employees turn the water off when they are finished with the sink. You may occasionally (although we hope not often) find sinks running that have no purpose to run and no one nearby—a pure waste of water. Kitchens occasionally install sink faucets that are activated by stepping on a peddle below the sink. When the peddle is pressed, the faucets are turned on; when the peddle is released, the water turns off. The advantages of the peddle-operated faucet are reduced water consumption and also a no-contact operation of the faucet. This feature is nice because it allows the worker to turn the faucet on without touching it with his or her hands, thereby reducing the opportunities for cross-contamination.

Water only upon request: Many restaurants will institute a "water upon request" program during drought events or other water shortages. This is the only time that water-saving measures impact the guest in the dining room. Water will not be served to the guest automatically; the guest must request a glass of water. This saves not only water but ice as well.

Laundry

On-premises laundry facilities (OPLs) are laundry operations that the hotel operates on-site. The alternative to an OPL is contracting with a laundry service that cleans and prepares linens, towels, and uniforms off-site. Properties that operate OPLs have many opportunities for water savings. The first opportunity is to use front-loading washing machines rather than top-loading machines, which are the type that most people have in their homes. Front-loading machines not only use less water but also require less detergent to clean the materials. Front-loaders also provide better extraction, which is the removal of water from the linens and towels during the final spin cycle. This leads to reduced drying times for the materials, thus lowering energy bills.

Newer washing machines also come in high-efficiency models. High-efficiency models are available in both front-loading and top-loading machines. These high-efficiency machines also require less water and fewer chemicals for operation.

Ozone laundry systems use ozone gas (O_3) to enhance the cleaning and sanitizing cycles of laundry systems. Ozone consists of three oxygen atoms bound together (rather than just two atoms, which is the form of oxygen that we require to live). This gas is very effective at killing microbes and, once used by the wash cycle, returns to our atmosphere as pure oxygen (O_2), meaning there are no residual chemicals. Benefits of ozone laundry systems include the need of fewer chemical additives to clean the laundry, less chemical output in the wastewater (good for the environment), and less water than traditional systems. In addition, the water temperature does not need to be as hot as a traditional washer. The result is lower energy and chemical costs for the property. The wet laundry coming out of the washers contains less water that needs to be removed by dryers, also saving energy costs.

Swimming Pools/Spas

Water savings can be found for swimming pools and spas. First, both pools and spas require the water filters to be flushed to provide efficient filtering. Instituting a sensible schedule and duration for backflushing the filters will save many gallons of water per day. Your pool maintenance manual or a local pool contractor will be able to help determine the proper schedule for your equipment's size and usage.

Second, warmer water evaporates more quickly than cooler water. Keeping your pool at a lower temperature will slow evaporation. However, lowering the temperature too far will hurt guest comfort and satisfaction, so this policy must be instituted with care. Finally, installing a cover over the pool water during hours when the pool is not in operation will slow evaporation and, in cooler weather, heat loss. However, as discussed earlier in this chapter, pool covers are not legal in some jurisdictions. Check your local laws before ordering a swimming pool or spa cover.

Landscaping/Water Features

City center hotels and restaurants may not have enough property to provide landscaping. However, many suburban, rural, and resort properties have extensive landscaping schemes. The landscaping may, in fact, be a major attraction of the property. For example, many resorts offer one or more golf courses. These are major users of water! Some properties also offer additional amenities that use water, such as fountains and car washes.

Water conservation is important in good landscape irrigation management. The easiest way to save water is to ensure that the landscaping is watered on the correct basis for the types of plants, trees, and shrubs on the property. Many properties over-water, simply because the employees responsible for setting the irrigation system and timers do not know how to set the system properly. Good sources of information include the local water utility, water authority, and landscaping contractors.

Proper watering systems are a good first step. A more effective alternative that is growing in popularity is ensuring that the plants used in the landscaping are plants that are native to the area. These plants are often highly adapted to the type of weather, water, and pest conditions that exist in the area. Use of native flora can reduce watering requirements and also reduce the use of fertilizers and pesticides, which will save money and lessen the impact on the environment.

Landscapers can take the landscape plan one step further in water-saving potential and install a landscape based on **xeriscaping** (pronounced zeer´-i-skāping). A xeriscape is a landscaping scheme that intentionally uses plants that require little water and are drought-tolerant. The use of grass is minimized, since grass requires a great deal of water to live. Many jurisdictions in areas with chronic water shortages or drought conditions, particularly in the western and southwestern United States, have strict restrictions on the type of landscaping that can be used in new construction and require the

FIGURE 5.12
Xeriscaping.
Source: Dina Zemke.

property to use a xeriscaping plan. Check with your landscaping contractor to see what types of xeriscaping options are available in your area[4] (Figure 5.12).

Many hospitality properties' landscaping will include **water features**. The term "water features" encompasses a wide variety of accents that use water, such as ponds, fountains, and manmade streams. Water features offer the guest a beautiful environmental amenity, and a sensible operation of the water features can save water. For example, fountains have a high rate of evaporation while in operation, but this evaporation can be reduced by turning the fountain off during off-hours, such as late at night when guests are unlikely to see the fountain.

RECYCLING WATER: GRAYWATER SYSTEMS **Graywater** is all water that has been used in the building, except for water from toilets. This includes water from sinks, bathtub and showers, and also laundry, kitchen, and dishwasher use. This water, while not potable, only requires minor treatment to render it suitable for outdoor use in landscaping and water features. Many properties have installed graywater systems to collect the water, filter it, and then use it in landscaping. For example, nearly all of the golf courses in Las Vegas, Nevada, are watered using graywater collected either from the resorts that operates them or the local communities in which they are located.[5]

HEALTH AND SAFETY CONCERNS

The major safety concerns about water supply and removal are potability, temperature, and in the case of swimming pools and spas, chemical balance. One additional safety concern with water is proper disposal of hazardous chemicals. An unfortunate, but common, situation that hospitality managers may experience is employees dumping hazardous materials into the storm sewer system. A classic example is disposing of kitchen grease by dumping it into the storm sewer. Grease at room temperature or cooler will coagulate, clogging pipes. Some unscrupulous or lazy foodservice operators have been caught dumping grease into the storm sewer. Any chemical that goes into the storm sewer ends up in the environment, and either leaches into the groundwater or flows into local lakes and streams, potentially contaminating the water supply. Grease, paint, cleaning chemicals, and any other waste should **never** be disposed of in the storm sewer system. Local Departments of Public Works usually accept hazardous chemical disposal and there are many vendors that will remove chemical waste for a fee. Kitchen grease should be disposed of via a grease removal contractor.

Summary

You should now have a reasonable understanding of how water gets to a building, leaves the building, and all of the things that we need to do to water so that it is safe to use while in the building. You should also have a good basis for evaluating a building's water usage and be able to identify ways in which your company can save water. Some experts predict that water will become such a precious commodity in the future that countries will go to war over it. While we fervently hope that this will not be the case, we can probably assume that effective, efficient water management will become increasingly important throughout your career.

Key Terms and Concepts

Aquifers *104*
booster heater *113*
city sewer system *108*
constant pressure
   systems *104*
consumption charge *121*
domestic hot water *111*
effluence *108*
ejector pumps *108*

electric water heater *112*
fire-tube boiler *113*
fixture *103*
float valve *104*
flushometer *123*
gallons per minute
   (gpm) *103*
gravity-fed systems *104*
graywater *128*

ozone laundry
   systems *126*
potable water *104*
pounds per square inch
   (psi) *103*
pressure *103*
P-traps and S-traps *110*
sanitary sewer
   system *107*

septic field *109*
septic tank *109*
sewer charge *121*
storm sewer system *107*
water features *117*
water softener *111*
water-tube boiler *113*
xeriscaping *127*

Discussion and Review Questions

1. Research your local codes for building and operating a swimming pool at a hotel or residential property. Identify the rules for shutting the pool down during the winter months, requirements for lifeguards to be present, and signage.

2. Why is it important for the manager of a hotel or restaurant to know where the ejector pumps are?

3. What does a grease trap do?

4. Identify and describe six ways that you can conserve water in a hotel.

5. Go to a local hotel or restaurant kitchen. Survey the kitchen to find possible areas where water is being wasted. What sorts of measures could be taken to improve water efficiency?

6. What type of toilet do you have in your home (or dormitory)? What type of toilet is in the public restroom in your school building? How do they work?

7. Why is the p-trap such a great invention?

Notes

1. More information on Rid X, available at http://www.reckittprofessional.com/find_a_product/products/ridx.html
2. How Stuff Works.com, available at www.howstuffworks.com
3. Anonymous. (Dec. 7, 2004). Survey: Scalding water found in nearly 90% of hotel rooms; Legionella also a risk. Hotel Online Special Report, retrieved March 16, 2005 from http://www.hotel-online/News/PR2004_4th/Dec04_ScaldingWater.html.
4. www.xeriscape.org
5. www.greywater.net

6

Electrical Systems

CHAPTER OBJECTIVES

After reading this chapter, you should be able to:

- define the physical properties of electricity and light.
- describe the various ways that electricity is generated.
- describe the pros and cons of alternative energy sources.
- discuss electrical safety measures that should be taken at the property level.
- read electrical meters and calculate electric bills.
- understand the concept of electrical demand management.
- describe the types of lamps available.
- discuss group relamping programs and calculate the cost savings associated with running one.
- select the right lamp for a given situation, including a quantitative analysis.

INTRODUCTION

Imagine a world without electricity . . . we would depend on candlelight for lighting in dark conditions. We would probably have to get water from wells and physically transport it into our buildings. We would not have elevators. We would not have telephones, computers, or any other electronic equipment that we depend on so heavily today.

Hospitality facilities use a great deal of energy—approximately 80% of that energy is in the form of electricity. Electricity is extremely useful and important to any facility, but is it also dangerous. You, as a hospitality manager, should never work with electricity or electrical systems unless you are trained to do so. This chapter is intended to provide you with the tools to understand basic electrical systems in buildings, how to manage your electricity costs, and to have an intelligent conversation about electrical systems with your building engineer and/or electrical contractors.

PHYSICAL PROPERTIES

Before we discuss electrical systems in hospitality buildings, we must first understand many of the key principles and properties of electricity. A short lesson in physics is in order.

Electricity is created as a result of the negative charges of electrons and the positive charges of protons in an atom. Electrons repel other electrons; protons repel other protons. This effect of repulsion generates an electrostatic charge, which is electricity.

The first electrical term that you should know is **volt** (V), which is a measure of electrical pressure. This is the force that causes electricity to flow. Electricity flows in units called **amperes**, or amps (A). Electricity encounters friction, or resistance when it travels through electrical wires and when it arrives at an appliance or machine that requires electricity to operate. This resistance is measured in units called **ohms**, often abbreviated with the Greek letter Ω (omega). An analogy that will help illustrate these terms is comparing electricity to water. In the previous chapter, we measured water pressure in pounds/square inch (psi). Electrical pressure is measured in volts. We measured water flow in gallons/minute; electricity flows in amps. Water experiences friction while it travels through pipes and pumps. We do not have a term for water resistance, but we do consider pressure drop associated with water resistance. Electrical resistance is measured in ohms.

One of the primary principles of electricity is **Ohm's Law**. Ohm's Law is an equation that will allow you to calculate the number of volts, amps, or ohms for a specific situation, if you have values for two out of the three variables. The equation for Ohm's Law is as follows:

$$\text{Volts} = \text{Amps} \times \text{Ohms}$$

You can use this equation to calculate volt, amps, or resistance. For example, say you need to determine how much electrical current (i.e., the number of amps) that a particular appliance will use on a 20-amp circuit. You know that you have a 110-V circuit and that the television's resistance (ohms) value is 91. You will calculate the amps by using the following equation:

$$A = \text{volts}/\text{ohms}$$
$$A = 110/91$$
$$A = 1.2 \text{ amps}$$

You will then calculate the amp usage for the rest of the appliances that will be operated using this electrical circuit, such as lamps, radios, computers, or stereo equipment. You should add up all of the amp values to see if a 20-amp circuit will provide enough power to operate all of the equipment at once. If the equipment amps exceed the number of amps in the circuit, turning all of the equipment on at once will cause the fuse or circuit breaker to trip and there will be no power available.

A **watt** is a unit of power. Watts are calculated using the following equation:

$$Watts = Volts \times Amps$$

Again, we can use this equation to calculate any of the three variables, as long as we have information for the other two. Using our television example from above, we know that the television will use 1.2 amps. If we connect the television to a 110-V power circuit, we can calculate the number of watts that the television will use while it is operating.

$$Watts = 110 \text{ volts} \times 1.2 \text{ amps}$$
$$Watts = 132$$

One thousand watts equals one **kilowatt (kW)**. The kilowatt is one measure that power utility companies use to bill commercial customers for electricity, by measuring the greatest amount of electricity demanded over a short amount of time, usually a 15-minute period. Electric utilities also bill customers for the amount of power used over the entire billing period, usually one month. This measure of overall consumption is called a **kilowatt-hour (kWh)**. We will explore demand and consumption billing in greater detail later in this chapter.

Electrical current can be supplied in two forms: direct current and alternating current. **Direct current**, usually referred to as **DC current**, is the type of electrical current that is generated by a battery. It is called direct current because it is supplied at a constant time rate at either a positive or a negative polarity (positive *or* negative electrical charge) (Figure 6.1a). For example, the drawing below shows current flow in a DC circuit, which maintains a positive polarity.

In the past, power utility companies supplied DC current power as well as AC current power. Commercial buildings used the DC power to operate mechanical equipment, most commonly motors, since DC power permitted a smooth speed control of the motor. Most utility companies today provide only AC power; few, if any, provide DC power.

Today's electronic control technology has made it possible for building managers to control the speed of motors using AC power. **Alternating current**, usually referred to as **AC current**, is an electrical current that is supplied with *both* positive *and* negative polarity (Figure 6.1b). The current

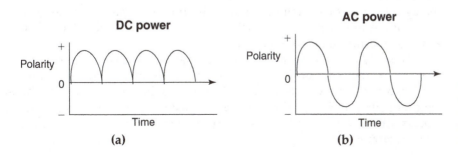

FIGURE 6.1 (a) Direct Current (DC) Power. (b) Alternating Current (AC) Power. *Source:* Dina Zemke.

alternates between a positive and a negative electrical charge, hence the name alternating current. The figure demonstrates the alternating current flow in an AC circuit. Notice that this flow forms a sine wave.

AC current can be generated with different frequencies of positive–negative cycles per second. This is referred to as the **frequency** of the electrical circuit. Frequency is also referred to by the term **Hertz** (abbreviated as **Hz**).

Different parts of the world use different frequencies as standard supply for electrical equipment. For example, the North American standard is a 60-Hz supply, while Europe uses a 50-Hz supply. Not only do North American and European utilities provide electricity at different frequencies, they also provide it at different voltages. Most household electrical outlets in the United States supply 110 V/60 Hz, while most European outlets supply 220 V/50 Hz. This is why travelers need to use power transformers while traveling to different countries. For example, plugging in an American hair dryer in Europe will cause the dryer to work incorrectly and may ruin the dryer. European appliances will run too slowly if connected to a North American power supply.

ELECTRICAL GENERATION AND DELIVERY

Now that you are familiar with some of the physical properties of electricity, we turn to how electrical power is generated. Electricity is made in a generator. The generator uses metal coils that are attached to a shaft. The shaft spins in a tube that is lined with magnets. The movement of the metal across the magnet generates the electrical charge. The shaft holding the metal coils is turned by a turbine, or a machine whose sole job is to turn the shaft.

Electricity is made in large power generation plants. Most of these plants use some form of fossil fuel, such as coal, natural gas, or petroleum (oil). The most common of these is coal. Approximately 51% of the United States' electricity is generated in coal burning plants. Natural gas generates about 16% of the electricity, while oil only generates about 3%. The next most common source of electricity is nuclear energy. About 20% of the United States' electrical supply comes from nuclear reactors.

Fossil fuel and nuclear power plants all create waste byproducts that require disposal. In addition, the fuel required to run these plants is usually not renewable, which may lead to future fuel shortages. Alternate sources of energy that do not use nonrenewable fuels and which do not create byproducts that require disposal exist. These sources include hydroelectric, solar, wind, geothermal, and biomass power.

The only one of the alternate sources that is a significant source of electricity is hydroelectric power. Hydroelectric power makes use of the flow of water in a river or a waterfall to turn the turbines that create electricity. Thus, the fuel source is free and there are no waste byproducts created in the process. Approximately 7% of the electricity in the United States is generated using hydropower.

The remaining alternative sources—solar, wind, geothermal—each contribute less than 1% of the electrical power in the United States. **Solar power** uses heat from the sun to create steam that turns the turbines used to generate electricity. Solar power may also be created through **photovoltaic cells (PV)** (Figure 6.2), which are semiconductor chips that convert sunlight into electricity. **Wind power** is generated using large windmills that use our abundant, free wind energy to turn the turbines. **Geothermal power** uses heat and water that are located deep in the earth to create steam to turn the turbines. Biomass-generated power generates about 2% of the electricity used in the United States. **Biomass generators** of electricity burn waste material, such as household garbage from a municipal dump, or agricultural garbage, such as wheat straw, to create the heat to operate the turbine.

While these methods are attractive because they do not deplete our finite supply of fossil fuels, they each have their shortcomings, which have prevented us from fully utilizing their potential. For example, solar power will only work in regions where there is adequate sunshine. Fortunately, most regions of the United States, including unexpected locations such as Upstate New York, receive enough sunlight to make these systems work. However, at the time of this writing, the photovoltaic equipment used to generate solar power is quite expensive, particularly because of a raw material shortage of silicon, the primary ingredient in manufacturing the semiconductor chips that make up the PV cell. The equipment also takes up a great deal of space in relation to the amount of power that is generated, sometimes rendering it an inefficient use of a building's exterior space. However, recent technology improvements and rebate programs offered by utility companies are making

FIGURE 6.2 Rooftop Photovoltaic Array. *Source*: Adam Blakeslee.

solar energy more cost-effective in many areas, particularly in the southwestern United States.

Wind power also has its shortcomings. The windmills are sometimes considered to be unsightly and may make a loud humming noise while they are operating. There is also some concern from environmental advocates about birds flying into the blades of the windmills (with bad outcomes for the birds). There have also been reports of the propeller blades flying off the windmill, posing a hazard below. In addition, many of the locations where there is adequate wind to operate the windmills are located far away from the North American electrical grids. This obstacle requires the power that is generated at the windmill to travel a long distance to reach the grid.

Power Distribution

Once power is generated, it needs to travel through power lines until it reaches the building. High voltage power is sent to the main power grid and is then distributed to wherever it is needed. For example, typical overhead power lines may carry 15,000 V or more! The power company sends high-voltage electricity throughout its system to substations and switching stations. Local substations will reduce the voltage to transmit medium-voltage electricity, in the 2,400–13,000-V range, to specific buildings. Once it arrives at the building, the voltage is reduced again to a relatively low voltage for distribution within the building. Since we know that our normal household appliances use 110 V, we need to reduce the voltage quite a bit before we use it.

Electrical voltage is reduced using a transformer (Figure 6.3). Transformers also make use of magnets—electrical wire is coiled around an iron core to reduce the voltage. This type of transformer is called a **step-down transformer**, because it steps the voltage down. Voltage can be increased in much the same way using a **step-up transformer**. Typical voltages that are present in a large building, such as a hotel, will include 600 V, 440 V, 220 V, and 110 V. The higher voltages operate large equipment such as motors, air-conditioning systems, and elevators. Many appliances such as washing machines, dryers, and refrigerators use 220 V, and most small household appliances and fixtures use 110 V. Electronic equipment often operates at very low voltage. This type of equipment usually has its own step-down transformer either built into the equipment or uses a special electrical plug that reduces the voltage.

Transformers in commercial buildings are usually located on the building's property, either above or below the ground. Above-ground transformers are located outside the building's exterior and will usually be housed in a metal box. Below-ground transformers are housed in a **transformer vault** that is dug into the ground and covered either with a metal grate or metal doors (Figure 6.4). Hospitality managers need to know where their transformers are located for an important reason: transformers generate a great deal of

FIGURE 6.3a
Transformer—Above
Ground. *Source*: Dina
Zemke.

FIGURE 6.3b
Transformer—Above
Ground. *Source*: Dina
Zemke.

heat and occasionally catch fire. The manager, whether it is the Chief Engineer
or the Front Office Manager who is acting as manager on duty, needs to
communicate with the Fire Department in the event of a fire, particularly
if the fire is in the transformer. Since transformers generate heat, they need to
be cooled. Older transformers often use a type of oil for cooling, and many of
these oil-cooled transformers still exist. Older oil formulations contained

FIGURE 6.4
Transformer Vault in the
Sidewalk. *Source*: Dina
Zemke.

chemicals called PCBs, which are hazardous to humans because they have
been known to emit carcinogenic substances when burned. It is important
information for the Fire Department so that they can extinguish the fire as
quickly as possible to ensure safe air quality and to protect the building from
a serious, lengthy loss of power.

ELECTRICAL DISTRIBUTION SYSTEMS

Now that the electricity has reached the building and has been stepped down
to an appropriate voltage, it must be distributed throughout the building.

Electricity will travel throughout the building through a network of electrical wires at a set voltage but at varying amperages (currents). Circuits with
higher current travel to **electrical panels** that then distribute the power to
various rooms or sub-circuits. The electrical panels use fuses and/or circuit
breakers to ensure that each circuit is providing a safe amount of current
(Figure 6.5). If there is too much demand for electricity on one circuit (i.e.,
drawing too many amps at once), the fuse or circuit breaker will break the
circuit, discontinuing the power to the appliance.

Fuses are good for only a one-time use. When they have been exposed
to too great a current, they burn out and must be replaced by a new fuse.
The old fuse is discarded. **Circuit breakers** also break the circuit when
exposed to too much current. However, circuit breakers do not burn out
with one use—they may be reset many times before they wear out and must
be replaced.

What we normally call an "electric outlet" is technically called a "receptacle." There is one type of receptacle that offers overcurrent protection that
exceeds the protection offered by a circuit breaker. This receptacle is called a

FIGURE 6.5a Circuit Breaker Panel. *Source*: Craft Construction Company.

FIGURE 6.5b Circuit Breaker Panel in Hotel Guestroom. *Source*: Dina Zemke.

FIGURE 6.6 Ground Fault Circuit Interrupt (GFCI) Receptacle. *Source*: Dina Zemke.

GFCI (ground fault circuit interrupt) receptacle (Figure 6.6). It monitors the power coming in and going out of the receptacle and, if an inconsistency is found, cuts off the circuit. This usually happens much quicker (relatively speaking) than it would if the circuit discrepancy was detected at this circuit breaker panel. We install GFCI receptacles in wet areas, such as kitchens, bathrooms, laundries, and pool areas, where the presence of water increases the risk of electrocution. You'll notice the receptacles have two push buttons which are not found in normal receptacles—they are labeled "test" and "reset." They provide the opportunity to test to make sure the receptacle works properly, which should be done once a month, and also to allow the receptacle to be reset if the circuit blows.

Wiring

Electrical wires are made of copper, which offers very little electrical resistance, permitting the flow of electricity to occur without friction. The wires are wrapped in a plastic insulation, both for safety reasons as well as to keep two separate wires from touching each other, which would cause them to create a short circuit and burn up. Older buildings used a type of cloth insulation over the wires. If you find that you have cloth-wrapped electrical wiring, you may want to consider having an electrician rewire using modern wire. The cloth insulation tends to dry out and can either crumble or burn, which could lead to a short circuit (if you are lucky) or to a fire (if you are not lucky). While many building owners have replaced the original cloth-wrapped wiring, some have not, and you must consider this carefully if you are purchasing or leasing an older building if the building has not yet renovated the wiring system.

In addition, older buildings often used aluminum wiring, before copper wiring became the standard. Aluminum wiring wears out over time and is subject to burning and melting. If you find that your building has aluminum wiring, you should definitely consider replacing it with modern wiring as soon as possible.

The electrical wires are usually pulled through the building in a bundle that travels through some type of piping (Figure 6.7). Local building codes determine the type of extra protection that the bundle of cables needs. The most common types of wire protection include:

- Non-metallic sheathed cable, or cable that is wrapped in a plastic sheath: This is usually only used in smaller commercial buildings and in residential buildings. This type of cable is often called Romex. Local codes usually prohibit its use in larger commercial buildings.
- Cable wrapped in a sheath of steel tape: This type of cable is called armored cable, or BX.
- Closed raceway: Raceway is a term used for different types of electrical pipe, similar to piping used in plumbing. The bundle of cables is pulled through the pipe. Examples of a raceway include:
  - a rigid conduit, which is a steel pipe that is either attached to the walls or ceiling or is run through a concrete floor.
  - a flexible metal conduit, or cables wrapped in a segmented, armored sheath. The sheath looks a little like the armored shell of an armadillo. This is often referred to as "Greenfield."

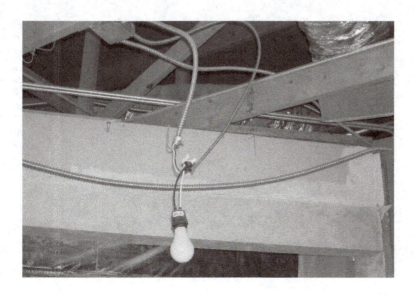

FIGURE 6.7 Wiring. *Source*: Craft Construction Company.

- Surface or floor raceways, which are long metal channels that are installed either in the floor or are attached to the outside of a wall or ceiling.

Emergency Power Systems

Most hospitality facilities have some form of emergency power system in the event of a power outage. The type of system and the amount of power that needs to be generated depends on the type of building occupancy, the consequences that the building will face in the event of a power outage, and in some cases, local codes. Smaller buildings may use a battery-operated system. This type of system would provide enough power to operate emergency exit lights, exit signs, and fire and life safety systems.

A large hotel may be required by code to have a more extensive emergency power system. The larger systems use a diesel-powered generator located somewhere on the property (Figure 6.8). The system may need to be turned on manually or it may automatically turn on when a power outage is detected. The size of the system will depend on how large the building is and how much equipment is connected to it. The equipment that *must* be operated by the system includes fire and life safety systems, emergency lighting, and telecommunications. However, the property may decide that more equipment needs to operate during a blackout. The specific equipment will depend on what management thinks is "essential equipment." What is essential in a building?

FIGURE 6.8a Diesel-Powered Emergency Generator. *Source*: Dina Zemke.

FIGURE 6.8b   Diesel-Powered Emergency Generator.   *Source*: Dina Zemke.

FIGURE 6.8c   Diesel Fuel Storage Tanks for Generator.   *Source*: Dina Zemke.

It depends! Typical essential equipment for hotels includes computer systems, particularly for reservations and the front office, refrigeration equipment, and elevators. However, some properties may have a broader definition of what is essential. For example, many casinos believe that the entire gaming floor, including slot machines, contains essential equipment that must continue to receive power during a blackout.

Poor definition of essential equipment can have unexpected results. The massive power outage that affected the eastern United States and parts of Canada in August 2004 brought some of the shortcomings of hospitality properties' systems into the limelight. Examples include:

- Guestroom locking systems: Many card key systems require a small electrical current to operate. Hotel guests were able to walk up the stairs to their guestrooms, only to find that they could not get in the room because the lock did not work. The electronic locks either lacked batteries or the batteries were dead.
- Infrared faucets and toilets: Restaurants and airports found that the sinks and toilets in the restrooms would not work because the new water-saving infrared fixtures would not operate without electricity. They should also have a back-up power source.
- Elevators. Many hotels do not have their elevator systems connected to the emergency power system. Guests and residents of high-rise buildings had to walk up the exit stairs to get to their rooms—sometimes as many as fifty floors.
- Cash registers. Most businesses do not have cash registers on emergency power. Some businesses had to shut down completely, although they had goods to sell, because their cash registers would not work and employees were not trained to work without cash registers. Emergency power (or hand-held calculators) should have been present.
- Gas pumps: Most gas stations were not open because the pumps are not on emergency power, preventing access to gasoline.

Uninterruptible Power Supply systems, or UPS systems, are often found to provide emergency power to electronic equipment for a short time, ranging from 15 to 60 minutes. This short time period usually provides a business manager the opportunity to shut down the electronic equipment safely, insuring the safety of data files that would be lost in the event of a total power outage. These UPS systems operate as follows:

- The UPS unit receives power from the building's normal AC power supply.
- It converts the power to DC current, using a rectifier.
- The DC current is stored in a battery (unlike AC current, DC current can be stored, which is why batteries provide DC current).
- The UPS unit draws power out of the battery and converts it back to AC power, via an inverter.
- The electronic equipment, such as a computer, is plugged into the UPS system and draws the AC power.

A UPS system performs two functions. First, it provides a constant power source that will not be interrupted by a power outage. It also provides very clean, consistent electricity to electronic equipment. Most electrical equipment is not very sensitive to variations in voltage, such as sags, surges, and other problems. However, electronic equipment is sensitive to these variations. A computer that receives wild variations in voltage or a lot of static (noise) on the electrical supply will operate incorrectly and may lead to lost data files and corrupted software programs. A UPS system's clean power eliminates the problems posed by untreated electricity.

PURCHASING ELECTRICITY

We purchase electricity from an electric utility company. Residential properties will usually have only one meter that the electric company representative reads once a month (or once a quarter). Residential customers are usually only billed for the amount of electricity that they use. Commercial properties, on the other hand, are charged two ways for their electricity. These charges are the consumption charge and the demand charge.

The first step in understanding electric costs is to understand the electric meter. The meter is a device with several dials with numbers ranging from 0 (zero) to 9. A commercial building will have two of these meters, one measuring consumption and the other measuring demand, on each electrical supply line entering the building. The two types may also be combined into a single meter, as shown in Figure 6.9. The **consumption meter** measures the amount of electricity used in kilowatt-hours (kWh). The property pays for the total amount of electricity used over a month's time. It's intuitively easy

FIGURE 6.9 Electric Meter with Both Consumption and Demand-Dials. *Source*: Craft Construction Company.

to understand this part of the meter, because we are simply paying for what we use over the billing period.

The second meter, the **demand meter**, does not measure the total amount of energy used during the month, but the maximum *rate* at which the property draws electricity during any 15-minute period during the monthly billing cycle. The demand meter measures the greatest level of **electrical demand** in kilowatts (kW). In essence, the electric company charges the property for the 15-minute period when the property's electrical needs are the greatest. You might think of it as the cost for the privilege of meeting our highest need for power at the moment we need it.

For example, imagine we are operating a full-service hotel in Memphis, Tennessee, in July. Our property is relatively quiet during the night and does not use a large amount of electricity. However, as morning arrives, our guests begin to rise and our day-shift employees arrive for work. As the day progresses, the sun shines on the building and the outdoor temperature rises. The building heats up, requiring more air-conditioning to cool the building. The laundry is in full operation, the kitchens are producing lunch for the banquets and restaurants, computers are operating, and motors are running. Between 12:30 and 12:45 P.M., all of the equipment in the building is running at full capacity. This level of operation requires more electricity than it did at 3:00 A.M. The power company charges us a premium for the energy used at this time because all other buildings in the area require this large volume of electricity at the same time. This is the demand charge that measures the highest spike in energy drawn during a 15-minute period.

Electrical power is increasingly expensive. Our demand for electricity rises each year but the electric utility company has a limited amount of power it can provide out of a single plant. The demand charge penalizes businesses that use power during peak hours. The more the electric demand, the greater the penalty. The prices for demand charges will add a significant expense to your electric bill.

Electric Rates

CONSUMPTION CHARGE The consumption charge is calculated a variety of different ways, depending on the specific rate schedule you are using. For example, one utility company may calculate consumption costs using a tiered structure, where increasingly high amounts of consumption get charged increasingly high rates per kWh. Another utility company might base the consumption rate on the time of day that the building hit its peak demand for the month, linking the rate to the demand meter.

DEMAND CHARGE The rate for the demand charge will vary according to the time of year and possibly the time of day. For example, since electrical demand is highest during the summer, many utility companies have a high peak and a low peak season. The demand charge is higher during the summer than during the winter. The time of day demand charge will break each day into sections of low, medium, and high demand. In this instance, the electrical demand cost will be highest in the late morning and early afternoon and lowest during the night.

RATCHET CLAUSE—THE CLAUSE THAT KEEPS ON TAKING Some utility companies include a ratchet clause (sometimes called the "facilities charge"), which is also based on demand. The **ratchet clause** states that the demand charge will be based on the highest demand amount that occurred over the last twelve months, rather than the normal demand charge based on the previous month. For example, the Los Angeles Department of Water & Power bill includes a Facilities Charge on the rate schedule for General Service buildings. The Facilities Charge is $2.25 per kW, in addition to the demand charge of $13.78 per kW during the high season from June through October. These charges are determined on a "rolling basis" where hitting a high peak demand in July will cause you to be billed the facilities charge based on that particular high peak for the next 12 months. That is, unless you hit a new high demand in August. In this case, you will pay the facilities charge based on the August demand for the 12 months following August (the start and end dates roll forward every time you hit a new high demand). If you do not hit a new high peak demand before August of next year, then the facilities charge resets with next August's demand charge. Needless to say, the effects of one bad 15-minute period can penalize you for an entire year, so we have a big incentive to manage our demand charges, which is discussed in the next section.

OTHER CHARGES The electric company will also list additional charges, such as a base service charge, universal energy charge, transmission line charges, delivery charges, power factor surcharges, and various state and local taxes.

Each electric company offers different levels of electrical service. Consult with your electric company representative to determine the correct service contract for your facility to insure that you get the best rate schedule possible and to insure that you understand what your charges mean.

Electrical Peak-Shaving

Hospitality facilities have options to reduce their peak demand. The process of reducing the peak demand is called peak-shaving. **Peak-shaving** occurs when equipment is turned off during peak usage times to reduce the spike in electric demand, thus reducing the demand charge on the electric bill and avoiding the ongoing penalties of the facilities charge. The tasks being performed can sometimes be rescheduled for off-peak periods. For example, if a hotel has an on-premises laundry, the laundry operation can shut down during the day and rescheduled for the evening shift, when peak demand rates are lower.

Peak-shaving can be performed manually by designating an employee to physically turn off the equipment during the peak hours. However, humans are not always available or reliable. Automated **load-shedding systems** monitor the actual demand at the demand meter in real time. These systems use computers to monitor electric demand and when a preset demand profile is reached, the computer system will shut down equipment in the building automatically, then return it to service once the peak period has passed. A load-shedding system is much more reliable than a manual system and can provide the proper timing for equipment shutdown and return to service. The key to implementing a successful peak-shaving system in a hospitality facility is to select the equipment and duration of the shutdown that will have the least negative impact on guest comfort and satisfaction.

Deregulation

A relatively recent development in electrical supply is deregulation. The electric company has traditionally held a monopoly in its service area. The company was a publicly held company and the local government operated it. However, as utility companies began to privatize and as energy rates rose, customers began to request competition to get the best pricing possible. State governments began to deregulate the electric companies in the 1990s, with the intention of providing greater choice and purchasing power to customers through increased competition. Today, approximately thirty states have some sort of deregulated power.

The electric customer selects a power generation company. That company then supplies power using the pre-existing power transmission lines from the public utility. The customer may join a co-op to take advantage of lower electric rates or may contract directly with the electric generation company. If your property is in a deregulated state, you and your chief engineer should review your electric service contract and compare it with other companies to ensure that you are getting the best rate structure and service possible for your facility.

POWER QUALITY

One additional issue in electrical supply is that of power quality. Power quality refers to the consistency of the voltage and current provided by an electrical circuit. A small amount of variation is to be expected—for example, have you ever experienced the lights in a room dimming when a vacuum cleaner or a hair dryer is turned on? This is an example of a temporary reduction in power on the circuit and is what a UPS system cures for electronic equipment. Many hospitality facilities are located in areas with power quality problems. Some of the key issues include:

- *Surges:* Too much voltage occurs. This is also called "overvoltage."
- *Transients:* These are intense bursts of high voltage that may come from the utility company or from lightning.
- *Sags:* This is the opposite of a surge. Too little voltage is provided, also called "undervoltage."
- *Brownouts:* These are electrical sags that are 5% or greater drops in voltage from the electric company.
- *Blackouts:* These are complete losses of power.
- *Electrical "noise":* Noise refers to static on the electrical line, which can affect electronic equipment.

Electronic equipment needs a very steady, consistent electrical supply. For example, exposing a computer system to fluctuating current and voltage may result in lost data and system shutdowns. The display screen may show the effects of fluctuating current as well, where the screen images may become wavy, change color, or shift around on the screen.

There are two ways to ensure that your computer equipment is not exposed to poor power quality. First, you can install a UPS system. Second, your electrician can install a **dedicated line**, which is an electrical supply circuit that is only used by the computer system. No other equipment is plugged into the circuit that could draw power and possibly affect the electricity delivered to the computer.

LIGHTING

What is a good lighting design? A good lighting design accomplishes several goals at the same time. First, a good design will provide lighting levels that are bright enough for people to accomplish their tasks and activities in space. General lighting provides an overall ambient light in a space but may be too dim for people to perform specific tasks. Task lighting provides targeted light to assist people in performing tasks. For example, a restaurant's lobby area may use dim lighting to provide a romantic atmosphere. It is enough light to allow guests to walk through the space and get to their tables. However, it may be too dark for the host/hostess to see the seating chart. A small light in the ceiling directly above the podium can shine down to provide a brighter surface as task lighting for the host/hostess to work.

Next, a good lighting design will highlight objects or areas in the space to add to the décor. A good design will also provide light at the correct color to maintain the integrity of the interior design, meaning that the space looks the way that the designer intended it to appear. The light must be provided at an angle that will illuminate a surface but will not create glare, which is fatiguing to the eye.

What is Light?

Light consists of energy waves at a specific range of frequencies. The human eye detects energy waves in the range of 380 to 780 nanometers. Ultraviolet light waves falls below this range, while infrared waves fall above this range. Neither is visible to the naked eye. Objects and people absorb light waves. We detect color by seeing a particular light wavelength that is not absorbed by the object; the light is reflected off the object and we detect the light as color. White light, such as that of a typical light bulb, is light that contains all of the colors in the visible spectrum. In contrast, if we mixed a gallon of paint that contained all of the colors in the spectrum, the result would be black paint.

Before discussing lighting design, we must first familiarize ourselves with several lighting terms.

- *Lamp:* A lamp, when discussed by a lighting professional, actually refers to a light bulb, not the lamp that the light bulb works in (Figure 6.10a).

- *Lamp life:* Lamps have a rated life, specified in the number of burn hours. The lamp life is an approximation of the number of hours that 50% of a large batch of that type of lamp will burn before failing (burning out). Any given lamp may fail sooner or later than the rated lamp life. Lamp life ratings will range between 800 hours and 10,000 hours, depending on the type of lamp.
- *Fixture or luminaire:* A lamp housing or an overhead light that uses light bulbs is called a fixture or a luminaire (Figures 6.10b and c).

FIGURE 6.10a
Example of Two Fluorescent Lamps in an Overhead Fixture. *Source*: Dina Zemke.

FIGURE 6.10b
Example of a Luminaire (or Fixture).   *Source*: Dina Zemke.

FIGURE 6.10c Ceiling Fixture. *Source*: Dina Zemke.

- *Lumens and lux:* The amount of light that a lamp emits at the source is measured in lumens in the United States. In other parts of the world, it is measured in **lux**.
- *Efficacy:* The efficiency of a light source is called efficacy. It is measured in the number of lumens generated per watt of electricity consumed (lumens/watt).
- *Footcandles:* The amount of luminance at the surface of an object that is being lit is measured in footcandles. We use a footcandle meter to measure this.
- *Footlamberts:* The amount of light that the eye actually registered is measured in footlamberts.
- *Color Rendering Index (CRI):* A lamp's color rendering index is a measure of how closely a light source matches the color of light emitted by the sun. Color rendition is graded on a scale of 0–100, with a rating of 100 being a perfect match with the light spectrum provided by the sun.
- *Correlated Color Temperature (CCT):* The Correlated Color Temperature (CCT) is the color of the light source itself. The term "temperature" describes the various temperatures a piece of black metal will turn as it is heated. For example, an electric stove coil is black at room temperature. However, as it heats up, it begins to change color, first turning red, then yellow. If the coil temperature continued to rise, it would eventually turn

white, then blue, then violet. The CCT of a lamp compares its color to the black metal color at various temperatures using the Kelvin scale. This differs from the color rendering index, which measures the color of the light itself. CCTs range from warm (yellowish) at 1500 kelvins to cool (bluish) at 9000 kelvins.

Types of Lamps

There is a wide variety of lamps available to the facility manager. The proper lamp selection will depend on the desired end result of the lighting scheme. There are three categories of lamps: incandescent, electric discharge, and light emitting diode (LED). Figure 6.11 presents a variety of different lamp types.

INCANDESCENT LAMPS   Thomas Edison invented the **incandescent** lamp in the 19th century. Figure 6.11a shows a typical incandescent lamp, which consists of a closed glass bulb, a metal **lamp base**, and a metal filament wire. The filament wire has a high electrical resistance. When electricity contacts the wire, heat is generated. The heat is so intense that the wire begins to glow, producing light. The area inside the bulb is a vacuum, because the wire will burn up if exposed to oxygen. Incandescent lamps are made in a variety of shapes and sizes.

Incandescent lamps are inefficient sources of light. The lumen output ranges 4–20 lumens/watt. Incandescent lamps also have a relatively short rated lamp life, averaging 800–1,000 hours of burn time.

Tungsten halogen (TH) lamps use a tungsten filament in a gas-filled capsule to provide light (see Figure 6.11b). These lamps provide exceptional CRI (100) and a low-to-medium CCT, making them ideal for situations where

FIGURE 6.11a
Incandescent Lamp.
Source: Dina Zemke.

FIGURE 6.11b
Tungsten Halogen Lamps.
Source: Dina Zemke.

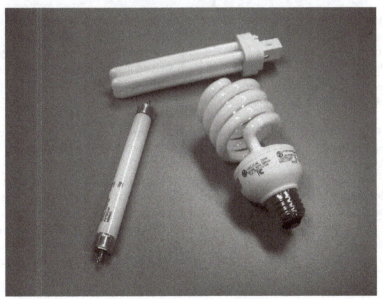

FIGURE 6.11c
Fluorescent Tube and
Compact Fluorescent
Lamps (CFL).   *Source*:
Dina Zemke.

good color rendering is important. They work well in restaurants to illuminate people and food, and can provide focused light to accent or highlight objects in a room. The lamps are dimmable and they are much more efficient and have longer rated lives than incandescent, basically providing the advantages of incandescent without some of the drawbacks.

However, TH lamps do have drawbacks. First, the lamps are quite expensive compared to other types of lamps. Second, if you need general, diffuse

FIGURE 6.11d Metal Halide Lamp.
Source: Dina Zemke.

lighting, TH lamps will not perform well because the light is focused. Next, they give off a lot of heat and, if they break while lit, they can pose a fire hazard. If heat generation is a problem and causes spaces or objects to heat up, there are TH lamps available with a **dichroitic coating**, which directs the heat up through the lamp housing rather than directing it down onto a surface, such as on people or food.

ELECTRIC DISCHARGE LAMPS **Electric discharge lamps** work by heating an inert gas inside the closed glass bulb, rather than heating a filament wire. The inside surface of the bulb is coated in a variety of **phosphors** that create the color temperature of the light. Electricity is supplied to a **ballast** that is located inside the light fixture. The ballast uses the electricity to generate an electrical arc, often via a small amount of mercury, that is exposed to the inert gas in the bulb. The heated gas emits ultraviolet rays, which contact the phosphors inside the bulb and cause them to glow, which then creates light. There are two major types of electric discharge lamps: fluorescent and high-intensity discharge.

    Fluorescent Lamps.   We are all familiar with fluorescent lamps. Most offices, hallways, and classrooms use them. Fluorescent lamps come in a variety of sizes, wattages, CRIs, and CCTs. Fluorescent lighting is more efficient than incandescent lighting. A typical 40-watt compact fluorescent lamp will provide 65 lumens/watt. Compare this with a 40-watt incandescent lamp that provides only 11.75 lumens/watt. Fluorescent lamp lives often range 8–12 times more than those of incandescent lamps. Some newer models of fluorescent lamps offer dimming capability and three-way lighting options.

    Fluorescent lamps are manufactured in a wide variety of shapes (Figure 6.11c). Ceiling lighting fixtures usually use a straight, linear fluorescent tube, although some use a circular tube. The ballast is located in the fixture, so you simply insert the tube into the ballast and the fixture is lit.

Another class of fluorescent lamp contains its own integral ballast. These are called **compact fluorescent lamps (CFL)**. CFLs may use a regular screw-type base, similar to the ones used for incandescent lamps, and can easily replace a incandescent lamp in most fixtures. Other CFLs use a base consisting of two or more pins. These are popular when a new energy-efficient lighting system has been installed and the property manager wants to ensure that employees do not replace the CFLs with incandescent lamps in the future.

Past complaints about fluorescent lighting included poor lighting color and flickering. Today's fluorescent lights offer significantly better CRIs and CCTs. Older fluorescent lamps flickered because the magnetic ballasts in the fixtures were inefficient and did not control the electrical arc very well. Today, the ballasts are electronic and provide much better control of the arc, eliminating the flickering problems. Today's ballasts are also much more energy efficient than in the past. New electronic ballasts consume as little as three to four watts.

High-Intensity Discharge Lamps.   The other category of electric discharge lamp is the **high-intensity discharge lamp (HID)**. The light color quality of these lamps is generally poor and they are usually used in places where good color rendition is not important.

High-pressure sodium vapor lamps give off a yellowish light, due to the vaporized sodium that is used to generate the light. Sodium burns with a yellow color, and sodium vapor lamps provide a poor CRI of approximately 20. However, they are very energy-efficient, emitting 64–133 lumens/watt. They also have relatively long lamp lives, ranging from 16,000 to 24,000 hours. The poor color rendering index of the sodium vapor lamp makes it undesirable for indoors applications where color representation is important. These lamps are often used outdoors in parking areas and for street lighting.

Low-pressure sodium vapor lamps also give off a yellowish light and are energy-efficient. However, this lamp uses a higher level of mercury in the vapor mixture, which poses health and environmental risks. These types of lamps are being replaced with other HID options

Metal halide lamps use a crystal arc to provide the electric sources to argon and mercury gasses in the enclosed bulb. They can offer a variety of CRIs, often rated in the 80–90 range, and various CCT options as well. These lamps produce approximately 75 lumens/watt. While not as efficient as high pressure sodium vapor lamps, their improved color rendition index has made them popular for indoor use in big box retail stores and public spaces. Lighting manufacturers are exploring new ways to use this highly efficient and versatile technology.

Mercury vapor lamps are an older type of lamp that is being phased out of use due to its mercury content and potential environmental hazards. These lamps were the least efficient of the high-intensity discharge family and offered relatively poor color rendition, with CRIs ranging from 45 to 50. The light emitted is a bluish-green color. These were often used in street lighting and parking lot applications, due to their extremely long lamp lives that operated in excess of 24,000 hours.

LIGHT EMITTING DIODES (LED'S) **Light emitting diodes** do not use bulbs at all. The LED is a semiconductor chip that emits light when an electrical current is applied to it. They are highly efficient, with some LEDs producing more than 131 lumens/watt. Because virtually all of the electricity is converted to light, very little heat is generated. They also have lamp lives in excess of 50,000 hours. LEDs are available in five colors; red, green, blue, yellow, and white. The white LED is actually a blue LED with a coating that converts part of the blue light to yellow, producing a white light. Earlier white LED's consisted of an array of red, green, and blue that combined to produce white.

There are many applications for LEDs in the hospitality field. New emergency exit signs use LEDs instead of incandescent or fluorescent bulbs, partially because the long lamp life renders it virtually maintenance-free, but also because the latest exit sign fixtures use only one watt of electricity. LEDs are also used to provide signage lighting, directional lighting, and lighting for swimming pools and spas. This technology offers the opportunity to create many special effects in a wide variety of colors. Look for LED technology to become more popular in the future.

Which Lamp to Use?

The choice of lamp depends on the goal of the design. The designer needs to consider the general and task lighting requirements of the space. In addition, a good design will also consider maintenance and energy conservation.

Many hospitality properties, particularly hotels, have replaced incandescent lamps with compact fluorescent lamps and have realized large savings in energy costs. While energy conservation is always important, replacing all incandescent and tungsten halogen lamps with compact fluorescent is not necessarily the right choice. Newer fluorescent lamps provide greatly improved color rendition, but still tend to have a relatively high color temperature. This combination results in an accurate depiction of color but the overall tone of the light is on the cool side. Our lodging guests are often accustomed to a warmer, incandescent light in their living rooms, bedrooms, and bathrooms. If we want our property to feel like home-away-from-home, we need to provide the warm ambient light that our customer has at home.

How do we address this problem? Careful selection of lighting sources can result in energy efficiency as well as an attractive atmosphere. For example, rather than just purchasing a compact fluorescent lamp, research your vendor's product catalog to find the right combination of CRI and CCT. A CFL with a high CRI and a low CCT can provide light that will please guests and reduce your energy costs.

Restaurants can also use a combination of incandescent and CFL lighting. For example, in a typical full-service restaurant, the workers in the kitchen require high levels of general and task lighting but do not require perfect color rendition. Fluorescent lighting provides appropriate lighting with the advantage of energy savings. The dining room lighting design might use incandescent or tungsten halogen lighting for the guest areas. This warmer lighting makes food look more appetizing and people look more attractive, which would enhance the experience for the restaurant's guests. However, lighting the entire dining room with tungsten halogen would be inefficient, expensive, and might provide too bright an atmosphere. Some restaurants address this issue by combining a soft general lighting system using fluorescent lamps and using halogen or incandescent lamps to accent the dining room tables and décor items.

Maintaining Lighting

Proper maintenance of a lighting system will provide the facility with cost savings. Some of the important steps are:

CLEANING FIXTURES   Lighting fixtures (e.g., table lamps, overhead lights, or spot lights) attract airborne dirt and dust, which collects on the lamp and the fixture's surface. This dirt will decrease the lumen output of the fixture. The dirt may also shorten the life of the bulb, if the dirt prevents the fixture from venting and results in abnormally high operating temperatures. Your housekeeping and maintenance personnel should have a regularly scheduled cleaning routine in place to safeguard your investment in the lighting system. The fixtures have a slight electrostatic charge that is not dangerous, but does result in dirt that may require special cleaning products for removal and air-drying, to avoid generating a new electrostatic charge.

RETAINING DESIGN INTEGRITY   All too often, the person responsible for ordering replacement supplies will order the first lamp that presents itself in a lighting catalog, rather than matching the light characteristics to the original design. This results in an uneven level and color of lighting and may negatively affect the appearance of the hotel. Restaurants have the same problem, but poor replacement lamp choices can also degrade the appearance of the food served. Property managers need to ensure that the ongoing replacement of burned-out lamps uses the same lamp specifications.

Group Relamping

Say that your hotel has a guest room floor corridor that had all of its lamps installed at the same time. A couple of lamps have burned out. What do you do? Common sense tells us to just replace the ones that are burned out now and replace the others as each burns out over time. However, a better option is actually to replace all of the corridor's lamps at the same time. This process is called **group relamping**.

How can this be a good idea? Why should we throw out lamps that may have hundreds of hours left to burn? Yes, group relamping is a counterintuitive process. However, it can result in large cost-savings in the long run. The costs involved in replacing a light bulb go far beyond the cost of the bulb itself. The burnt out bulb must be reported to the engineering department, which requires an employee to create a work order. The work order is assigned to one of the engineers, who needs to get the new lamp out of inventory, travel to the location of the burnt out lamp, get a ladder, change the lamp, return the ladder to its storage area, and return to the engineering department office. In a larger property, this process can consume 30 minutes of the employee's time.

If the property had a group relamping system in place, the Chief Engineer would assess the timing of the relamping. If this is the correct time to do so, the employee might spend one hour replacing 30 lamps in the corridor. Plus newer light bulbs may burn brighter, which might look strange when mixed with older ones in the same corridor.

ENERGY CONSERVATION

The rapid increase in energy prices during the past few years has created an awareness of the need for energy conservation in the hospitality industry. The following measures for energy conservation in lighting are not just helpful during times of high energy costs, but they are always useful in controlling costs while not affecting guest satisfaction. Energy conservation for heating and air-conditioning is addressed in their specific chapters.

Switch to Fluorescent

The discussion of lighting earlier in this chapter covered many of the pros and cons of switching from incandescent lighting to fluorescent. This is a convenient way to save 50% or more on a property's **electrical consumption** for lighting. If replacing incandescent lamps with fluorescent, the hospitality manager must be precise in specifications to insure that the quality of the light is adequate to provide warm light with good color rendition.

Controlling Operation

The other key way of reducing lighting energy consumption is to provide lighting when it is needed and to turn it off when it is not. This can, of course, be accomplished manually. However, relying solely on employees to turn off lights is not the most efficient option, because people do forget to turn them off. The following equipment provides a more effective method of control over lighting operation.

The first three measures are relatively inexpensive and easy to install. They can be implemented using most typical operating budgets, rather than scheduling them into the capital budgeting process, and they provide immediate results.

- *Occupancy sensors:* Occupancy sensors use infrared beams to detect people in a space. They are relatively inexpensive and easy to install and maintain. Occupancy sensors will permit lights to be on when people are in the space, but will turn lights off when the space is empty.
- *Timers:* Timers are also an easy-to-install, inexpensive method to control lighting. They turn the lights on and off at a preset times. One caveat

is changing the settings on timers. If the area being lit is an outdoor area that is lit only when it is dark, the timer must be reset several times a year to account for changes in sunrise and sunset times, as well as adjustments for daylight savings time.

- *Photocells:* Photocells are switches that make contact with an electrical source when they detect light. This contact prevents an electric current from being completed between the electrical source and a piece of equipment. As light decreases, such as while the sun is setting, the electrical charge decreases and the current is completed, turning the equipment on. For example, once it gets dark enough, a photocell will turn outdoor lights on and then turn them off again once daylight approaches. Photocells are inexpensive and easy to install and have the advantage of never having to be reset. They are available with a wide variety of operating options, such as turning lights on 30 minutes after sunset or turning lights or equipment off after six hours of operation.

The next three energy conservation measures are more expensive than the previous measures. They would be most appropriate during a new construction or a renovation project.

- *Programmable lighting control systems:* Programmable lighting control systems are similar to sophisticated timer systems. These are often found in public spaces in hotels and, on a smaller scale, in restaurants to provide preset lighting designs to achieve certain effects. For example, a hotel ballroom with a programmable system might have seven or eight different lighting schemes in the system to provide environments ranging from a romantic atmosphere for dinner and dancing to a very bright environment for a corporate training session. The system can be programmed to turn the lights on and off at preset times, saving electricity. Another major advantage to programmable lighting controls is that the lighting scheme is consistent—never too bright or too dark—and not at the discretion of employees who may not provide consistent settings, which might harm the overall design of the space.

- *Photovoltaic systems (PV):* Photovoltaic systems use solar energy to create electricity. These systems use a series of photovoltaic cells to convert sunlight into power. They work well in areas with ample sunshine and a dry (non-rainy) climate, although they will generate electricity in less sunny climates too. It is unlikely that, at this time, a PV system would be able to provide all of the power for a typical hospitality operation in the United States. However, PV systems could help alleviate some of the peak demand levels to reduce peak load charges and would certainly reduce the amount of electricity used overall.

  Baseline PV systems only generate electricity while the sun is shining. Batteries are available to store electricity, but these should be approached with caution due to the maintenance requirements and the possible exposure to hazardous materials that are used in making the battery.

These systems are very expensive and should be analyzed for cost-effectiveness. At this time, the average cost per watt generated is approximately $9 per peak watt. A typical system for a residential property will cost between $18,000 and $50,000 or more to install. A hospitality property using hundreds of watts during peak demand periods may not see significant financial benefits from a photovoltaic system. However, smaller lodging properties, restaurants, and properties in remote areas may find that this is a good option. Some electric companies will purchase excess electricity that a PV system produces. For example, if a homeowner has a PV system that generates electricity while no one is home to use the electricity, the electric company will buy that electricity. If this option is available, it should be included in the financial analysis.

- *Daylighting:* Daylighting is a method of building design that orients the building to intentionally take advantage of the sun to provide light to the interior. It should provide light without imposing too much heat on the building's air conditioning system, which would eliminate any cost savings from reduced lighting needs. This type of system is best implemented during new construction or building an addition onto an existing building. Not all architects and designers are familiar with the technical aspects of daylighting. If you are interested in this type of design, find an architect who is experienced with working with daylighting.

HEALTH AND SAFETY ISSUES

Electricity is a dangerous thing. It has the potential to hurt or kill us. Electrically operated equipment also poses threats to our health and safety. Implement the following measures in your property's operational procedures to help protect your employees and your guests.

Employees

Your employees are your most valuable asset and keeping them safe is not only the right thing to do, it is a legal priority. If you or your employees will be working around electricity and/or mechanical equipment that uses electricity, your policy should include the following items:

- Wear sensible, close-fitting clothing. Loose fitting clothing will not only get caught in moving machinery and kitchen equipment, but it may also catch fire from contact with an electrical wire.
- Long hair should be tied back and secured to prevent contact with the equipment.
- Jewelry, especially rings, should not be worn around electrical equipment and electrical panels. Electricity has been known to arc out of the cabinet and make contact with metal jewelry, which can hurt the wearer or even result in death.

- Employees who work around electrical equipment should wear rubber-soled shoes to minimize the risk of electrical shock.
- Safety glasses should be worn around electrical equipment, if possible, to minimize the risk of eye damage.

Your engineering and/or maintenance personnel should have their own departmental procedures for working with electricity. Some of the standard procedures include:

- *Replacing fuses:* Always replace a burned-out fuse with a new fuse that has the correct amperage rating for the circuit. Do not put a larger amp fuse than the amperage of the circuit or a fire may occur. In addition, plastic fuse tongs should be used to pull the old fuse out and insert the new fuse. Your employees should not do this with their bare fingers, due to the risk of shock.
- *Circuit breaker reset:* When resetting a circuit breaker that has tripped, look away from the panel when flipping the switch. Electricity can arc out of the panel and cause eye damage.
- *Lock-out/tag-out program:* Shutting down large pieces of equipment for repair or maintenance requires the equipment's electrical circuit to be shut off. The circuit breaker or cut-off switch is often located out of sight of the equipment itself. If the shut down equipment is inconveniencing other hotel personnel or guests, a motivated employee sometimes addresses the problem by turning the electricity back on, without knowing the reason why it was off in the first place. The employee fixing the equipment might be working on the equipment at that moment. The sudden start of the equipment could electrocute the employee, or his or her fingers, tools, or clothing might become caught in a motor that suddenly turns on, resulting in tragedy. The Occupational Safety and Health Administration (OSHA) requires running a lock-out/tag-out program to prevent such accidents. This program involves employees padlocking a de-energized energy source (electrical circuit, steam line, gas line, or mechanical equipment) which prevents anyone else from turning the equipment on—this is the lock-out component. The employee also attaches a tag to the lock (tag-out), explaining the circumstances behind turning the energy source off, ensuring communication. This program has been successful in reducing the incidence of on-the-job injuries and deaths. The materials for a lock-out/tag-out program are shown in Figure 6.12.
- *Equipment check:* All equipments that use an electrical cord should be checked prior to and after use for frayed cords or other damage, to prevent fires and electrocution.
- *Keep it clean:* A good cleaning program will prevent dust and dirt from building up near an electrical current. Dust and dirt are flammable and dirty equipment may cause a fire.
- *Only purchase UL-rated lamps and extension cords:* The Underwriters' Laboratory (UL) tests products under a variety of dangerous conditions

FIGURE 6.12a Lock-Out/Tag-Out. *Source*: Dina Zemke.

FIGURE 6.12b Lock-Out/Tag-Out Program in Action. *Source*: Circus Circus.

before the products are released to the market. Purchasing products with a UL rating will minimize the risks of faulty equipment, electrocution, and fire.

- *In case of fire:* One of the first things that you or your employees should do in the event of a fire is to turn off electricity to the area that is burning. If the fire is an electrical fire, the situation could worsen if the electrical current is still present. However, this should only be done if it does not put the employee in danger.

Summary

Energy is the largest utility expense for most hospitality properties. Since we have relatively little control over the rates that our utility company charges us for consumption (per kWh) and demand (per kW), we need to manage our electrical usage to minimize the effects of electrical costs on our bottom line. Electrical systems also play a significant role in our property's safety and security. We need to ensure that electricity is available during emergencies to protect the property and our guests and employees. Electricity can also be dangerous, so it's important to train employees that work around electricity in approved methods and safety measures to reduce injuries or fatalities, ultimately reducing the premiums that we pay to our insurance company.

Lighting plays a critical role in hospitality facilities. We need to be able to provide the correct quality and quantity of light for employees and guests. Traditionally, the fluorescent lamp was frowned on for use in guest areas, due to the poor light quality it provided. However, recent improvements in fluorescent lighting, as well as in other types of lamps, such as tungsten-halogen, light emitting diodes (LEDs), and metal halide, are providing options that can save significant amounts of electricity while supplying adequate light quality for front- and back-of-house uses.

Key Terms and Concepts

alternating current
    (AC current) *133*
amperes *132*
ballast *154*
biomass generators *135*
circuit breakers *138*
Color Rendering Index
    (CRI) *151*
compact fluorescent
    lamp (CFL) *155*
consumption
    meter *145*
Correlated Color
    Temperature
    (CCT) *151*
dedicated line *149*
demand meter *146*
dichroitic coating *154*

direct current
    (DC current) *133*
efficacy *151*
electric discharge
    lamps *154*
electrical
    consumption *158*
electrical demand *146*
electrical panels *138*
fixture/luminaire *150*
footcandles *151*
footlamberts *151*
frequency *134*
fuses *138*
geothermal power *135*
ground fault circuit
    interrupt (GFCI) *140*
group relamping *157*

Hertz (Hz) *134*
high-intensity
    discharge lamp
    (HID) *155*
incandescent *152*
kilowatt *133*
kilowatt-hour *133*
lamp *149*
lamp base *152*
lamp life *150*
light emitting diode
    (LED) *152*
load-shedding
    system *147*
lock-out/tag-out
    program *161*
lumen/lux *151*
Ohm's law *132*

ohms *132*
peak-shaving *147*
phosphors *154*
photovoltaic *135*
ratchet clause *147*
solar power *135*
step-down
    transformer *136*
step-up transformer *136*
transformer vault *136*
tungsten halogen
    (TH) *152*
Uninterruptible Power
    Supply system (UPS
    system) *144*
volt *132*
watt *133*
wind power *135*

Discussion and Review Questions

1. Electronic equipment needs a very steady, consistent electrical supply. Discuss the ways to ensure that computer equipment is not exposed to poor power quality.
2. Explain how a GFCI receptacle provides increased protection against electrocution over the protection provided by a circuit breaker.
3. Explain the difference between electrical consumption charges and electrical demand charges.

If a ratchet clause is present, how is it affected by demand?

4. Think of a typical restaurant. What types of equipment would you want to connect to an emergency power supply?
5. The owner of a hotel property asks you why the property should implement a group relamping program. How would you explain it to her?

Notes

Lamp Manufacturers:
  Osram Sylvania www.sylvania. com
  General Electric www.gelighting.com/na/
  business_lighting/lighting_applications/
  hospitality/index.htm

How to read electrical meters:
  www.nyseg.com/MediaLibrary/2/5/Content%
  20Management/NYSEG/YourAccount/PDFs%
  20and%20Docs/ReadingYourMeter.pdf

7

Heating Systems

CHAPTER OBJECTIVES

After reading this chapter, you should be able to:

- describe the different types of heat and heat energy transfer.
- describe the components of the "human comfort zone."
- describe the components of heating systems, including thermostats, controls, and methods of generating and distributing heat.
- describe the safety components in a heating system.
- describe the operational requirements to operate a safe heating system.
- discuss the pros and cons of each of the three types of piping arrangements for centralized heating systems.
- list and describe some common ways to conserve energy in an existing heating system.
- list and describe ways to design energy conservation into a new building.

INTRODUCTION

As hospitality managers, we are concerned with providing a safe, comfortable environment for our guests and employees. The next three chapters focus on the ways we provide comfortable human environments in our buildings, through heating, ventilation, and air conditioning (HVAC) systems. This chapter will explore building heating systems.

What is heat? It is a form of energy. Heat is detected when this energy is transferred from one body to another. For example, if you were to stand outside your classroom building, the outside temperature right now is the difference between the heat projected by the sun and your body. Before we begin exploring building heating systems, we must first know several basic definitions and principles of physics.

Sensible heat is heat that you can feel. It is measured by a typical thermometer, which measures the dry-bulb temperature of the air or an object. Sensible heat does not account for any sensation of heat that is influenced by the humidity in the air.

Latent heat is sensible heat plus the effects of the quantity of water in the air. It is affected by relative humidity and is measured in terms of the wet-bulb temperature.

Relative humidity refers to the quantity of water vapor that is in the air compared to the total amount of water that the air could hold before the water condenses. A relative humidity (rh) value of 40% means that the air is currently holding 40% of the moisture that it can hold before dew or condensation forms on the ground or on walls. Relative humidity values vary based on the actual temperature of the air. Higher temperatures can hold more water, while lower temperatures can hold less water. The same amount of water in the air will yield a higher relative humidity at lower temperatures than it would at higher temperatures.

It is important to note that water vapor always moves to equalize the relative humidity between two spaces. For example, if a building is located in a cold climate, the heated air in the building will have more water in it than the cold air outside. The moisture in the air will attempt to travel to the outside to equalize the relative humidity of both spaces.

The **dew point** is the temperature at which the humidity in the air will condense into a liquid (e.g., turns to dew). As air cools, the water in the air condenses. It is at this temperature that the air is completely saturated with water (or 100% relative humidity). If an outdoor environment has reached its dew point, it is likely that the area will be foggy.

Evaporation is the transformation of liquid into a vapor or gas. Water evaporates into the air to add moisture to the air. Evaporation increases with air movement. If a fan blows across a bowl of water, the water will evaporate more quickly than if the fan was not blowing.

Air-conditioning is not necessarily cooling air! It is a term that technically (and correctly) refers to *conditioned air*. This is air that we have manipulated to achieve certain qualities to meet our needs. Air-conditioning includes managing the sensible heat, the relative humidity, the cleanliness of the air, and the movement of the air.

HUMAN COMFORT

Hospitality managers are concerned with providing environments with air quality that achieves human comfort levels through comfort air-conditioning. The American Society of Heating, Refrigeration, and Air Conditioning Engineers (ASHRAE) defines comfort air-conditioning as "... the *process of treating air* so as to *control simultaneously* its *temperature, humidity, cleanliness,* and *distribution* to meet the comfort requirements of the occupants of the conditioned space."

To begin to understand the ways that facilities managers condition the air in a building, we must first examine the ways that heat is present in our buildings. The most important concept in this chapter is the notion of **heat energy transfer**. The definition of heat states that heat is the difference in temperature between two spaces or objects. Nature will always attempt to achieve equilibrium in temperature. If one room is cold and the room next to it is warm, the air in the two rooms will attempt to arrive at a common temperature. This happens through heat transfer, where the heat in the warmer environment will travel to the cooler space to equalize the temperature. There are three types of heat transfer that humans experience: radiant, convection, and evaporation.

Radiant heat is the simple movement of heat from one object to another, without the effects of air movement or liquid evaporation. This is the type of heat provided by the sun. In a hotel, radiant heat is generated by lighting fixtures and human beings. Touching a cool object results in radiant heat transfer—the heat in your hand travels directly into the cooler object. In a kitchen, radiant heat can be found in a standard oven or over a burner on the stovetop.

Heat transfer by **convection** involves temperature and air movement (Figure 7.1). It is a natural process that evolves in a space with uneven heat. We know that air rises as it gets warmer and sinks as it gets cooler. This will lead to a cycle in a room where air begins to circulate through the room in a circular form. A common example of convection heating in a lodging facility is baseboard heating.

The air is heated at the baseboard and rises toward the ceiling. The warmed air spreads across the ceiling, transferring its heat to the area. Once the heat in the air begins to decrease, the air begins to sink toward the floor. Once the now-cooler air reaches the floor, it is drawn toward the baseboard, reheated, and sent up to the ceiling once again.

Convection heat transfer is also found in the kitchen. Convection ovens use radiant heat with a small fan that blows the heat in a circular pattern around the cooking food. This method of cooking can reduce the overall cooking time of food and is called forced convection, since a fan is used to force the convection flow.

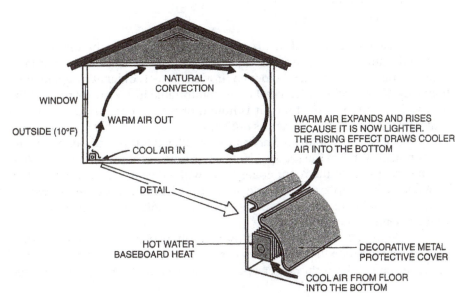

FIGURE 7.1 Convection.
Source: Thomson Delmar.

The sensation of heat transfer also occurs through evaporation. There is a sensation of cooling as moisture from one object travels to another (or into the air). For example, misters are often used in warm climates to increase the comfort of guests who are dining or meeting on an outside patio. There is no actual change in the temperature, but the water droplets fall on the skin and evaporate, making the environment feel cooler. Another example is air blowing across perspiring skin—again, there is no actual change in temperature, but it feels cool and refreshing due to evaporation.

COMFORT ZONE

Now that we understand how to detect heat and heat transfer, we need to explore the range of conditions that are generally acceptable for human comfort. The hospitality manager needs to consider a variety of factors to provide the right set of conditions. These factors include the sensible heat (in the form of the dry-bulb temperature), the relative humidity and latent heat, the season (heating or cooling), and how people on the property are dressed.

Since we know that air near the ceiling is warmer and air near the floor is cooler, how do we get a good measurement of the current conditions? We measure it through a sensor, such as a **thermostat** or a thermometer that is installed at the room's **breathing line**, which is approximately five feet above the floor. It is called the breathing line because it is the range where many peoples' noses are located.

Once we measure the existing conditions, the air needs to be treated to fall in the comfort zone. The ideal "ambient condition" ranges are:

Humidity: 20%–60% rh

Dry-bulb temperature: 68–78°F

Air movement/fan speed

The balance of conditions is achieved by measuring the temperature against the humidity. Warm environments feel even warmer if they are humid than do drier environments. Colder environments feel colder at a high relative humidity. Conversely, we can feel more comfortable in a warmer room if the relative humidity is low. If the air is humid or we are perspiring, it will feel cooler if we feel air blowing across our skin.

The hospitality manager needs to consider the types of people in the environment. What is the season? How are guests likely to be dressed? What are the occupants of the room going to do while they are in the room? How crowded will the room be? People adapt to seasonal conditions, so we are more comfortable in cooler temperatures in the winter as well as in warmer environments in the summer.

Some research has suggested that men have faster metabolisms than women, leading men to prefer cooler conditions. The research is inconclusive. However, one of the author's personal experiences and training have resulted in the following rule of thumb for comfort control in meeting rooms, ballrooms, and dining rooms:

1. If men are removing their jackets, it's getting warm
2. If the ladies are removing jackets, it's getting *really* warm
3. If the men have removed their jackets, but the ladies have not—it's just right!
4. If both the men and ladies have their jackets on, it might be too cold (especially if someone is shivering)

Please note that this rule of thumb should be taken with a grain of salt and with some common sense. If all of the guests in the room are men, the optimal comfort conditions will be different than if the guests are a mix of men and women.

The activity of the occupants will also affect optimal comfort levels. For example, if a group of meeting participants is sitting in a conference room and they do not move around very much, they are more likely to prefer a slightly warmer environment. On the other hand, if a wedding party in a ballroom has many guests on the dance floor, the guests will probably be more comfortable in a cooler environment because the dancing makes them warm.

The tricky part of comfort levels for hospitality managers is finding the right balance between guest comfort and employee comfort. An all too common scenario is at a restaurant in the summertime when the air-conditioning is on. The guests are freezing because they are sitting still. However, the wait staff (who control the thermostat) are comfortable as they move around the dining room and in and out of the kitchen. The result: unhappy guests, but happy wait staff! Should your guests be comfortable at the cost of employee comfort? That is the challenge.

Thermostats

How do we control air temperature? We use a thermostat, a device that senses changes in air temperature and communicates with the heating and cooling system to adjust the temperature of the air being supplied. There are two types of thermostats: mechanical and digital (Figure 7.2).

Mechanical

Older thermostats and newer, very inexpensive thermostats are mechanical. The thermostat uses a bimetallic strip wound into a coil to sense temperature changes, and then it activates or turns off the heating system when a preset temperature is reached. The bimetallic strip consists of two different pieces of metal laminated to each other. The two metals have different expansion properties, so one will have greater expansion at a given temperature than the other. When one side of the bimetallic strip tries to expand and the other does not, the entire strip bends. The bent strip activates a switch that turns on the

FIGURE 7.2a
Mechanical Thermostat.
Source: Dina Zemke.

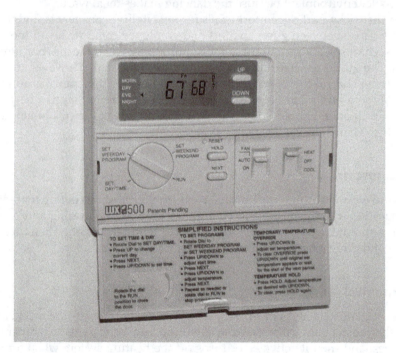

FIGURE 7.2b Digital
Thermostat. *Source*:
Dina Zemke.

heating system. As the heat in the space increases, the other metal side begins to expand until both sides unbend and the strip is again straight. At this point, the switch is turned off, because the room has reached its desired temperature. As the room cools, one of the metal sides contracts and the other doesn't, which causes the strip to turn the heat on again.

Mechanical thermostats are inexpensive and easy to install and maintain. Over time, however, they may lose calibration, meaning the temperature that the lever is set at no longer matches up with the bimetallic strip's winding location. It becomes difficult to set the thermostat to the desired temperature, since the lever's location is inaccurate. The mechanical thermostat also does not offer programmable capability.

Digital

Digital thermostats use a device called a thermistor. The thermistor produces an electrical charge that changes depending on the temperature that the thermistor senses. This electrical charge activates the on/off switch for the heating system. Digital thermostats were once expensive, but current prices are only slightly higher than for mechanical thermostats. The price difference is inconsequential, once the potential energy savings of the digital thermostat is considered. Digital thermostats provide the user with the ability to program different temperature settings for various days and times. For example, you can set the temperature on the heating system to a cooler level during the night while you are asleep and do not need as much heating, and thus you can save money. The thermostat can be programmed to provide the right amount of heat when you need it, but less heat when you do not.

WHERE DOES COLD AIR COME FROM? HEATING LOADS

Now that we know the ways that heat is transferred and guest comfort is defined, we need to identify the ways that spaces become cold and need to be heated. Objects or processes that take away heat are creating a **heating load**. Heating loads can be internal or external to the building.

There are not very many **internal heating loads** for most hospitality buildings. Sources of internal heating loads may include open doors to coolers or freezers in the kitchen, or very cold objects being brought into the building. Frozen food that is thawing creates a heating load; the frozen object absorbs heat from the ambient conditions in the kitchen.

In contrast to internal heating loads, there are many **external heating loads** for most buildings, particularly in cooler climates. The major factor is the outdoor air temperature and relative humidity. A warm building surrounded by cold air continually transfers heat to the cold air outside. The humidity in both environments is also trying to achieve equilibrium.

The building's walls are a major conductor of heat to the outside. Windows provide even less insulation than do walls. Since heat rises in every structure, a great deal of heat can escape through the roof. Finally, **infiltration** can occur. Infiltration happens when cold air from the outside gets into the building through the opening and closing of exterior doors, and from poor seals and cracks in the building's walls and windows. Infiltration can be thought of as hot air leaking out of the building (although it feels like cold air is leaking into the building).

HEATING SYSTEMS

When the building gets cold, we need to condition the air to provide the correct comfort level for our guests and employees. Heating systems for hospitality buildings can either be decentralized or centralized. These systems are often combined with the building's cooling system, which will be covered in the next chapter.

Electric heating is a form of decentralized heating, because the operation and control of the heating system is completely self-contained and does not interface with other building systems. One form of electric heating is the electric heat units that are sometimes mounted at floor level that look like baseboards. Another is the portable ceramic heating units, that operate when an electrical current is sent across a metal coil. The coil has a high resistance, which results in a great deal of heat being generated as the electricity tries to pass across the coil. The hot coil provides radiant heat into the space and should also result in a natural convection cycle in the room.

A common type of heating and air-conditioning unit is the **package terminal air-conditioning unit (PTAC)** that you will often see in smaller hotels (Figure 7.3a). These are also sometimes referred to as "through-the-wall" units, because they are mounted in the exterior wall of the guest room. Part of the PTAC is exposed to the outside elements. These units will combine both heating and air-conditioning into one single piece of equipment. The advantage to using PTACs is that they are relatively inexpensive to purchase, easy to replace, and easy to maintain. The property's engineering department does not need to operate large, complex equipment that might require special training and specialized personnel to operate it. When a room's PTAC has operating problems that require time-consuming or expensive repairs, the unit

FIGURE 7.3a Package Terminal Air Conditioning (PTAC) Unit. *Source*: Circus Circus.

FIGURE 7.3b Rooftop Package Unit. *Source:* Craft Construction.

can be removed and replaced with a new unit that the engineering department can keep in its inventory.

One other common type of electric heating is a **heat pump**. Heat pumps work like a typical window air-conditioning unit. However, in addition to providing cooling in warm weather, the mechanical cycle reverses in cool weather and can provide heat during the winter. Heat pumps work best in locations where winters are relatively mild or in a facility that is closed during the coldest months of the heating season. This topic will be covered in greater detail in Chapter 8–Air-Conditioning.

The advantages of electric heating systems are that they are relatively inexpensive and easy to purchase, install, and maintain. A company can purchase them in large volumes for a lower cost than purchasing them on an as-needed basis. However, the major disadvantage to this type of system is that electricity is expensive and electric heating is a very inefficient way to generate heat (as discussed in Electrical Systems). Electric heat is not desirable for most large hospitality operations. It may be feasible for:

1. smaller properties (200 rooms or less).
2. a property in a location where the winter weather is generally mild and the heating season is relatively short.
3. a property that experiences low occupancy during the heating season.
4. properties whose maintenance personnel have limited skills in heating and refrigeration maintenance skills.

While the disadvantages are substantial, PTACs are actually the most common type of HVAC system for hotel guest rooms in North America. The benefits of ease of maintenance and replacement often outweigh the disadvantages.

"Package Units"

A typical PTAC unit is usually adequate for a guest room, a small office, or a meeting room. Larger spaces require heating systems with a larger capacity than PTACs can provide. The type of system that is used for medium-sized spaces, such as larger meeting rooms, offices, and other public spaces, is called a **package unit** (Figure 7.3b). This type of heating and air-conditioning system is similar to a forced-air system that you will find in a home or apartment. The heating portion of a package unit is supplied with the hot water circulating through the building's heating system or with an electrical heating unit of its own. A fan blows air across the hot coils through a system of air ducts that supply the space with heat. The mechanics of the air supply system will be discussed in Chapter 9—Ventilation Systems.

A package unit will usually be housed in a mechanical closet close to the office or rooms that it heats. Separate pieces of equipment for the air-conditioning function are usually located on the roof or on the ground outside the building. The presence of the unit's own cooling source, rather than using a centralized chilled water system, is the distinguishing feature of a package unit.

CENTRALIZED SYSTEMS

Centralized heating systems provide heat through either hot water or steam that is heated in one location of the building—usually the engineering department or the "engine room." The hot water or steam is then circulated throughout the building through a piping system and delivered to the guest room via a baseboard heater, a fan coil unit, or a radiator. The methods of heating water were addressed in Chapter 5—Water Systems. You should review this process before continuing with this chapter.

Steam Heat

Converting water into steam for steam heating applications is similar to the system for heating hot water. The water is placed in a boiler, where heat is introduced via natural gas or electricity to heat the water beyond its boiling point. The steam that is generated circulates throughout the building through a series of pipes and provides heat in the room by heating a radiator. Radiators are not common in newer buildings, but older hotels, motels, and resorts that have not been completely modernized often still have a radiator system.

Radiators tend to be difficult to operate to provide good customer comfort because it is very hard to control the heat. The only way to regulate how much heat is in a room is by regulating the amount of steam that travels through the radiator with a steam valve. Older valves provide very little flexibility in steam control—the guest will often have the option of having the heat on or off, but not much in between. Newer valves provide better control but often must be adjusted manually, which may be frustrating for the guest if he or she needs to continually adjust the valve until the room temperature is just right. The valves also have a tendency to fail sooner than expected.

The outer radiator coils are the same temperature as the steam inside the pipe and can present a significant burn hazard for guests that accidentally touch the pipe.

Fan Coil Heating Systems

A more common type of centralized heating system is the fan coil system. A fan coil is a piece of equipment that has water, heated or cooled, circulating through a series of pipes (coils) (Figure 7.4). A fan blows air across the pipes to provide heating or cooling to the room. The water in the pipes is water that was heated or cooled in a central location and circulated throughout the building. Figure 7.4a shows a fan coil unit whose cover plate has been removed; the object in the top section is the fan. The middle section are the pipes that supply hot or cold water to the unit. Finally, the bottom of the photo shows the air filter, which removes dust from the air that is heated or cooled. Figure 7.4b shows the unit, minus its filter. We can see the coils through which the hot or cold water flows.

Air Handling Systems

The final type of centralized system that is used for large spaces, such as large meeting rooms, ballrooms, arenas, and other public or open spaces that require conditioned air, is called an **air handling system**. These systems work

FIGURE 7.4a Fan Coil Unit. *Source*: Dina Zemke.

FIGURE 7.4b Fan Coil Unit. *Source*: Dina Zemke.

using the building's hot water (or chilled water for the cooling season) to circulate through the building, with fans that blow air across the coils to provide the heat to the space. Figure 7.5 illustrates the flow of one of these systems. In the upper left-hand corner, you see a room with a man on an exercise bicycle (think of this as a Fitness Room in a hotel). The difference between an air

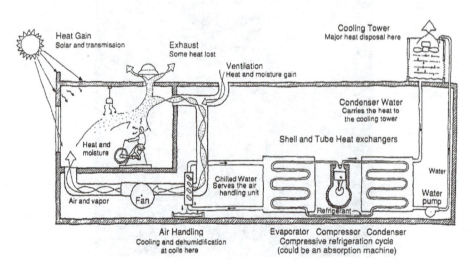

FIGURE 7.5 A Complete Air Handling Unit System. *Source*: Stein & Reynolds.

handling system and a package unit for a public space is the use of centrally provided heating or cooling water. For example, to heat a ballroom, a package unit would simply have an electric resistance heating coil and the fan would blow the air across the coil. In contrast, an air handling system will use a large bank of hot water coils placed downwind of the fan, which will blow air across the coils, through the ductwork and into the ballroom. Air will be sucked out of the ballroom by the fan through the return ductwork, and then blown across the hot water coils again, creating a cycle of supply and return air.

Air handling system equipment can be quite large. Many air handling units' water coils will be ten-feet high and several feet across. Your maintenance personnel can easily stand inside the air handling unit.

HEALTH AND SAFETY ISSUES

Steam and hot water generation provide some safety challenges for the property, due to the type of processes and equipment that are used. First, hot water and steam boilers use closed vessels to heat water or to make steam. One of the principle laws of thermodynamics states that as water heats up inside a vessel, the pressure inside the vessel will increase. Therefore, boilers operate at higher pressures than the normal atmosphere. If the water or steam is overheated, the pressure can increase enough to the point where the boiler will begin to leak or even explode. Heating systems require careful maintenance and monitoring to insure that a catastrophic failure does not occur.

One of the tools that heating systems employ to prevent boilers from operating at too high a pressure is a **pressure relief valve (PRV)** (Figure 7.6). The PRV looks like a trigger on top of the boiler. This valve is set to open up and release steam from the boiler if the pressure exceeds a certain level.

FIGURE 7.6   Pressure Relief Valve. *Source:* Dina Zemke.

Another safety measure that a property will use is to employ qualified employees to monitor, maintain, and operate the boiler. There are training programs available through state organizations that can train your employees for safe boiler operation.

Many jurisdictions require properties with boilers over a certain capacity—usually 15 psi or higher—to hold a Boiler Operator's License. This licensing is offered through most states and requires the employee to have a specified level of experience and to complete classroom instruction before taking the exam. Candidates for a position that requires a **boiler operator's license** may have to be paid a higher hourly wage than the rest of the engineering staff. General Managers of hotels need to keep costs down to return a profit on the property and may balk at hiring employees at a higher wage rate. The General Manager may need to be instructed on the reasons why a higher wage employee needs to be provided for the property. If you are the General Manager of a property and your Chief Engineer asks for funds to pay for training and licensing, take the request seriously, because inadequately trained and licensed staff can result in costly and deadly consequences for your guests and employees.

One of the byproducts of the boiler's heating process is carbon monoxide. Carbon monoxide is an odorless, colorless gas that is deadly to human beings. The system is vented to the outdoors. The boiler itself needs to be monitored for proper seals to keep the gasses out of the machine room and other interior spaces. One problem that occurs more often in residential homes, but can also occur on a commercial property, is where the vent gets covered with snow or debris, preventing the gas from venting properly. The gas then backs up into the boiler room, providing a dangerous environment for people in the area. Your property personnel, not only from the engineering department but any employee that is outside the building frequently, should always check the vent pipes to ensure that they are clear of obstructions.

Any area with a boiler, both in your business and in your home, should have **carbon monoxide detectors** installed to provide early warning in case of a leak. Carbon monoxide detectors are an inexpensive and easy way to avoid a potentially catastrophic event.

HEATING SYSTEM MAINTENANCE ISSUES

System chemical balance and cleanliness is an important issue for heating systems. Minerals and other chemicals in water precipitate as the water temperature increases. Acid levels and heat-tolerant (thermophylic) bacteria in the water corrode the pipes at an accelerated rate. A well-maintained heating hot water system or steam system requires additional chemicals to balance the pH and mineral content to extend the life of your boiler and heating system. Most commercial chemical suppliers that provide water-balancing chemicals will act in a consultative role to help the property manager determine the best mix of chemicals and maintenance measures to operate the system efficiently. This service is free to their contract customers.

Boilers wear out over time. The primary culprit is a mineral build-up on the tubes inside the boiler chamber. Two problems occur with the mineral build-up. First, the minerals form a coating, called "**scale**," that insulates the heating element from the water that needs to be heated. This forces the boiler to work harder to provide water at the correct temperature, resulting in wasted energy and money. The second problem is the corrosive effect that the minerals and other chemicals and bacteria in the water have on the tubes. The tubes begin to deteriorate and will eventually develop leaks that may shut the boiler down for emergency repairs to install new tubes in the boiler. Murphy's Law tells us that this tube failure will happen at the least convenient and most expensive time possible. A good preventive maintenance and replacement system will permit the facilities manager to save money and to schedule the work for a time that is least disruptive to the hotel and its guests.

OPTIONS FOR GUEST COMFORT

Public spaces, such as ballrooms and offices, are often monitored for temperature and air quality using a computerized system that provides communication between the space's thermostat and the heating equipment. The guests themselves cannot adjust the temperature or ventilation rate of the system. However, guests should have control inside the guestroom to maximize customer comfort and satisfaction. Guestroom heating and cooling systems either use a thermostat or control switches on the unit's operating panel that the guest can adjust to his or her liking.

One very common heating system problem occurs during a winter thaw in northern climates. The weather in the northern United States and Canada is very cold during the winter. However, it is not uncommon for the area to undergo a mid-winter thaw, where temperatures suddenly rise into the 50s or 60s. Hotels that have PTAC units in the guestroom usually do not get complaints, as the PTAC has both heating and cooling within the unit. However, hotels using a fan coil system for guestroom heating and cooling face a greater challenge. Let's look at the three types of piping systems that are found in hotels with fan coils (Figure 7.7).

Two-Pipe System

A two-pipe system uses two pipes: one to supply water to the fan coil unit and one to remove the water and return it to the boiler. These are called supply and return lines. During the heating season, a boiler provides the heating needed to generate hot water. When the cooling season arrives, the connections to the boiler are shut down and the water is routed through the chiller system to generate cold water. The changeover process may take several days. A sudden warm spell during the heating season may result in unhappy guests because it simply isn't possible to switch the system over to cooling quickly enough before temperatures drop again.

The two-pipe system is quite common because it is the least expensive to install, since there is less piping for the heating contractor to install. It's also efficient to operate because the building does not need to operate both heating and cooling equipment simultaneously. However, its major downside

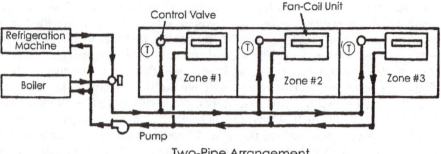

Two-Pipe Arrangement

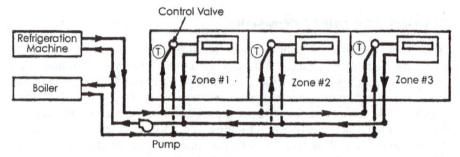

Three-Pipe Arrangement

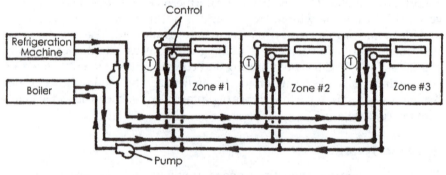

FIGURE 7.7 The 2-Pipe, 3-Pipe, and 4-Pipe Heating and Cooling Systems. *Source*: BOMI.

Four-Pipe Arrangement

is that it is the least responsive piping arrangement for customer preferences and satisfaction.

Three-Pipe System

A three-pipe system uses both a hot water supply and a cold water supply line. There is a single return line. This system is better for customer satisfaction because the customer can get heating or cooling whenever they want it. However, it is more expensive to install due to the increased piping requirement. It is much more expensive to operate, since the single return line mixes both hot and cold water. This return water needs more energy to heat it for heating and more energy to chill it down to the proper chilled water temperature. Three-pipe systems are relatively uncommon. If you manage a building with a three-pipe system and it is time to renovate the building, you should consider switching to either a two-pipe or a four-pipe system in order to improve energy efficiency and cost.

Four-Pipe System

The four-pipe system is ideal for customer comfort and energy efficiency. There are two supply lines, one each for cold water and hot water. There are also two return lines; the cold water supply uses the cold water return and the hot water supply uses the hot water return. This system has the most piping to install and is therefore the most expensive during construction. However, it offers excellent guest comfort control as well as better energy efficiency than the three-pipe arrangement.

ENERGY CONSERVATION FOR HEATING SYSTEMS

Heating systems are the major users of energy in hospitality buildings. Since the hospitality industry does not operate on huge financial margins, any decrease in energy consumption will provide profit directly to the business's bottom line. Conversely, any increase in energy prices or consumption will have a direct negative effect on the bottom line. Energy prices in recent years have increased rapidly and are projected to continue doing so. The smart hospitality manager finds ways to conserve energy and manage utility costs while continuing to provide the appropriate levels of service and comfort for his or her guests. In this section, energy conservation for heating systems will be approached from a maintenance/repair perspective, including some minor equipment upgrades, and then from a design and renovation perspective.

Maintenance/Repair

The following maintenance and repair measures are activities that will save energy and money without affecting guest service at all.

MAINTAINING HEATING EQUIPMENT   Dust accumulating on heating pipes and mineral scale deposits in boiler equipment prevent efficient heat transfer. Keeping equipment clean will permit the systems to work at their most efficient level and will keep energy costs down.

INSULATING DUCTWORK AND PIPES   Buildings with centralized heating systems should insulate the heating hot water pipes and the supply ductwork to help retain heat within the system and prevent it from escaping to areas that do not need to be heated, such as machine rooms or the ceilings through which the ductwork travels. Figure 7.8 shows supply and return water pipes for a centralized air handling system. In this particular example, the supply pipes are insulated but the return pipes are not.

FIGURE 7.8 Insulated Supply and Uninsulated Return Pipes. *Source:* UNLV.

WEATHERSTRIPPING Exterior doors are a major source of cold air infiltration into the building during the heating season. Weatherstripping consists of rubber or rubber foam strips that attach to the doorframe that create a tight seal when the door is in the closed position, preventing warm air from leaking outside. Larger doors, typically the main entrances to the building, will have a solid piece of metal with a rubber wiper on the bottom that slides into a channel at the bottom of the door. Your maintenance staff may be able to replace these or, for more complicated door designs, a professional service company may need to be hired to do this.

DOOR CLOSERS Exterior doors should have devices installed on them to automatically close the doors. The closers are either located in the upper corner of the door next to the top door hinge or are located embedded in the door sill near the bottom hinge. These closers will get out of adjustment over time and may fail to hold the door firmly against the door jamb or may fail to close the door at all. A loose door seal will permit warm air to escape outside. A good maintenance program will check the operation of the closers and adjust them accordingly.

SEALING THE BUILDING Every autumn, your engineering staff should inspect the exterior of the building and replace any caulk around windows or fill any cracks in the exterior finish. Small breaks in the seals around windows and in the exterior can provide an escape route for warm air in the winter, which wastes energy. These repairs will also close off an entry path for insects and other unwelcome pests.

WINDOW REPLACEMENT If your building has thermal pane windows, which use two pieces of glass with a space between them that is vacuum sealed, your staff should report any windows that are fogging up the space between the two pieces of glass. The vacuum seal acts as insulation and once it is broken, the window no longer provides a proper barrier to heat loss. The window will need to be repaired or replaced.

In addition, older windows may warp over time and will be unable to close completely or provide a tight seal against the elements. These windows should be considered for replacement as soon as it is financially feasible.

OVERHEAD FANS   Many hospitality properties have overhead ceiling fans in public areas with high ceilings. While most of us are familiar with using ceiling fans during the cooling season to provide a cooling air movement in the room, these fans are also useful during the heating season. Ceiling fans operate in two directions: one that pulls air up from the floor and one that draws air down from the ceiling, pushing it to the floor. Since warm air rises, winter operation of the ceiling fan will draw the warmer air from the ceiling level and force it downward to the floor level, reducing heat lingering in the upper part of the room.

SETBACK THERMOSTATS   Digital thermostats with programmable capabilities are relatively inexpensive and are easy to install. Replacing older, non-programmable thermostats with new, programmable ones will permit the property to automatically provide heat to areas when they are occupied and will reduce the need for heat when the areas are not occupied. Setback thermostats work best in areas where the occupancy is predictable and maintains relatively stable patterns, such as offices and small meeting rooms.

OCCUPANCY SENSORS   Occupancy sensors are mounted on the ceiling, usually in the middle of a room. An infrared beam is projected into the room. When the beam detects a movement in the room, or detects a heated object (such as a human being), the sensor signals the thermostat to raise the room temperature. If, after a preset length of time, the sensor does not detect the heat or the motion, it will turn the heating system off or to a temperature setback position. Occupancy sensors work well in most spaces, but particularly well in areas with occasional use where the people in the room do not remember to adjust the thermostat when they leave the room, such as meeting rooms with infrequent usage and storage areas.

Building Design and Renovation

The following issues are most appropriately addressed during the design phase for a new building or a major renovation. They will require capital expense budgeting and, for renovations, should be included in the CapEx planning at least five years in the future.

DESIGN FOR SOLAR EXPOSURE   If designing a new building or an addition to an existing building, you should ask your architect about providing the right orientation and exterior design and finishes to capitalize on the free heat that the sun provides. Done correctly, the sun could provide heat for the building during the heating season that will reduce energy costs significantly. This is a form of passive solar heating.

SOLAR HEATING SYSTEMS   Solar heating systems also use the sun to provide heat. Rather than just relying on the building itself to absorb solar heat, a property could also install a solar heating system. This type of system runs heating hot water (and/or domestic hot water) through black tubes that are located on the exterior of the building. The dark tubes absorb the sun and the solar heat transfers to the water. In some areas, this type of system may be able to provide all of the building's heating needs. At a minimum, the pre-heated water will require less energy in the boiler to heat it to the desired temperature for the heating system, and thus will save money. A note of caution: a hospitality manager that wishes to install a solar heating system will need to check local building construction and design codes to insure that this type of system is permitted in that jurisdiction. Some communities' Architectural Review Boards have determined that the rooftop equipment used in solar heating is not attractive and will not permit it to be installed.

RADIANT HEAT   Radiant heat works by running heating hot water tubes through a room's floor. The floor is usually concrete and the tubes are buried in the concrete. An attractive flooring finish can be installed on top of the concrete. Many people like this type of heat because it heats the entire room evenly, it is quiet, and there are no drafts due to convection. In addition, people usually feel warmer if their feet are warm. The radiant heat transfer also directly heats objects in the room, such as chairs. Floors are usually cold, since heat rises, so this type of system can operate at a lower supply temperature than other systems, and thus save money. However, since the tubes are buried in the concrete, maintenance issues could arise if a tube begins to leak or if one gets clogged.

Another form of radiant floor heating is electrical. An electric resistance mesh is installed below the floor finish in the wall. The heating mesh is controlled by a switch on the wall of the room where the mesh is located. This is an upscale design option for newer residential and hotel properties and is typically found in the bathroom. The amenity provides a nice, warm floor in the bathroom. We recommend that if you install electric radiant heat in the floors or walls of a room, you install the switch on a timer. Electric resistance heat is very inefficient and you do not want the system operating when it is not needed.

REVOLVING DOORS   Revolving doors are not just for crowd control! If a building entrance is expected to manage a high traffic volume, revolving doors are used to save energy. A revolving door loses less heat, on a per entry basis, than a traditional swing door. Maintenance and installing weather-stripping on these doors can be complicated. You may need to hire a service company to do annual winterizing of the doors, as well as for normal maintenance.

INTEGRATED PMS/FO SYSTEMS   If your property is considering an upgrade of the front office's property management system (PMS), many vendors now offer wireless communication with guestroom thermostats. These systems will turn a guestroom's temperature back to a setback temperature while the room is vacant. Once a guest checks into the room, the PMS will signal the guestroom thermostat to increase the room temperature. The guest will have full control of the thermostat while he or she occupies the room. Once the guest checks out, the PMS system returns the thermostat to the setback position. Many properties currently ask the housekeeping staff to manage the thermostat. An automated system removes some of the human error and guesswork.

KEYCARD SYSTEMS   A traveler to Europe these days is likely to check into a hotel where the electricity and heat to the guestroom is only activated while the guest is physically in the room. These systems require either the electronic room key card or a specially shaped key to be inserted into a device on the wall. As long as the key is in the slot, the power is on. This is highly effective in providing energy management. However, the hotel will often only provide one key. If two guests are staying in the room and one leaves for a while, the other guest will either sit in the dark or will have to wait for the first guest to come back. The hotel may balk at providing a second key because the guest may then leave the electricity on while he or she is not in the room! A good hospitality manager will work to balance the need for energy conservation against the need for guest satisfaction.

ENERGYSTAR® BUILDINGS AND LOCAL UTILITY HELP   The U.S. Department of Energy's EnergyStar® program (www.energystar.gov) provides guidelines and assistance for design and construction of energy-efficient buildings. Local utility companies also have programs and funding available for energy conservation upgrades. You should take advantage of these services to provide maximum energy efficiency while also providing maximum comfort and satisfaction for your guests and employees.

Summary

Heating systems involve the transfer of heat from a heat source to a space that needs to be heated. Other aspects of human comfort include humidity, air movement, and the cleanliness of the air. A common problem in hospitality properties is to find the right balance of temperature conditions to satisfy both guests and employees. For smaller spaces, such as guest rooms, the guest usually has some degree of control over their air-conditioning either via a PTAC or a fan coil unit. Larger spaces that find employees and guests sharing the space, but using it differently, can be more challenging to condition to suit everyone's needs.

In your career, you will usually work in an existing building, rather than be involved in selecting a type of system for new construction. This means that you need to be able to figure out what type of system you have, understand its strengths and weaknesses, and manage the system to provide the best possible comfort while conserving energy.

Key Terms and Concepts

air handling system 175

air-conditioning 166

boiler operator's license 178

breathing line 168

carbon monoxide detectors 178

convection 167

dew point 166

electric heating 172

evaporation 166

external heating loads 171

heat energy transfer 166

heat pump 173

heating load 000

infiltration 000

internal heating loads 171

latent heat 166

package terminal air-conditioning unit (PTAC) 172

package unit 174

pressure relief valve (PRV) 177

radiant heat 167

relative humidity 166

scale 179

sensible heat 165

thermostat 168

Discussion and Review Questions

1. If a four-pipe heating and cooling system provides much better guest control and comfort than a two-pipe system, why are two-pipe systems more common?
2. How does a radiant heat system work?
3. Describe the human comfort zone, including the range of temperatures and the range of relative humidity that are generally acceptable.
4. Discuss the measures that can be taken to save energy in an existing building's heating system.
5. How can energy conservation be designed into a new building?

8

Cooling Systems

CHAPTER OBJECTIVES

After reading this chapter, you should be able to:

- define the physics concepts behind the refrigeration process.
- identify cooling loads.
- discuss how the refrigeration cycle works.
- discuss decentralized cooling systems, including the pros and cons of each.
- discuss centralized cooling systems, including the pros and cons of each.
- describe the maintenance challenges behind refrigeration.
- describe energy conservation measures in cooling and refrigeration.

INTRODUCTION

In the not too distant past, warm weather was simply something to be endured. Warm indoor spaces were cooled by opening windows and hoping for a breeze to create enough air movement to have a cooling effect. Fans have also been used for millennia to cool spaces. Food was kept cool by either immersing it in a cool river or stream (in a sealed container) or by using ice. Ice was harvested from frozen lakes and rivers and stored in an "icehouse," where large blocks of ice were packed in sawdust to insulate them. Ice vendors sold ice to businesses and homeowners, who put the ice in an icebox, the precursor to today's refrigerator/freezer. However, this method was inconvenient and not too reliable.

As cities grew and population density increased, the concrete and brick used for buildings and for paving roads increased the amount of heat that was retained after sunset. Working conditions in the heat caused poor productivity. In addition, increasing amounts of mechanical equipment in factories and offices generated more heat. The need for a convenient, reliable system for cooling buildings became critical.

We can thank Willis Haviland Carrier for creating a viable cooling system for comfortable indoor spaces during hot weather. In 1902, Carrier developed a practical mechanical system for cooling rooms. Prior to Carrier's invention, mankind relied on simple evaporation created by fans for cooling. The same system led to the creation of refrigeration and freezing equipment for food storage.

Cooling is just like heating in many respects. Both systems involve moving air over a source that changes the temperature of the air. In heating, the air blows over a hot coil carrying either an electrical current, hot water, or steam. In cooling, the air blows over a pipe carrying cold water or a **refrigerant** gas. The types of equipments used in the lodging industry—window air conditioning units, fan coils, PTACs, heat pumps, package units, and air handling systems—were discussed in Chapter 7—Heating Systems. In this chapter, we will focus on how the refrigeration cycle works and how we apply it in lodging and food and beverage applications.

We will discuss a few general principles behind refrigeration and cooling. However, one important distinction needs to be made. Most people call systems that introduce cool air into an occupied space "air-conditioning" systems. This term is actually incorrect. When any characteristic of air is altered, it is considered to be "conditioned air," since the air is conditioned to provide human comfort or to fit some criterion for equipment operation. We will use the terms "cooled air" and "cooling system" in this chapter. Before we begin our exploration of the world of cooling systems, we will define several concepts so that we are prepared to discuss cooling systems.

DEFINITIONS

HEAT   Remember that heat always flows from a warmer object to a colder object, including warmer air flowing towards colder air. Heat's goal is always to equalize the space's temperature, including objects within the space, such as furniture, flooring, and walls. If a space is cooler than the surrounding environment, heat will transfer into the space to achieve an even temperature.

Let's review some of the concepts of heat that were presented in Chapter 7. First, the temperature that we read on a thermometer is a measure of sensible heat, or the heat that is detected by the thermometer. This temperature is referred to as the dry-bulb temperature. However, the dry-bulb temperature may not accurately reflect how we actually feel in a space. Humidity can change how we perceive the comfort of the space. We measure the latent heat of the space via the wet-bulb temperature to account for both sensible heat and humidity. Air's ability to hold water vapor depends on the dry-bulb temperature of the air. Warmer air is capable of holding more water vapor than cooler air. The amount of water vapor the air is currently holding, relative to its temperature, is called relative humidity.

COLD   There is no such thing as cold! Cold is merely the absence of heat. Cooling is a heat removal process. If a space is too warm, a colder substance is introduced to absorb the excess heat. This is a crucial aspect of cooling systems.

HUMAN COMFORT   We know that our perception of the temperature of a space varies based on the dry-bulb temperature, the relative humidity, and air movement in the space. We need to determine the acceptable parameters that will provide the most comfort in the most efficient way possible. **Psychrometrics** refers to the study of air and its qualities. Engineers use a **psychrometric chart** (also called a "psych chart") to determine how a space feels, air comfort-wise, under different combinations of temperature, relative humidity, and air movement. A building engineer will use a **psychrometer** to measure the relative humidity in the air.

BRITISH THERMAL UNIT (BTU)   One **BTU** is the amount of heat that must be added to one pound of water to raise the temperature one degree Fahrenheit. In refrigeration, it is the reverse: one BTU equals the amount of heat that must be removed from one pound of water to lower its temperature one degree Fahrenheit. Most small cooling systems and window air-conditioning units display their capacity in terms of the number of BTUs the system provides.

COOLING TON   A single BTU is a relatively small amount of energy. The cooling capacity of a large cooling system is usually expressed in terms of the "tons" of cooling generated. One cooling ton is equal to 12,000 BTUs.

CAPACITY   While room cooling systems are described by the amount of BTUs generated, refrigerator and freezer capacities are described in terms of the number of cubic feet of interior space that the unit offers.

EVAPORATION   Evaporation is the transformation of liquid into a vapor or gas. Evaporation is increased with air movement. Evaporation is also a stage in the refrigeration cycle that results in a cold substance that can cool air or water.

COOLING LOADS   The amount of heat that must be removed from a space is called a "cooling load." There are many heat sources that contribute to creating a cooling load, and may be internal or external sources.

External cooling load sources.   There are several ways that heat from the outdoors enters the building. For example, solar energy from the sun is absorbed through the building's walls, windows, and roof. The outside air temperature transfers through the building's exterior to equalize the temperature of the indoors and the outdoors. The building will also experience **infiltration**, which is where warm air from the outside seeps into the building through cracks and unsealed spaces around windows and doors, as well as air coming in through doors as they open and close.

Finally, all building codes require outside fresh air to be introduced into the air supply system to keep the air from becoming stagnant. This is called "outside air" or "mixing air." If the outside air is warm, we need to cool it to provide a comfortable environment for our guests and employees. We will discuss outside air in the next chapter, Ventilation Systems.

Internal cooling load sources.   There are many ways that cooling loads are generated inside a building. Humans, with a normal body temperature of 98.6°F, are usually warmer objects than the building's interior. Heat is transferred from human bodies to the air. Humans also add humidity to the air through breathing, talking, and perspiring. The humidity will affect the sensation of heat in the space. Lighting adds radiant heat to the space. Computers are an increasingly important source of internal cooling loads today as well.

Internal loads also sneak in from one area of the building to another through internal infiltration. For example, a kitchen is a warm, humid environment, while the dining room should be cooler and drier. Every time the kitchen doors open, warm, moist air from the kitchen infiltrates the dining room. In addition, the doors do not provide a tight seal for the entire door opening, and air infiltrates the dining room through these cracks as well.

A building's mechanical equipment is also a major source of internal heat loads. Motors and other equipment, such as boilers, electrical systems, the domestic hot water system, cooking, and candles add heat to the interior environment.

REFRIGERATION CYCLE

The next step in understanding how air cooling systems work is to explore the way that cold is generated to remove heat from the air in a space. This process is called the **vapor-compression refrigeration cycle**, which we will simply call the refrigeration cycle. This cycle is a "closed" cycle, because no part of it is exposed to the surrounding environment or mixes directly with air or water.

Refrigeration is possible because of **Boyle's Law**, which states:

At a constant temperature, the volume of a gas is inversely proportional to the pressure upon it.

What does this mean? Let's explore it step by step:

At a constant temperature . . . We know that objects expand as they get warmer and contract as they get cooler. This is true of liquids and gasses as well. The constant temperature indicates that any change in size or volume is due to factors other than temperature.

. . . the volume of a gas . . . The volume of a gas refers to the amount of space that it takes up. The actual amount of gas remains unchanged.

. . . is inversely proportional . . . Inversely proportional means that it moves in the opposite direction of something else.

. . . to the pressure upon it. Pressure refers to the amount of force imposed on the gas in terms of pounds per square inch (psi).

Let's rephrase Boyle's Law now.

If the temperature in the room stays the same, this gas will take up less space if there is high pressure present and more space if there is low pressure present (e.g., small space/high pressure and big space/low pressure). This is illustrated in Figure 8.1.

The refrigeration cycle uses Boyle's Law to first compress, then decompress gas in a closed cycle. Vapor-compression refrigeration systems use a refrigerant gas to facilitate heat transfer from one place to another. The cycle has four basic elements, as illustrated in Figure 8.2.

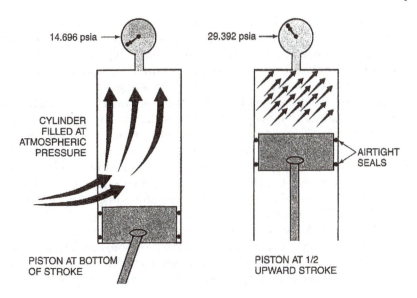

FIGURE 8.1 Boyle's Law. *Source*: Thomson Delmar.

1. *Compressor.* The refrigerant gas is **compressed** into a hot, high-pressure gas by a compressor. A compressor essentially crushes, or compresses, the gas from a large volume into a much smaller volume, which increases the pressure.
2. *Condenser.* After the gas is compressed, it travels to a condenser, where it is cooled. As the refrigerant cools, it condenses into a liquid state. The liquid is cooled by surrounding the pipe containing the refrigerant with cool

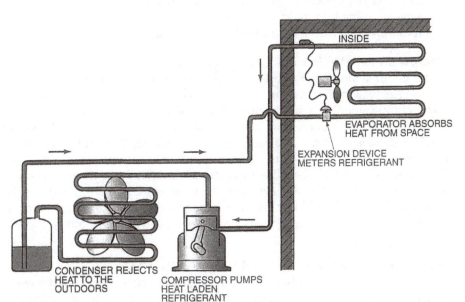

FIGURE 8.2
The Refrigeration System.
Source: Thomson Delmar.

water or air, which absorbs the heat from the refrigerant. We know that gases condense as they cool, similar to air at 100% relative humidity forming dew on grass. The refrigerant is now a warm, high-pressure liquid.

3. *Expansion valve.* The warm, high-pressure liquid passes through the pipe to an expansion valve (also called a metering device) that allows the refrigerant to enter a chamber called the evaporator at a controlled rate. The pressure on the evaporator-side of the expansion valve is much lower than on the condenser-side. The refrigerant expands in volume as it passes through the expansion valve, in accordance with Boyle's Law.

4. *Evaporator.* The refrigerant suddenly expands and returns to a gaseous state, e.g., it evaporates. This change in state, **from liquid to gas**, is possible because refrigerants boil at very low temperatures under the right pressure conditions. The refrigerant at this point becomes very cold and is now able to absorb heat. When warm air or warm water passes over the pipe containing the refrigerant, the cold gas in the pipe absorbs the heat in the water or air. The refrigerant gets warmer and returns to the compressor as a cold, low-pressure gas to be compressed again and repeat the cycle.

That's really all there is to refrigeration. The refrigeration process described above is virtually identical for all cooling applications, including building air-conditioning, refrigerators, and freezers. We will now turn to the varieties of cooling equipments that you will find in a typical hotel or restaurant.

DECENTRALIZED SYSTEMS

The three types of systems below are considered to be decentralized systems, because they are not part of a central heating and cooling system. They may also be called **DX systems**, which stands for "**Direct expansion.**" This is because the air going into the space comes into direct contact with the evaporator pipes through which the cold refrigerant gas passes.

WINDOW UNITS Window units are the type of air conditioners that we might install in our windows at home. In a hotel or restaurant, the unit may also have an electrical resistance coil that provides heat during the heating season. The cooling system in a window unit consists of the components listed above: a small compressor, a condenser (this is the part that hangs outside of the window), an expansion valve, and the evaporator, which is the part that is inside the window. As cold refrigerant passes through the expansion valve and into the evaporator, a small fan in the unit sucks air in from the room and blows it over the evaporator. The refrigerant in the evaporator coil absorbs the air's heat, and the cooled air blows back out into the room. Some units provide an option to either use inside air only or to permit the air from outside to be drawn into the room.

PTACs Package Terminal Air Conditioning units (PTACs) are similar to the window unit, but are usually installed through the wall instead of in the window (Figure 8.3). The PTAC is fitted into a sleeve which is a frame built into

FIGURE 8.3a Package Terminal Air Conditioning Unit (PTAC). *Source*: Dina Zemke.

FIGURE 8.3b PTAC in the Shop for Repairs. *Source*: Circus Circus.

the wall that is designed to hold the PTAC in place. The sleeve that goes through the wall is a permanent fixture, but the PTAC unit itself is easy to remove and replace.

PACKAGE UNITS Package units were discussed in Chapter 7—Heating Systems. For heating, a package unit might provide its own heat using an electric coil, or it may be integrated with a building's heating hot water system.

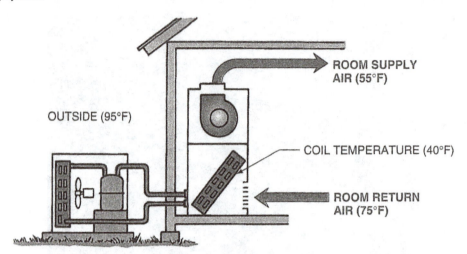

ROOM SUPPLY
AIR (55°F)

OUTSIDE (95°F)

COIL TEMPERATURE (40°F)

ROOM RETURN
AIR (75°F)

FIGURE 8.4 Split System. *Source:* Thomson Delmar.

However, the unit provides its own cooling system. If you will recall the discussion of package units in Chapter 7, you may remember that these systems are located inside the building, usually in a mechanical closet that is located not too far from the space that is being heated and cooled. All of the system's equipment, including the compressor, condenser, and evaporator, might be located in this one mechanical closet. However, some systems are **split systems**, where the evaporator is in the closet and the compressor and condenser are installed outside the building, as illustrated in Figure 8.4.

The air surrounding a condenser pipe absorbs heat from the refrigerant, and the surrounding air can get quite hot. If the cooling load is high enough, it will be undesirable to keep this hot equipment inside the building. Condensers are located outdoors to allow the heat from the refrigerant to transfer directly outside, resulting in a much more energy-efficient operation. Most central air conditioning systems inside homes are split systems; "central air-conditioning" is the residential term for a split system. You will find the condenser sitting on a concrete pad outside the house (Figure 8.5a) or on top of the roof (Figure 8.5b). In commercial applications, they are commonly used in offices and restaurants, as well as for public space and function space air-conditioning in hotels.

CENTRALIZED SYSTEMS: CHILLED WATER SYSTEMS

The next type of cooling system in a hospitality property will be found in larger buildings. It is called a chilled water system (CHW). These systems are only in large buildings because of the amount of piping that needs to be installed to carry the chilled water through the building as well as the large refrigeration plant.

Recall that the DX system operates by blowing air directly over the evaporator coils. This is an effective and efficient method for cooling smaller spaces. However, the equipment necessary to do this on a large-scale basis

FIGURE 8.5a   Rooftop
Split System.   *Source*:
Dina Zemke.

FIGURE 8.5b   Split
System with Compressor
and Condenser Next to
Building.   *Source*: UNLV.

would be unwieldy, expensive, and inefficient. A chilled water system uses a **chiller** to cool water to between 40°F and 45°F, using the refrigeration cycle. It essentially works by passing the chilled water over the evaporator coils; thus, the cool refrigerant absorbs heat in the chilled water (lowering the water's temperature). The chilled water is circulated throughout the building. Fans in public spaces and/or guest rooms blow air across an array of chilled water coils to send cool air to the space being cooled. Chilled water systems use the same basic principles of refrigeration as DX systems do, but use water to extract heat from the room and, in the condenser, from the refrigerant.

CHILLER The main refrigeration unit is called a chiller (Figure 8.6). The type of compressor used in a DX system is a reciprocating compressor, which has plungers that squish the refrigerant gas into a chamber. These moving parts are somewhat inefficient and may experience operational problems at high volumes, so the air-conditioning industry usually uses a centrifugal compressor in a chiller. A centrifugal compressor spins the gas in a small chamber that basically throws the gas to the end of the chamber, thereby compressing it.

After the hot refrigerant gas is compressed, it travels to the condenser. A large chiller system immerses the condenser coils into a tank of cool water, which removes the heat from the gas more efficiently at high volumes than air would. The water is called condenser water.

FIGURE 8.6a Chiller.
Source: Las Vegas Hilton.

FIGURE 8.6b Chiller.
Source: UNLV.

CONDENSER WATER AND COOLING TOWER The water that cools the condenser coils is called **condenser water**. This water now needs to release the heat that it picked up from the refrigerant. The condenser water travels to the **cooling tower**, which is located outside the building (Figure 8.7a). You will see cooling towers either on the roof or next to the building. In the summer, you may notice steam rising from the cooling tower. This is because the condenser water does not flow through a closed system. It pours from a pipe at

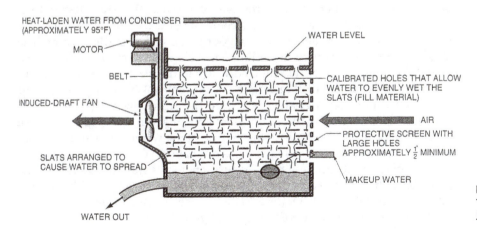

FIGURE 8.7a Cooling Tower—Section View.
Source: Thomson Delmar.

FIGURE 8.7b   Cooling Tower. *Source*: Dina Zemke.

the top of the cooling tower and drips down racks that are exposed to the outdoors (Figure 8.7b). The heat that is released from the condenser water is warm enough that part of it escapes as steam. The cooled condenser water collects in a pool and returns to cool the refrigerant in the condenser once again. Since the system loses water over time due to evaporation, an important piece of equipment in the cooling tower is a **float valve**. This is a valve that is closed unless the water level in the cooling tower gets too low. If it is too low, the valve opens and introduces **make-up water** to the tower, to make-up for the water lost to evaporation.

EVAPORATOR AND CHILLED WATER   The evaporator in a chilled water system also works slightly differently than the evaporator in a DX system. Rather than air blowing across the evaporator coils containing the cold refrigerant gas, the evaporator coils are immersed in a tank of water called **chilled water**. The chilled water travels through the building in a closed loop system (it is not exposed to the outdoors), providing cold water to the air handling equipment in large spaces or to fan coil units in the guest rooms. Warm air passing over the chilled water coils transfers heat into the chilled water (Figures 8.8a and 8.8b). Since the air also contains water vapor, the cold coils (Figure 8.9) will also reduce the air temperature to the point that the water vapor starts to condense on the outside of the coils and drips down into a drain pan. This process provides dehumidification, which, in turn, increases human comfort in the space. Once the chilled water has picked up heat from the air (although the water is not so chilly now), it returns to the evaporator tank to get cooled again, by releasing its heat into the cold refrigerant gas.

FIGURE 8.8a Chilled Water (CHW) Pipes. *Source:* UNLV.

FIGURE 8.8b Chilled Water Supply; Condenser Water Return Pipes. *Source:* UNLV.

MAINTENANCE ISSUES IN REFRIGERATION

Cooling systems use a great deal of electricity, primarily consumed by the compressor and the fan motors. Therefore, these systems should be well-maintained to prevent emergency breakdowns (these always happen at the

FIGURE 8.9 Chilled Water Coils. *Source*: Dina Zemke.

worst possible and most expensive time), wasted energy, and increased operating expenses.

REFRIGERANT LEAKS Refrigerant gas runs through a closed-loop system, meaning it is not exposed to air. However, the piping may develop a small hole or a piping connection may shake loose over time, creating an escape route for the gas. Losing refrigerant gas is bad for two reasons. First, losing gas will decrease the system's ability to transfer heat. This will result in the system working much harder than it usually does to create the desired temperature. This is highly inefficient and, more importantly, it wears the compressor out prematurely.

Refrigerant leaks may also cause environmental damage. In the past, an older family of refrigerant gasses was found to destroy the ozone layer in the earth's upper atmosphere. Most refrigeration and cooling systems have been retrofitted to use a newer class of refrigerant gasses that is not harmful to the ozone layer. However, these refrigerants are harmful to humans. OSHA and the EPA both require continuous monitoring and proper storage, handling, and disposal of refrigerants to protect both the environment and the people working around the refrigerants. Larger systems have sensors that will warn the operator if a leak is occurring. If you are working in a restaurant or a smaller hotel, you may have a refrigeration service contractor who will periodically inspect and maintain the equipment.

CLEANING Cleaning is very important in the efficient operation of cooling equipment. Coils that are covered in a layer of dust, dirt, or mineral build-up are, in essence, insulated. This insulating layer prevents proper heat transfer, so the system will have to work harder to achieve the desired results. In this instance, the compressor is working harder than it should, which leads to early failure and increased electricity costs.

Coils on all guest room heating and cooling equipment should be inspected and cleaned periodically. This should be part of a preventive maintenance routine and, preferably, a guest room maintenance program. The coils should be vacuumed and wiped free of any other debris. The coils in coolers and freezers in the kitchen should also be dusted regularly.

CHEMICAL TREATMENT Coils that are immersed in water, such as those for condenser water and chilled water in a chilled water system, also get dirty. Minerals present in the water, typically calcium and magnesium, can build up inside the water pipes, forming an interior insulating layer that prevents proper heat transfer and eventually blocks the pipe altogether. This layer of scale also provides a harborage for any microbes in the water, providing a docking point for them to multiply. The presence of undesirable minerals and organisms in the water is corrected by adding chemicals to the water to balance the mineral content and the pH level, and to kill any microbes. However, chemical levels need to be monitored regularly, usually once a week. Chemical vendors provide training and may also provide monitoring services to help maintain the proper chemical balance.

One area of particular concern for building managers is the condenser water and cooling tower. Recall that the condenser water travels to the top of the cooling tower and is then poured over a rack that is exposed to the outdoors. This water picks up many different kinds of pollution, such as pollen, algae, mold spores, bacteria, leaves, and twigs. In addition, birds, insects, and perhaps small animals can get into the cooling tower area, leaving "organic" matter behind. Also, the make-up water that is introduced into the cooling tower to compensate for water lost to evaporation comes directly from the water utility company. It has not yet been treated to correct any chemical/mineral imbalances.

The warm, wet environment of the cooling tower is a perfect environment for all sorts of problems. Microbes will thrive under these conditions and may be released into the atmosphere with the steam that is emitted by the warm water. Some bacteria that live in the condenser water produce a corrosive byproduct that can eat through the system's components, leading to leaks and other equipment damage. If wood is one of the structural components of the cooling tower or other parts of the building adjacent to the tower, mold and other fungal growth can eat away at the wood, destroying structural supports and rotting components of the system. Finally, many people have an allergic reaction to mold. If the cooling tower is too close to the building, your employees and guests may have a less than optimal reaction.

Until the late 1970s, cooling tower water treatment chemicals were fairly effective at controlling the mineral scale, pH, and microbe issues. However, these chemicals were found to be dangerous to human health and were removed from the market. Newer chemicals are safer but may not be as effective at keeping the system clean, or may loosen scale that has accumulated inside the pipes. This means that you or your chief engineer will need to ensure that

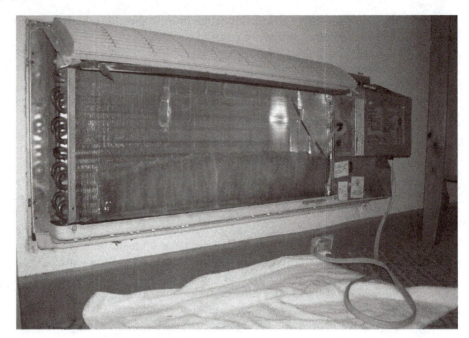

FIGURE 8.10
This PTAC was Too Cold and Water Vapor in the Air Formed Ice on the Coils. As the Ice Melts, the Water Fills the Drip Pan, Which is Overflowing.
Source: Dina Zemke.

the condenser water chemical levels are correct and the cooling tower is cleaned and monitored regularly.

DRIP PANS AND DRAIN LINES   In all cooling systems, the heat transfer from the air to the evaporator will result in water condensation from the humidity in the air. The condensate is collected in a pan under the evaporator coil and drains out through a drain line. A common problem is the drain lines get clogged with dirt or dust, causing the drip pan to fill (Figure 8.10). The water will turn stagnant and may be a good environment for mold or microbes to thrive. The pans could rust and develop leaks. The pans may also overflow. This usually results in damage to the ceiling and space below the machine room. You or your engineering staff need to inspect these systems regularly and clear the drain lines of debris to ensure proper drainage. Check the pans for any sign of mold or microbe growth (the pan will look slimy). Building managers place algae inhibitor tablets in the drip pan to prevent growth.

CAPITAL BUDGETING ISSUES FOR COOLING SYSTEMS

SIZING A COOLING SYSTEM   Many hospitality facilities have problems with the cooling system not creating the desired level of cooling. If a maintenance engineer examines the system and finds that everything is operating correctly, the problem may lie in the system not being big enough to provide enough cooling for the required space.

The process of determining how much cooling capacity a building needs is conducted long before the building is constructed. An HVAC consultant discusses the anticipated use of the building with the owner and architect and then determines the maximum amount of cooling load that the building should experience. The system is sized to accommodate this maximum load.

Over time, however, the use of the building may change. Space might be added to the property, exterior and interior finishes may change, and landscaping that provided shade from the sun might be removed, creating an increased solar load on the building. Most significantly, many older buildings that have not yet been renovated were not built to accommodate the abundant use of electronic equipment, such as computers, which generate a great deal of heat. The cooling system may have been perfectly adequate when it was installed, but may not be able to serve the current needs.

If you are planning new construction, it is crucial that you meet with your architect and any other operational consultants, to develop an accurate assessment of the building's occupancy, activities, and location of the activities. Try to anticipate any medium or long-term changes in usage. This may prevent problems in the future. If you are involved in a renovation, you may find that the HVAC system needs to be replaced. This will probably be very expensive. As in new construction, it is important to assess the actual building usage and anticipated future usage. It is not unusual for larger properties to begin planning for this in their capital expense budgets as far as ten years in advance.

RETROFITTING   If you are retaining your old HVAC equipment during a renovation, you may have to upgrade it to meet current code requirements. This may include retrofitting, or replacing some of the old equipment with new equipment, such as the compressor or other parts of the system. The compressor is designed to accept only one formulation of refrigerant. If the refrigerant needs to be replaced with a newer type, it may require replacing the entire compressor and other parts of the system. Meet with your HVAC consultant or your refrigeration contractor to determine what you are required to do and the best way to do it.

ENERGY CONSERVATION IN COOLING SYSTEMS

The greatest measure that a manager can take to improve energy conservation in cooling systems is to keep the system clean and well-maintained. However, there are other opportunities for energy savings.

CEILING FANS   We know that air blowing across our skin causes evaporative cooling, resulting in a cooling sensation. It is surprising how many people believe that turning on a fan actually lowers the air temperature! We can use this to our advantage by installing ceiling fans when appropriate. The fan should have two operational settings, one for winter mode and one for summer mode. When the fan works in the summer mode, the fan rotates to draw air upwards from the floor. The airflow will make the room seem cooler than it actually is. Some managers have found that using a fan can reduce the perception of the temperature by 5°F to 10°F. These fans use far less energy than the cooling system, since the main electrical load is from the compressor. The winter mode reverses the fan's rotation and draws warm air from the ceiling, pushing it to the floor. Fans require ceiling heights of at least ten feet to be fully effective and work best if there is at least three feet between the fan blades and the ceiling.

THERMOSTATS Programmable thermostats provide control over the HVAC system by ensuring that the system is operating when needed and is off when it is not needed, thereby saving energy. Programmable thermostats also provide **setback** capabilities, where the temperature is lowered (in the winter) or raised (in the summer) to save energy when the space is unoccupied.

PROPER SYSTEM BALANCING Package and central heating/cooling systems use ductwork to move conditioned air through the building. The process used to ensure that the right amount of air flow occurs throughout the space is called "balancing." An improperly balanced system wastes energy and creates discomfort and frustration for the room's occupants. Balancing is covered in greater detail in the next chapter.

LIGHTING Incandescent lamps, particularly halogen lamps, generate a great deal of heat. Fluorescent lighting produces much less heat than incandescent does. Replacing incandescent lamps with fluorescent (where appropriate for aesthetic purposes) will save not only electricity in lighting but will also reduce energy usage by removing a large internal cooling load. You might argue that lamps providing heat would be helpful in the winter. However, the benefits of the heat generated in the winter will be far outweighed by the increased cooling load in the summer, because it is generally more expensive to provide cooling than it is to provide heat.

Summary

Cooling systems permit us to work in comfort during hot, humid weather. They also allow us to preserve food products via refrigerators and freezers. Cooling works by transferring heat out of a space and into a refrigerant chemical. The heat is then removed from the refrigerant and eventually ends up outdoors. Most of the cooling systems that you will encounter will probably involve this vapor-compression cycle, although you may work in a building that uses an absorption chiller. (We did not cover these in this text, because they are not common in most hospitality properties.)

Running a cooling system requires us to operate a compressor. Since compressors run on electricity, a cooling system will be one of the major consumers of electrical energy in your building. As stated throughout this text, it is crucial that we provide cooling that is adequate and not excessive, to help us control our electrical costs, both in consumption and in demand. You will need to understand the type of system that your workplace has so that you can do this effectively.

Centralized cooling systems use a cooling tower to expel the heat from the building. We need to maintain the tower properly, to save energy as well as to reduce the risk of pathogens being sent into the surrounding air via water vapor evaporating out of the tower. These pathogens, such as b. Legionella, can be sucked into a building, exposing occupants to potentially deadly health risks.

Key Terms and Concepts

Boyle's Law *190*
British Thermal Unit
    (BTU) *189*
capacity *189*
chilled water *194*
chiller *196*
cold *188*
compressor *191*
condenser *191*
condenser water *196*
cooling loads *189*

cooling ton *189*
cooling tower *197*
direct expansion (DX)
    systems *192*
evaporation *188*
evaporator *192*
expansion valve (or
    metering device) *192*
external cooling load
    sources *189*
float valve *198*

human comfort *188*
infiltration *189*
internal cooling load
    sources *189*
make-up water *198*
Package Terminal
    Air Conditioning
    units (PTACs) *192*
package units *193*
psychrometer *189*

psychrometric
    chart *189*
psychrometrics *189*
refrigerant *188*
setback *204*
split systems *194*
vapor-compression
    refrigeration
    cycle *190*
window units *192*

Discussion and Review Questions

1. Carefully describe the refrigeration cycle. Identify the heat transfer process at each step of the way.
2. How can ceiling fans reduce your electric bill in the summer months?
3. If PTACs are not as energy-efficient as other types of heating and cooling systems, why are they the most popular type of HVAC system in North American hotels? Describe five advantages of PTACs in detail.
4. Package units in commercial buildings are also known as split systems. What makes them "split"?

Notes

American Society of Heating, Refrigeration and Air Conditioning Engineers www.ashrae.org
Carrier Corporation www.carrier.com
Trane Corporation www.trane.com

Whitman, W. C., Johnson, W. M., & Tomczyk, J. A. (2000). Refrigeration and air-conditioning technology: Concepts, procedures, and troubleshooting techniques (4th ed.). Albany, NY: Delmar Thomson Learning.

9

Ventilation Systems

CHAPTER OBJECTIVES

After reading this chapter, you should be able to:

- describe the basic components of the ventilation system.
- describe how we can realize energy savings through efficient ventilation operation.
- describe indoor air quality and its importance in the hospitality industry today.
- describe maintenance issues in the ventilation system.
- describe common problems that arise from poor ventilation.
- describe Legionnaires' Disease, where it comes from, and how we can prevent exposure to it.

INTRODUCTION

In the previous two chapters, we examined the various methods of heating and cooling buildings, focusing on the actual heating and cooling systems. Once we have established a system for heating and cooling, we must distribute our conditioned air throughout the targeted space using a ventilation system. Ventilation systems also address many issues related to air quality.

VENTILATION CONCEPTS

Ventilation may be defined as supplying air that does not have any noticeable odors or pollutants to a space in a building. We can ventilate a building either naturally or mechanically. A natural method of ventilation is opening windows and doors or opening a vent grille that permits air from the outdoors to come into the building. This method of ventilation is adequate for many homes but is usually inadequate for commercial hospitality properties. This chapter will focus on the mechanical methods of ventilation where mechanical equipment is used to supply and remove air from a space.

Ventilation does not simply refer to air movement. We must also consider the air speed, humidity, pollutants, and odors. The broad definition of these issues is called **indoor air quality (IAQ)** and is a very important subject in hospitality facilities management today. Many people have allergies or respiratory illnesses that are either triggered or exacerbated by poor air quality. Hospitality customers demand good air quality as part of our total service offerings and many customers will take their business to our competitors if the air quality in our establishment is not good.

Relative humidity has a significant impact on human comfort. The recommended range for an indoor space is 40–60% relative humidity. Remember, water travels to where there is none in order to achieve equilibrium. The human body is composed of 70% water, while the air's relative humidity is usually not that high. Relative humidity above 60% will cause the air to feel sticky and uncomfortable, due to the reduced ability of the human body to evaporate perspiration. Relative humidity below 40% will cause rapid evaporation of perspiration and will result in the occupants of the space feeling cool and perhaps getting thirsty or dehydrated, since their body's water content is trying to achieve equilibrium with the air in the room.

Humidity can also work in our favor. A property that is located in a hot, dry area can supply air at higher temperatures than a property in a hot, humid location can, since the dry air feels cooler than it actually is. This provides energy savings during the cooling season, since the dry-bulb temperature does not have to be as low.

AIR SPEED   Ventilation systems use fans to push air into a room and then remove it. The speed of the airflow will affect human comfort. If the air speed is too slow, it will cause the air to feel stagnant and the room to feel stuffy. If the relative humidity is high and the air speed is slow, not only will the occupants feel uncomfortable, but also the furniture and the other objects in the space will feel sticky and paper will be limp. Increasing the air velocity will help people in the space to feel cooler, because the air movement will increase the evaporation of moisture from the skin. Conversely, air speeds that are too high will cause people in the room to feel cold and may even blow paper and other objects around the room.

POLLUTANTS AND ODORS   Air contains a variety of solids, microbes, and gasses that must be removed to provide truly good indoor air quality. Common solids found in the air include dust, dirt, dust mites, and smoke particles from cigarettes or fireplaces. Microbes in the air often include bacteria, viruses, and mold and mildew spores.

Examples of gasses include fumes from pesticides and cleaning chemicals, perfumes and scents from personal care products, air fresheners, and painting products. One gas that is common but not usually associated with ventilation systems is radon, a naturally occurring gas that is often found in basements and ground levels of buildings. Some of the gasses that are currently in the public eye include paint fumes, dry-cleaned clothing, and gasses

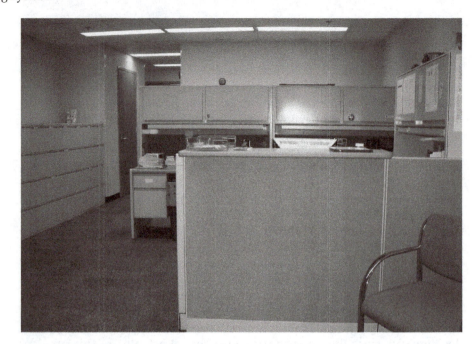

FIGURE 9.1 Office Finishes, such as Carpet, Cubicle Walls, and Furniture Can Off-Gas. *Source*: Dina Zemke.

emitted in cigar or cigarette smoke. Synthetic carpeting and upholstery fabric emit gasses that some people are sensitive to through a process called **outgassing** or **off-gassing**. New or renovated buildings frequently use construction products or furniture made of pressed wood. Pressed wood is manufactured using glue to hold the wood particles together (Figure 9.1). This glue usually contains formaldehyde, which also off-gasses into the building's interior and can cause sensitivity or allergic reactions for the building's occupants.

VENTILATION SYSTEMS AND EQUIPMENT

The primary components of a ventilation system are fans, ducts, grilles and diffusers, filters, and humidifiers.

FANS   These mechanical pieces of equipment push the air through the system. There are two general categories of fans in a ventilation system. The first is a supply fan, which pushes air through the duct system and into the space being ventilated. The second type of fan is an exhaust fan, which pulls air out of a space and expels it to the outdoors.

DUCTS   Ducts, or **plenums**, are the metal channels through which air travels. They may be made of metal or fiberglass and are installed in the ceiling, the walls, or through the floor of a building. **Supply ducts** supply air to the space, while **return ducts** remove air from the space and return it to the heating/cooling coils, where it is conditioned and sent to the supply ducts.

Ducts may be round or rectangular. Round ducts have the advantage of quieter operation than rectangular ducts. A piece equipment called a **damper** is installed inside the ducts. Dampers are slats of metal that operate like mini-blind window coverings. If the dampers are in the closed position, the airflow in the duct is completely blocked. If the dampers are in the open position, the airflow is unimpeded. Older damper systems required the damper position to be set manually. Today's dampers use small motors to open the dampers to any position between fully open and fully closed to regulate the airflow through the ductwork.

GRILLES AND DIFFUSERS   Grilles and diffusers are the covers installed at the room-end of a piece of duct. **Grilles** are perforated coverings, like screens, that may be used on both the supply and return ducts. **Diffusers** are used only on the supply ducts. They use a set of louvers and directional slats to disperse the incoming air evenly throughout the space. This provides airflow that is even, less breezy, and quieter than a grille could provide (Figures 9.2a and 9.2b).

FILTERS   Filters are usually installed in the supply duct just past the fan so that the air travels through the filter before continuing onward toward the space. Filters are used to remove pollutants or odors in the air so that the air supply is fresh and clean (Figure 9.3). There are three types of filters: mechanical, electronic, and ion-generators.

Mechanical filters are made of either paper media or a reusable, washable steel grid that is designed to trap particles in the air, such as dust, hair, or smoke particles. Household air-conditioning and forced air heating systems

FIGURE 9.2a   Grille—for Supply or Return Air.   *Source*: Dina Zemke.

FIGURE 9.2b Diffuser—for Supply Air Only. *Source*: Dina Zemke.

usually use a paper filter. Paper filters are disposable and must be changed regularly (usually every three months) to retain their effectiveness, as the paper fabric tends to clog up with dirt and dust over time. Paper filters would be an expensive option for a typical hospitality facility, which will need to move larger volumes of air that is usually dirtier than the air in a house.

FIGURE 9.3 A Filter Bank in an Air Handling Unit. *Source*: UNLV.

Larger ventilation systems use washable steel grids due to their durability and cost-effectiveness.

Mechanical and paper filters only trap particles that are floating in the air. Another type of filter, the **activated charcoal filter**, is used to trap odors and gasses in the air. Activated charcoal filters remove gas and odors through a process called adsorption. *Absorption* refers to the process of one substance absorbing another, as a sponge absorbs water. *Adsorption* refers to a process where one substance sticks to another substance, forming a thin film or coating over the second substance. Activated charcoal filters provide a surface that attracts odors and other gasses and then causes the gas to stick to the charcoal surface. A typical restaurant using an activated charcoal filter as part of the ventilation system traps cooking odors, cleaning chemicals, and cigarette smoke in the filter.

You may have heard the term **HEPA filter** before. High Efficiency Particulate Arrestor (HEPA) filters are used to provide the best level of particle filtration possible. Normal mechanical filters will trap airborne particles that range from 20 to 30 microns in diameter. These are very small, because there are 25,400 microns to an inch. However, many particles and microbes are smaller than 20 microns. A HEPA filter uses special materials to capture particles that are as small as 0.3 microns. HEPA filters are often used in homes or guestrooms where the occupant suffers from severe allergies or respiratory illnesses. For example, the Las Vegas valley has a recurring problem with PM-10, which is fine particulate matter that is ten microns or less in diameter. PM-10 is generated by construction activity.

Electronic air cleaners use an electrostatic process to capture particles in the air. The cleaner contains one set of metal plates with a positive electrical charge and another set with a negative electrical charge. As particles pass through the filter, the particles are charged with the positive electric charge. The positively charged particles are attracted to the negatively charged plates, causing them to stick to the negative plate. Most properties will use an electronic air filtration system in combination with an activated charcoal filter to adsorb gasses and odors.

Ion-generating filters work by generating ions that cause the air particles to have an electric charge. The electric charge makes the particle sticky, but instead of adhering to the filter system, the particles stick to objects in the room, such as walls, draperies, and furniture. Heavier particles fall to the floor and can then be removed by vacuuming the room. While these were popular for a while, research is now finding that filtration systems that generate ions, or ozone, are actually harmful to people with respiratory diseases. Caution is advised before installing one of these systems.

HUMIDIFIERS   Humidifiers are used to increase the amount of moisture in the air. These are useful not only for properties in dry climates, but also for most buildings during the heating season. Heating air reduces the overall relative humidity and can provide air that has too little moisture for human comfort. People in the building may experience dry eyes or nasal passages, making them susceptible to illness.

The most common type of humidifier is a stationary **evaporative humidifier**. A screen is placed in the supply ductwork after the filter. Cleaned air is blown across the filter screen, which has water trickling down it. The air picks up moisture as it passes through the humidifying screen and continues its trip to the room.

Commercial **atomizing humidification systems** work by spraying a fine mist of water into the air after it passes through the filter. An atomizing humidifier is not appropriate for every application. The water used in an atomizer system needs to have a very low mineral content. If the water is "hard," or has a high mineral content, the water tubes and the misting nozzle will clog with mineral build-up. In addition, the atomizer should always be shut off when the air handling equipment is off, to prevent excessive water collecting and becoming a harborage for mold, mildew, bacteria, and virus growth.

High humidity levels are as bad as low humidity levels. Some systems use a desiccant compound, which is a substance that absorbs water. However, most systems use chilled water or a DX coil to cool the air below its dew point so that the moisture condenses into drain pans, leaving the air dry. Operating a cooling system during the cooling season achieves this automatically. If the cooling system is not operating, some HVAC systems use a supplemental cold water line to extract water from the air.

HOW MUCH VENTILATION DO WE NEED?

The amount of ventilation that a system can provide is measured in **cubic feet per minute (cfm)**. This refers to the number of cubic feet that the system can supply to the room during peak operation. A professional heating, air-conditioning, and ventilation consultant needs to know the size of the space and its use to ensure the correct quantity of air movement. The starting point in calculating the amount is to check with the American Society of Heating, Refrigeration, and Air-Conditioning Engineers (ASHRAE), which publishes guidelines for various types of building uses, such as restaurants, bars, and other hospitality buildings.

The local government will also provide minimum requirements for a certain number of **air changes per hour**. Air changes per hour means the number of times that the room's volume of air is exchanged in a one-hour period. Typical air change numbers run from five to twenty per hour, depending on the type of activity that will occur in the room. Some jurisdictions' codes may specify air exchange based on the square footage or the number of occupants expected in the space.

A system should be sized for the maximum amount of load that is expected in the space. However, the system will not need to operate at full capacity all of the time. A common way of managing this is through a variable air volume (VAV) system. This control system adjusts the duct's dampers based on the amount of ventilation needed at a given moment. The controllers monitor the room's environment using a series of sensors located in both the supply and return ducts. When the sensors detect that the room is outside the desired conditions, it signals the damper motors to open or close as needed.

Older ventilation systems use the fan motor operating either at full speed or completely turned off. However, newer technology has alleviated this issue. A newer VAV system does not adjust dampers but instead adjusts the fan's speed. This is accomplished using variable voltage with variable frequency (VVVF) drive motors that can operate at almost any speed between the off position and the full speed position. A system using VVVF motors will save electrical costs by both reducing overall electrical consumption as well as the peak demand. They also offer better temperature and humidity control, and may result in less overall system maintenance by decreasing the need for damper motors.

"OFFICE WARS": SYSTEM BALANCING

Almost every office that uses more than one air supply duct experiences uneven comfort control. This leads the workers who are hot to turn the temperature down on the thermostat. This action results in the employees in the cold areas getting colder, and they turn the temperature up. A comical, but common, scenario has employees sneaking around each other's backs to control the thermostat. Sometimes shouting ensues, leading to "office wars."

Balancing is a process that corrects the amount of airflow to spaces in the HVAC system. A badly balanced system will result in noisy, drafty, uncomfortable spaces. Some areas in the system will be too hot, while others will be too cold. This is what leads to office wars. When the ventilation system is installed, a professional HVAC engineer balances the system so that the airflow is strong enough at the end of the duct but not overpoweringly strong near the fan. However, as furniture locations change and personnel change, this balance of airflow might not be appropriate. In addition, the systems themselves lose calibration over time. If a space in your hospitality property experiences numerous complaints about unsatisfactory heating or cooling, it is probably time to bring in a HVAC balancing expert to adjust the system. This is common in restaurant dining rooms and back-of-the-house offices.

Another method used to address this complaint is installing a zoned system. A zoned system will have two or more spaces connected to the main duct system. Smaller ducts will branch off the main duct to heat individual areas. Each area has its own thermostat, permitting the occupants in that area to control their own HVAC. The thermostat will signal a fan that services only that particular section to provide either heated or cooled air. While this offers good comfort control and satisfaction, it is more expensive to install and operate than one of the simpler systems.

BATHROOM VENTILATION

Bathroom ventilation is important to prevent retaining too much humidity over time. An overly humid environment will result in mold growth and damaged finishes, such as peeling wallpaper. Commercial buildings, particularly larger hotels, have dedicated ventilation systems that remove odors and humidity from their public restrooms and bathrooms. An airshaft runs up through the building alongside each stack of bathrooms. An exhaust fan at the top of the shaft draws air out of the bathrooms and vents it out at the top of the building. The air in the bathroom is freshened with air that is in the guestroom or from the corridor via the space under the bottom edge of the guestroom door. This also helps to circulate air through the interior of the building, providing fresh air throughout the facility.

VENTILATION SYSTEM MAINTENANCE AND OPERATION

The following points are important in the safe and efficient operation of a ventilation system:

MOTORS   Your ventilation system's motors need a scheduled maintenance program to ensure efficient and reliable operation.

DUCT CLEANING   Ducts will accumulate dust, dust mites, and dirt over time. Poorly maintained systems may have rodents or insects nesting in the ductwork. Standing water in the ductwork can lead to bacteria and other microbe growth. All of these problems can cause bad odors, health problems, and reduced system efficiency. Ducts have access panels, which permit periodic inspection for problem conditions. If problems are found, the facility manager must have the ducts cleaned. On-site personnel may not be qualified to do this work and an outside contractor should be brought in to do it. This may also provide an opportunity to rebalance the system.

DRAIN PANS   Water in the air condenses as it passes over cooling coils, collecting in a drain pan below the coils. Drain pans are notorious for their drain lines becoming clogged with dirt, microbes, or algae that grow in the water. If the drain line is clogged, not only do more organisms and dirt accumulate, but the pan may overflow and cause a surprising amount of water damage to the space below the mechanical room. Microbes mold, or mildew may grow there. Airflow will carry these organisms to the area being supplied and cause health and comfort problems for the people in the space. Equipment can also corrode, due to exposure to the stagnant water and other substances.

A good preventive maintenance program will include weekly inspections of the drain pans to ensure that the lines are not clogged during the cooling season. Drain pans in a system with a humidifier will also need to be inspected frequently, particularly since the air temperature during the heating season will provide a warm, comfortable environment for microbe growth. Microbe and algae growth can be prevented by using an anti-microbial product in the drain pan. These products are shaped like large lozenges and are placed directly in the pan. They slowly release a chemical that kills those organisms.

INSULATION   Ducts, particularly air supply ducts, should be insulated to prevent heat from escaping through the ductwork. Traditional fiberglass blanket insulation may be used, although the installers should wear safety glasses and gloves while handling the fiberglass, which can embed fibers in the skin and thus cause irritation.

FRESH AIR SUPPLY Every building requires the addition of fresh outdoor air to the conditioned air inside the building. The purpose of this is to help exhaust dust, microbes, and gasses. Many buildings can achieve this by opening guest room windows. Installing a window air conditioner, a heat pump, or a PTAC unit will provide a path for fresh air to enter. Fresh air enters guest rooms through the space under the door to the corridor. Smaller restaurants may have enough fresh air entering through the exterior doors opening and closing (Figures 9.4a and 9.4b).

Local codes dictate how much fresh air needs to be provided. This fresh air, called **outside air**, must make up anywhere between 10% and 30% of the system's total air volume. If the passive air exchange is not adequate, then mechanical systems need to be put in place. This is most common with a larger package unit or central chilled-water air handling unit system.

It seems inefficient to exhaust perfectly good pretreated air and bring in new untreated air from the outdoors, which needs to be heated or cooled and humidified or dehumidified. However, introducing outside air into the system keeps the building's air from becoming contaminated and stagnant.

Outside air is supplied by two vent panels that are located in the return duct system. The first vent removes part of the return air and exhausts it to the outdoors. The second vent, which should be located some distance away from the exhaust vent, brings in fresh air from outdoors and introduces it into the system.

FIGURE 9.4a Dampers for Outside Air Intake. *Source*: UNLV.

FIGURE 9.4b Dampers for Outside Air Intake. *Source*: Dina Zemke.

LEGIONNAIRES' DISEASE

The intake duct should also be located far from the cooling tower, if the property has one. The cooling tower can be a breeding place for all sorts of microbes and flora. One notorious case occurred in 1976, when an American Legion convention was held at the Bellevue-Stratford Hotel in Philadelphia. A few days after the convention ended, 221 of the attendees became seriously ill with a pneumonia-like infection. Thirty-four of the victims died. The culprit was eventually found to be the hotel's cooling tower.

Cooling towers remove heat from water in the central chiller system by running the water over a frame that is outdoors. Some of the heat that is released contains water vapor and is exposed to the outdoor elements. The warm, wet conditions provide a good breeding ground for mold, mildew, and germs. The water vapor from the Bellevue-Stratford's cooling tower was sucked into the air handling system. Unfortunately, the water in the cooling tower was contaminated with the bacterium that caused the illness. Legionnaires inhaled the infected air and became ill. It took two years for researchers to discover the bacterium and its source. The causative bacterium was named *Legionella pneumophilia*.

The risk of Legionnaires' Disease, as it is known, is still present. Chemicals developed after the first outbreak of the disease controlled organism growth in cooling towers (Figure 9.5). However, these chemicals were eventually found to be hazardous and were banned.

FIGURE 9.5 Cooling Tower. *Source*: UNLV.

Today's chemicals are safer overall, but not as effective in preventing microbe and flora growth in cooling towers, so the threat of Legionella still exists. Cooling tower chemical levels need close monitoring, and a sensible design of new buildings should avoid air intake that could include harmful substances.

Summary

Ventilation and indoor air quality are very hot issues in the hospitality industry. As more state and local governments consider banning smoking in public spaces, many restaurants, bars, and casinos have raised concerns about the effects that a smoking ban will have on their business. However, one study found that the air inside a typical hospitality venue was more polluted than the air that turnpike toll collectors breathe.[1] In this study, the air in the bars, restaurants, and a casino contained substances that some people believe cause cancer and respiratory problems. There is great debate about the effects of second-hand smoke on health. Regardless of whether or not you support smoking in restaurants and other public spaces, good hospitality managers need to find the right balance between providing a desirable environment for their customers and providing a safe, healthy, and desirable environment for their employees.

The general standards that influence the local and state codes are developed by ASHRAE under Standard 62. Representatives of ASHRAE and various hospitality organizations are working together to write an addendum to Standard 62 that will pertain to the unique needs of the hospitality industry. Ideally, the addendum will offer methods of implementation that will permit businesses to continue to allow smoking while supplying filtration methods to provide a clean, safe environment for employees and patrons.

Key Terms and Concepts

activated charcoal
filter *211*

air changes per
hour *212*

atomizing humidifica-
tion systems *212*

balancing *213*

cubic feet per minute
(cfm) *212*

damper *209*

diffusers *209*

electronic air
cleaners *211*

evaporative
humidifier *212*

grilles *209*

HEPA filter *211*

indoor air quality *207*

Legionnaires'
Disease *216*

mechanical filters *209*

off-gassing *208*

out-gassing *208*

outside air *215*

plenums *208*

relative humidity *207*

return ducts *208*

supply ducts *208*

variable air volume
(VAV) *212*

ventilation *206*

Discussion and Review Questions

1. You are the general manager of a hotel. The Marketing and Sales departments are located in a suite containing several individual offices and some open, shared space. The employees are constantly adjusting the thermostat up and down, because some of them are too cold and some are too hot. What is the likely cause of this problem? How would you solve it?

2. Why is it important to provide good filtration?

3. How can we adjust our ventilation systems to save money during the cooling season?

4. What would be the consequences of providing too much air flow in a space?

5. What is Legionnaires' Disease? Where can we find it? How can we prevent it?

6. Local codes require buildings to eject perfectly good, conditioned air and replace it with unconditioned air from outdoors. Is this efficient? Why do we have to do this?

Notes

www.eurekalert.org/pub_releases/2004-09/mba-vib090804.php

1. The American Society of Heating, Refrigeration, and Air Conditioning Engineers. Available at www.ashrae.org

2. The Indoor Air Quality Association, Inc. Available at http://www.iaqa.org/

10

Life Safety and Security

CHAPTER OBJECTIVES

After studying the chapter, the student should be able to:

- identify the reasons why there has been a significant decrease in the number and severity of hotel fires in the United States over the past two decades.

- list the components of the Fire Tetrahedron, the byproducts of combustion, and the five classifications of fires.

- describe the role of the National Fire Protection Association.

- identify and describe the major United States hotel fires in the 20th and 21st centuries.

- chronicle the history of the 1990 Hotel and Motel Fire Safety Act.

- list at least six elements of an emergency response plan, who should serve on the safety committee, and sources of information and assistance for developing an emergency response (or action) plan.

- list and describe the various types of fire, each fire's alphabetical symbol and the suppression agents used on each type of fire.

- describe the various types of fire suppression equipment, fire control equipment, and fire detection and notification equipment that may be found in a hospitality facility including installed and portable equipment.

- describe the three types of accident prevention programs.

- describe the impact of slips and falls on properties.

- list common guestroom security equipment.

- list the various security systems maintained by the engineering department.

INTRODUCTION

Guests trust us to keep them safe and secure during their stay. Since Medieval times, the inn's first duty was to protect the wayfarer from harm. A traveler who did not make it to the inn by nightfall was said to be "benighted," or able to travel no further because of the dark. This was a less than enviable situation. The hazards of being robbed and perhaps killed were far greater after the sun had set. The inn provided sanctuary to anyone who was able to pay the innkeeper for the night's stay. The traveling poor who were not able to pay for a stay at an inn sought the protection of the local church and the traveling aristocracy stayed at the castle of the local ruler.

The modern guest of today may expect a higher level of quality as far as accommodations when compared to the Dark Ages, but the expectation of protection from harm while at the inn remains. This responsibility for the safety and security of the guests and the employees of the establishment rests not only on the shoulders of top management, but is shared by everyone in the employ of the property.

However, it is management's responsibility to ensure that the entire property is prepared to provide an adequate and proper level of safety and security. In larger properties, the coordination of all safety and security issues often rests with the risk manager. In smaller properties, the coordination of efforts falls on the shoulders of the general manager with the aid of the executive committee. The role of the chief engineer and the engineering department typically revolves around the installation and maintenance of safety and security equipment and systems. In some instances, particularly where there is no risk management department, the chief engineer may be called upon to chair the hotel's safety and security committee.

Certainly, safety and security is a major responsibility of the engineering department. Coordination and communication on a daily basis between the engineering department and the rest of the hotel's departments, particularly security, the front office, and housekeeping, are an absolute must.

DISASTER PREPAREDNESS AND RISK MANAGEMENT

November 21, 2005, marked the 25th anniversary of a date many of the citizens of Las Vegas would just as soon forget. It was the second deadliest hotel fire in American history. On November 21, 1980, the M.G.M.–Grand Hotel and Casino (now Bally's) reported a fire at 7:16 A.M. When it was over, 87 people died of injuries associated with the fire. Three months later eight people died and 198 were injured at a fire started by an arsonist at the Las Vegas Hilton. The next great hotel fire happened on December 31, 1986, at the Dupont Plaza Hotel and Casino in San Juan, Puerto Rico. That fire resulted in 97 fatalities and 140 injuries.

Since the Dupont fire in 1986, the hotel industry has been spared a similar occurrence. Unfortunately, the same cannot be said for all aspects of the hospitality industry as evidenced by The Station nightclub fire on February 20, 2003, in which 100 club patrons died.

Fortunately, after the hotel fire tragedies of the 1980s, the industry finally reacted to the need for more planning and better preparedness. In Las Vegas the Clark County Commission passed the historic hotel retrofit code that demanded sprinklers and smoke detectors throughout all high-rise properties. Although immediately after the first fire, many properties objected to the estimated $2 million cost per property to retrofit, they were soon silenced by the Hilton fire three months later. The retrofit code was later adopted by numerous municipalities and counties throughout the country.

On the national level following these conflagrations, many hotel chains did not want to repeat these tragedies, so (some say at the prodding of their insurance companies) they began to develop new strategies to prepare for disasters, particularly fire disasters.

Many joined the **National Fire Protection Association (NFPA)** and became actively involved in the NFPA code-making process, such as the Fire Prevention Code, the Life Safety Code, the National Fire Alarm Code, and the Installation of Sprinkler Systems code. Today these and other National Fire Protection Association codes are referred to throughout the hotel companies' operating policies and procedures.

The only federal disaster legislation impacting the hotel industry to any degree was the **1990 Hotel and Motel Fire Safety Act**. After the Dupont Plaza fire, many members of Congress wanted to see a comprehensive piece of legislation enacted that would prevent the reoccurrence of major hotel fires. As originally conceived, it mandated automatic sprinkler systems and hardwired smoke detector systems in all United States hotels. However, the hotel industry lobbied effectively to get the proposed legislation amended. What finally passed was but a shadow of the initial legislation. The Act stated that all hotels that desired business from the federal government had to install hardwired, single station smoke detectors in all guest rooms. It also required sprinkler systems with a sprinkler head in each guest room. Hotels with three stories or fewer were exempted from the automatic sprinkler requirement. Participating properties were to be entered into the Federal Travel Directory that all federal employees consult when using United States hotels. Hotels that did not desire federal business were not mandated to make any retrofits. The Act was also conceived as being self-enforcing. That is, no per diem would be withheld if a federal employee stayed at an unapproved hotel and there were no other penalties involved.

Today, it is estimated that 90% of all high-rise hotels and 45% of all hotels and motels have sprinklers in their guest rooms. Although, this record may be less than perfect, the hotel industry has made great strides in preventing future fire disasters. This is not to say that hotel fires and fatalities no longer happen. In January 2004, a fire at the Comfort Inn of Greenville, South Carolina claimed six lives and a dozen guests were injured, and in Reno, Nevada, on October 31, 2006, six people were killed and dozens of others were injured in an arson-related hotel fire at the Mizpah Hotel. Neither of these hotels was sprinkled.

Planning for Emergencies

The U.S. Department of Labor's Occupational Safety and Health Administration's (**OSHA**) Hazardous Waste Operations and Emergency Response standard of 29 CFR 1910.120(q) clearly stipulates that all businesses that require some or all of their employees to respond and assist in case of a hazard or emergency must have a written **emergency response plan** and that plan must contain the following elements:

- Pre-emergency planning and coordination with outside parties
- Personnel roles, lines of authority, training, and communication
- Emergency recognition and prevention
- Safe distances and places of refuge
- Site security and control
- Evacuation routes and procedures
- Decontamination
- Emergency medical treatment and first aid
- Emergency alerting and response procedures
- Critique of response and follow-up
- Personal protective equipment (PPE) and emergency equipment

In addition, the plan must be available to employees for their inspection and copying, and also available to employee representatives and OSHA.

Furthermore, according to OSHA's 29 CFR 1910.157, any facility (including hotels) where fire extinguishers are required must have an **emergency action plan**. The plan should contain preferred procedures for reporting an emergency; information on notification alarms in place; an evacuation policy, procedures, and escape route assignments; procedures for "sheltering-in-place"; procedures for employees who remain on site; procedures to account for employees; the duties and responsibilities and names of employees who are assigned to rescue and to perform medical tasks; a description of how employees will be informed of the contents of the plan; names, titles, and phone numbers of employees who can be contacted for further information about the plan; and a list of key personnel who can be contacted for emergencies 24 hours a day, seven days a week.

Although not a requirement, astute operators would be wise to include the establishment of an alternate communications center and a secure on- or offsite location to store financial and legal documents, emergency contact lists, and all other essential records. It is best to involve employees from all departments in the emergency planning process. Top management should designate one person who is in charge of this process and is responsible for the coordination of all aspects of the process including communication and training. This may be the hotel's **risk manager**, chief engineer, director of security, or a number of other individuals employed at the property.

Several associations and agencies, such as the American Hotel & Lodging Association, the Occupational Safety and Health Administration, the National Fire Protection Administration, the Department of Homeland Security, and the Red Cross, among others, have resources to aid in the planning process. Chain hotels and franchisors also have loss prevention or risk management departments that can provide resources to individual properties that are designing emergency preparedness plans.

Other community resources can be incorporated into the planning process. Contact your local fire department and have them do a walkthrough inspection of your facility so they are familiar with the property in case of an emergency, and also to point out any hazards that can be corrected. Contact local ambulance services and arrange for readily available emergency transportation should the need arise. Make arrangement with hospitals and clinics in the area if the need develops. Contact local and county agencies that provide disaster-related assistance for expertise on how to prepare for other natural disasters common to your area. Contact your local Red Cross or other community provider of training for first-aid training of your employees, and remember that emergencies can happen at any hour, on any day of the week, so be sure to have trained people on duty round-the-clock. Consult with local service providers and vendors on the proper first-aid equipment to have on the premise along with the proper personal protective equipment for employees who are administering aid. Consult with your local police and sheriff's department on possible security and safety concerns immediate to your area, such as current criminal activity.

OSHA has a particularly good Emergency Action Plan Checklist at their website http://www.osha.gov/SLTC/etools/evacuation/eap.html#plan. It includes four areas: general issues, evacuation policy and procedures, reporting emergencies and alerting employees in an emergency, and employee training and drills. Other essential issues that should be addressed by the plan include a description of the alarm system, the site of an alternative communication center if the entire facility needs to be evacuated, and the location of a secure on- or offsite location to store original or duplicate copies of all important records.

Every emergency action plan must be tailored to the area where the hotel resides. Although the possibility of certain emergencies and disasters are fairly universal (e.g., fire, assault, robbery), others are specific to a particular region (e.g., flooding, hurricanes, tornadoes, earthquakes, blizzards) and do not need to be addressed in areas where their occurrence is highly unlikely (e.g., hurricanes in North Dakota). Brainstorming on possible emergency incidents and how to best handle these incidents is a particularly good activity for the emergency action plan committee.

Critical incident response teams are an integral part of any emergency action plan. A property may have different teams for different emergencies. One team may be in charge of medical emergencies (e.g., heart attacks, choking, slips, and falls, etc.) and other teams may respond to natural disasters and fires. Whatever the incident might be, the team must be properly trained and outfitted to meet the challenge.

A **post-incident program** is another essential part of an emergency action plan. Post-incident programs may include everything from public relations concerns, such as the production of press releases pertaining to an incident at the hotel to contracting with a bio-hazard cleaning company to clean a guest room after a shooting. Other post-incident activities might include, but are not limited to the following:

• arranging accommodations for guests after a fire, flood, hurricane, tornado, explosion, or other disaster that has damaged the hotel

- hiring building contractors to secure and rebuild damaged facilities
- hiring cleaning specialists to restore a facility that has suffered flooding or smoke damage
- contacting insurance companies and bonding agencies
- filing police and fire department reports
- arrangements for additional security to guard the damaged facility
- communicating with owners, corporate headquarters, and employees

Once an emergency response or action plan is developed, it must be implemented. Training programs need to be developed, teams need to be formed, and the entire organization must be put on notice, through proper and regular communication, that safety and security have the highest priority at the property. Too often, one sees the subject of safety and security introduced to new employees during orientation and then the subject is never addressed again. This approach is a recipe for failure. A property may not be able to prevent emergencies and disasters from happening, but with proper training and the use of drills to monitor the readiness of the staff, the property can effectively mitigate their impact on the lives and assets of the hotel and its guests.

An Ounce of Fire Prevention versus a Pound of Burnt Cinders

To be truly prepared for an emergency or disaster, a property must take all reasonable precautions to prevent an occurrence. Here are some of the more common precautions the various departments might take to avoid a fire. To begin with, in the kitchen, a regular program of cleaning filters, hoods, fans, vents, and broilers of grease should be implemented. Filters should be cleaned every day by passing them through the dishwasher at the close of the restaurant. The frequency of cleaning hoods, fans, and vents should be in relation to their level of use. Kitchens that depend heavily on their deep fat fryer should obviously be done much more frequently than, say, a vegetarian restaurant with no fried items on the menu. For heavy frying kitchens once every month is not unusual and for the other extreme, once a year will probably suffice.

In the banquets department, the most common source of trouble used to be the practice of emptying ashtrays onto the table cloths and then throwing them into the dirty laundry bin. Thankfully, this insane practice is seldom seen these days because of the demand for smoke-free food functions. Lit Sterno cans that are not properly extinguished after a function remain as a major source of trouble.

Housekeeping departments that allow guest room attendants to empty ash trays into the trash may not know it, but are requesting a "command performance" from their local fire department. Housekeeping departments also have the bad habit of letting linen bins block the back-of-the-house hallways and emergency exit doors, which prevents a quick exit from the property in case of an emergency and also impedes firefighters who are on their way to the source of a conflagration. In the laundry, lint screens on dryers should be cleaned daily—no exceptions. Another dangerous practice is letting dirty linen pile up in satellite and main linen rooms, thus providing ample fuel for a carelessly tossed cigarette or an opportunity for a potential arsonist.

In the engineering department, overheated equipment, soldering guns left on, and blow torches used around flammable materials are only a few of the mistakes that may lead to a fire. Fires are also quite common during periods of property remodeling and expansion. Contractors should be required to take all possible precautions and the property should monitor their practices to make sure they are practicing **due diligence**. Welding and trash fires are two of the more common occurrences. Unfortunately, construction fires often turn into major disasters because either the automatic sprinkler and alarm systems are not operable, or the fire is located in an area not serviced by these systems. One example would be a fire starting in a false ceiling or on a roof where the sprinkler system would not be triggered. Two casinos close to Las Vegas burned to the ground, one in 1998, and another in 2003. In both instances the casinos had sprinklers, but the roofs were completely engulfed in flames causing the structures to collapse and burn before the sprinklers were tripped.

In all departments, practices, such as, overloading circuits, smoking in nondesignated areas, and the specter of disgruntled employees starting fires to harm the business are, unfortunately, too common. Regular inspections need to be made throughout the property by management to reduce the odds of a fire on the premise.

The Fire Tetrahedron, Products of Combustion, and Fire Classifications

You probably first learned about it in grade school where it was called the "**Fire Triangle**." There were three sides to it, as there is to any triangle. They were labeled "fuel," "oxygen," and "heat." It took all three of them to make a fire. Now we have added a fourth side (making it a tetrahedron). The fourth side is a "chemical reaction" (i.e., oxidation) that takes place and causes a fire to start. If the chemical reaction is very fast, it is an "explosion," and if is exceedingly slow, we call it "rust."

Every material has an **ignition temperature**. When a product is heated to its ignition temperature, that product will burst instantly into flames. An open flame is not necessary; the heat alone will cause the material to combust. This is what happened in the casino fire at the MGM-Grand in Las Vegas. When the smoldering fire finally burst through the ceiling, many of the furnishings in the casino—even the mirrors—were made of plastics that had a low-ignition temperature. Thus, before the flames even reached these materials, the heat from the fire made them ignite spontaneously, which then caused the fire to advance at about 19 feet per second through the casino. That is about 13 miles an hour, which is far faster than most people can run. Today, most construction companies will not install furnishings and fixtures that have low-combustion temperatures, but management (and sometimes, guests) may introduce items after construction that have low-ignition temperatures, and that compromises the fire retardant nature of the property.

Another concern is the **products of combustion** emitted by a fire. Management should be aware of what has been used in the construction and furnishing of the building and what will happen if there is a fire and these materials burn. Again, at the MGM—Grand fire in Las Vegas, many of the materials were made from plastic in the casino and when they burned, they emitted highly toxic gases that undoubtedly led to a higher loss of life. The products of combustion are heat, light, smoke, and gases. Even with a common wood fire, the smoke and gases can be deadly, but with burning chemicals and petroleum-based products, the toxicity of the byproducts can be increased.

One of the deadliest gases to be found in most fires is **carbon monoxide (CO)**. Carbon monoxide results from incomplete combustion and is odorless, tasteless, and colorless. The problem with carbon monoxide is that it displaces oxygen in its victims' hemoglobin. A low level of poisoning will result in flu-like symptoms (200 **ppm**); at higher levels the victim will have a headache and will become sleepy and disoriented (800+ ppm). Victims have actually been found crawling toward a fire, rather than away from a fire, due no doubt, to the effects of carbon monoxide. In high enough concentrations, carbon monoxide will kill (3,200 ppm). Treatment involves the administration of oxygen to displace the carbon monoxide attached to the hemoglobin. In extreme cases, the victim will be placed in a hyperbaric chamber, a pressurized tank containing oxygen, in order to drive the carbon monoxide out of the victim.

When confronting a smoke-filled corridor with no other way out of the building, people should crawl to safety because the fresh air containing oxygen will be concentrated at the floor and the smoke and hot gases (e.g., carbon monoxide) will be on top of this narrow band of fresh air.

Smoke, one of the other products of combustion, is also deadly for two reasons. First, breathing the particulates along with the hot gases can cause injury and immediate death. Second, smoke is composed of materials that have not completely burned. When the temperature in a space rises to the level where these particulates and all other furnishings and materials will ignite, one has **flashover, or rapid fire development**. When flashover occurs, no one in the room will survive. However flashover is not a true explosion, there are no shockwaves. The effect is similar to a backdraft which is an explosion. A backdraft occurs when the level of oxygen is so low in the room that the fire cannot be sustained. There is still fuel present in the form of smoke particulates and partially combusted furnishings, and the temperature level is still high enough to support a fire. When oxygen is introduced through the opening of a door or window, a backdraft occurs. The resulting explosion can be enormous.

This author had a student in his facilities class at the beginning of a semester. One week later the student died entering his apartment. He had just moved in a few weeks earlier and had noticed a short in an electrical switch in the bathroom, but he only told a friend about it. According to the fire department, his apartment had caught on fire, but most of the oxygen was consumed and the fire was reduced to embers. It was at that point he entered the apartment (which had an outside entrance) and was confronted with thick black smoke from the top of the ceiling to almost down to the floor. No doubt, the outside door he entered through was hot, probably almost too hot to touch. At the instant he walked inside, the fresh air coming in from opening the door triggered an explosion that propelled two 200-pound men sitting on a couch in the above apartment over six feet into the air. My student died instantaneously.

Perhaps, if it had been later in the semester, he would have remembered that when confronted with a hot door or doorknob, do not open it even if there may be victims in the room. If the door is hot to the touch, then they are most assuredly dead, and opening the door will only serve to spread the fire and perhaps cause a backdraft explosion. One should instead, sound the alarm and report the fire.

Heat, another byproduct of combustion can be another killer. Since heat rises, the temperature of a room on fire can vary considerably from ceiling to floor. At the ceiling, the temperature may be over a thousand degrees Fahrenheit, several hundred degrees Fahrenheit five to six feet off the floor and less than 100 degrees Fahrenheit two feet off the floor. A person crawling in this environment would survive, but if the same person stood up, he or she would be dead instantly.

Light, the final byproduct of combustion may not pose a risk to occupants, but there is a considerable misunderstanding among the public about how much light is produced in a building fire. As Tim Szymanski, Public Information Officer for Las Vegas Fire and Rescue describes it, "If Hollywood were to portray a fire in a building accurately, the screen would be black." The smoke effectively hides what light there is produced in most building fires.

That is a description of the Fire Tetrahedron and the byproducts of combustion, and that brings us to the most important lesson to be learned in this section: the five classifications of fire. Everyone who may ever be called upon to fight even the smallest of fires must know these five classifications and must be able to instantly recognize their symbols. The five classifications are "A," "B," "C," "D," and "K." "A" fires are fueled by combustibles, such as wood, paper, and cloth. "B" fires are flammable liquids and gases such as kerosene, gasoline, and propane. "C" fires are electrical fires, and "D" fires are metal fires such as magnesium, potassium, and sodium. Class "K" fires, a relatively new classification, is a subset of class "B" fires and involves cooking oils and fats. Class "A" fires are the most common classification of guest room fires, class "K" fires are the most common for restaurants, and class "D" fires are extremely rare in the hospitality industry.

Fire Suppression Chemicals

With a class "A" fire, one needs to remove either the heat or the oxygen from the fire to effectively put it out. Water serves as the suppression agent for class "A" fires because it does both; the fire is cooled and smothered by the water. Never use water on a class "C" fire because water will conduct electricity and the operator may be electrocuted. Water is also not appropriate for "B" and "K" fires because the water will serve only to spread the burning liquid, making the fire worse.

Ammonium phosphate also known as a multipurpose dry chemical is effective on "A," "B," and "C" fires. The ammonium phosphate interrupts the chemical reaction, which extinguishes the fire. It is less than ideal on class "A" wood fires. The heat retained in the wood can reignite the fire if the fuel is not completely covered. The agent does not conduct electricity, but it is corrosive so it will harm electronic equipment. The extinguishing agent leaves a considerable residue and should be cleaned from all surfaces as soon as possible after use. The pressure of the agent leaving the extinguisher is quite high, so it can spread liquid combustibles and thus contribute to the spread of a fire. Finally, the release of the agent in a confined space will severely obscure vision.

Sodium bicarbonate, known as simply "dry chemical," is rated for class "B" and "C" fires. It will not effectively extinguish deep-seated wood fires. It is considered to be nontoxic. If there is moisture in the extinguisher, the agent will cake and will not discharge from the extinguisher. Other disadvantages are the same as those associated with ammonium phosphate.

Carbon dioxide (CO_2) is used on "B" and "C" fires. Carbon dioxide will not burn and it displaces oxygen. The vapor is extremely cold and will cause frostbite. Never spray another person with a CO_2 extinguisher. When using a CO_2 extinguisher, the operator must stand closer to the fire than with other extinguishers.

Wet chemical agents used on class "K" fires are usually potassium acetate with potassium citrate, or potassium carbonate. The extinguisher sprays out the agent as a fine mist, which serves to cool the fire, and the potassium salts "saponify" the surface of the burning oil as a layer of foam forms over the oil surface to keep it from reigniting. This agent only works on animal and vegetable oil and is ineffective against class "B" fires.

There are literally dozens of other extinguishing agents on the market, but these are the ones most commonly found in hospitality facilities. Some of the other agents have been discontinued due to their toxicity (e.g., carbon tetrachloride) or their harm to the environment (e.g., Halon).

Fire Suppression Equipment

Fire suppression includes sprinkler systems, hoses, portable fire extinguishers, and all of the supporting equipment needed for the equipment to function. In hospitality operations there are principally two types of sprinkler systems, **dry pipe** and **wet pipe**.

Figure 10.1 is a diagram of a dry pipe sprinkler system and ten steps about how to operate it.

Water is transported up a **riser** from the main. In-line pumps may supplement the city water pressure so that the water can be lifted to upper floors (see Figure 10.2). Typically, the water pressure should be at least 120 lbs. per square inch, or whatever is required by local code. In the riser servicing an automatic sprinkler system, there will be a valve. That valve will either have water on both sides of the valve (a wet pipe system), or it will have water on one side and pressurized air on the other side of the valve (a dry pipe system). The dry pipe system is favored in cold climates where there is a chance that water in the system might freeze and would thus compromise the system. Most city and county fire codes mandate that these valves may be turned off

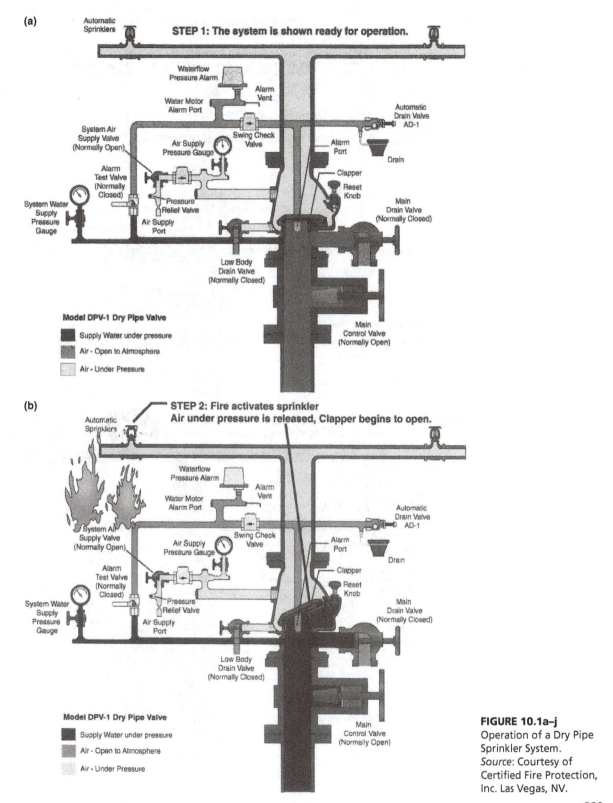

(a)

Automatic Sprinklers

STEP 1: The system is shown ready for operation.

Waterflow Pressure Alarm

Alarm Vent

Water Motor Alarm Port

Automatic Drain Valve AD-1

System Air Supply Valve (Normally Open)

Air Supply Pressure Gauge

Swing Check Valve

Alarm Port

Drain

Alarm Test Valve (Normally Closed)

Clapper

Reset Knob

System Water Supply Pressure Gauge

Pressure Relief Valve

Main Drain Valve (Normally Closed)

Air Supply Port

Low Body Drain Valve (Normally Closed)

Main Control Valve (Normally Open)

Model DPV-1 Dry Pipe Valve

Supply Water under pressure

Air - Open to Atmosphere

Air - Under Pressure

(b)

Automatic Sprinklers

STEP 2: Fire activates sprinkler
Air under pressure is released, Clapper begins to open.

Waterflow Pressure Alarm

Alarm Vent

Water Motor Alarm Port

Automatic Drain Valve AD-1

System Air Supply Valve (Normally Open)

Air Supply Pressure Gauge

Swing Check Valve

Alarm Port

Drain

Alarm Test Valve (Normally Closed)

Clapper

Reset Knob

System Water Supply Pressure Gauge

Pressure Relief Valve

Main Drain Valve (Normally Closed)

Air Supply Port

Low Body Drain Valve (Normally Closed)

Main Control Valve (Normally Open)

Model DPV-1 Dry Pipe Valve

Supply Water under pressure

Air - Open to Atmosphere

Air - Under Pressure

FIGURE 10.1a–j
Operation of a Dry Pipe Sprinkler System.
Source: Courtesy of Certified Fire Protection, Inc. Las Vegas, NV.

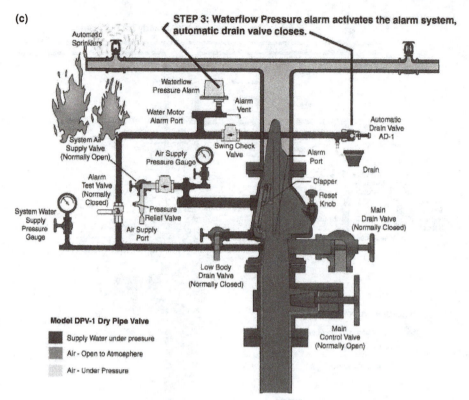

(c)

STEP 3: Waterflow Pressure alarm activates the alarm system, automatic drain valve closes.

Automatic Sprinklers

Waterflow Pressure Alarm

Alarm Vent

Water Motor Alarm Port

Automatic Drain Valve AD-1

Swing Check Valve

Drain

System Air Supply Valve (Normally Open)

Air Supply Pressure Gauge

Alarm Port

Alarm Test Valve (Normally Closed)

Clapper

Reset Knob

Main Drain Valve (Normally Closed)

System Water Supply Pressure Gauge

Pressure Relief Valve

Air Supply Port

Low Body Drain Valve (Normally Closed)

Main Control Valve (Normally Open)

Model DPV-1 Dry Pipe Valve

- Supply Water under pressure
- Air - Open to Atmosphere
- Air - Under Pressure

(d)

STEP 4: Sprinkler releases water
Note: Only sprinklers activated by the fire will operate.

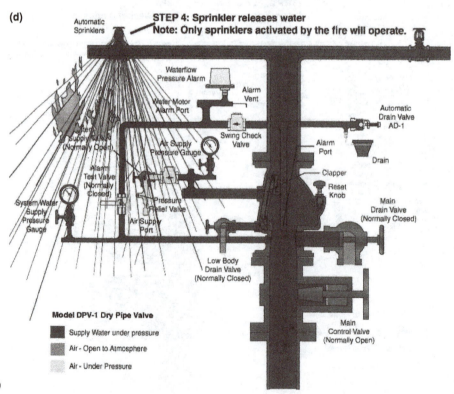

Automatic Sprinklers

Waterflow Pressure Alarm

Alarm Vent

Water Motor Alarm Port

Automatic Drain Valve AD-1

Swing Check Valve

Drain

System Air Supply Valve (Normally Open)

Air Supply Pressure Gauge

Alarm Port

Alarm Test Valve (Normally Closed)

Clapper

Reset Knob

Main Drain Valve (Normally Closed)

System Water Supply Pressure Gauge

Pressure Relief Valve

Air Supply Port

Low Body Drain Valve (Normally Closed)

Main Control Valve (Normally Open)

Model DPV-1 Dry Pipe Valve

- Supply Water under pressure
- Air - Open to Atmosphere
- Air - Under Pressure

FIGURE 10.1 (*continued*)

230

(e)

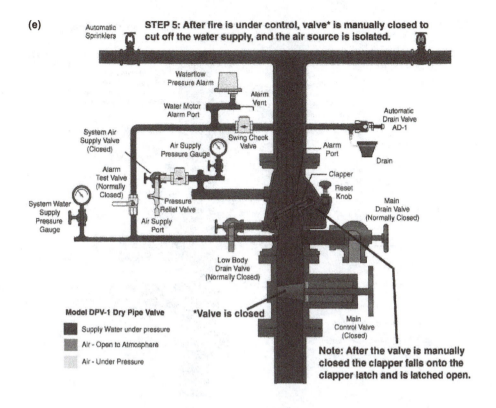

STEP 5: After fire is under control, valve* is manually closed to cut off the water supply, and the air source is isolated.

Automatic Sprinklers

Waterflow Pressure Alarm

Alarm Vent

Water Motor Alarm Port

Automatic Drain Valve AD-1

System Air Supply Valve (Closed)

Air Supply Pressure Gauge

Swing Check Valve

Alarm Port

Drain

Alarm Test Valve (Normally Closed)

Clapper

Reset Knob

System Water Supply Pressure Gauge

Pressure Relief Valve

Main Drain Valve (Normally Closed)

Air Supply Port

Low Body Drain Valve (Normally Closed)

Model DPV-1 Dry Pipe Valve

Supply Water under pressure

Air - Open to Atmosphere

Air - Under Pressure

*Valve is closed

Main Control Valve (Closed)

Note: After the valve is manually closed the clapper falls onto the clapper latch and is latched open.

(f)

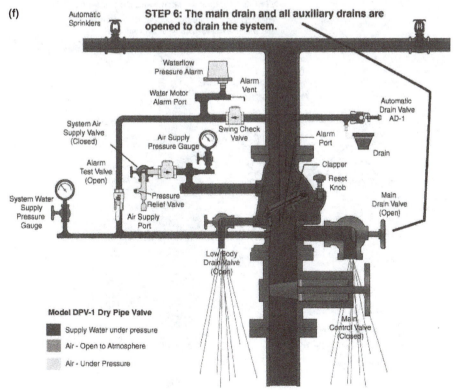

STEP 6: The main drain and all auxiliary drains are opened to drain the system.

Automatic Sprinklers

Waterflow Pressure Alarm

Alarm Vent

Water Motor Alarm Port

Automatic Drain Valve AD-1

System Air Supply Valve (Closed)

Air Supply Pressure Gauge

Swing Check Valve

Alarm Port

Drain

Alarm Test Valve (Open)

Clapper

Reset Knob

System Water Supply Pressure Gauge

Pressure Relief Valve

Main Drain Valve (Open)

Air Supply Port

Low Body Drain Valve (Open)

Model DPV-1 Dry Pipe Valve

Supply Water under pressure

Air - Open to Atmosphere

Air - Under Pressure

Main Control Valve (Closed)

FIGURE 10.1 (*continued*)

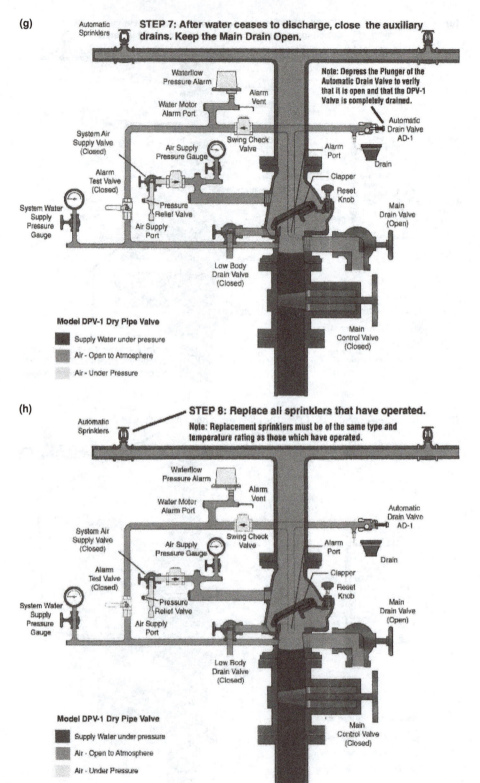

(g)

Automatic Sprinklers

STEP 7: After water ceases to discharge, close the auxiliary drains. Keep the Main Drain Open.

Waterflow Pressure Alarm

Alarm Vent

Water Motor Alarm Port

Note: Depress the Plunger of the Automatic Drain Valve to verify that it is open and that the DPV-1 Valve is completely drained.

System Air Supply Valve (Closed)

Air Supply Pressure Gauge

Swing Check Valve

Automatic Drain Valve AD-1

Alarm Port

Drain

Alarm Test Valve (Closed)

Clapper

Reset Knob

System Water Supply Pressure Gauge

Pressure Relief Valve

Air Supply Port

Main Drain Valve (Open)

Low Body Drain Valve (Closed)

Model DPV-1 Dry Pipe Valve

Supply Water under pressure

Air - Open to Atmosphere

Air - Under Pressure

Main Control Valve (Closed)

(h)

Automatic Sprinklers

STEP 8: Replace all sprinklers that have operated.

Note: Replacement sprinklers must be of the same type and temperature rating as those which have operated.

Waterflow Pressure Alarm

Alarm Vent

Water Motor Alarm Port

Automatic Drain Valve AD-1

System Air Supply Valve (Closed)

Air Supply Pressure Gauge

Swing Check Valve

Alarm Port

Drain

Alarm Test Valve (Closed)

Clapper

Reset Knob

System Water Supply Pressure Gauge

Pressure Relief Valve

Air Supply Port

Main Drain Valve (Open)

Low Body Drain Valve (Closed)

Model DPV-1 Dry Pipe Valve

Supply Water under pressure

Air - Open to Atmosphere

Air - Under Pressure

Main Control Valve (Closed)

FIGURE 10.1 (*continued*)

232

(i)

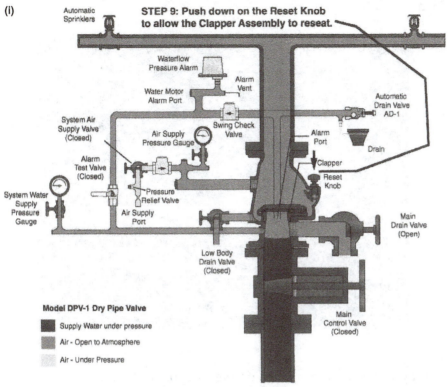

STEP 9: Push down on the Reset Knob to allow the Clapper Assembly to reseat.

Automatic Sprinklers

Waterflow Pressure Alarm

Alarm Vent

Water Motor Alarm Port

Automatic Drain Valve AD-1

System Air Supply Valve (Closed)

Air Supply Pressure Gauge

Swing Check Valve

Alarm Port

Drain

Alarm Test Valve (Closed)

Clapper

Reset Knob

System Water Supply Pressure Gauge

Pressure Relief Valve

Air Supply Port

Low Body Drain Valve (Closed)

Main Drain Valve (Open)

Model DPV-1 Dry Pipe Valve

■ Supply Water under pressure
■ Air - Open to Atmosphere
░ Air - Under Pressure

Main Control Valve (Closed)

(j)

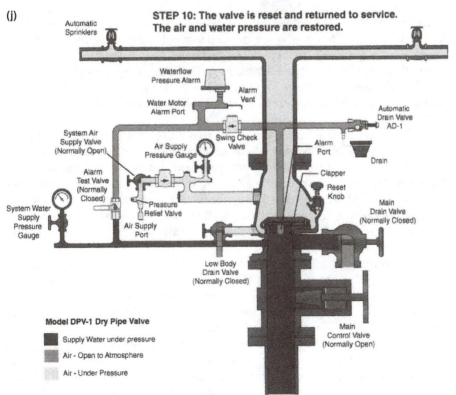

STEP 10: The valve is reset and returned to service. The air and water pressure are restored.

Automatic Sprinklers

Waterflow Pressure Alarm

Alarm Vent

Water Motor Alarm Port

Automatic Drain Valve AD-1

System Air Supply Valve (Normally Open)

Air Supply Pressure Gauge

Swing Check Valve

Alarm Port

Drain

Alarm Test Valve (Normally Closed)

Clapper

Reset Knob

System Water Supply Pressure Gauge

Pressure Relief Valve

Air Supply Port

Main Drain Valve (Normally Closed)

Low Body Drain Valve (Normally Closed)

Model DPV-1 Dry Pipe Valve

■ Supply Water under pressure
■ Air - Open to Atmosphere
░ Air - Under Pressure

Main Control Valve (Normally Open)

FIGURE 10.1 (*continued*)

233

FIGURE 10.2
Emergency Diesel Engine
and Rotary Pump for Fire
Suppression System.

only by the fire department even if there is a sprinkler head discharging water
when there is no fire in the vicinity. To turn off the valve would compromise
other sprinkler heads in other rooms where a fire may occur while the sprinkler head is reset. That is why the fire department wants to be present to turn
off a valve. Alarms are often connected to valves so that the property is made
aware that a sprinkler head is discharging. The alarm may not indicate exactly
which sprinkler head serviced by the riser is discharging, so the management
and the fire department personnel will have to knock on many doors and inspect
to find the problem.

The water moves from the riser to **cross mains**. From the cross main the
water flows to the **branch lines** where the sprinklers are attached. Traditionally,
sprinklers come in three basic types; **pendant**, **upright**, and **sidewall** (see
Figure 10.3). Pendant sprinkler heads hang from the pipe and disperse water
in a 360° arc. Upright sprinkler heads are installed on the top of the pipe, but
operate the same as the pendant. Sidewall sprinklers extend from the wall of
a room and the water cascades out of the sprinkler head in an 180° pattern
wetting the room and the wall.

The water, or air in the case of a dry pipe system, is held in check by a
stopper that is kept in place by a bulb filled with liquid or a fusible link (see
Figure 10.4). When the air temperature surrounding the sprinkler head
reaches the rated temperature of the head (135°F–225°F), either the link melts
or the bulb shatters. The pressure of the air or water behind the cap then forces
the cap off, and water begins to flow out of the sprinkler head. The delay of a
dry pipe system is usually only a few seconds. Despite what is shown in
Hollywood movies, only one sprinkler head closest to the fire will activate unless the fire continues to spread. If the heat buildup continues, then the next

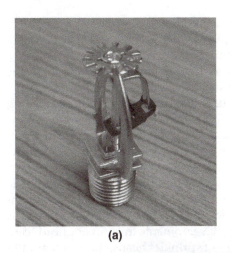

(a)   (b)

(c)

FIGURE 10.3
(a) Pendant, (b) Upright,
& (c) Sidewall Sprinkler
Heads.

FIGURE 10.4   Liquid
Filled Bulb Stopper on
Sprinkler Head.

closest head will activate, and so on and so forth. Most seasoned fire fighters have never seen more than one or two sprinkler heads activate. They are simply that effective if the fire is below the sprinkler head.

As previously mentioned, only the fire department in many locales is allowed to shut off the riser valve, so what should the property do when a sprinkler head is dispensing hundreds of gallons of water a minute damaging furnishings, walls, and floors? One option is to have the engineering department (or the manager on duty) slow the flow by inserting a wedge and wrapping the head with a cloth and placing a bucket underneath to catch the slowed flow of water. Rest assured that whoever does this will get thoroughly soaked in the process. It should also be noted that the water in an automatic sprinkler system is a static supply so it will be black, smelly and may even contain antifreeze to prevent freezing in cold climates. It is definitely not potable.

There have been some interesting developments in sprinkler head technology. One advance is the development of sprinkler heads that automatically shut off when the ambient temperature falls below a predetermined level. If the fire happens to start again, the sprinkler head will reactivate. Another is disguised sprinkler heads that pop out of ceiling fittings. This is a purely aesthetic advancement, but can often be seen in many hotel lobbies. Another advance is the use of mist fire suppression systems. These systems dispense far less water, but they do it under very high pressure. They may also be linked to smoke detectors, so they activate at much lower temperatures than traditional sprinkler heads. With less water released, the damage to the room is minimized.

Hotel hose systems are being phased out in many facilities in favor of automatic sprinklers. A hotel fire hose is two inches in interior diameter and is typically stored in a cabinet on hooks and can be operated by trained members of the staff. A valve in the cabinet releases the water. To begin with, the hose should be removed from the cabinet by taking the hose nozzle proceeding in a direction AWAY from the fire until the hose is fully extended and out of the cabinet. Then return to the cabinet and turn on the water. Nozzles may have one or two settings. If there are two, then one is a stream to be aimed at the base of a fire. The other setting is a fog setting. The fog setting is used to push back flames, smoke, and hot gases so a victim can be reached and rescued. A minimum of two people should man a hotel fire hose. A fire should never be fought until an alarm is turned in. The property will also have hose connectors throughout the property for four-inch hoses brought by the fire department.

One should never attempt to put out a fire with a portable extinguisher in the free burning stage. Ideally, the fire should be in the **incipient stage** and should be no larger than the proverbial breadbasket. The size of a fire extinguisher is either rated in the number of pounds of agent in a dry chemical extinguisher or the volume of a liquid agent.

Effective portable fire extinguishers must be:

1. approved by a recognized testing laboratory. (Extinguishers manufactured in the United States are generally approved by Factory Mutual (FM) and listed by Underwriters' Laboratories, Inc. (UL).)

2. of the proper type for the class of fire expected.
3. located where they are readily accessible for immediate use and in sufficient quantity and size to deal with the expected fire.
4. inspected and maintained on a regular basis so that they are kept in good operating condition.
5. operated by trained personnel who can use them effectively.

All employees should know the P.A.S.S system of fire extinguisher operation (see Figure 10.5). Furthermore, one should never attempt to fight a fire that is between you and the exit.

FIGURE 10.5
Remember the "PASS" Word.

CLASSES OF FIRES	TYPES OF FIRES	PICTURE SYMBOL
A	Wood, paper, cloth, trash & other ordinary materials.	
B	Gasoline, oil, paint and other flammable liquids.	
C	May be used on fires involving live electrical equipment without danger to the operator.	
D	Combustible metals and combustible metal alloys.	
K	Cooking media (Vegetable or Animal Oils and Fats)	

FIGURE 10.6 Fire Extinguisher Symbols. *Source*: Courtesy of Certified Fire Protection, Inc. Las Vegas, NV.

The use of certain extinguishing agents on the wrong type of fire can have a disastrous effect. Everyone should know the following symbols used on portable extinguishers (Figure 10.6). A numerical rating may also appear on an extinguisher, such as, "5A:20B:C." The number "5" in front of the "A" represents an equivalent of 6.25 gallons of water extinguishing capacity (i.e., 1 = 1.25 gallons of water). The "20" in front of the "B" means that the extinguisher has 20 square feet of coverage. There is never a number in front of a "C" classification.

Portable fire extinguishers must be visually inspected monthly. The inspection should assure that:

1. fire extinguishers are in their assigned place.
2. fire extinguishers are not blocked or hidden.
3. fire extinguishers are mounted in accordance with NFPA Standard No. 10 (Portable Fire Extinguisher).
4. pressure gauges show adequate pressure (CO_2 extinguisher must be weighted to determine if leakage has occurred).
5. pin and seals are in place.
6. fire extinguishers show no visual sign of damage or abuse.
7. nozzles are free of blockage.

Maintenance of a portable extinguisher means a complete examination and involves disassembly and inspection of each part and replacement when necessary. Maintenance should be done at least annually or more often if conditions warrant it. Hydrostatic testing of portable fire extinguishers is done to protect against unexpected in-service failure. This can be caused by internal corrosion, external corrosion, and damage from abuse, etc. Hydrostatic testing must be performed by trained personnel with proper test equipment and facilities.

Fire Control Systems

Fire control systems start at the fire-rated door. Whether the door is steel or a solid core wood door, the door and its frame should be fire-rated. The length of time a fire can impinge on that door is noted in its rating. For example a guestroom door might have a **fire rating** of 45 minutes. That means fire can be at that door for a full 45 minutes before it burns through. Modern hotels are, for the most part, a series of compartments that should be closed off during a fire, in order to impede its progress and give the fire department additional time to fight the fire. That is one of the reasons we have **door closures** on guest room doors. Another, more sophisticated variety of a simple door closure system is the **automatic door closure** that trips when a fire alarm sounds. They are typically found between guest room corridors and lobbies.

Other fire control systems include **smoke and fire dampers** that are activated during a fire closing down ventilation ducts that could transport the smoke and fire to other parts of the building. U.S. District Judge Philip Pro who worked as a magistrate on the M.G.M.–Grand fire carries a small **fusible link** from the ventilation system of the M.G.M. It was intended to melt and close off a ventilation duct during a fire. However, the link was improperly installed and was one of the causes of the smoke migrating throughout the guest room tower, killing and injuring hundreds of people.

Another more sophisticated control device is the use of fans that can be engaged to pressurize areas in a property, such as fire stairwells to prevent smoke from migrating. When reversed, these **pressurization systems** can suck smoke out of a room and expel it to the outside of a building. These devices are often designed to work automatically with manual overrides.

Many hotel fire control rooms have the ability to shut off power to the entire property with one switch. If the entire property were engulfed, the fire department commander might decide to take such action. It should be remembered that all electrical fires become class "A" fires if the power is cut, making them far easier to extinguish.

The vertical movement of fire in a high-rise building is one of a building operator's worst nightmares. Consequently, elevator shafts, seismic joints, plumbing chases, and even escalators can be sealed beforehand or are designed to seal during a fire automatically. Elevator cars should automatically be called to a floor where there is no fire and then open and lock off out-of-service. Escalators can be designed to seal with a closure device that operates similarly to an automatic door closure. Of course, this does not work if the escalator is located in an atrium.

Fire Detection Systems

There are three basic types of fire detection systems that apply to hospitality facilities. There are smoke detectors, heat detectors, and flame detectors. Flame detectors have a limited application. Possible uses would include storage areas where highly flammable materials are located that may not give off a particularly high degree of smoke, such as certain cleaning chemicals and paints.

Smoke detectors are the most frequently used detection system, because they provide early warning, and most hotel fires are class "A" fires which produce the most amount of smoke. Smoke detectors are further broken down into two major categories, photoelectric and ionization detectors.

Photoelectric detectors, as seen in Figure 10.7, employ a photocell and a light emitting diode (LED) in a chamber. In one type, smoke entering the chamber blocks the LED's beam of light from the LED and sets off the alarm. In another type, the light from the diode does not hit the photocell because of a diaphragm blocking the light. Smoke entering the chamber refracts the light allowing it to hit the photocell, thus turning on the alarm.

Normal Condition in Clear Air

LED

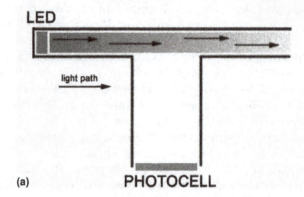

(a)   PHOTOCELL

Photocell Active Condition in Smoke

LED

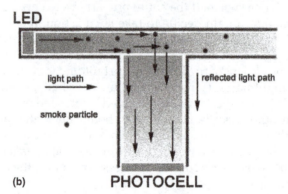

FIGURE 10.7 Diagram of Photo Electric Detector—Standby and Alarm Mode. *Source:* Courtesy of Certified Fire Protection, Inc. Las Vegas, NV.

(b)   PHOTOCELL

Ionization detectors (Figure 10.8) employ an ionization chamber containing a trace amount of radioactive americium-241, which is a source of alpha particles. Inside the chamber are two plates separated by a centimeter. A battery or other electrical source applies a voltage to the plates, making one plate positive and one plate negative. The alpha particles knock electrons off of the atoms in the air, ionizing the oxygen and the nitrogen. The positively charged oxygen and nitrogen atoms are attracted to the negatively charged plate and the electrons are attracted to the positively charged plate. This completes the electrical circuit, which allows current to flow. When smoke enters the chamber the particles attach to the ions and neutralize them, which disrupts the circuit so that an alarm is tripped.

There is considerable debate about which is better. The truth is they both work and either may be considered as long as the unit has been certified by the Underwriters Laboratory (UL). Ionization detectors typically respond more quickly to fires that produce considerable flame and photoelectric detectors work slightly faster with smoldering fires. Ionization detectors are typically not as expensive as photoelectric, but they are known to give more "false

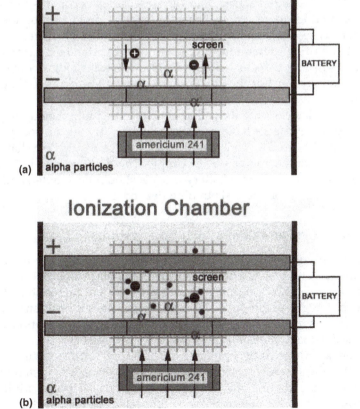

FIGURE 10.8 Diagram of Ionization Detector—Standby and Alarm Mode.

positives" from normal cooking operations. Many of the current generation of smoke detectors have an additional feature. When someone burns the toast or lights a cigar, the heavy plume of smoke used to trip the alarm. Now we have smoke detectors that will not trip immediately. They have a delay, typically 30 seconds, when they will sample the air again to determine if conditions have changed. If so, they will not sound the alarm, but if the conditions remain the same, the alarm is sounded.

The heat detector has its own niche. In kitchens where there is considerable smoke and vapors, a smoke detector would give too many false alarms. A unique variation of a heat detector, the rate-of-rise heat detector, trips only when the temperature in the room increases swiftly. If the temperature climbs slowly (as in most kitchen operations), the alarm does not sound.

Detector placement, number, and spacing are determined by many variables, such as the manufacturer's recommendations, engineering surveys, tests, and recommendations from testing laboratories. In general, one detector should be placed in each room, storage area, or hallway. Detectors should go as close to the center of the ceiling as possible. Detectors should be placed at the top of stairways.

Over time, dust, dirt, and other foreign material can build up inside a detector's sensing elements, resulting in reduced sensitivity, which can limit the amount of warning time given during a fire. Dirty or dusty detectors can also result in unwanted alarms that can desensitize occupants to the alarm system or produce more serious behavior (such as disconnecting the system altogether). Therefore, maintenance is an absolute must. Fire detectors should be tested according to manufacturers' and N.F.P.A. standards. Unreliable or reduced sensitivity detectors should be cleaned, adjusted, and maintained by qualified personnel. If the units cannot then be recalibrated, they should be replaced.

The best detectors are those that are hardwired into the building's electrical circuitry and also have a battery backup in case of power failure. Although not required by code, an ideal alternative would be to have all detectors on an uninterruptible power supply. The backup batteries should be changed twice a year. Simple battery models should be avoided and are not acceptable by most commercial building fire codes.

Fire Notification and Communication Systems

Fire alarms are typically integrated in a modern building into a number of other different systems. Obviously horns, visual alarms (strobes), and communication systems, are an integral part of a fire detection system, but they may also be integrated into sprinkler valves, other fire suppression equipment, HVAC systems, doors, water flow switches, manual pull stations, carbon monoxide detectors, and computers.

There are three basic strategies for building alarms: 1) single station alarms; 2) multiple station alarms; and 3) remote alarms. Single station alarms sound only at the location of the fire detector that has activated. Multiple station alarms have all the detector-alarms connected together so that when one trips, the rest sound an alarm and they also alert a central panel or fire control room. Many times in large buildings, the multiple station alarms are interconnected within a given zone and the property may have multiple zones. So, the alarm will only sound within a zone if the operator does not wish to evacuate the rest of the facility. Remote alarms are also connected to a remote location, such as the nearest fire station. This helps to eliminate human error if the fire department is not contacted by the property.

Such an occurrence once happened to the author. A broiler in the kitchen was engulfed in flames (the cooks had not been properly cleaning the broiler). I was the first on the scene and I was attempting to put out the fire with a handheld extinguisher. The dry chemical hood system activated and extinguished the broiler fire. The hood system had a remote alarm to the local fire department. At that moment the General Manager arrived and ordered an assistant to call the fire department to tell them we had everything under control. There was a $500 charge if the fire department truck was called to your property. The fire department responded that they had already left the station and they would continue to our property to check things out. It was good that they did, because the fire had burned through the hood flue and was burning in the false ceiling directly above our heads, but we were completely unaware of the problem. We could have had a similar situation to what happened to the MGM–Grand.

Fire alarms should have redundant power systems, so that if power is cut because of an outage, there is a backup. The backup is usually a self-charging battery that supplies power the instant the electrical power supply is interrupted. Fire alarms should also have "trouble reporting" capabilities. In other words, if the system is compromised in any way, the system would notify the operator. For example a "trouble" might include a dead backup battery, a wiring fault, such as a loose wire on a smoke detector, or a closed valve on a sprinkler riser, a horn, or any other type of alarm.

Panels in the main fire control room or in satellite locations throughout a property may indicate the approximate location of the fire or trouble, or they may pinpoint the exact location of the problem. Those systems that can pinpoint the exact location are called **addressable systems**. Those that can only approximate the location are known as **remote annunciation systems** and are older generations of alarm systems. The addressable systems use transponders to communicate the exact site of the fire or trouble to the firefighters or the hotel staff. There are also LED screens and printer systems that can communicate the location of a problem. Figure 10.9 is the main fire command and control center at the Las Vegas Hilton.

The use of voice communication systems in addition to bells and horns can direct occupants to safety. They may either use prerecorded messages or they may broadcast a live message from a central command and control center. Some hotels even have the flexibility to broadcast a message to an individual guest room or the entire hotel depending on the circumstances. Visual alarms, such as strobes, are used in disabled guest rooms (ADA rooms) and may also be in public areas for hearing impaired guests and to augment the audio alarms. The use of a voice communication systems are essential in

FIGURE 10.9 Fire Command and Control Center at the Las Vegas Hilton.

casino properties, because guests will often ignore a horn or bell alarm and continue to play.

NATURAL DISASTERS

Natural disasters may be of metrological, biological, or geological origin. Common disasters would include blizzards, earthquakes, floods, hurricanes, epidemics, thunderstorms, and tornados. Obviously, the prospects of certain natural disasters are not as prevalent in certain regions as are others. Hurricanes, for example, are impossible in the midwestern United States and earthquakes are highly unlikely in Minnesota. Consequently, a property should prepare for the most likely occurrences that could happen in that region. Certainly, some disasters can occur anywhere, such as, norovirus outbreaks.

As has already been discussed, to be prepared for any disaster, a plan is critical. The plan should have a strategic component that addresses the vision, mission, goals, and objectives of the program. It should have a response component that assigns responsibilities to individuals and units to carry out specified actions at the appropriate time when a disaster occurs. It should also have a mitigation component to eliminate hazards or reduce those hazards that cannot be eliminated. A recovery component is necessary for the restoration of the property, its infrastructure, and its services and products. Finally, a continuity component that identifies critical applications, vital records, processes, functions, personnel, and procedures is needed while the damaged facility is being repaired.

Emergency communication and warning procedures need to be developed, operational procedures must be devised, personnel need to be trained and drilled, emergency equipment and supplies should be in place, and the property needs to coordinate all emergency and disaster plans and programs with the appropriate federal, state, and local public agencies.

ACCIDENTS AND COMMON EMERGENCIES

Fortunately, the prospect of a massive disaster is not common for most hospitality facilities. However, this is not the case for accidents and medical emergencies. It has often been said that any human calamity can and will happen in due course at any hotel.

Some properties are admittedly more successful than others in preventing accidents. Less successful properties are often known as *accident cycle properties*. The *accident cycle* is typically found at reactive properties—that is, properties that only respond when the accident rate increases. When the accident rate is low the need for accident prevention is not on anyone's radar. One usually sees fluctuating numbers of accidents at these properties. In some months it is increasing, and at other times it is decreasing. There are often predictable changes in the recorded rates of accidents. When the property is sponsoring accident prevention programs because of a recent series of accidents, the rate falls and when the property is doing nothing about accidents, the rate starts spiraling upward. There are no continuing efforts and no continuous improvement. In this crisis-driven environment, management is inconsistent in its support of safety.

Usually, only one department is responsible for safety (e.g., engineering). Arbitrary numerical goals are often in place. Special meetings are held for reactive training. For example, someone is injured in the laundry department, and then a program is set up to train laundry workers on how to operate laundry equipment safely. Accident investigations are adversarial. The goal is usually to determine who was at fault, not how can this incident be prevented in the future. Finally, any disciplinary action is often inconsistently applied.

Better properties are known as *plateau properties*. They have continuous efforts, but they do not show continuous improvement. There is usually good improvement at first, but in spite of continuous efforts, performance levels off and plateaus. In these properties, the safety "pressure" is constant and goals are numbers-driven. Line supervisors are often held accountable for the safety numbers and there is a lack of agreement between top management and the front line on what constitutes a truly safe facility. There is a sporadic department-specific accident focus. There is also a reliance on lots of posters and signs through the back-of-the-house promoting safety. Finally, accident investigations still focus on faultfinding and the assignment of blame.

The best properties practice *continuous improvement*. Performance improves continuously. Management is committed to accident prevention and that commitment and support for safety is consistent. Both management and hourly wage workers agree that safety is important. The safety initiative at these properties is focused on *upstream* measures, prior to incidents. There is meaningful employee involvement and performance accountability at all levels of the organization. In the safety meetings, there is ongoing, data-driven problem solving and action planning by the members. Statistics are used properly to evaluate results and direct site-wide activities. There is a heavy reliance on an inventory of objectively defined, critical safety-related behaviors. Finally, accident investigations are not concerned with faultfinding. Instead, they use multilevel participation and are oriented to data gathering and establishing mechanisms to summarize results for directed problem solving.

Slips and Falls

One of the most ubiquitous accidents to befall employees and guests alike is slipping and falling. Four percent of all workplace deaths are from a slip and fall that takes place on one level. Falls account for over eight million hospital emergency room visitations. A slip and fall is the primary reason for lost days at work and is also the leading cause of workmen's comp. claims.

According to the Consumer Products Safety Commission, floors and flooring account for more than 555,000 slips and falls a year in the United States. Slips and falls happen to guests and customers in addition to employees. Approximately 30% of all Americans over 65 experience a slip and fall every year. Of those seniors who fall, approximately 10% are serious falls.

Showers and bathtubs should always have either mats or should have an abrasive coating that raises the static slip coefficient. Bathroom, hall, and lobby floors should also have a special coating to help protect people from slipping and falling. Make certain that all cleaning agents do not remove these abrasive coatings. A static slip coefficient rating of 0.5 or greater is considered to be a safe floor. Of course, any level floor surface that is completely wet has a slip coefficient rating of zero. Care should also be taken to note the static slip coefficient rating of any floor finishes and sealers used. Kitchen tiles should either have an abrasive coating, rubber anti-slip fatigue mats, or both. Grease combined with water can cause an extremely hazardous surface. Pool areas are also a major concern and should have an anti-slip deck coating installed. Failure to use a reasonable amount of care that results in injury or death to guests will most assuredly bring a negligence suit against the hotel.

Medical Emergencies

Cuts, burns, heart attacks, drowning, and choking are extremely common in all hotels and restaurants. The property cannot prevent all medical emergencies, but much can be done to mitigate their impact. In larger properties, full-time security personnel are typically trained in all first aid techniques. However, training in first aid does not have to be limited to just security personnel. Competent individuals in all departments should be identified and selected for first aid training, including the Heimlich maneuver for choking, cardio-pulmonary resuscitation techniques, and the use of automated external defibrillators (A.E.D.). There should be properly trained personnel on duty seven days a week on all shifts.

Emergency equipment and supplies should be properly inspected and maintained. Expired supplies should be replaced as needed. The location of first aid kits and A.E.D.s should be communicated to all employees.

SECURITY

Safety implies the protection of human beings from harm. Although security also implies the protection of employees and guests from harm, it also implies the protection of the assets of the guests, employees, and the hotel's property. To fulfill this function, those involved in the security of the property, including engineering, must foresee and evaluate threats and then make recommendations to top management on the appropriate action to take to safeguard the property and the lives of guests and staff.

In addition, personnel in all departments must alert management of any imprudent actions or situations that could be considered negligence on the part of the company. Security, like safety, is everyone's responsibility. One of the most important concepts that should be taught to every employee is to report anything that is *JDLR* (just doesn't look right), and management should be taught never to ignore or disparage any employee who does report anything that *JDLR*.

It is hard to conceive of many other businesses that are more vulnerable to security hazards than lodging properties, particularly ones with restaurants and cocktail lounges. It is a business that attracts large numbers of people who are, for the most part, unknown by management and who may pose a security threat to other guests, employees, and the property, and, on occasion, the threat may come from inside—an employee or employees.

Theft and Vandalism

Theft is an ever present concern in the modern hotel. It may come from guests, employees, or uninvited trespassers. Engineering's responsibility is to provide and maintain security equipment in the hotel that helps to protect against theft. Security within guestrooms is maintained with the following equipment:

- automatic door closures on solid core doors
- automatic latching devices on all exterior guestroom doors that require a key or keycard to open and unlock the door
- deadbolts that extend at least ¾″ into the frame of the door and are set from the inside, but can be opened from the outside with a special emergency passkey
- a door chain or other locking device that is set from the inside of the room
- a peephole installed in the outer guestroom door that allows the occupant a 180° view both vertically and horizontally
- drapes that fully close and completely obstruct any view of the room from the outside
- locking latches and bars on all sliding glass exterior doors
- a card entry system for the primary door lock that allows the reprogramming of the lock with every new guest arrival

Card entry systems have simplified and greatly improved guest security, and should be adopted by all hotels. Most of the systems are designed around the premise that when a guest checks into the hotel, a plastic card which has a magnetic code impressed into the strip is given to the guest. The card unlocks the guestroom door with a combination that has been assigned to the new guest. When the previous guest checked out, their code has been effectively obliterated from the system. Housekeeping and other master cards can be reset in an instant when the need arises.

Many of the locks can be *interrogated*, that is, the lock can report when the room was entered and whose key was used to enter the door. This capability can be tremendously important when a theft is reported. This feature may well help to exonerate an employee, such as a guestroom attendant, who has been accused of pilfering an item from a guestroom.

The guestroom television is often the most pilfered item in a hotel. One of your authors has physically chased some television thieves at a property where she was working at the time. Some hotels have even taken to locking down the remote control so that it does not disappear into guest suitcases. In making the decision to lock down the remote controls, engineering has to calculate the savings to the hotel versus the imposition to the guest and the corresponding increase in guest dissatisfaction.

However, locking down the television is an almost universal practice. Many hotels are currently upgrading their televisions to liquid crystal display (LCD) or plasma sets that are far more expensive than the traditional cathode ray tube sets. A theft of one or more of these sets constitutes a serious loss to the hotel. Televisions should be bolted down to cabinets, table tops, or walls so that their removal requires special tools and keys.

Vandalism, particularly graffiti can be far more than a minor inconvenience to the property. Fences and exterior walls are particularly vulnerable. Chemicals have been developed to ease the process of graffiti removal. Sealants have been formulated to repel paints and dyes to aid in cleanup. Cleaning agents have also been developed to remove unwanted paints from surfaces quickly and relatively painlessly.

Bomb Threats, Crimes of Violence, and Other Dangerous Activities

Bomb threats often require a complete search of the premises. Engineering departments are often asked to lead search teams because of their familiarity with the property. It is also a good idea to make sure the property is kept neat, clean, and orderly so that there is a reduced chance that a device can be hidden. Tools and equipment should always be placed in their proper storage areas. Chemicals should not be left lying around so that an opportunistic arsonist can use them to start fires.

Terrorist activities are also based on opportunistic circumstances. Doors to equipment rooms should be kept locked. Ventilation systems are particularly vulnerable to a terrorist who may want to injure or kill his victims by placing chemical or biological agents into the ventilation system in order to spread illness or death throughout the hotel. The Department of Homeland Security has urged all building operators to move their building's ventilation intake dampers off the first floor and relocate them to upper floors so that a passerby cannot compromise the hotel's indoor air quality.

Another recent trend is the use of hotels by illegal drug makers to make methamphetamine. Many of the chemicals used in the process are extremely dangerous and if released into the environment can easily kill or injure people. Engineering and housekeeping departments should be on the lookout for guests who refuse any service. They should also look for fire detectors that have been compromised (wrapped in plastic or disconnected). Another telltale sign is a room that is running its air-conditioning in winter and there is a strong chemical smell emanating from the room. If a lab is discovered, cleanup should not be the responsibility of housekeeping or engineering. Specially trained cleanup crews should be used and the room should not be rented until the proper authorities certify it to be habitable once again.

Security Systems

The engineering department may not be in charge of operating the closed circuit television cameras in the hotel, but they will assuredly find themselves in charge of their maintenance and perhaps even their installation. Recording onto hard drives has started to replace the video cassette recorders (VCRs), which makes the process far easier. The resolution of the cameras now is simply remarkable. Stories of reading a watch on a patron from 75 feet away are now quite common. Cameras should be located in hallways, lobbies, entryways, elevators, parking lots, meeting rooms, restaurants, and lounges. Properties should never use the empty camera housings instead of a real camera system. When guests see these empty housings, they believe they are more secure because they are being watched by cameras, but unscrupulous employees and outsiders may well know that the housings are empty, which gives them a decidedly unfair advantage over unsuspecting guests.

Other security systems would include communication systems, lighting in parking lots and public areas, landscaping, fences, elevators that take a special card or code to operate, and locks on exterior doors.

Summary

Management's responsibility in the area of safety and security is clear, and must not, under any circumstances, be abdicated in favor or the belief that nothing of an emergency nature could ever happen to the hotel or to their guests and employees. Lax attitudes or the mistaken belief that money spent on safety and security is a waste will usually end in disaster. Remember: if nothing ever happens, security is doing a good job.

Key Terms and Concepts

1990 Hotel and Motel
  Fire Safety Act *221*
addressable
  systems *243*
automatic door
  closure *239*
backdraft *226*
branch lines *234*
carbon monoxide
  (CO) *226*
critical incident
  response teams *223*
cross mains *234*

door closures *239*
dry pipe *228*
due diligence *225*
emergency action
  plan *222*
emergency response
  plan *222*
fire rating *239*
Fire Triangle *225*
flashover *226*
fusible link *239*
ignition
  temperature *225*

incipient stage *236*
National Fire Protection
  Association
  (NFPA) *221*
OSHA *221*
pendant sprinkler *234*
post-incident
  program *223*
ppm *226*
pressurization
  systems *239*
products of
  combustion *225*

remote annunciation
  systems *243*
riser *228*
risk manager *222*
sidewall sprinkler *234*
smoke and fire
  dampers *239*
upright sprinkler *234*
wet pipe *228*

Discussion and Review Questions

1. What is the difference between safety and security?
2. Explain the benefits of a card entry system over the hard key method traditionally employed.
3. List the type of security systems the engineering department might have to maintain.
4. Describe the elements of a competent emergency action plan.
5. List the products of combustion and explain why they can be so deadly.

11

Vertical Transportation

CHAPTER OBJECTIVES

After reading this chapter, the student should be able to:

- identify the basic types of elevators and escalators.
- describe how each type of elevator operates.
- describe the major components of elevators and escalators.
- discuss the proper application for each type of elevator or escalator.
- describe the safety mechanisms and systems present in elevators and escalators.
- describe how to respond to a variety of elevator emergencies.
- discuss the components of a vertical transportation maintenance contract.

INTRODUCTION

Man has needed to move people and materials upwards for millennia. There is evidence of elevator-like devices being used to move gladiators and animals through the Coliseum in ancient Rome. Most vertical lifting devices prior to the 1700s used a rope and pulley system, with animals or people performing the hoisting tasks. Eventually, elevator systems incorporated some type of mechanical power to perform the hoisting, often using water pressure and counterweighting. However, all early vertical transportation systems posed a hazard because they were unsafe. If a hoisting rope were to unravel, break, or come untied from its anchor, the platform or bucket in which materials and people were loaded would crash.

This problem was solved in 1854 when Elisha Graves Otis introduced the first "safe" elevator to the world at the Crystal Palace Exposition in New York City. This elevator incorporated a safety device that gripped the elevator's guiderails when the hoisting rope was severed, and it consistently prevented the elevator from plunging into the hoistway pit. This invention revolutionized modern architectural design. The technology to build tall buildings was always present, but the physical exertion necessary to move people and materials rendered tall buildings impractical.

The creation of a safe elevator was soon followed by the design and construction of the first skyscrapers, and the modern urban landscape emerged.

Vertical transportation is a blanket description for equipment and systems that move people and materials up and down a building. Common components of a hospitality facility's vertical transportation system include passenger elevators, dumbwaiters, freight elevators, and escalators. We will address each type of equipment in this chapter, with a focus on safety devices and procedures. We will also briefly examine vertical transportation maintenance issues.

ELEVATORS

There are two basic types of elevators: passenger elevators and freight elevators. **Passenger elevators** are designed with many safety features that protect the general public from harm while using the elevator system. **Freight elevators** are large elevators that have reinforced framing to accommodate extremely heavy loads that move horizontally across the elevator floor. Freight elevators generally do not have as many safety features as passenger elevators and could pose a danger to members of the general public. These elevators should not be available for use by guests or by employees who have not been properly trained to operate them. **Dumbwaiters** are small elevators that do not have any of the safety features necessary for transporting people or animals; they are only used to move material. There are several components that are common to all elevators.

HOISTWAY   First, all elevators travel up and down a hoistway, or elevator shaft. They are guided up and down the hoistway along guiderails. The bottom of the hoistway is called the **elevator pit**, which contains a type of safety equipment called a **buffer**. The buffer breaks the elevator's descent into the pit if it travels too far down.

MACHINE ROOMS   Elevators also have **machine rooms** which contain the mechanical equipment that makes the elevator go up and down. Machine rooms may have **hoisting machines**, hydraulic tanks and pumps, controllers, and various pieces of safety equipment in them. The **controller** is the "brain" of the elevator system and controls how fast the elevator travels, which direction it travels, where it is located, and where it needs to stop. It also controls other functions, such as opening and closing doors, operating the position and direction indicators that tell passengers where the elevator's location is in the hoistway and its direction of travel, and operating the elevator during emergency situations.

ENTRANCES   Elevators make stops at floors up and down the building. Each stop is called an **entrance**. A typical elevator entrance includes a frame, doors, **hall buttons** that passengers push to call the elevator, and markings on the elevator entrance that indicate the floor number (Figures 11.1a and b). Some elevator entrances include lights or digital read-outs that indicate the current

FIGURE 11.1a   Elevator Entrance.   *Source*: Dina Zemke.

FIGURE 11.1b   Elevator Entrance with a Trompe l'oeil Finish to Look Like Bookshelves. *Source*: Dina Zemke.

location of the elevator, its current direction of travel, and hall lanterns that indicate the direction that the elevator will travel after it stops at the floor.

ELEVATOR CAB   The part of the elevator that passengers ride in is called the elevator cab. The interior of the cab will have several control and indicator features. First, the **car operating panel** contains the floor buttons that passengers push to indicate the floor they wish to travel to (Figure 11.2). The car operating panel will also have a car position indicator that tells the passenger which floor the elevator is passing or where it has stopped. Tones sound as the

FIGURE 11.2   Car
Operating Panel.
Source: Dina Zemke.

elevator is passing floors, to indicate to sight-impaired people the location of the elevator. The elevator should also have a telephone unit with a hands-free operation in the elevator car operating panel that will allow trapped passengers to communicate with someone outside if the elevator is stuck. Finally, the car operating panel contains some safety features that allow the fire department to use the elevator in an emergency.

Other components of the elevator cab include lighting and **emergency lighting** that works when the elevator system loses power, such as in an electrical blackout. The cab should have a handrail to comply with the Americans with Disabilities Act. There is a **door operator** mounted on the top of the elevator cab. This piece of equipment opens and closes the elevator car door as well as the hallway entrance doors. The doors in the car and in the hallway will not open unless they are opened by the door operator or with special equipment used by elevator professionals.

DOOR EQUIPMENT   The elevator door also has a safety device that prevents the doors from closing on passengers or equipment in the entrance to the elevator. Older systems use a mechanical edge that retracts when it comes into contact with a solid object, sending a signal to the elevator controller to reopen the door. Newer systems do not require contact with the object to cause the doors to reverse direction. These systems usually use beams of infrared light that crisscross the elevator entrance. When one of these beams is broken by the presence of an object in the entrance, the signal is sent to the controller to reverse the door operation.

COMMON TERMS

There are three common terms used to describe the operating features of an elevator. They are described below.

Capacity

First, the elevator may be described according to its **capacity**, or the amount of weight that it is designed to carry. Capacity is specified in pounds in the United States, and in kilograms in areas that use the metric system. Typically capacities for passenger elevators range from 2,000 to 5,000 pounds (908–2,270 kg).

Speed

Next, elevators may be described by their **speed** of travel. This is specified either in feet/minute or in meters/second. Typical elevator speeds range from 100 feet/minute (0.50 meters/second) to 1,400 feet/minute (7 meters/second) or higher.

Travel

Finally, elevators are often described by the number of stops that they make or the distance that they travel. The number of **stops** often equals the number of floors in the building, but not in all cases. There are many elevators that are prevented from stopping at certain floors in the middle of the hoistway, which means that there are fewer stops than there are floors. The elevator's **rise** is the distance (in feet or centimeters) that the elevator actually travels from the bottom landing to the top landing. The elevator's rise will always be less than the building's height. An elevator's rise can range from only a few inches to over a thousand feet.

TYPES OF ELEVATORS

There are two basic methods of moving elevators: hydraulic and traction.

Hydraulic Elevators

Hydraulic elevators are the most common type of elevator in the world. Hydraulic equipment uses liquid to move objects. Hydraulic elevators consist of a **piston and cylinder** that have traditionally been buried in the ground below the elevator hoistway. The piston travels up and down the surrounding cylinder when oil is pumped in or out of the cylinder. If oil is pumped in, it displaces the piston and the piston rises. Similarly, if oil is let out of the cylinder, then the piston descends into the cylinder. The piston is attached to the elevator cab, causing the elevator to rise or descend (Figure 11.3).

The hydraulic oil is contained in a tank in the elevator's machine room, which is usually located next to the elevator hoistway at the bottom landing.

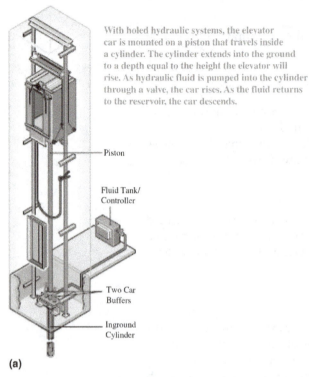

With holed hydraulic systems, the elevator car is mounted on a piston that travels inside a cylinder. The cylinder extends into the ground to a depth equal to the height the elevator will rise. As hydraulic fluid is pumped into the cylinder through a valve, the car rises. As the fluid returns to the reservoir, the car descends.

Piston

Fluid Tank/ Controller

Two Car Buffers

Inground Cylinder

(a)

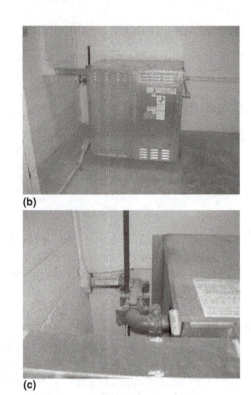

(b)

(c)

FIGURE 11.3   (a) Section View: Hydraulic Elevator System.   *Source*: Otis Elevator. (b) Hydraulic Elevator Tank with Front-Mounted Controller. (c) Piping from Hydraulic Tank to Elevator Hoistway.   *Source*: Dina Zemke.

The oil is pushed into the cylinder by a pump connected to the tank. When the elevator needs to travel in a downward direction, a valve into the tank opens and the weight of the elevator cab pushes the oil back into the tank by gravity. This means that the pump only operates when the elevator is traveling in the up direction.

Traditionally, the hydraulic elevator's piston and cylinder were buried in the ground. The piston needs to be as long as the total rise of the elevator and thus must be buried in a hole in the ground that is as deep as the elevator's rise. Drilling a very straight, very deep hole can be both tricky and expensive. The driller can run into underground streams that cause the hole to collapse or flood. Sometimes the driller encounters large boulders that are difficult to penetrate. The need to excavate the hole limits the rise that the elevator can travel. Elevator companies have addressed this problem for relatively low-rise projects by developing **holeless hydraulic elevators** that use telescoping pistons and cylinders, eliminating the need for a hole. More recently, elevator companies have developed a **roped hydraulic elevator**, which is a hybrid type of equipment that uses both a buried piston and cylinder as well as hoisting ropes to operate the equipment and thus allows a higher rise of travel in the system.

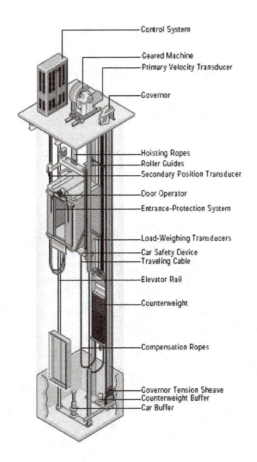

Control System
Geared Machine
Primary Velocity Transducer
Governor
Hoisting Ropes
Roller Guides
Secondary Position Transducer
Door Operator
Entrance-Protection System
Load-Weighing Transducers
Car Safety Device
Traveling Cable
Elevator Rail
Counterweight
Compensation Ropes
Governor Tension Sheave
Counterweight Buffer
Car Buffer

FIGURE 11.4 Section View: Traction Elevator System. *Source*: Otis Elevator.

Traction Elevators

Traction elevators are hoisted using **ropes** or cables. They are often also called **cable elevators** or **electric elevators**. There are two basic types of traction elevators: geared and gearless. The type used for a building project is determined by how fast and how far the elevator needs to travel (Figure 11.4).

Most traction elevators have a machine room that is located at the top of the elevator hoistway. You may occasionally see older traction elevators that have the machine room located at the bottom landing, adjacent to the hoistway. The machine room contains the elevator hoisting machine and brakes, the elevator controller, and the overspeed governor, a safety device that shuts down the elevator if it is traveling too fast. Here are some basic elements of a traction elevator:

ELEVATOR ROPES Traction elevators are moved up and down the hoistway by cables that are attached to the top of the elevator cab. These cables are called **ropes** in the elevator industry, because the cable consists of a hemp rope or some other type of flexible core that is wrapped by many strands of metal wire. Every traction elevator will be hoisted by at least three ropes and as many as eight ropes. Each rope is capable of lifting the elevator by itself; if one rope should break (which rarely happens), the elevator is not in danger of falling to the bottom of the hoistway.

TRACTION ELEVATOR MACHINES   The ropes attached to the top of the elevator cab run up the hoistway and over a grooved sheave that is similar to a pulley in the machine room (Figures 11.5a and b). The machine is connected to a motor that turns the sheave to move the elevator. The other end of the rope is attached to a **counterweight**, which is a large rack of weights that moves up and down the hoistway in the opposite direction of the elevator's travel. The counterweight

FIGURE 11.5a Hoisting Machine. *Source*: Dina Zemke.

FIGURE 11.5b Hoisting Ropes. *Source*: Dina Zemke.

reduces the amount of work that the elevator hoisting motor has to do to turn the sheave.

The traction elevator also has a set of **brakes** on the hoisting machine. The brakes do not slow down and stop the elevator. Instead, this is done by slowing the machine down electrically. Once the sheave has stopped turning, the brakes are set in place to prevent the elevator from moving until the controller tells it to move to another floor.

GOVERNOR AND SAFETIES   The elevator **governor** is a mechanical device that prevents the elevator from traveling too fast. If the governor detects that the elevator's speed is too fast, generally 115% of rated speed, the governor will first attempt to shut down the elevator by disconnecting power to the motor (Figure 11.6). If the elevator continues to travel, even though there is no power, at 125% of rated speed, the governor will mechanically engage the "**safeties.**" Safeties are clamps that will grab onto the guiderails in the hoistway if the elevator is traveling too fast. These are a modern version of the same safety devices that Elisha Graves Otis demonstrated during the Crystal Palace Exposition. The elevator usually only travels a few feet between the time the overspeed condition is detected and the engagement of the safety devices. The safeties must be manually reset before the elevator can move again.

Geared Elevators

Geared elevators are used for medium-rise, medium-speed projects. A typical application for a geared elevator will be a building with anywhere from 6 to 20 stops. The elevator will travel at speeds that could range from 250 to 400 feet per minute. A geared elevator could be used for a taller building but it would

FIGURE 11.6 The Governor Protects Against Overspeed Situations. *Source*: Dina Zemke.

take a long time for the elevator to travel completely up the hoistway, which would result in unhappy passengers.

This type of traction elevator is called a "geared" elevator because the hoisting machine uses a worm and gear arrangement to take the energy from the machine's motor and turn the sheave upon which the ropes travel.

Gearless Elevators

Gearless elevators are used for higher-rise, higher-speed applications. Typical gearless applications have 15 or more stops and the elevator travels at speeds that could range from 400 to 1,500 fpm. For example, the Stratosphere Tower in Las Vegas, Nevada has a bank of gearless passenger elevators that travel 1,800 feet per minute. These elevators travel to the observation deck at the top of the 1,149-foot tower in less than 30 seconds.

Gearless elevators are called "gearless" because they do not use a worm and gear arrangement to turn the hoist rope sheave. The sheave is turned directly by the elevator motor. This type of elevator is mechanically more complex than a geared elevator and therefore costs more to install and maintain.

SAFETY IN ELEVATORS

Elevators are one of the most secure forms of transportation in the world, thanks to the many devices and procedures that have been developed to ensure the safe transport of passengers. Some of the safety devices and procedures include the elevator safeties, the periodic testing of the safeties, the firefighters' service functions, the leveling control, and the improved design of the hydraulic piston and cylinder.

GOVERNORS, SAFETIES, AND TESTING   The traction elevator's overspeed governor and safety devices, discussed earlier in this chapter, provide a way to stop the elevator in its tracks in the event that it is traveling at a dangerously high speed. It is, of course, important to maintain this equipment. Most jurisdictions require periodic testing of the devices to insure that they will work properly in a real emergency. Two types of tests are conducted: the **no-load test** and the **full-load test**.

The no-load test involves overriding the elevator's normal control function of the speed, allowing the elevator to go into a free fall. This free fall condition should trip the overspeed governor, which will activate the safety clamps that grip the elevator guiderails and then it will stop the elevator. The test is called a "no-load" test because it is conducted without adding weight to the elevator. The no-load safety test should be conducted once a year. The "full-load" safety test is conducted every five years. It requires the mechanic to load the elevator cab with the full, rated weight capacity of the elevator. The elevator is then sent into a free fall to test if the safety devices operate properly while carrying a full load.

FIREFIGHTER'S SERVICE   We have probably all seen signs in or near an elevator that indicate that the elevator should not be used in the event of a fire. This is because the elevator may stop at the floor where the fire is occurring and could put passengers and property in danger. However, some people still try to use elevators in a fire emergency, sometimes with tragic results. Local, state, and national standards now require elevators to have a special operation system that is activated when a fire is detected, to insure passenger safety and also to allow trained firefighters to use the elevator during the emergency.

Firefighter's service is a two-phase operation. Phase One is activated by a smoke detector that is located in the vicinity of the elevator. These smoke detectors are located at the elevator landing at each building floor, and also at the top of the hoistway and in the machine room. These smoke detectors are connected directly to the elevator controller and only these detectors should initiate firefighter service. The building's fire detection system should not trigger the elevator's firefighter service (Figures 11.7a and b).

FIGURE 11.7a
Firefighter's Service—
In-car.   *Source*: Dina
Zemke.

FIGURE 11.7b
Firefighter's Service
Keyswitch in the Hallway.
Source: Dina Zemke.

When the controller receives the fire signal from the smoke detector, the elevator travels immediately to the main landing for the elevator, which is the landing that allows quickest access to exit from the building. This floor is usually (but not always) at the ground or lobby level of the building. The elevator opens its doors at the main landing and will not move, preventing passengers from traveling up into the building. The elevator will only move again if it is reset by authorized personnel.

Phase Two provides access to the upper floors for firefighters and other trained personnel. A switch, activated by a special key, is turned on, and the trained personnel can travel up near the floor where the fire has been detected. This also allows the fire department to move its equipment up to the trouble area quickly and efficiently. While managers of hospitality properties should not use the elevator during a fire emergency, it is important that they know where the keys are located to help the fire department during an emergency.

LEVELING A major source of passenger injuries in elevators is the result of poor **leveling**. Leveling refers to the elevator's ability to stop at a floor, level with the floor landing. If the elevator stops slightly below or above the floor level, a tripping hazard is produced. Passengers often trip as they enter or exit the elevator, and sometimes experience serious injuries. Older elevators were installed in compliance with leveling standards that are not acceptable today. Newer elevator systems have improved control that provides leveling to within 0.25 inches of the floor level (Figure 11.8).

SINGLE-BOTTOM CYLINDER FAILURE Hydraulic elevators, as previously discussed, use a piston and cylinder arrangement that is buried in the ground. Some older cylinders have been found to corrode over time, due to a combination of ground water and minerals in the water. The minerals, water, and the metal in the cylinder itself generate an electrical charge and a process called **electrolysis** that eventually eats holes in the cylinder. The cylinder contains

FIGURE 11.8 Leveling—Modern Elevators Should Level to Within +/– 1/4".
Source: Dina Zemke.

the hydraulic oil that is used to raise and lower the elevator, but the holes allow the oil to seep into the surrounding soil.

Leaking cylinders are bad for two reasons. First, the oil may create an environmental contamination hazard in the surrounding soil and perhaps even in the groundwater supply. More seriously, the elevator may also experience a **catastrophic failure**. This failure occurs when the hole in the elevator cylinder is large and suddenly breaks loose. The result is that all of the oil in the cylinder would gush out into the soil at once, which would cause the elevator to make an uncontrolled descent (a.k.a., a crash). This problem can cause severe building damage as well as serious injury or death for passengers.

Your elevator company should maintain records on how much oil the system contains and make a note if it appears to be losing oil. There are several ways for a hydraulic elevator to lose oil. They should all be investigated. However, your elevator company may determine that there is a leak in the cylinder. The only way to fix this problem is to dig up the old cylinder and replace it with a new one, which is a very costly, time-consuming, messy process. However, it is the only option. Newer hydraulic elevators are constructed with special materials and design features to prevent this problem from occurring. The replacement cylinder should be equipped with a double-bottom construction to prevent the catastrophic failure, as well as being housed in a PVC (polyvinyl chloride) case to prevent electrolysis from occurring.

ESCALATORS

Escalators are another way of moving people vertically through a building (Figure 11.9). Escalators were originally called "moving stairways." The first patent for a moving stairway was granted in 1859. However, the first moving stairway available for public use was built by Jesse Reno in 1895 and installed at

FIGURE 11.9 Escalator—a Spiral Version.
Source: Dina Zemke.

Coney Island in New York. Another elevator manufacturer, Charles Seeberger, joined with the Otis Elevator Company in 1899. The term **escalator** is actually a brand name for Otis Elevator Company's early version of a moving stairway. The term entered the public domain as a generic term for all moving stairways in 1950.

Escalators are used to move large numbers of passengers up or down a relatively short distance. Some escalator systems are capable of moving thousands of passengers per hour. Some of the basic components are the truss, which contains the motors, chains, and controller; the steps; the handrail; and numerous safety devices (Figure 11.10).

TRUSS   The escalator **truss** is the structural assembly in which the escalator travels. This is usually assembled in the factory and dropped into place using a crane during the building's construction. The truss provides the framework for the escalator's steps and machinery. The escalator's machine room is located in the floor at the top of the escalator. The machine room contains the escalator's controller panel as well as all of the motors that drive the moving parts of the escalator.

STEPS   The first major moving part of the escalator is the **steps**. These are pulled up or down by chains that are driven by a motor. The steps' surfaces are grooved for two reasons. First, the grooves, or **combs**, provide a measure of slip protection for passengers. Second, the combs provide safety as the passengers enter or exit the escalator by protecting objects such as shoes, shoelaces, fabric, or packages from getting caught in the equipment at the top or bottom landing of the escalator.

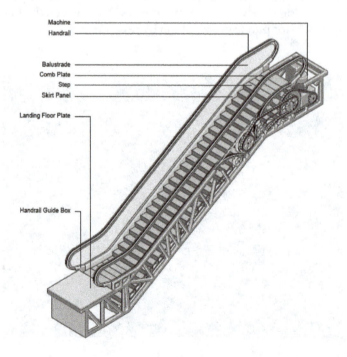

FIGURE 11.10   Section View: Escalator.
Source: Otis Elevator.

HANDRAILS AND BALUSTRADES   The next major moving part of the escalator is the **handrail**, the rubber-like rail that passengers grip while riding the escalator. Handrails are driven by a motor and chain system in the machine room. The handrail rides along the escalator's **balustrade**, which is the vertical element of the escalator, similar to a wall in appearance. Balustrades may be sheathed in metal or may be constructed of glass.

SAFETY FEATURES   Escalators have numerous moving parts and gaps, which create some fairly serious safety hazards for passengers. Safety devices are provided to protect passengers from harm, including demarcation lights, emergency stop switches, and skirt panel protection. **Demarcation lights** are lights that glow at the top and bottom landings of the escalators. They provide a visual cue for passengers that they are about to enter or exit the escalator so the passenger can focus on moving safely onto or off the escalator. **Emergency stop switches** are provided to allow a person at one of the escalator landings to quickly stop the escalator if an emergency arises (Figure 11.11).

The part of the escalator where the steps and the balustrade meet is called the **skirt panel**. There is usually a small gap between the step and the skirt panel, which creates a serious hazard for passengers because it is easy to get shoes, shoelaces, and loose clothing caught in the equipment. This hazard has caused serious injury to passengers in the past, particularly to small children who sat on the escalator step and got fingers or clothing caught in the equipment. New developments in escalator safety include ultra-slick skirt panels that reduce the likelihood of material catching on the gap as well as devices that close the gap between the step and the skirt panel.

HOSPITALITY ESCALATORS   One final note on escalator safety: the escalator should never be used to transport equipment, carts, baggage, or strollers. There have been many past incidences where hotel employees find it quicker to take a luggage cart up the escalator instead of waiting for an elevator. A guest may find it quicker or more convenient to take a child's stroller up the escalator.

FIGURE 11.11
Escalator Emergency Stop Switch.   *Source*: Dina Zemke.

Alas, it is uncommon, but not unheard of, for escalators to stop suddenly. The law of inertia states that an object in motion tends to stay in motion. If the escalator stops suddenly, the passengers, baggage, and other materials on the escalator will keep moving and serious injury or death could occur.

In addition, escalators are especially dangerous for children. Their clothing, hair, limbs, shoes, or other parts might get caught in the equipment and it could lead to loss of limb or life. If you see children playing on or around escalators, you should see that they are moved to another area. This may require you to explain to their parents why the escalator is very dangerous. If the parents become indignant or upset, it is a small price to pay compared to the costs of injuries, death, lawsuits, and negative publicity.

ELEVATOR AND ESCALATOR MAINTENANCE CONTRACTS

The complex nature and the importance of maintaining the safety of elevator and escalator equipment require this equipment to receive regular inspection and maintenance. There are three basic types of maintenance contracts: 1) lubrication and inspection, 2) lubrication, inspection and small parts, and 3) full maintenance.

LUBRICATION AND INSPECTION The lubrication and inspection contract offers minimal coverage for the elevator system. A mechanic visits the equipment on a periodic basis—usually monthly, quarterly, semi-annually, or annually—and performs a visual inspection of the equipment. Moving parts are oiled and greased, provided the lubrication is accessible on a superficial basis (i.e., parts do not need to be disassembled for access). The mechanic will then write up a list of repairs that the elevator requires, which can be performed at an additional cost.

This is the least expensive planned maintenance option. However, if anything goes wrong with the elevator, the repair or replacement work must be done at an additional cost, which is difficult to predict. Newer hydraulic elevators may be suitable for this type of maintenance, since their controllers are electronic and do not contain as many small moving parts and electrical contacts as their predecessors. It will probably be more expensive to maintain older hydraulic elevators as well as traction elevators, because the increased number of moving parts may lead to more frequent unplanned maintenance and repair expenses. Due to the complexity of escalator systems and the owner's exposure to liability for injury, the lubrication and inspection contract is not recommended for escalators.

LUBRICATION, INSPECTION, AND SMALL PARTS This type of contract covers the same lubrication and inspection items as the previous contract but also includes **minor repairs**, adjustments, and **small parts**. This contract may also allow a set number of **trouble calls**, or calls for service when the elevator is malfunctioning. The caution for the building owner or manager is that the definition of "minor" repairs and "small" parts can be quite restrictive. The building manager might find that virtually every problem with the elevator is not considered to be a minor repair or a small part, and the additional repair expenses might be quite costly. Again, the complexity and liability issues surrounding escalators make this type of contract unsuitable for escalator maintenance.

FULL MAINTENANCE   A full maintenance contract will cover lubrication, inspection, and all repairs that arise from normal wear and tear. This type of contract is appropriate for elevators and escalators. This type of contract usually includes unlimited maintenance calls during regular business hours.

CONTRACT OPTIONS   Elevator contracts may come with a variety of optional coverage. One such option is the inclusion of **overtime callbacks**, or calls for emergency service outside of regular business hours. This may be added to a full maintenance contract at an additional cost.

Other options on today's elevator maintenance contracts may offer discounts for remote elevator monitoring, billing terms, and extended contract length options. Some elevator companies will install monitoring equipment on the elevator that will automatically notify the elevator company if some aspect of the elevator is performing incorrectly. This saves money for the elevator company in the long run, so the company might offer a discount for this type of service.

Elevator maintenance companies' costs are reduced if they need to invoice the customer less frequently and if the customer pays bills promptly. Some companies offer customers discounts for quarterly, semi-annual, or annual billing frequencies, rather than issuing invoices on a monthly basis. Additional discounts might be available if the customer is willing to pay an invoice automatically via direct debit electronic fund transfer, rather than sending the invoice through the billing department and waiting for a check to be cut and sent to the elevator company.

ELEVATOR MAINTENANCE CONTRACT MANAGEMENT   The building owner or manager should always obtain at least three bids from reputable companies for elevator and/or escalator maintenance. Once the bids are obtained, the owner/manager should carefully examine the proposals and compare them. Some of the items that should be specifically examined are the following items.

BILLING TERMS   How often will the customer be invoiced and for what price? Companies will bill at different frequencies, so the price shown on the proposal needs to be broken down into comparable units, usually a per month amount.

CONTRACT LENGTH   What is the length of the contract term? One year, two years, and five years are common contract lengths.

CANCELLATION POLICY   When and how does the customer cancel the contract? Some states in the United States allow **rollover contracts**, where the contract automatically "rolls over" into another contract cycle unless the customer explicitly cancels the contract within an acceptable length of time.

PARTS AND SYSTEMS COVERED   Examine the contracts carefully to see if one contractor excludes parts or systems in the elevator or escalator from coverage. A price that is too low is usually an indicator that the contractor is excluding components from coverage.

VISIT FREQUENCY   Compare the contracts to determine the extent of the coverage and the frequency of the mechanic's visits.

TROUBLE CALLS   Examine the contracts to determine the times and extent of coverage for trouble calls. Different contractors will have different coverages specified in the contract.

MODERNIZATION OF ELEVATORS

Elevators and escalators can typically operate for many years with adequate preventive maintenance. However, all systems must eventually be renovated, as dictated by changing customer tastes, regulatory issues, or through wear and tear. An elevator system will usually operate well for 20–25 years with good maintenance, but may then need to be modernized. Modernization can include updating the appearance of the elevator's interior and operating fixtures, controller operation, door operation, and safety devices. The entire elevator might be modernized at one time or the modernization may be broken down into phases, which may be a more affordable way to spread the expense of the project over time. Each modernization project is unique and should be included in the property's capital budgeting process. A good resource for planning for the future modernization of the equipment is your elevator maintenance company's representative.

Summary

Elevators and escalators allow us to occupy very tall buildings. There are two types of elevators: hydraulic (the most common; for low-rise buildings) and traction (for medium- to high-rise buildings). While elevators are one of the safest forms of transportation available, they are also frequently misunderstood. If your building has elevators, there is the possibility that a problem will arise, including a passenger entrapment. You need to know the various components of elevators and how they work to communicate effectively with trapped passengers, frustrated employees, and your elevator service provider. Elevator maintenance is expensive but extremely necessary not only to ensure the safe operation of the building and the compliance with codes, but also to ensure high productivity in the building—you and your employees cannot do your jobs if you are waiting around for an elevator!

Escalators pose some unique safety risks because there are several points in the system where passengers can get pinched or caught in moving parts. It is, of course, important to have high-quality maintenance performed. However, it is equally important, particularly in hotels, to ensure that your employees use the escalator correctly—i.e., no bellcarts on the escalator—and that they enforce safe riding procedures among the guests, particularly children.

Key Terms and Concepts

Balustrade 265	cable elevators 257	catastrophic failure 263	counterweight 258
brakes 259	capacity 255	combs 264	demarcation lights 265
buffer 252	car operating panel 253	controller 252	door operator 154

Discussion and Review Questions

1. Describe how a hydraulic elevator operates, including the function of the piston and cylinder.
2. Describe how a traction elevator operates, including the function of the counterweight.
3. What are some of the clauses you need to compare between vendor bids when assessing proposals for an elevator maintenance contract? What does each clause cover?

4. Let's say you have a hotel guest trapped in an elevator and the guest is panicking! How would you talk to the guest to assure him/her that the elevator is safe? Make sure you describe the safety features built into elevators.
5. Should you ever personally ride in a dumbwaiter? Why or why not?
6. How does an elevator's governor work?

Notes

How Stuff Works.com—these two topics in How Stuff Works are animated!
    http://science.howstuffworks.com/elevator.htm
    http://science.howstuffworks.com/escalator.htm
    Kone Corporation: www.kone.com
Goodwin, Jason. (2001). *Otis: Giving rise to the modern city*. Chicago, IL: Ivan R. Dee, Inc.
Otis Elevator Company: www.otis.com

Schindler USA, The Elevator Company: www.us.schindler.com
ThyssenKrupp Elevator: www.thyssenkruppelevator.com
www.elevatorworld.com—look for the Saf-T Rider program for escalator safety.

12

Foodservice and Laundry Systems

CHAPTER OBJECTIVES

After studying the chapter, the student should be able to:

- describe equipment selection considerations for foodservice equipment.
- identify all foodservice equipment and describe relevant options for each item.
- describe the maintenance considerations for different types of foodservice equipment.
- describe the vapor-compression process that is used in most refrigeration equipment.
- identify equipment needed to operate a laundry in small and large hotels.
- describe the steps in planning a hotel laundry.
- describe examples of laundry design considerations.
- describe non-equipment and engineering considerations when building a laundry.

INTRODUCTION

This chapter examines two specialized building systems that are common to hospitality facilities: food service and laundries. We will explore the factors influencing the selection of equipment, the types of equipment normally found in these areas, the operation of the equipment, and also energy, maintenance, and sanitation considerations.

FOODSERVICE EQUIPMENT

This section focuses on the selection, care, and maintenance of foodservice equipment to optimize its performance, prolong its life, and minimize its operating cost. Everything starts with the operation's menu. For it is the menu, along with the type of service offered (see Table 12.1), that will determine the proper kitchen and dining room equipment needed to produce the items on that menu. Ideally, the menu should be developed before the structure is designed and built because it

TABLE 12.1 Styles of Service	
American Service	Food is plated in the kitchen and the server brings it to the table and places it in front of the guest. In diners and coffee shops, the plates may be carried by hand. In more upscale surroundings, a tray and a jack stand may be used. The plates are placed on a waiter's tray, which the server carries on one shoulder balanced with one hand, and in the other hand the server carries a jack stand which is a portable stand that will hold the tray when the server arrives at the table. This arrangement eliminates multiple trips to and from the kitchen.
English Service	Food is placed on serving dishes in the kitchen. Then the serving dishes and serving utensils are brought to the table. The serving dishes are passed around by the guests who serve themselves, sometimes with aid of a food server.
French Service	A food cart known as a *guéridon* is essential to French service. Food is placed on the cart in the kitchen and then is transported to the table where it may be carved or cooked in front of the guest on a *rechaud* (i.e., tableside grill), before it is served. *Flambé* work is a common type of tableside cookery in French service.
Russian Service	Food is placed onto serving dishes in the kitchen. Carved meats are made to look whole by the chef. The food server takes the dishes to the table and serves each guest from the serving dish.

will impact the allocation of space in the dining and kitchen areas as well as the facility's décor.

Equipment Selection Considerations

The first consideration in equipment selection is *need*. Is the equipment needed to produce items on the menu, will it reduce operating costs if purchased, or will it enhance the quality or quantity of the menu items produced? A microwave oven may be essential to a diner or coffee shop, but may be totally out of place in an exclusive French restaurant. A grill may be indispensable to a fast food restaurant featuring hamburgers, but completely superfluous to a tea room featuring baked goods, soup, and salad sandwiches.

Proper *sanitation* and *safety* of the equipment is crucial. The National Sanitation Foundation International (NSF) is an independent, not-for-profit organization committed to the health and safety of the American public by certifying goods and equipment used in the food, water, and consumer goods industries. A quick search of their web site www.nsf.org will give operators, lists of equipment that has passed NSF certification. Also, look for the NSF label on any prospective equipment.

Sharp edges on equipment and any moving parts should be shielded so that operators and customers cannot come in contact with them and suffer injury.

The adequate venting of flue gases from the combustion process should be included in the design of the equipment. Rough surfaces or hard-to-clean areas that could harbor bacteria should not be present on equipment. All electrical wiring should be properly grounded, and the wiring should not be exposed to fraying, which could cause shock hazards. Look for the Underwriters Laboratory (UL) certification mark on electrical and gas-fired appliances. Corners of appliances should be rounded to minimize injury if inadvertently hit by operators and the public. Hot water heaters on dishwashers and steam-jacketed kettles should have pressure release valves in case the thermostats of these units malfunction. These cautions are by no means complete, but they are some of the more important safety and sanitary issues to consider when selecting equipment.

Durability or the *reliability* of equipment is also an important consideration. Equipment designed for residential use simply does not hold up to the use and abuse encountered in a foodservice operation. Recently, commercial appliances have been making its way into residential kitchens, not only for their increased durability and performance, but also for the increased status of having commercial brands in one's kitchen at home. One should not exclusively rely on the word of the salesperson about an appliance's durability, but one should also confer with other operators, or other third parties about the equipment's durability.

Construction materials may be Monel metal, aluminum, wood, plastic, iron, or stainless steel. Monel is two-thirds nickel and one-third copper. It can be polished to a high sheen, but it has been largely replaced by stainless steel. Aluminum is light, but dents fairly easily and can corrode when exposed to acids. Wood is relatively lightweight, but is susceptible to moisture and can support bacteria. Stainless steel, specifically No. 304 stainless steel, which is composed of 18% chromium and 8% nickel, is highly prized because it has a high impact strength and a very high corrosion resistance.

The author of remembers very well a situation when a competitor purchased a very expensive pour control system for its bar and lounge. The unit was a one-button operation that would dispense, mix, and ring up an ordered beverage. The problem was that it was very sensitive to the slightest changes in voltage in the electrical system (i.e., transients). When the system went down, it effectively closed the bar. The company had no way to manually fix a drink for a customer. All the liquor and mix came through hoses linked to 1.75 liter bottles and most of the bartenders did not know the common drink recipes. To bring the system back up took a qualified repair person who was 1,500 miles from the hotel. Finally, after three catastrophic outages, management installed a sophisticated uninterruptible power supply (UPS) system, connected the pour control system to it, and the problem was finally solved after the loss of thousands of dollars in revenue. Reliability is often compromised when the level of complexity increases.

Performance of equipment is another concern to the operator. Does the unit function as it is intended to function? Is it easy to clean? Can it be easily disassembled and assembled for servicing? Does it need continual maintenance? Equipment that goes out of adjustment easily is usually costly to maintain.

The *appearance* of equipment is another factor to consider. It should blend in with the other equipment and should be attractive. Form should follow function as architect Ludwig Mies Vander Rohe once proclaimed.

Weight of the equipment can be a factor. The load capacity of the building's floors, walls, and ceilings should not be overloaded.

Most equipment depends on one or more of the following items: an energy supply (e.g., propane, methane, electricity, etc.), hot and/or cold water, connection to a sewer, and a ventilation system. Water in a kitchen is usually delivered at 140°F (60°C), but may then be increased with the aid of booster heaters, as in the case of dishwashers where water for rinsing and sanitation may be increased to 180°F (82.3°C). In the United States, natural gas (methane) is still considered to be the best value (more British Thermal Units for the dollar), so if there is a choice on the type of energy, natural gas is the prudent choice if all other factors are equal. Ventilation systems exhaust heat, moisture, and the waste products of combustion from the kitchen. The ventilation system maintains a negative atmospheric pressure in the kitchen. Odors, heat, and moisture should not pass from the kitchen into the dining room, but the airflow should be from the dining room to the kitchen and then out through ventilation hood system.

Food Preparation Equipment Considerations

Prior to cooking, food may be measured, mixed, cut, sliced, chopped, and peeled. This entails the use of the following equipment:

- cutters and choppers
- cutters and mixers
- extruders
- food processors
- scales
- slicers
- vegetable peelers

Every kitchen and dining room option should practice *clean as you go*. Those who dirty equipment should be expected to clean the equipment they used on every shift and, when necessary, clean the equipment multiple times during a shift. Kitchen personnel should also be trained to perform all light maintenance, such as the oiling of gears and the inspection of belts. These procedures can save the operation considerable time and money, plus it builds respect for the equipment on the part of the very individuals who use the equipment.

CUTTERS AND CHOPPERS   The commonly named "buffalo chopper" has a rotating bowl, a lid that forces the food into knives that are usually stainless steel in construction. It is a tabletop piece of equipment that can chop a wide assortment of foods. Figure 12.1 is an example of a 14-inch model. The size of the cut is determined by the length of time the chopper is operated. The knives will cycle at approximately 1,700 rpm. For safety's sake the knives

FIGURE 12.1   Buffalo Chopper 14″ Bowl.

should not operate if the cover is not properly attached so that no one can inadvertently come into contact with the knives.

Another important selection factor is a design that ensures proper sanitation. The unit should have rounded corners and be able to be dismantled for the complete cleaning of the bowl, cover, attachments, and knives. It should also have a plastic plunger to force the food into the knives. Attachments for the making of French fries, grinding, slicing, and shredding foods are available. The equipment should be cleaned frequently (at least once daily), and knives should be sharpened as specified in the manual. Shafts, bearings, and cutting heads should be lubricated. The lubricant in the gear case should be checked at least weekly. Gears should be greased semi-annually, or at least annually, depending on use.

CUTTERS AND MIXERS   There are three general categories of mixers: vertical mixers, vertical cutter/mixers, and spiral mixers. There are floor and counter-top models. A floor model is featured in Figure 12.2 and a countertop model is shown in Figure 12.3. Capacities can run from 15-quart to over 100-quart models. The mixer bowl should be made from stainless steel. They can have several speed settings and may even have timer controls. In vertical mixers there may be six or more different types of beater attachments as can be seen in Figure 12.4. There are also several types of optional equipment, such as splash covers, pouring chutes, and a dolly to move large-capacity bowls. Large mixers can have bowl lifters that bring the ingredients up to the beater. Spiral mixers are designed for very heavy doughs. The bowl rotates and the dough arm spins on its own axis. Vertical cutter/mixers have the motor mounted on the bottom of the bowl. They can be used to make everything from coleslaw to pie dough. They are much faster than ordinary vertical mixers and they have a lockdown lid.

Maintenance of mixers includes a weekly inspection of transmission oil levels, a monthly inspection of belts, and the application of grease to the gears.

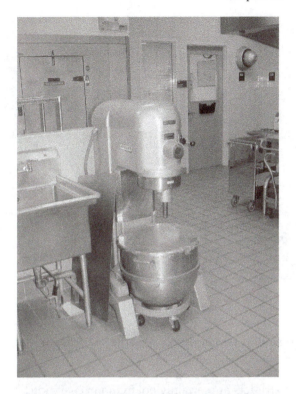

FIGURE 12.2   Floor Model Mixer.

FIGURE 12.3
Countertop Mixer.

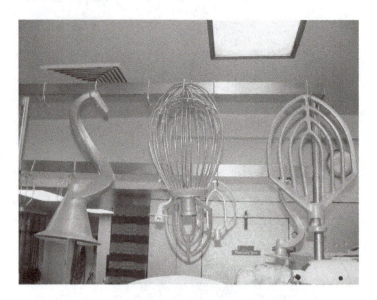

FIGURE 12.4 Mixer Beater Attachments.

The oil pump should be inspected, and the old transmission oil should be replaced at least every six months.

EXTRUDERS Extruders are certainly not found in every kitchen, but if you are making your own hamburger, sausage, pasta, or frosting for a large number of cakes, you probably have an extruder. However, the extruder for frosting cakes, also known as a pastry bag, resembles a pasta or sausage extruder in name only. Most pasta and sausage extruders use a single screw, but some of the larger and costlier models use a double screw. Pasta extruders can have literally dozens of dies and attachments so they can produce a plethora of pasta shapes. Extruders should meet NSF standards and should also be able to be broken down for cleaning. Common maintenance includes the oiling of bearings on the electric motors. Frequency will vary depending on the use and model.

FOOD PROCESSORS The food processor is very similar to the buffalo chopper or vertical cutter/mixer. With the proper attachments, these units will chop, slice, dice, shred, grate, mix, and whip. The bowls of the commercial units are typically from four to six quarts. Most of the units are tabletop models. Safety features do not allow the units to operate until the cover is properly attached. Domestic processors are usually made from plastic, but the commercial model housings and bowls are made from aluminum with clear plastic bowl tops so that the contents can be seen without removing the lid as shown in Figure 12.5. Depending on the ingredients, food processors should be cleaned from every use to once a day. Maintenance includes lubricating the bearings and shafts weekly to monthly depending on use. The unit's blades should also be sharpened as needed.

FIGURE 12.5 Food Processors.

SCALES Every kitchen needs a scale. Other than cleaning, the chief concern with scales is their accuracy. Spring scales should be calibrated frequently. Frequent cleaning is, of course, a necessity. The scale on the left in Figure 12.6 measures items in ounces and the scale on the right measures them in pounds.

SLICERS Slicers are commonly found in a number of different kitchens, from delis to gourmet restaurants. There are manual, semi-automatic, and fully automatic models. There are variable speed units because some foods need to be sliced slowly and others can be sliced at full speed. Thickness of cut can vary from razor thin to over an inch. The dial in the front of the

FIGURE 12.6 One Pound (L.) and Five Pound (R.) Scales.

FIGURE 12.7   Manual Slicer.

slicer in Figure 12.7 varies the thickness of the cut. Options for slicers include scales, counters, blade sharpening attachments, and special trays for shredded lettuce and cabbage. To avoid cross-contamination, slicers should be cleaned frequently, so they should be designed for ease of disassembly and cleaning. A good unit should have numerous safety features to protect the operator. Manual slicers are definitely more dangerous than automated models.

VEGETABLE PEELERS   Vegetable peelers have lost their appeal in many restaurants because of the prevalence of processed vegetables, particularly potatoes. They vary in size from tabletops to floor models. Some are mounted on casters so they can be wheeled in and out of the production area. Belts need to be inspected and tightened. Bearings should be inspected and lubricated, and the abrasive disks that do the peeling should be changed according to the unit's manual.

Cooking Equipment Considerations

In the area of cooking equipment, there have been some tremendous changes over the past five decades, but some methods and equipment have not changed one iota during this time. Pizza purists will insist that their pies be baked by deck ovens fired not by gas or electricity, but by coal. In addition, any BBQ restaurant worth its salt will insist that their ribs and pork shoulders are cooked "low and slow" using the same wood fired ovens installed by their founder a hundred years prior.

Cooking equipment can be categorized as follows:

- broilers, rotisseries, and salamanders
- fryers
- ovens
- ranges and griddles

- steamers
- steam-jacketed kettles
- tilting skillets
- toasters

Within these categories lies a vast assortment of specialty items, each with its own purpose and design. The primary heat sources for kitchen cooking equipment are usually electricity and natural gas, but as mentioned above, even coal and wood still have some applications.

BROILERS, ROTISSERIES, AND SALAMANDERS   Broilers use infrared or radiant heat sources to cook food at high temperatures. The most intense are infrared broilers that can produce temperatures over 1,500°F. Food is normally cooked only on one side of a broiler, but there are units that have heating elements on both sides, so that food can be cooked on both sides at the same time. Charcoal broilers (char-broilers) allow the meat juices to drip down onto the heat source allowing for a unique flavor to be imparted to the meat. These broilers may actually use charcoal or wood (see Figure 12.8), or they may use gas burners with artificial briquettes or lava rocks. Cleaning up these types of broilers is particularly difficult and the briquettes or rocks have to be replaced frequently. Wood fired or charcoal fired broilers are banned in a number of communities because of their release of gases and particulates into the environment.

Grease can build up in broilers and easily catch on fire, which could cause a disastrous situation. At one restaurant, where the author worked, a fire started in a dirty broiler. Almost immediately the entire unit was engulfed in flames. The flames spread to the hood and up into the duct. Finally, the automatic fire control system tripped and the entire kitchen was bathed in a fine

FIGURE 12.8   Portable Charcoal Broiler.

dry chemical powder residue. The broiler fire was almost extinguished, but the fire had already burned through the duct and was in the false ceiling above the kitchen. Luckily, the fire department was able to extinguish it before it spread. However, it ended up costing the hotel thousands of dollars, and all because of negligence. When questioned, the cooking staff could not remember when they had last cleaned either the broiler or the grease filters in the hood. The policy was to do both of them daily.

Since broilers use so much energy, it is wise to shut them down whenever they are not needed. Most models take only a minute or two to heat up to cooking temperatures. Some are designed to heat in zones to save heating the entire broiler for a single item. Maintenance consists of cleaning the units frequently and replacing the worn-out heating elements on the electric models. Gas models require the cleaning, inspection, and adjustment of the burner components.

Rotisseries allow for the broiling of food on a rotating spit. Burners are located on the back or the center of a unit. Rotisseries are often found in show kitchens where the sight of the food inspires diners to make a selection of an item cooked in the rotisserie. As in the case of broilers, rotisseries can have grease concerns. Rotisserie surfaces along with the skewers used on the food items should be designed for easy cleaning. Some rotisseries have holding areas for the food once it is cooked. Cleaning of the units, along with the maintenance of belts, chains, motors, burner, or infrared components is required. Figure 12.9 is a photo of a gas rotisserie. In addition to a central gas flame, there are also gas flames on either side of the front opening. Meat is hung by hooks that not only rotate in a circle around the central flame, but also spin on their own axis as they rotate. A water spigot can fill the bottom of the unit to provide moisture to the cooking process.

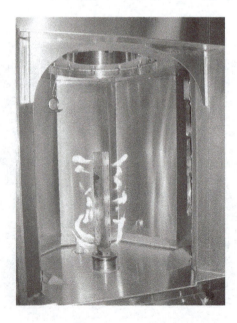

FIGURE 12.9 Gas Rotisserie.

The salamander, named after the reptile because it was once thought to be impervious to fire and heat, is nothing more than a small broiler usually mounted on a shelf above a range or griddle. A salamander is pictured in Figure 12.10. It is used to melt the cheese on onion soup and other small jobs. The heat in a salamander is directed downward.

FRYERS   There are four basic kinds of fryers: deep-fat fryers (Figure 12.11), pressure fryers, conveyor fryers, and one that is not a true fryer, the air fryer. Some deep-fat fryers use a pump to convey the hot oil from the burner element to the food; these *convection* deep-fat fryers cook food in far less time in comparison to the *natural draft* deep-fat fryers. Pressurized fryers also speed the cooking process and limit the absorption of grease into the food. Pressurized fryers are commonly found in chicken restaurants. *Broasted Chicken*® fryers is one well-known line of pressurized fryers. Conveyor fryers

FIGURE 12.10
Salamander.

FIGURE 12.11   Deep-Fat Fryer.

are found only in very high-volume operations. The food product is carried through the fry tank in baskets and deposited on a collection station at the end. The air fryer gives food the appearance of being fried but no oil or grease is used in the process, and thus it creates a healthier, lower calorie product.

Some deep-fat fryers have no drains, thus requiring a manual removal of the fat from the fryer which is a potentially hazardous and dirty process. Deep-fat fryers that have efficient filtering systems will save the operation considerable money by reducing the number of fat changes needed by 25%–50% and they also increase the quality of the products fried. Gas and electrical models should be given monthly inspections. For the gas models, burner components should be cleaned, inspected, and calibrated monthly. On all of the natural gas appliances, the flame should be blue with perhaps a slight hint of yellow at the top of the primary (interior) cone of flame. If the flame is yellow to yellow-orange, incomplete combustion is taking place and carbon monoxide may be produced by the appliance. A competent technician should be called to service the unit. For electric models, a monthly inspection and service of all electrical connections should be conducted. For both units, the high-limit thermostat should be inspected. The high-limit thermostat prevents an uncontrolled rise in the oil temperature to the point of combustion. The proper operation of this safety device is essential, for without it the deep-fat fryer could literally explode if the temperature controls malfunction. Filters and filter pumps must be cleaned and changed often according to manufacturers' specifications to ensure a continued satisfactory operation.

OVENS   There are combi-ovens (combination ovens), convection ovens, conveyor ovens, cook and hold ovens, deck ovens, microwave ovens, reel ovens, and wood and coal ovens. The combi-oven was introduced approximately 35 years ago and is a versatile piece of equipment. It can cook with steam, with air (convection), or with both steam and hot air (Figure 12.12). There are countertop, stacking, and roll-in models. Combi-ovens are available as either gas or all-electric models. The biggest maintenance concern with these ovens is the problem of **scale** buildup. In-line water filters help to decrease the frequency of cleaning and descaling of the unit. The units may also be used as holding units.

Convection ovens have been around for over 50 years. They are ovens with built-in fans (**forced convection**) that circulate the air inside the oven over the food. Pictured in Figure 12.13 is an interior of a convection oven with the fan on the rear wall of the unit. Their advantages are that they cook faster, provide for greater heat distribution, do an excellent job of browning food, and are more energy-efficient than conventional ovens. Gas units should undergo monthly inspections of the burner components. Electrical components should also be checked monthly and the ovens should be cleaned as needed, including daily if used heavily or if spills happen.

In conveyor ovens, food is placed on a moving belt and when it emerges at the other end, the food is cooked. Although these ovens can come in a wide variety of sizes, the smaller units (e.g., 18" × 24" tunnel lengths) are the ones

FIGURE 12.12
Combination Oven (Top)
Blast Chiller (Below).

FIGURE 12.13
Convection Oven Interior.

most often found in restaurant kitchens as opposed to commercial bakeries. The ovens may be natural convection (i.e., no fan), forced convection (i.e., fan), infrared, or quartz. There are models that combine infrared and forced convection for extremely fast cooking. High volume pizza restaurants and delis are likely candidates for conveyor ovens. Regular maintenance needs to be performed not only on the heating elements, burners, fans, and electrical wiring, but also the belt needs to be regularly inspected.

Cook and hold ovens may be relatively new to the kitchen scene, but the technique of cooking "low and slow" has been around for many, many years. Cooking meats at lower temperatures reduces moisture loss, increasing yield by as much as 20%. The ovens come in either gas or electric models. Some of the electric ovens are mobile and they do not need to be placed under a hood, but one should first check with local codes to make sure a hood is not required. There are two types of cook and hold ovens: **natural draft convection** and forced convection. The natural draft ovens maintain a higher humidity level and operate at higher temperatures than the forced convection models, which have lower temperatures and correspondingly lower humidity levels inside the ovens. There are cook and hold units that have smoker attachments for barbeque meats. When these ovens first appeared about 40 years ago, there was some concern that these ovens would allow bacteria on the meat to thrive during cooking because of their low temperatures. This has not proven to be the case. However, to be safe, meats such as hamburger and chicken should be cooked at higher temperatures than beef roasts. Maintenance of these ovens is similar to other types of ovens. Electrical wiring should be inspected and gas burner components should be inspected, calibrated, and cleaned. The frequency of its cleaning depends on the frequency of its use. Figure 12.14 is an example of a portable cook and hold oven.

Deck ovens are stacked up to three ovens high (usually two). Here again, there are electric and gas models. The base fired gas models are hotter at the bottom than the top. The ovens can bake with bottom heating elements, broil with top heating elements, and roast with top and bottom heating elements. The height of the deck will vary depending on its intended purpose. For example, pizza ovens are usually no more than four to eight inches high, but

FIGURE 12.14 Portable Cook and Hold Oven.

deck ovens designed for roasting are 12″ to 15″ in height. Deck ovens designed for baking breads may contain a steam sprayer that will give a hard, chewy crust to the bread. Pizza ovens are fairly deep, so a **peel** is needed to insert and remove pizzas. Deck ovens can be made of steel, brick, or even ceramic materials in the case of pizza ovens, and coal or wood may be the fuel. As with all ovens, heavy use requires that the deck oven be cleaned daily. Electrical connections should be checked at least semiannually and gas burners should be inspected monthly.

The microwave oven generates heat inside the food, rather than from an external source. The heating is fairly uniform in most foods, as long as the food is not too thick. The oven's magnetron produces the microwave radiation that cooks the food. In a well-made, non-damaged oven, very little of the microwave radiation escapes. The first microwave oven was almost six feet tall, weighed 750 pounds, consumed 3,000 watts, and was water-cooled. Now the typical microwave oven consumes only a third of that amount of electricity. Microwave ovens now come with a host of added options, including browning with infrared lamps. Microwave ovens operate only at one energy level. To defrost or cook a food item slowly takes a timer switch that cycles the magnetron off and on during its operation. Microwaves can operate for many years with no servicing other than cleaning the unit. Abrasives should not be used to clean the unit. Microwaves do some things very well (e.g., heating water, reheating leftovers), and other things very poorly (e.g., baking, roasting without a browning element).

Reel ovens are rarely found in restaurants, but appear in many bakeries. Inside the reel oven are shelves that resemble a Ferris wheel or a merry-go-round. These ovens are designed for very high production. Since they are very large units, they often have access doors for cleaning.

Wood and coal ovens are often deck ovens for the cooking of pizza. However, seafood, poultry, and vegetables are often cooked in them to capture that rich, smoky flavor. The heat is more intense in these ovens that can reach up to 1,000°F. These ovens need specially designed ventilation hoods and ducts. Frequent cleaning of the oven, hood, and duct is essential to remove the buildup of creosote. If this is not done, the oven and the ventilation system will assuredly catch on fire, and may end up destroying the entire operation. The proper installation of these ovens and the materials used in the construction of the floor and ceiling adjacent to these units is a major consideration too. Another big negative is the cost of the fuel, particularly wood. Many municipalities have outlawed these ovens because of their environmental impact. Particulates, carbon monoxide, and other noxious gases are released by burning wood and coal.

RANGES AND GRIDDLES Ranges are cooking tops supported by a frame and an oven is usually placed beneath the range. Ranges can have open burner tops or grates on which pots and pans can be set. Another type of cooking top is the closed top. Open burner tops are more energy efficient than closed tops because there is not as much metal to be heated, but the closed top units provide an even heating surface. Figure 12.15 shows both closed top and open top ranges. Note the ovens beneath the ranges. Griddles are similar to closed

FIGURE 12.15   Close and Open Top Ranges.

tops, but they typically have a steel fence or a raised edge around three sides and a trough in either the front, one side, or the rear for grease and cooking waste. Figure 12.16 is an example of a griddle with the trough in the front. The units with troughs in the front of the unit are easier to empty than those that have troughs in the rear. Coved corners and edges on the griddle help to keep debris and grease from building up in those areas. Another selection consideration with griddles is whether to choose a thinner or thicker plate. Thinner plates heat quicker and use less energy, but are more prone to warping. Thicker

FIGURE 12.16   Griddle.

plates are stronger and retain heat longer, but respond more slowly to temperature adjustments. There are also chrome griddle tops. The chrome is a thin veneer on the steel plate. There are a number of advantages to chrome tops: they are faster to heat and easier to clean, they use less energy, and they do not have to be seasoned with oil, but unfortunately, they can be easily damaged.

A hybrid version is the ring top which can either function as a closed top or rings of steel can be removed so the unit functions as an open top. Finally, French hot plates are raised from the open top cooking surface. They provide a more even heating surface.

On open burner tops, drip pans are located beneath the burners to catch the grease. When selecting a range or griddle, it is wise to consider the relative ease of cleaning the unit. Ranges can be either electric or gas. There are specialty ranges available, such as, wok and taco ranges. Another technological innovation in ranges is the induction range. The cook tops are ceramic or glass and beneath the tops are electro-magnetic coils. The coil creates a magnetic field and when a steel or iron pot or pan is placed on the cook top, resistance is created in the pot or pan which heats the food. The cook top never warms up. Advantages to induction cook tops include less energy usage, faster cooking times, no chance of being burned by touching the cook top, and the reduction or elimination of ventilation.

STEAMERS   Steamers can be used for all types of food including seafood and vegetables. In Connecticut, steamed cheeseburgers are a regional favorite. The steam is generated either by a boiler near the kitchen, or a small self-contained steam generating unit next to the steamer. There are three types of steamers: high-pressure, low-pressure, and pressureless. Steamer models can be either electric or gas.

The pressureless steamer is unquestionably the most popular, because it has many advantages over the other two. The biggest advantage is that the unit can be opened at any time. Another advantage is that there is less chance that flavors will migrate from one food to another in the pressureless steamer. Some pressureless steamers contain a fan to help move the steam through the cabinet, which causes the food to heat faster. These units are called convection steamers.

Pressured steamers consume less water and energy during their operation. High-pressure steamers cook faster than low-pressure steamers and are preferred when the rapid heating of small batches of food is needed. Low-pressure steamers are rated at five **psi** and high-pressure steamers are 15 psi.

Maintenance includes "blow down" where the water is released from the boiler and the scale is removed by either chemical or physical means. Boilers need to be inspected to ensure that the low-water shutoff valves are operating properly. Safety relief valves also need to be inspected at least semi-annually to ensure their proper operation. Failure of any of these safety features turns the boiler into a bomb that can cause damage, injury, and possibly even death. Boilers operate on gas or electricity.

The steam that comes into contact with the food must be absolutely pure. There should be no additives or contaminants in the steam. The steamer must be thoroughly cleaned and dried every day. Leaks should be sealed immediately to prevent corrosion.

STEAM-JACKETED KETTLES   Steam-jacketed kettles can be used for a multitude of cooking operations, from heating vegetables to making soups, stews, and sauces. A steam-jacketed is actually two bowls, one inside the other. The bowls are sealed together and steam is introduced between the two kettles. The steam heats the inner bowl and its contents. The kettles can be stationary floor models, tilting units, or countertop models. A floor model is pictured in Figure 12.17. They can hold from a single quart to over 500 gallons. Valves and supply lines should be inspected weekly. The kettle should be cleaned with every use or at least daily if preparing the same product. Inspection of the steam line, high-pressure release valve, and gauges should be done daily. Steam traps and other valves and lines should be inspected at least weekly.

There are also kettles that use oil rather than steam. These thermo fluid kettles, as they are called, have several advantages over steam, including the fact that they cook at higher temperatures than steam and there is no corrosion or scaling.

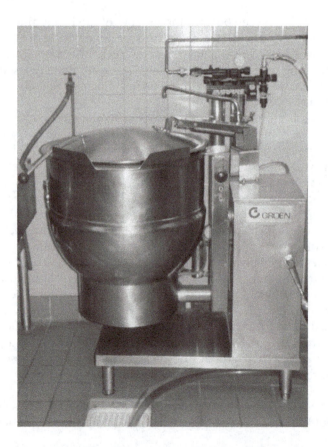

FIGURE 12.17   Steam-Jacketed Kettle.

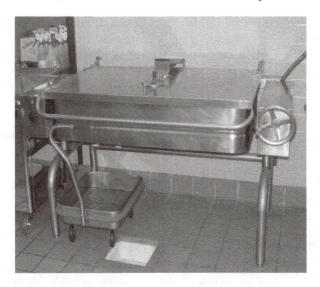

FIGURE 12.18 Tilting Skillet.

TILTING SKILLETS   The tilting skillet is one of the most flexible pieces of cooking equipment found in the modern kitchen (shown in Figure 12.18). It can braise, be used as a griddle, deep-fat fryer, stew pot, or range. It can even operate as a steamer with the aid of perforated pans and water in the bottom of the skillet. Tilting skillets come with covers and the energy source may be electric, gas, or steam. Daily cleaning with non-abrasive cleaners and a monthly greasing of the gears is required. Electrical connections, burner components, and thermostats should be inspected monthly.

TOASTERS   Pop-up toasters may contain either two or four slots. These units operate on electricity. Conveyor toasters can be either gas or electric. The daily cleaning of bread particles and the monthly lubrication of the chain in the conveyor models, along with monthly inspections of the gas burners and electrical contacts and wiring, are recommended.

Refrigeration Equipment Considerations

The vast majority of refrigeration equipment employs the vapor-compression process. A man-made chemical called **refrigerant** is employed. Refrigerant has the capacity to boil at a very low temperature. When it boils, heat is absorbed into the refrigerant. The refrigerant moves through two sets of coils with the aid of a **compressor**. The compressor draws the refrigerant from the **evaporator coils** and forces it under pressure into the **condenser coils**. The condenser coils are located outside of the refrigerated space and the evaporator coils are inside the refrigerated space. In the evaporator, the refrigeration boils at a low temperature because the pressure on the refrigerant is low. In the condenser, the pressure on the refrigerant is elevated, which causes the temperature to rise. This hot, high-pressure gas then gives off heat to the air or water surrounding the condenser coil. As heat is released, the refrigerant condenses from a gas to a liquid. As a liquid, it continues to release heat. The refrigerant then comes to a very narrow section of the coil called the **expansion valve**. Only a limited amount of refrigerant can pass through the expansion valve. This lowers the pressure on the refrigerant that has passed through the expansion valve. Instantly, approximately a quarter of the liquid refrigerant turns to a gas and, as the refrigerant passes through the evaporator coil, it continues to boil, absorbing heat from the area outside of the coil which is inside the refrigerated interior space. Once the compressor is shut down, the refrigerant will reach equilibrium between the two coils and heat will no longer be transferred.

Refrigeration equipment consists of reach-ins, walk-ins, ice machines, ice cream and yogurt makers, beverage equipment, and other miscellaneous refrigeration equipment. Reach-in refrigerators (coolers) are upright units with shelves. Reach-in freezers may be upright units (see Figure 12.19) or chest units. The chest units are more energy-efficient than reach-in units. Refrigeration equipment is categorized according to its capacity, rated in cubic feet. There may be sliding doors or hinged doors with magnetic strips on the frame to ensure a tight seal. The preferred construction material for all refrigeration equipment is stainless steel. Pass-through units have doors on both sides when the loading and unloading of products cannot be done from the same side. Equipment shelving is usually steel and should be adjustable. There may also be interior lights. All units should be well insulated to mitigate the effects of the **transmission heat load** that enters through the walls of the refrigeration equipment. Refrigerated units should have at least 3″ of insulation and freezers should have a minimum of 3″ to 6″ of insulation.

Blast chillers and freezers quickly lower the temperature of food for storage in other reach-in or walk-in units. This prevents the warming of other

FIGURE 12.19
Reach-In Cooler/Freezer
Combination.

foods and the growth of bacteria in the food if it cools more slowly. Since they consume far more energy than standard chillers and freezers, they should be turned off when not in use. Blast units typically use convection cooling (i.e., fans blowing across the evaporator coils) and may have water-cooled condenser coils to transfer the heat out of the units.

Walk-in units are often constructed on-site when the building is built, or they may be prefabricated and shipped to the kitchen for installation. They typically have tile floors, fiberglass interior walls, and aluminum ceilings. Walk-ins may also use convection cooling to increase the heat transfer from the food product to the evaporator coils. Kitchen personnel should not access walk-ins continuously during the shift. Every time the door is opened, heat enters the unit (**infiltration heat load**), and the cost of operating the unit increases. Limiting entry to six times during a shift is a reasonable goal. Food should be moved from walk-ins to reach-ins for preparation, and plastic door strips should be installed on all walk-ins to limit the infiltration heat load. Interior lights and fans used in convection cooling models create **appliance heat load**. Lights should be turned off when exiting. It is also a good idea to place motion detectors on these lights to eliminate the human element. A tremendous energy savings is also achieved when walk-in freezers are connected to walk-in coolers. Sharing one wall will reduce the transmission heat load for both the freezer and the cooler. If the freezer door is located inside the cooler, the energy savings are even more significant. In fact, up to a 20% energy savings can be realized with this arrangement.

The food itself can be a major source of heat load or heat gain (i.e., **product heat load**), particularly if it is at room temperature when it is delivered and placed into the coolers or freezers. Deliveries should be staggered so that the refrigeration equipment will not be overtaxed. Massive amounts of food product at room temperature may overwhelm the unit's ability to maintain optimum temperature for several hours leading to spoilage and the waste of energy. Food that is to be frozen should be delivered frozen, if at all possible. Food that needs to be chilled should be delivered in refrigerated trucks and immediately placed in the kitchen's coolers. It is also wise to instruct delivery personnel not to deliver during rush hours. Perishable food that is left on the dock or the kitchen floor because kitchen personnel are too busy to put it away properly is a wasteful and needless practice.

Ice machines can either be air or water-cooled units. The larger machines are more likely to be water-cooled. To extend the life of the equipment and correspondingly increase the quality of the ice, an optional water filtration system is a wise option, particularly when the water is very hard. There are bin machines, which are fine for kitchen operations, and there are dispensing machines with no accessible bin. The dispensing machines should be used when there is guest access. The danger of broken glass and contaminants entering an ice bin make guest ice machines with bins a very poor choice for guest foyers.

There are many options when it comes to ice shapes and sizes, but for most drinks, smaller is better. A quarter-inch square cube is a popular size and shape. Some machines are more energy- and water-efficient than others. These factors, along with production capacities (expressed in pounds per day), quality of construction, and, of course, cost, are considerations when purchasing. Maintenance of ice machines includes the weekly cleaning of the bin, lubricating fans, and the removal of scale every month. At least semiannually all of the ice-making components should be taken apart and cleaned.

Soft ice cream machines and yogurt makers should be cleaned daily. Once a month, electrical contacts should be checked and water filters cleaned or changed. Lubrication should be done according to the manufacturer's recommendations.

Refrigerated beverage equipment includes carbonated drink systems, juice dispensers, and smoothie makers. Daily cleaning of the equipment is a must. Health inspectors look for slime on dispenser nozzles, and in ice bins and cold plates.

One of the most important maintenance activities on all refrigeration equipment is the monthly cleaning of condenser coils so there is optimal heat transference. A monthly vacuuming is all that is usually necessary. In freezers, the evaporator coil should be defrosted if a quarter inch of ice forms on the coil. In both freezers and coolers the evaporator should be cleaned, as well.

Other Serving Equipment

Serving equipment covers a wide assortment of different types from steam tables, counters, coffee urns, cold bars, hot chocolate and espresso machines (see Figure 12.20), and infrared lamps to tables, chairs, and serving carts. All

FIGURE 12.20 Coffee/ Hot Chocolate/Espresso Maker.

FIGURE 12.21
Dishwasher.

equipment should be cleaned daily when used and other maintenance should be done according to manufacturers' recommendations.

Cleaning and Waste Equipment

This category includes dish, glass, and pot washers, garbage disposals, and pulpers. Dishwashers come in a multitude of sizes and configurations (see Figure 12.21). All require a daily cleaning after use. The removal of scale should be done every week in hard water areas. In addition, a weekly inspection for leaks and proper calibration of all thermostats and thermometers should be conducted. Garbage disposals should have their blades inspected weekly and foreign matter (e.g., metals, bones, plastics, etc.) should never be put down a disposal. Pulpers are similar to disposals. However, the ground-up garbage does not flow down the drain, but is expelled into a garbage can and to the landfill. Some pulper models can grind up aluminum foil, beverage cans, and even bones. Here again, blades should be inspected weekly and the manufacturers' maintenance recommendations should be followed.

THE LAUNDRY

Maintaining the quality of linens was resolved several years ago. Modern no-iron linens (cotton/polyester blends) now undergo a dual finish process that improves the molecular structure of the polyester fiber, resulting in linen that retains its no-iron properties throughout its normal life expectancy. Refined blended sheets now last three times as long as their cotton predecessors. In fact, the polyester fiber in new-generation no-iron linens tends to relax and actually increases in elasticity with use.

The no-iron linen industry has also perfected the equipment that processes the new-generation linens. The timing of wash-and-rinse cycles, temperature control, and the automatic adding of detergents, bleaches, and softeners have eliminated the problems of human error and operator inattention and the need for extensive employee training. There is a very strong case for having an economical on-premises laundry.

Planning the Laundry

Some managers of laundry facilities suggest that an on-premises laundry requires nothing more than installing a few washers and dryers in some remote space in the facility. Such inadequate planning usually results in laundries that must be re-engineered by qualified designers and laundry equipment contractors. This may require expensive modifications to fix the problems that could have been avoided with careful planning up-front.

Large laundries are not the only ones that are subjected to poor planning and insufficient engineering attention. It is often the owners of small properties who, after having made the decision to have an on-premises laundry, fail to give the consideration and planning that laundry operations warrant. Small properties may not require the detailed planning needed in larger properties; however, planning variables apply equally to small and large hotel laundries.

The first step in laundry planning is to determine the facility's laundry needs. For this step, there should be meetings with owners, architects, interior designers, engineers, and other project consultants to obtain all the data needed to sizing the laundry. Data includes the number of rooms, number of beds, expected occupancy, variety of services, areas of services, and budgetary restrictions. From these data, a report containing information about the size, type, and location of facilities is composed. This report describes the basic integration and development of the laundry in the overall hotel concept and design.

Once needs are defined, specialists concentrate on selecting the systems and components that are best able to handle the project requirements. Interrelationships of those allocated spaces are analyzed from a human engineering standpoint to eliminate costly extra steps or crossed traffic patterns. Many different approaches are considered in designing a system that optimizes efficiency and, therefore, economy of operations. Equipment layouts and labor-saving ideas are meshed with the most efficient work-flow patterns that can be designed within the given space. Alternate system components and layouts are investigated to ensure selection of the best possible system.

Next is the selection of the available options for the equipment that has been purchased. Costs are studied, including equipment installation and rigging equipment costs. Follow-up maintenance considerations are included, along with the expected life of the equipment. Budgets are finalized using standard specifications that allow fast tracking to early completion of the project.

Equipment connection schedules and mechanical, electrical, and ventilation details are defined, showing exact locations of all installations. Such drawings enable the contractor to rough-in utilities properly before the equipment arrives.

These steps expedite the connection and installation of the equipment. Detailed specifications for each piece of equipment are provided, reflecting every option selected. All mechanical and electrical requirements must be coordinated with architects, engineers, and contractors throughout this phase.

ESSENTIALS OF LAUNDRY DESIGN It may not be financially feasible for small property owners to use the services of a laundry consultant. When that is the case, owners need to know the basic considerations in the development of a small on-premises laundry operation.

The most commonly used and technically correct way of deciding the size and composition of the equipment is by analyzing linen poundage requirements. It is usual for laundry equipment manufacturers to design and specify equipment using this criterion. Thus, washers and/or dryers are available with load capabilities ranging from 25 to 600 pounds, which allows the selection of the most reasonably sized equipment for a given set of requirements. Most washers extract their own wash and rinse water; therefore, separate extractors are not necessary. Recognizing that labor costs will normally be the highest of all operating costs, it is desirable to specify the optimum-sized equipment that will minimize these costs.

Another consideration is that washing capacity, drying capacity, or handling capacity can provide the primary constraint for the laundry, and therefore these three constraints should be balanced. For example, a laundry with 400 pounds of washing capacity operating on a 30-minute cycle, 150 pounds of drying capacity operating on a 50-minute cycle, with adequate space for handling, storing, and folding linen, would be dryer-limited. However, a laundry with one 50-pound washing machine operating on a 30-minute cycle and one 100-pound dryer operating on a 1-hour cycle with adequate handling capacity would be properly sized.

In small operations, the number of dryers is normally related to the number of washers in a 2 to 1 ratio; for example, two 50-pound dryers to one 50-pound washer. This rule is based on the fact that a standard drying cycle is likely to be twice as long as a standard washing cycle.

Laundries equipped with ironers (a.k.a. flatwork finishers) do not require that sheets and pillowcases pass through dryers. In such operations, dryers are used only for terry linen. All of these factors enter into the planning of how much and what type of equipment needs to be installed.

Major Equipment Requirements

Let us consider a hotel with 100 guestrooms and linen requirements. The approximately 1000 pounds of daily laundered linen in this 100-room hotel will be used as a guide for determining equipment requirements.

Washer/extractor selection should be the best balance of machine capability and labor requirements; the best balance is the least machinery that allows for the smallest labor force (one person working an eight-hour shift is optimum). After setting a constraint that requires the production of 1 par linen (the total amount of linen required to cover every bed and supply every bathroom once) in one shift, we now select a mix of washing machine capacity that is most practical.

One 500-pound washer, washing two loads, which can be completed in about one hour washing time, can handle the 1000-pound requirement, but then the washer would be idle for seven hours (see Figure 12.22). The opposite extreme, one 50-pound washer working slightly less than a half-hour cycle, can produce the same amount of linen in ten hours of operation. Neither of these is the best choice. Two 50-pound washers can produce the 1000-pound requirement in about five hours, and two 50-pound-capacity machines cost considerably less than one 500-pound machine and require less energy and mechanical support.

There is another consideration, which is that all linens will not be washed using the same wash formula. Linens must be separated by linen types and degree of soiling. Wash formula refers to the combination of washing time, rinsing time, temperature control, and the automatic addition of chemical detergents, bleaches, and softeners.

Linens must also be weighed for proper washing. By analyzing the weights of each type of linen, we can find the most practical loading combination for a 50-pound washer. Two 50-pound washers, working one cycle of

FIGURE 12.22 Washer.
Source: Mission Industries.

approximately 30 minutes, can complete all wash operations in about five and one-half hours.

As we mentioned earlier, in a no-iron laundry, the number of dryers to the number of washers is typically a ratio of 2 to 1. At 100 percent occupancy, the production of up to 1000 pounds of washed linen (22 loads of wash) can be accommodated by three 100-pound dryers in a 6 and 1/2-hour period.

Of course, hotel operations are not always full. How, then, do we determine the hours of laundry production as related to hotel occupancy? For example, two 50-pound washers can generate the linen required for 100 percent occupancy in slightly more than five and one-half hours; 70 percent occupancy would require four hours of operation; lesser occupancies would require less time.

Additional Equipment

Having specified two washer/extractors and three dryers as basic machinery required for our 100-room example property, here is a list of other equipment that would be needed.

- 1 soak sink: double basin, plastic-formed, for soaking stained linens in special wash formulas for spot and stain removal.
- 1 folding table (4 by 6 feet): centrally located between dryers and storage shelving. It is used primarily for folding terry linens.
- 5 laundry hampers: either vinyl-coated canvas or plastic-molded hamper. Two hampers are used for soiled separated linen. One is to receive washed-wet linen, and two are for washed-dry linen. These hampers should not be used outside of the laundry.
- 6 linen storage carts: three carts should be in the laundry to receive clean linen throughout the day. These three carts are moved to satellite linen rooms for the next day's operation. Three mobile linen carts should be in the satellite linen rooms to accommodate soiled linen during the day. At day's end they are ready to be moved to the laundry for washing the following day. The total need for mobile linen carts is determined by the number of satellite linen rooms; two are needed for each linen storage area, one of which would be positioned in the laundry each day.
- 1 Extra Hand sheet/spread folders: one of several ways to fold sheets. The one used is normally determined by the size of the laundry workload. When workloads are low, capital expenditures for sheet folders would usually not be warranted or recommended, since two attendants working together can fold about 90 to 100 sheets per hour. For example, a small laundry load (50 percent average occupancy) in our 100-room example hotel yields a workload of about 150 sheets and requires two people to fold sheets for about one and one-half hours. If the workload permanently increases, it then becomes appropriate to consider purchasing an Extra Hand folder.

Laundry Equipment for Larger Hotels

The previously discussed equipment for our hypothetical 100-room hotel is probably sufficient, but what could be added to the mix in larger properties of several hundred rooms and multiple restaurant outlets? Obviously, the

FIGURE 12.23 Flatwork Finisher. *Source*: Mission Industries.

washers and dryers would have to increase in size and number, but what else is available to reduce our dependence on labor? To begin with, there are spreader/feeders. This device take laundered wet sheets, spreads them, and feeds them into an ironer. The purpose of this unit is to automatically dry and remove the wrinkles from the linen. The final stage is the automatic folding of the flatwork (i.e., sheets and pillowcases). Figure 12.23 is an example of a spreader/feeder attached to an ironer with a folder at the rear. There are also units that automatically fold bath and bed linen (e.g., towels, blankets, patient gowns, and underpads).

Nonequipment Factors and Requirements

About 4 square feet of space for each guestroom is required for the laundry facility itself, and an additional 4 square feet per guestroom is needed for linen handling and storage throughout the property. Soiled linens are first moved to a sorting and wash area. After washing and drying, linen is moved to the folding area. Both folded sheets and folded terry linen are then moved to linen storage carts for passage out of the laundry.

If a hot water system is not sufficient to accommodate two washers, a fast-generating hot water heater will be necessary. Gas hot water heaters must be properly vented when installed. Soak sinks provide the capability for soaking stained and spotted linen rather than using valuable washing time. There is also the need for folding tables. Even with proper drainage, washer spills and overflows will occur. It is therefore essential that the laundry floor be waterproofed (sealed).

Soiled sorted linen and even clean linen may be found on the floor occasionally, and as a result, the laundry floor must be damp-mopped daily. Linen on the floor is of no consequence, provided the floor has been sealed and is kept clean.

Engineering Requirements

When small facility equipment has been installed with no attention to engineering considerations such as electrical wiring, water supply and drainage, plumbing, and ventilation, it can create havoc. The greatest of these unrecognized problems is inadequate water disposal drainage caused by extraction cycles of several washing machines draining simultaneously. For example, can a 44-inch floor drain accommodate the drainage from three washers, each with a 3-inch discharge line? According to most specifications, the answer is no. A drain trough or holding basin that can hold 100 gallons of water can allow for the overload of effluent water under pressure and will allow time for the drain water to pass into the 44-inch floor drain over a period of several minutes.

Another requirement concerns the necessity to exhaust moisture-laden air from the three dryers out of the laundry room. Small properties usually have laundries with low ceilings, which compound the problem of dryer effluent exhaust. Most 100-pound dryers each exhaust about 800 cubic feet per minute (cfm) of air. Operating three dryers together results in 2400 cfm of this moist hot air.

Laundry rooms also require adequate space through regular doors to intake or supply an equal amount of fresh dry air. Without ample intake through regular doors or a separate forced dry air supply, dryers will not operate at specified efficiencies. Some modern dryers now provide for heat recovery equipment, which will reduce laundry energy requirements if provision is made for this type of accessory in advance.

It is absolutely essential that the laundry room and adjacent areas be kept clean and free of lint. Lint is a major fire hazard in laundry operations and must be dealt with accordingly. Not only must lint be removed from dryer air ventilation, but it also must be dusted away from overhead pipes and hard-to-reach areas. A regular campaign must be maintained to keep lint accumulation to a minimum.

Summary

These two highly specialized building systems, kitchens and laundries, each have very specific needs. There are a multitude of considerations when selecting equipment for these areas—not the least of which is cost. Commercial equipment is a major investment and it also constitutes a major business asset. Maintenance of that asset is essential for the protection of the investment. As in all other building systems, to defer maintenance is simply the wrong approach. Management needs to ensure that proper maintenance procedures are being followed.

The best approach is to have operators of this equipment perform routine maintenance, such as cleaning equipment, performing inspections, and lubricating parts. Then the engineering department will have more time for involved maintenance. There is also the added benefit that equipment operators who perform routine maintenance will develop a sense of ownership towards the equipment and will treat these assets with greater respect.

Key Terms and Concepts

appliance heat load
   291
compressor *289*
condenser coils *289*
evaporator coils *289*

expansion valve *290*
forced convection *282*
infiltration heat load
   291

natural draft
   convection *284*
peel *285*
product heat load *291*
psi *287*

refrigerant *289*
scales *277*
transmission heat
   load *290*

Discussion and Review Questions

1. Make equipment lists for the following different types of restaurants: 1) a 75-seat bakery/deli with extensive take-out; 2) a 120-seat Italian restaurant; 3) a 90-seat steak house. Compare your lists with your fellow students.
2. Visit with at least three kitchen stewards in your area and talk with them about their job of maintaining their kitchens. Arrange a tour of their facilities and compose a list, based on your conversations,

of the greatest challenges they face in the maintenance of their kitchen equipment. Give recommendations on what they could do to mitigate these challenges in your report.
3. Visit a commercial or hotel laundry. Comment on the layout and design of the facility and how it facilitates (or does not facilitate) the work flow. Also comment on safety considerations at the facility. Report to the class.

Building Planning and Design

13

The Building Envelope and Exterior Elements

CHAPTER OBJECTIVES

After reading this chapter, you should be able to:

- discuss the purpose of a foundation.
- describe different types of foundations.
- identify the four types of building loads.
- describe the different types of framing and where they are used.
- discuss the various types of exterior finishes for buildings, including each type's advantages and disadvantages.
- describe the importance of R-values.
- calculate the R-value of walls and roofs.
- describe the features of energy-efficient windows.
- discuss the importance of window safety.
- describe the various types of roofs and how they remove water.
- discuss the value of xeriscaping.
- discuss the reasons for renovation.

INTRODUCTION

The appearance of the exterior of a building and its surrounding grounds contribute heavily to the success or failure of a hospitality property (Figure 13.1). An unattractive exterior appearance can repel desirable customers, even if the service inside the building is excellent. The building's exterior elements also influence the energy efficiency, climate comfort, and visual pleasure of the

FIGURE 13.1 An Attractive Building Exterior Sets the Tone for the Business. *Source*: The Lark.

interior. A poorly constructed and/or maintained building will waste money through energy loss through the roof, walls, windows, and doors. A poorly insulated building will experience cold air drafts in the winter and will make it difficult to regulate cooling systems in the summer. Poorly planned windows can result in uncomfortable glare and the premature fading of fabrics and upholstery inside the building.

Poorly maintained building exterior elements, such as walls, windows, and roofs, also provide safety and building damage hazards. If brickwork on the building exterior is not periodically maintained, water leaks may appear. A poorly maintained roof will develop leaks. The exterior of the building requires continuous monitoring and repair to ensure that the property is appealing, is safe, and operates efficiently.

It is likely that you will work in a pre-existing building for part, if not all, of your hospitality industry career. You will inherit the building's strengths and weaknesses when you start at a new property. This chapter will provide a description of the most typical types of building components found in the hospitality industry, beginning from the bottom up. We will then discuss maintenance issues related to these components, followed by a discussion of building renovation.

FOUNDATIONS

When a new building is being erected, the building site must undergo a great deal of work before the casual observer sees something going up that resembles an actual building. This preliminary work is one of the most important work on the project, but these components may never be seen again once the building is complete. The **foundation** is the part of the building that meets the ground. Poor site preparation and foundation work can result in enormous physical and financial damage.

THE IMPORTANCE OF SOIL   The first component in constructing a building is to identify the type of soil that the building will sit on. A potential site for a building should be tested by a soil expert. The soil expert will take surface samples of the soil as well as drill core samples from various depths below the surface. The type of soil will tell you if the site will be able to support the type and size of building that is planned as well as the type of foundation that must be used to support the building properly. For example, if a soil test indicates that the site is over bedrock (a very hard, solid naturally occurring rock), the structural engineer will use the bedrock as part of the foundation itself. Very loose soil will require a different foundation. Sometimes the soil test will uncover a hidden underground spring or aquifer below the surface. The problem could be serious enough that the site cannot be built on at all. Soil with high groundwater content may freeze during the winter months. Frozen water expands and may crack the foundation or even cause it to bow inwards in the building's basement.

THE FOUNDATION OF THE BUILDING   The purpose of a building's foundation is to distribute the weight of the building evenly over the site. The weight of the building is transferred by the building's walls. Walls can either be load-bearing walls or non-load bearing walls. **Load-bearing walls** are the walls that transfer the weight of the building. They are necessary for structural support and for keeping the building intact. **Non-load-bearing walls** only serve as space separators.

There are two major types of foundations: deep systems and shallow systems. Shallow systems are foundations that do not penetrate very deeply into the ground. A shallow system consists of a **footing**, which is essentially a series of small platforms upon which the building sits. For example, a spread footing is made of long rectangular concrete blocks. They are arranged around the building's perimeter to form a shape that is slightly larger than the building's visible exterior. The building's load-bearing walls and vertical beams connect directly to the footing. The weight of the building travels down through the load-bearing walls to distribute the weight across the footings.

A **mat** (or **raft**) **foundation** uses a single slab of concrete that distributes the building's weight over the soil rather than just several footings. They are suitable for use in soil conditions that do not bear loads very well. You will see slab footings in hospitality buildings with a lower rise (building height). Residential homes and lower-rise apartment buildings usually use a footing system for the building's foundation. A basement in a house is a type of mat foundation.

Deep systems are building foundations that are installed deeper into the ground than mat foundations. A deep system will use a series of footings similar to a shallow system. However, the footings in a shallow system are the very bottom of the foundation, whereas additional components lie below the footings in a deep system.

The footings will rest on pilings. A **piling** is a long, straight section of concrete, steel, or wood that comes into contact with a solid object below the surface. The solid object is either bedrock or some type of soil that is firmer than the soil on the surface. Wood has been used for pilings for millennia. It is easy to use but it is difficult to obtain long, straight pieces of an appropriate diameter. Wood is also susceptible to insect damage and wood rot, so it is not common in commercial construction today. Today, we generally use steel or concrete to form pilings. Steel pilings are installed by dropping long pieces of steel that are coated with a waterproofing solution into the hole. The footings are then poured onto the steel pilings. Steel and wood pilings are installed using a pile driver, which is a machine that forces the pile down into the soil. Concrete pilings are installed by drilling a hole to the required depth and filling it with concrete. Once the concrete has cured, the footings are poured and the rest of the building can be erected. Concrete pilings may also come pre-cast, simply requiring them to be dropped into a pre-drilled hole.

Again, the purpose of a building's foundation is to distribute the weight of the building evenly over the site. If the wrong type of foundation is used, it is likely that the building will begin to settle unevenly, leading to sagging, cracking, doors and windows getting out of alignment, and water leaks. Problems that are the result of a bad foundation are very expensive and inconvenient to fix, because work needs to be done below the building, including using hydraulic jacks to lift the building and injecting concrete under it.

BUILDING LOADS

Building loads refer to the different types of weight that are imposed on the building's structure. Types of loads include live loads, dead loads, seismic loads, and shear loads. A **live load** is weight that moves through the building. For example, people walking through the building introduce a live load. Hand trucks moving produce from the loading dock to a storage area are another example of a live load. The structure must be able to not only handle the vertical weight of the people and the hand truck, but the horizontal movement of that weight as well. In contrast, a **dead load** is one that does not move and simply imposes a downward load. An example of a dead load is tile flooring in a bathroom. The tile's weight only travels in a vertical direction.

Seismic loads are loads that are imposed by movement of the earth below the building, especially earthquake movement. The building's wall system needs to be able to carry all of the dead and live loads as well as compensate for the building's shaking from side to side. Geographic areas are designated with a seismic rating that dictates the types of framing and reinforcement needed to manage seismic loads.

Finally, **shear loads** are loads imposed by wind. High-rise buildings are especially sensitive to shear loads. If you were to go to the top of a very tall building on a windy day, you might find that you can feel the building swaying in the wind. This is intentional, to help the building adjust to the force of the wind. If the building's framing and wall system are not built properly, it is possible that the building would topple over in a strong wind or during a hurricane.

FRAMING AND WALLS

Once the site preparation is finished and the foundation has been poured and set, the walls can be constructed. This chapter focuses on the exterior and other load-bearing wall systems of a building—the non-load bearing walls are less complex to plan and install.

Framing

Wall systems for most hospitality buildings are framed structures, meaning that the structure of the building consists of a frame that is covered with some sort of exterior finish material. The building frame is usually made of one of three materials: wood, structural steel, or concrete. The frame's purpose is to absorb all of the weight loads of the building and to transfer them to the foundation, which then transfers the weight to the soil below the building.

Wood framing is common in older buildings and low-rise buildings (Figure 13.2). Wood is easy to obtain, does not require special preparation or mixing, does not require special skills to handle, and is easy to install. Most residential construction today is still wood-frame construction. A wood frame consists of vertical members called posts and horizontal members called beams. Planks made of plywood or particle board are used to sheath the roof and the outer walls, and to form the floors and ceilings of the building. The planks handle the weight of the objects within the building, such as furniture and people. The weight from the planks is transferred to the beams upon which they sit. The beams transfer the weight to the posts, which then transfer the weight loads to the foundation.

If you work in a small hotel or restaurant, it is likely that you are in a wood-framed building. Wood framing is economical for smaller buildings, but becomes prohibitively expensive for higher rise buildings. This is because the weight of the building increases as the building's size increases vertically.

FIGURE 13.2 Wood Framing. *Source*: Dina Zemke.

The timbers needed to handle the loads of a tall building would have to be very large. Structural steel framing is a more economical option to handle these structures (Figure 13.3). Structural steel uses the same type of post-and-beam configuration as wood framing, but the posts and beams are made of steel. Structural steel offers the advantage of high strength, while at the same time weighing less than other options by reducing the dead load of the building. Another advantage is that it can be installed quickly.

Structural steel framing requires maintenance to prevent rust from corroding the frame over time. A regular program of rust-proofing and painting is necessary. In addition, steel is susceptible to failure at high temperatures and must be fireproofed to insure the frame's integrity in the event of a fire.

Concrete is an artificial stone made of Portland cement, aggregate (such as pebbles, small rocks, or sand), and water. It is highly durable and handles downward loads very efficiently. Because it is in a semiliquid form when mixed, concrete can be cast into different shapes, such as arches and domes, which can be transported as a whole to a building site for installation. It can also be mixed on-site and poured into forms to make foundations, floors, and walls. Interestingly, even though concrete is wet when it is poured, it doesn't actually dry. When the water mixes with the Portland cement, a chemical reaction takes place and the two substances form a new substance—the concrete. The correct term for the reaction is curing. Concrete is capable of curing underwater, so it definitely does not "dry"!

Concrete framing can be achieved using a form filled with concrete that cures into the desired shape. Concrete alone handles vertical weight very well as long as there is support underneath the slab (such as the soil below the foundation). However, if the slab needs to span a wide and unsupported horizontal distance the concrete which is actually quite brittle, will crack and break through the middle of the slab. This quality is overcome by reinforcing the concrete with steel reinforcing rods (also known as

FIGURE 13.3 Steel Framing. *Source*: Dina Zemke.

"rebar"), which provide the support needed to keep the floor from breaking apart. A concrete-framed building will have reinforced walls poured on-site. The floors of the building will use structural steel with steel decking for flooring, over which concrete will be poured to form the floor at each level of the building.

Pre-fabricated concrete slabs, called **pre-cast concrete**, are an alternative to concrete poured on-site. The concrete slabs are formed, poured, and cured in a factory, and then transported to the building site. Some advantages of pre-cast concrete include high quality control and quick installation, because the forms do not need to be made and the curing time does not need to be factored into the project schedule. Mixing concrete is a precise process that can be mishandled on-site, which wastes materials and could potentially result in a concrete mixture that will fail after construction is complete. Making concrete in a manufacturing facility ensures proper formulation, curing conditions, and conformance to standards. A disadvantage of pre-cast concrete is that it needs to be transported to the building site, which may prove to be expensive.

Concrete is a strong, durable material. Yet, it does require a regular maintenance program to prevent damage from water, normal wear and tear, and the formation of cracks due to the building shifting or settling.

EXTERIOR FINISHES

Once the foundation and the framing are installed, the building's exterior finish, or skin, is applied. The building's exterior finish performs a variety of functions including preventing the outdoor conditions (such as rain, heat, cold, and sunlight) from entering the building, acoustic protection from outdoor noise, and an attractive exterior appearance. We will discuss several types of exterior finishes that you will find in the hospitality industry.

Load-Bearing Exterior Finishes

CONCRETE   Building owners with buildings whose walls are formed from poured concrete may elect to leave the exterior wall unfinished, exposing the raw concrete. You may see this in storage or outbuildings on hospitality properties, such as those used for housing vehicles used in landscaping or transportation. While exposed concrete is often seen as an austere, utilitarian finish, it also offers designers a clean, modern look. Bare concrete should be sealed with a concrete sealant to prevent damage from exposure to water and chemicals. Once sealed, the concrete may be left bare, or it may be stained or painted. Concrete walls require regular maintenance to prevent corrosion and cracks resulting from the building's shifting and settling. This could lead to costly repairs.

Concrete block is the common term used for a **concrete masonry unit (CMU)** (Figure 13.4). CMUs are blocks formed from concrete. The blocks have holes that permit the mason to pick them up and transport them and also reduce the weight of the material. The blocks are stacked, with mortar (a cement-like paste) used to hold the layers of block in place. North Americans often also refer to a concrete block as a "cinder block," referring back to the days

FIGURE 13.4 Concrete Masonry Unit (CMU) Exterior Finish. *Source*: Dina Zemke.

when cinders left over from coal-burning processes were used in the concrete mixture to form the blocks. Concrete block walls are generally designed as load-bearing walls, so the exterior wall of the building is part of the framing itself.

Framed Construction Finishes

Buildings with wooden or steel frames are essentially boxes with an exterior layer applied to improve the appearance of the building's exterior. Preparing for the exterior finish is a four-step process:

1. The frame is erected.
2. The outer surface of the frame is covered with a sheath that consists of materials such as plywood, particle board, or other construction materials that are made in panels.
3. Insulation is applied to the inner side of the sheath.
4. A vapor barrier material that looks like a large sheet of plastic is applied to the outer side of the sheath to prevent outdoor moisture from penetrating the wall and entering the building.

Once the preceding steps are complete, the building is ready to receive its exterior finish. There are numerous types of finishes available. A list of the most common types of finishes appears below.

SIDING One of the most common exterior finishes is siding, which is composed of long strips of material made of vinyl, aluminum, or wood. The earliest type of siding consisted of strips of wood, called clapboards. The wood had to be stained or painted to prevent rot and it required repair when it was damaged by insects. Wood was flammable and relatively expensive to purchase. It also required constant maintenance. The 1940s saw the development of siding made of aluminum with a baked enamel finish. The aluminum siding

(a)

(b)

FIGURE 13.5   (a) Vinyl Siding. (b) A Close-up View.   *Source*: Dina Zemke.

never rotted or rusted and required little maintenance, which made it a popular alternative to wooden clapboards.

As the raw material prices for aluminum rose over time, however, aluminum siding became less desirable. In addition, many building owners were stuck with the original color of the siding, as most paint products at the time did not provide a durable finish on top of the enamel. The enamel on the siding also deteriorated over time. During the 1960s, many new uses for plastics developed, including the use of vinyl in place of aluminum for building siding. Vinyl siding gradually gained popularity and is now the most common type of siding. It is economical to purchase and easy to install. It requires little maintenance, and, because the vinyl siding is made of a solid piece, the color runs all the way through it and never requires painting (Figures 13.5a and b).

A new type of siding was recently introduced into the market and is rapidly gaining popularity. The siding is called **fiber-cement board**. It is composed of organic fibers mixed with a lightweight cement and formed into a variety of clapboards and panels. This product is somewhat more expensive than vinyl siding, but offers the advantages of having improved fire-resistance, greater durability, and paintability. It is also perceived to be a more upscale finish.

As a hospitality manager, you are likely to encounter each of the preceding types of siding. You should recognize the need for regular, scheduled maintenance not only for the wood siding, but also for the aluminum and vinyl siding.

MASONRY   Masonry is the term used to describe brick or stone finishes on a building or other project. The term is derived from the days when buildings were erected by masons, who worked with stone and brick. Some of the common types of masonry finishes used in the hospitality industry are brick and stone.

Bricks are masonry units made of vitrified clay and other substances. Like today's concrete block walls, brick walls were also designed as load-bearing walls in the past. However, bricks are relatively expensive compared to other building materials and are now used primarily as a cosmetic finish on a building's exterior.

(a)

(b)

FIGURE 13.6   (a) Brick Siding.   *Source*: Dina Zemke. (b) Brick Wall.   *Source*: The Lark.

The brick will be applied to the sheath as a thin exterior finish, similar to a wood veneer (Figures 13.6a and b). Stone blocks or panels, such as granite or limestone, can also be used as an exterior finish. The building's frame is sheathed, and then a thin sheet of stone is attached to the sheathing.

Bricks and stone both require mortar to be applied between each brick or stone to hold the material in place. Mortar is affected over time by exposure to water, temperature changes, and chemicals in the environment, such as road salt and smog. The mortar will eventually erode and require repair. The removal of failing mortar and the replacement of it with fresh mortar is called **tuck-pointing**, which means adding mortar to masonry after the bricks or stones are already laid. Tuck pointing is an expensive process, but building managers who do not maintain their exterior masonry can look forward to a great deal of interior wall damage due to water and insects entering the building through gaps in the mortar.

SHINGLES AND SHAKES   Shingles and shakes are rectangular pieces of wood that are individually installed and overlapped to cover the exterior wall or the roof of a building (Figure 13.7). Shingles are smoother and thinner than shakes, which are cut more roughly and are thicker to provide a more rustic appearance. Both shingles and shakes are generally made from cedar, which has a natural resistance to insects and is less affected by exposure to wind, sun, and precipitation. They do require some maintenance and a hospitality business manager will want to check for bee infestations, because these types of exteriors provide desirable conditions for bees and other insects when they are looking for a place to build their nests. The cedar may not be damaged, but guests generally do not enjoy the company of stinging insects.

GLASS   Many modern buildings use glass as an exterior finish, particularly high-rise buildings in metropolitan areas (Figure 13.8). This type of wall system is usually called a curtain wall, because the frame of the building, usually made of structural steel, carries the weight of the building and the glass walls simply act as a curtain to protect the interior of the building from wind, rain, snow, and heat and to provide privacy for the occupants. The building's

FIGURE 13.7
A Building Skinned in
Wood Shingles and
Clapboards. *Source*:
Dina Zemke.

FIGURE 13.8   Glass
Curtain Wall Building
Exterior. *Source*: Dina
Zemke.

foundation does not need to handle as much weight if glass is used in lieu of heavier exterior finish materials.

Glass curtain walls are relatively inexpensive to purchase and install, and they provide a clean, modern look. However, the able building manager will recognize the need for a continuous window-washing program to keep the exterior of the building attractive and to provide clean, clear windows for the occupants to enjoy. A window-washing program for a large, high-rise building will require specialized motorized scaffolding for the workers to use in a safe manner. Many larger properties contract out the window-washing services.

Glass curtain walls offer some safety hazards. The glass may break due to the building settling, which can cause the steel framing to shift slightly.

While it is designed to handle its own weight and the forces from strong winds, the glass can still break in a severe storm. Proper design and installation is crucial to keep the glass from popping out during a windstorm, which creates a vacuum that can pull the glass out of its frame.

Stucco and EIFS

Stucco is a type of cement or plaster that is spread over the building's exterior sheath to create either a smooth or rough surface. This type of material provides an attractive rustic finish that is used extensively in the southern and southwestern United States as well as in traditional Tudor-style half-timber construction. Stucco is relatively inexpensive and easy to apply, but it requires a significant amount of maintenance, depending on local weather conditions. It also tends to crumble or fall off in chunks if a heavy object hits the wall.

The trend today is to move away from the traditional stucco materials and instead to use an engineered exterior product called an **exterior insulating and finish system** (or **EIFS**, pronounced eef'-is). The new EIFS systems use durable, lightweight products that are easy to mix on-site and easy to apply. They are available in a wide range of colors and are easy to maintain (Figure 13.9). Some of the newer variations include the use of decorative

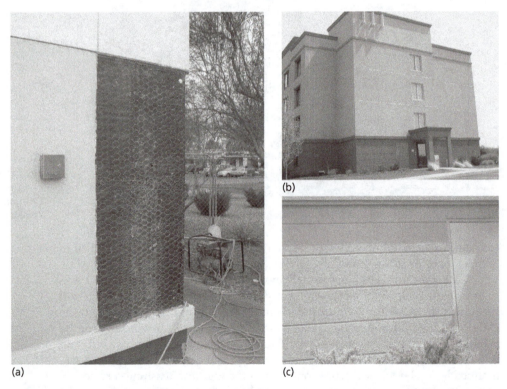

(a)

(b)

(c)

FIGURE 13.9   (a) Applying EIFS to a Restaurant's Exterior Wall. (b) A Hotel with EIFS as an Exterior Finish. (c) Close-up of EIFS.   *Source*: Dina Zemke.

crushed aggregate (stones), such as mixing in crushed granite or quartz, to provide a more deluxe appearance.

The use of these types of systems has spread from the southern and southwestern areas of the United States into northern areas, and you will very likely encounter it in one of the buildings you will manage in your career. One of the more common maintenance problems is staining from water used in landscaping. The water often contains minerals, such as iron, that can discolor the stucco or EIFS. Both finishes are susceptible to chipping as well. If you are responsible for a property that has a stucco or EIFS exterior finish, you should ensure that you or your chief engineer are familiar with the proper products necessary to clean, maintain, and repair these materials.

OTHER EXTERIOR FINISHES   The previous section discussed a variety of common exterior finishes for commercial and residential buildings. There are many others that you may encounter, including faux stone and brick, enamel panels, and a number of different types of wood siding. As mundane as the building's exterior seems, the knowledgeable hospitality property manager will understand that the outside of the building requires the same regular maintenance and repair as the interior finishes.

INSULATION

One of the most important issues in the building's exterior structure is one that is rarely seen—the building's insulation system. Insulation protects against energy loss and helps provide consistent, comfortable climate control for the building's occupants. If you have been in a drafty building, it was due to poor insulation and/or inefficient windows. (Windows will be discussed in the next section.)

The purpose of insulation is to provide a barrier against heat transfer. You may recall from our earlier discussions of heating and cooling systems that heat energy always moves from a warmer area to a cooler area. Hence, if the building is warm inside and the outside is cold, the heat from inside the building will try to escape to warm up the outside. The reverse is true during the cooling season.

Insulation should be installed in the roof and in the exterior walls. Not all buildings require the same quantity of insulation. For example, buildings in colder climates require thicker layers of insulation than those in warmer climates.

Insulation works by creating an empty space, or a series of smaller empty spaces, that provide an insulating barrier against heat transfer. If you think of a piece of fiberglass insulation, you know that it is like a very fluffy, thick blanket. The paper backing on the insulation is used to attach the insulation to the wall or in the ceiling. The wooly part of the insulation provides the small empty spaces, or voids, that trap the heat and prevent it from traveling to the cooler environment. If insulation is compressed, the voids disappear and the insulation loses its insulating value.

An insulation material's ability to inhibit heat transfer is measured by its **R-value**, which stands for its thermal resistance value. All building materials have an *R*-value. A comprehensive list of *R*-values for most building materials is available through the American Society of Heating, Refrigeration, and Air Conditioning Engineers (ASHRAE).

To determine what a wall's R-value is, simply add the combined R-values of all of the materials. These should include the building's skin, sheathing, insulation materials, framing, and interior wall materials. For example, let's say that we have a wall made of the following components.

Component	R-Value
$\frac{1}{2}$ inch gypsum board	0.45
Wood stud framing	0.00
$3\frac{1}{2}$ inches of fiberglass insulation	11.00
$\frac{1}{2}$ plywood sheathing	0.87
Exterior Insulating Finishing System (EIFS)	0.00
Total R-value	**12.32**

The higher the R-value, the greater the insulating power. However, more insulation is not always better. Additional insulation eventually provides diminishing returns, so too much insulation is simply a waste of money. The U.S. Department of Energy provides an R-value calculator through the Oak Ridge National Laboratory. You will need your building's zip code, the framing type (metal, wood, or concrete) and the type of heating system. When checking the results, remember to include both the building sheathing and the cavity values. You can exceed the recommended R-value somewhat and see cost-savings, but too much insulation will not be beneficial.

A variety of insulation materials are used in hospitality buildings. Some of the most common are fiberglass or mineral wool blankets, urethane-based insulating foams, shredded cellulose that is blown into wall cavities and overhead ceiling spaces, Styrofoam boards that are attached to the building sheath, and foil products. The foil products do not provide insulating void spaces, but instead work by reflecting the radiant heat waves either back into the building (during the heating season) or away from the building (during the cooling season).

WINDOWS AND DOORS

FENESTRATION The term **fenestration** refers to the system of windows in the building. Windows provide protection from the outside elements but also permit daylight to enter and allow building occupants to view the outdoors. Windows that open may also be used to ventilate the building. There is a large variety of windows that you will encounter in your hospitality career.

HOW ARE WINDOWS MADE? Windows basically consist of a frame and glass or other transparent material that is placed in the frame. For purposes of this discussion, we will refer to the transparent material as glass, although various types of plastic may be used as well. Frames are usually made of aluminum,

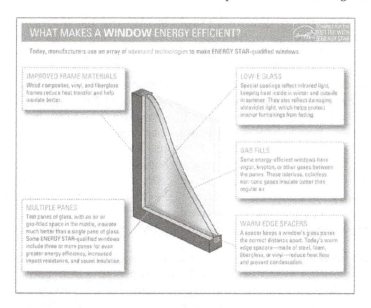

FIGURE 13.10 What Makes a Window Energy Efficient? *Source:* EnergyStar.

wood, vinyl, or fiberglass, and may be clad in metal or vinyl. Wood frames may be stained or painted. Today's frames provide a good seal, are insulated, and do not need a great deal of maintenance.

The glass in windows can consist of anywhere from one to three panes of glass. This is referred to as the window's **glazing**. A single-glazed window has a single pane of glass, a double-glazed window has two panes, and a triple-glazed window has three panes. Empty spaces between the panes of glass are called **thermal breaks**. As with wall insulation, these thermal breaks create a layer of insulation (Figure 13.10). Once the glass is set in the frame, the air is pumped out of the window and the unit is sealed. The thermal breaks are vacuums, which provide additional insulation value. Most windows now also contain some form of inert gas, usually argon or krypton, that adds to the insulating value. The surface of the glass may also have an invisible metallic coating that reflects heat and light outwards for added energy efficiency. Ultraviolet (UV) rays are reflected, which reduce fading in carpet, upholstery, and fabric. Windows that are energy-efficient are called low-E windows. Low-E is short for "low emissivity," meaning that the window permits relatively little solar heat to pass through the window (http://www.inspectionprotection.com/info/WindowsDoors.pdf). These windows keep heat out of the building during the cooling season and keep heat inside the building during the heating season. The thermal breaks, if properly designed, also add acoustic insulation to the window, which creates a quieter indoor environment.

Old-fashioned windows provided protection from rain, snow, and insects and they permitted occupants to see outside. However, they were not very energy-efficient. Today's technology permits windows to provide insulation that, while perhaps not as good as a solid wall, minimizes energy loss. A window's insulating value is measure by its *U*-value. The *U*-value is the inverse of the *R*-value used in measuring a wall's insulation value. If a material has an *R*-value of 2, its *U*-value would be ½. Therefore, in contrast with the *R*-value of a material, the lower the *U*-value, the better the insulating power.

WINDOW SAFETY   As hospitality business managers, we must be concerned about potential safety problems with our building finishes. In addition to being a potential point of entry or exit for intruders, windows may also provide access to people who wish to jump out of the building or for children to fall out of the window. Many high-rise hotels have windows that do not open at all. If a hotel's windows do open, they should be fitted with hardware that restricts the opening size. Even with limits on the window opening, however, hotel managers must also be concerned with small children accidentally falling out of windows. **Window guards** come in a variety of styles for different types of windows. One of these should always be installed.

WINDOW MAINTENANCE   An active cleaning program must be implemented to insure the attractiveness of the building's appearance from both inside and out. Most windows that open, however, have mechanical parts that need to be repaired or replaced from time to time. Double-hung windows have slide mechanisms, and casement windows use cranking mechanisms, both of which should be checked for safe operation. Double-hung windows whose slide mechanisms fail may result in the lower window crashing down onto the sill, possibly hitting an employee or a guest. This sometimes results in broken bones and, in one recent residential case where the window closed on a child's head, death.

Double-glazed and triple-glazed windows will, over time, develop leaks in the vacuum seals, resulting in vapor build-up between the panes of glass and possible deterioration of the window structure. If the damage is not too extensive, the glazing can be repaired and the vacuum reinstituted. However, the entire window itself may need to be replaced. New windows will come with a warranty from the manufacturer. Due to the large number of windows that populate many hospitality properties, particularly hotels, the knowledgeable hospitality manager will track window performance and work with the manufacturer to repair defective products.

Doors

Doors provide protection from the elements as well as security for the building. Some of the major components of doors for entrance and egress (exiting the building) are fire-rating, closers, and locking devices.

Many of the doors in a commercial building, whether a hospitality facility or not, are required to be fire-rated. Fire-rating means that the door has been tested in a laboratory to determine how long it will remain intact during a fire. This measure is intended to compartmentalize an area that is on fire in order to prevent the spread of the fire to other parts of the building.

We should not depend on our guests and employees to close doors behind them. Many people simply do not remember to do it. An open door is an invitation for the outside weather, insects, animals, and criminals to enter and damage the premises. Exterior doors, as well as interior doors in commercial buildings, have closers to automatically close a door left ajar. Most door closers are located at the top of the door and use a pneumatic device to ensure a slow, controlled closing. Some closers are imbedded at the bottom of the doorframe or in the sill.

Exterior doors have special hardware that most interior doors do not. First, we want our guests to enter the property through designated entrances without difficulty. However, there are many doors on the property that should remain closed all of the time and should only be used when a specific need arises. For example, emergency exit doors should only be used to evacuate the building, not for everyday entry and egress. Emergency exit doors often have alarm devices that are activated when the door is opened. These alarms serve a threefold purpose. First, the alarm deters people from casually using the door as an exit. Second, the alarm deters people from opening the doors to let other people in. Many criminals in the past have entered the building and opened the exit stairwells to let accomplices in or to remove property in a clandestine manner. Finally, the alarm also alerts the security personnel that the door has been opened, which should initiate an investigation of the reason for this occurrence. Faster detection of a fire, medical emergency, or crime in progress is desirable.

Much of the door hardware inside the building, such as doorknobs, requires twisting a knob or pressing a lever-type opener to access the interior areas. However, exterior doors are required by code to utilize **panic bars** to open the doors (Figure 13.11). These are necessary because fires or other emergencies often cause panic and irrational thinking. A person would have to find the doorknob and turn it in the proper direction to exit the building. Moreover, a panic bar will open the door when an object, like a body, simply crashes into it, which eliminates the need for people to search for and manipulate a door knob.

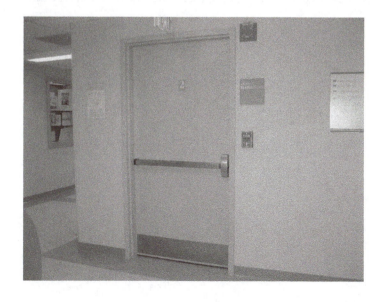

FIGURE 13.11   A Panic Bar on an Exit Door. *Source*: Dina Zemke.

ROOFS

The final element of all building exterior systems is the roof. Roofs consist of two main elements. The first element is a framed structure that shapes the roof and manages the weight of precipitation and equipment that may accumulate. The second element is a waterproof membrane to prevent water and wind from entering the building. There are two general types of roofing that you will encounter in the hospitality industry: sloped roofs and flat roofs.

Sloped roofs are roofs that are commonly used on relatively low-rise buildings (Figure 13.12). They are the most popular type of roof for residential construction. In the hospitality industry, you are more likely to see this type of roof on a restaurant or on a lodging facility that is only a few stories high. Sloped roofs consist of a structural frame, decking that is applied to the outside surface of the frame, a waterproof membrane, and shingles made of a variety of materials, such as asphalt felt embedded with sand or mica granules (what we normally think of as shingles), clay tile, slate, or wooden shingles. The slope of the roof causes water and snow to drain off the roof. The edges of the roof may be lined with gutters, which are metal or plastic channels that collect the water and move it away from the building through downspouts. The choice of roof finish material is largely determined by aesthetics, although some materials may be required or prohibited based on local codes and rules.

Flat roofs, also referred to as **built-up roofs**, are also common. These roofs do not use shingles but instead use a synthetic membrane to seal the roof surface. They are common on hospitality buildings, particularly on high-rise lodging properties (Figure 13.13). They consist of a structural frame, some sort of decking such as plywood or steel decking, and several layers of materials that are applied one at a time. These layers consist of either asphalt or coal tar, aggregate (sand or small stones), and decking felt. The layers merge together during the curing process to create a single, integral membrane that is waterproof. Other synthetic materials are often used to

FIGURE 13.12   Sloped Roof, with Asphalt Shingles.   *Source*: Dina Zemke.

FIGURE 13.13   Flat
Roofing System.   *Source*:
Dina Zemke.

create the membrane, including elastomers, polyvinyl chloride sheeting, and polyurethane compounds.

Flat roofs are often less expensive to install than sloped roofs. They do not add vertical height to the building, which is an important consideration in jurisdictions that limit the maximum building height. The architect can maximize the amount of available space in the building's design, which the owner can then use as saleable square footage. These roofs frequently have the advantage of being hidden from view, so the building manager does not need to be concerned with maintaining a pleasing appearance.

Flat roofs require significant upkeep. If improperly installed or maintained, they are susceptible to developing leaks. The surface can be very delicate and may break if walked on. Many buildings have walkways installed on a flat roof's surface to minimize random foot or equipment traffic that would damage the roof. Built-up roof surfaces also deteriorate over time, so periodic maintenance and resurfacing are required.

Periodic inspection of the roof from both the exterior and the interior attic space can help identify when the roof is beginning to deteriorate. If your property is in a location that is prone to strong winds, you should inspect the roof frequently, particularly after heavy storms. The most important element in roof maintenance is ensuring that the waterproof membrane remains intact. Breaks or penetrations into the membrane can result in leaks that cause a great deal of interior damage. Unplanned roofing repairs are very expensive. The sources of leaks can be extremely difficult to diagnose because water that enters a tear in the membrane in one area of the roof may travel across the membrane and come out of the ceiling below in a completely different spot. The ceiling below may be capable of holding a great deal of water before the leak begins to appear in an occupied space. In this instance, the damage might be so extensive as to require replacement of the ceiling. The ceiling below may also collapse, which could cause significant damage to the space and its occupants.

DRAINAGE **Roof drains** and **gutters** (Figures 13.14a and b) are integral parts of good roofing systems. Flat roofs have drainage systems that are located either around the perimeter of the roof or down the center of the roof deck. The roof's surface should be very slightly sloped toward the drains. Water goes down the drains and is carried down and away from the building by a system of drainage pipes. Drainage systems should be inspected to insure that they are clear of obstacles and that drainage occurs efficiently. A clogged drain on a flat roof will result in roof flooding. Water will always find a way to go down, thanks to gravity, and will seep into the building's interior. If the water does not leak downwards, it may accumulate on the roof to the point where the roof collapses due to the water's weight.

Gutters are installed at the edges of sloped roofs, where the sloped roof directs water into the gutter and away from the building via downspouts (Figure 13.14c). The water exits the building out onto the grounds, preferably downhill from the building. This prevents water from accumulating alongside the building's foundation and basement. Concrete is porous and water may penetrate the foundation or basement walls and result in mold

(a)

(b)

(c)

FIGURE 13.14 (a) Roof Drain. (b) An Outlet for a Roof Drain. (c) Gutter on a Sloped Roof.
Source: Dina Zemke.

or water in the basement and structural damage to the foundation itself. Many building managers do not like gutters because gutters require maintenance to ensure that they are not clogged with debris, such as leaves or moss.

Gutters should also be maintained to insure that they do not leak. Leaking gutters are unsightly and pose a safety problem as well. Snow and melting ice in the winter can fill clogged or leaking gutters. If the temperature drops, the water in the gutter will turn to ice and may form icicles. While icicles are pretty, they can also be deadly. High-rise buildings in many cities have had to block their sidewalks to pedestrian traffic because large icicles fell from great heights at unpredictable times. The icicles often injure, and sometimes kill, passersby. A good inspection and maintenance program can minimize the potential for property damage and injury to people in the area.

SNOW   Snow can add a great deal of weight to a roof. People in very snowy climates, such as in Northern Europe, have traditionally designed their buildings with steeply sloped roofs that prevent snow from accumulating. You may occasionally see metal bars or spikes project up from the roof surface. The purpose of the bars is to collect solar heat that will melt the snow in the surrounding area, allowing the snow to move off the roof. If temperatures are warm enough during a snowstorm, the snow may contain a great deal of water, which makes the snow very heavy. (Those of you who ski may be familiar with the terms "Sierra sludge" and "mashed potatoes.") If this snow accumulates, it is possible that the roof structure will be unable to handle the weight and collapse. If you experience very heavy snow conditions, you may need to manually remove the snow by shoveling it off the roof.

GARAGES AND PARKING

Most hospitality facilities provide parking areas for their employees and guests. In locations where land is relatively inexpensive, the parking lot may be one large horizontal area. In areas where enough land for a parking lot is either not available or prohibitively expensive, the facility may own and operate a parking garage.

The number of parking spaces that the property must have is usually determined by local codes. This number may be based on the building's square footage or maximum occupancy. The local code may also require that a certain percentage of the parking lot square footage be filled with landscaping. Local codes may also govern whether or not a parking structure is permitted and if so, the maximum height and size of the structure. If you are building a new facility, make sure that these issues are considered during the planning stage of the project.

The size and layout of the parking spaces may also be governed by local codes. In general, a standard parking space, or bay, is approximately 8 to 9 feet wide and 18 feet long. The space is designated by painted stripes. Location of landscaping islands and lighting requirements will also be dictated by local building codes.

HANDICAPPED PARKING The Americans with Disabilities Act Accessibility Guidelines (ADAAG) dictates the number and size of parking spaces for handicapped drivers. These spaces are wider and include walkways that permit drivers to exit and enter their cars if more space is needed, as well as accommodate drivers or passengers who use wheelchairs. Each handicap bay must be a minimum of 96" wide and must be adjacent to a walkway that is at least 60" wide for automobiles and 96" wide for vans.

Parking spaces for the handicapped must also be designated with signage that is outlined in the ADAAG. The parking space must be striped with blue paint and the accessibility symbol. There must also be upright signage indicating that the space is designated for a vehicle for the handicapped.

The route between the parking spaces for the handicapped and the building entrance must provide a route that does not require people to climb up onto curbs or step over other obstacles. If there is a change in elevation between the parking area and the building entrance, ramps must be provided with a gentle enough slope (a maximum of 1:20 ratio) that a person in a manually operated wheelchair can easily use the ramp.

PARKING GARAGES Hotels located in the center of larger cities often do not have access to enough land to provide a surface-level parking lot. Some hotels and center city restaurants do not provide parking at all, but instead direct guests to nearby on-street parking, metered parking, or public parking garages. Yet, some properties do own parking garages for the convenience of their guests. Most city hotels with parking garages use the garage as a source of revenue, charging either an hourly fee for non-guests or a daily fee for hotel guests. The property may choose to operate the garage itself. Yet, because of the insurance and liability risks, most properties subcontract the garage operation to vendors that specialize in garage operation.

A parking garage may consist of a single level or many levels. The garage may be completely underground or aboveground. Some parking garages are located on top of a building, but most are either below or alongside the building. All garages have ticket dispensing equipment, cashiering equipment, gates to restrict entry and exit, parking bays, and lighting. Many garages require ventilation equipment to ensure safe air quality. Some garages use automatic counting equipment to determine the number of parking spaces available, to avoid the frustration a guest may experience when driving around looking for a parking space in a full lot.

Some garages operate by offering valet parking. In these instances, an office is necessary for customers to turn keys over to the valet parkers, obtain tickets, and pay for car retrieval. A waiting space for guests while the car is being retrieved is also necessary. Valet parking offices require secure storage for customers' keys, to insure that the automobiles are not stolen. If the parking fees are applied to the customer's guestroom folio, the cash register system should be compatible with the hotel's front office property management system.

Safety is a major concern in parking garages. The narrow aisles and parked cars provide limited visibility for oncoming traffic and cars backing out of the bays. Both of these actions could create potential property damage to other cars. Perhaps of more concern, however, is the potential for criminal behavior. If your property is responsible for a garage, you will need to ensure that security personnel actively monitor the garage, both in person and by using closed circuit television or other types of electronic monitoring equipment. Adequate lighting is critical to help drivers see potential hazards and to deter or identify criminals following a crime. Having the right kind of security equipment will deter crime or will at least facilitate in filing incident reports and provide backup in the event of a lawsuit.

WALKS AND CURBS Most hospitality properties with parking lots or other exterior grounds facilities must provide sidewalks. The parts of the property that are adjacent to roads, driveways, or parking lots will usually have curbs to delineate the grounds from the paved areas. The dimensions of sidewalks and curbs are often dictated by local building codes and can range from plain and utilitarian to highly decorative elements of the landscaping design.

SIGNAGE

Signage is one of the most important elements of the facility. The term "wayfinding" refers to the process that an individual goes through in navigating a new space. While we are discussing exterior signage in this chapter, the same principles apply (perhaps even more strongly) to interior signage as well. Signage alerts guests to the location of the property and its entrances and exits, directs traffic through the property, provides warnings for possible hazards, and may serve as a decorative element. Unfortunately, many hospitality properties suffer from poor signage. The signage systems are usually designed during the construction of the building and often go untouched after the building's grand opening. Signage should be evaluated periodically to ensure that it:

- has an attractive appearance and is well maintained.
- has been revised to reflect changes to the property and building.
- provides excellent, clear direction.
- complies with local codes, which change over time.

Poor exterior signage can result in accidents, injury, and guest frustration. If signage around driveways and parking areas is poor, pedestrian and automobile collisions may occur. Poor signage can frustrate guests who are trying to locate a particular entrance or area of the property, which can result in dissatisfaction with the hotel or restaurant before the guest ever enters the building!

LANDSCAPING

The exterior landscaping of a hospitality property serves a largely aesthetic function. The landscaping design and maintenance project messages about the property to the public. Good landscaping helps people form assumptions about the quality of the hotel or restaurant. For example, a building surrounded by attractive landscaping beckons customers and helps them assume that the product and service inside are of good quality. In contrast, if we use the same building and provide identical product and service inside but have a poorly designed or maintained landscape outside; prospective guests may form the assumption that the quality of the establishment is poor.

In addition to the aesthetic function, landscaping also serves a practical function. Properly placed trees and shrubs can serve as shade devices or windbreaks. Grass and shrubs cool off more quickly in the summer than pavement, which can help reduce cooling needs. The pleasing appearance of plants also helps people in the environment feel cooler in the hot weather than if they only see pavement. Some hotels and restaurants use their own personnel to perform landscape maintenance. However, many hotel managers may find that hiring a local landscaping contractor is more cost-effective than having the hotel staff members perform the maintenance tasks themselves. In addition, landscaping contractors often provide snow removal services in the winter months.

While green, leafy foliage is always pleasing to the eye, it is not always the best choice for landscaping. Landscaping can be expensive to maintain. First, landscaping needs to be mowed, trimmed, raked, and otherwise tended. In addition, most landscaping requires water, which is expensive and depletes water levels in wells and aquifers. This does not mean that properties in desert climates cannot have landscaping that is both attractive and easy to maintain.

The system of landscaping using native plants that do not require a great deal of water is called **xeriscaping** (Figures 13.15a, b, and c). Using plants that are native to the area means that these plants are accustomed to the area's typical rainfall patterns and have adapted over time to survive arid or drought conditions. These plants are also acclimated to the area's soil conditions, such as pH levels and mineral content, which eliminates the need to amend the soil to provide the right growing conditions. These plants still provide beautiful foliage and can be used to create spectacular landscapes, without all of the maintenance and water use—it just requires thoughtful design.

Many areas in the southwestern part of the United States have instituted codes that require xeriscaping and penalize residential and commercial properties that install water-consuming landscaping. Yet, xeriscaping is not just for hot, desert climates. Every building is located in an area that was originally covered with native flora, which evolved to thrive in local conditions. All building owners can save money, natural resources, and labor hours by xeriscaping with indigenous plants that are native to the local environment. Most areas of the United States and Canada provide resources to help gardeners and landscapers select appropriate plants for their region. You can usually find these resources through your local water utility company, state or provincial college's agriculture or horticultural programs, or local landscaping companies.

FIGURE 13.15(a–c)   Xeriscaping Examples.   *Source*: Dina Zemke.

BUILDING RENOVATION

All buildings must eventually be renovated. Equipment breaks down, occupancy patterns shift, additions to the building are erected, building codes and laws change, and aesthetic tastes change. Building renovations should be considered investments in the main asset of a hospitality property. Renovations can improve the appearance, efficiency, and profit margin of the building. However, a successful renovation requires enormous planning, scheduling, and careful management. Planning for a minor renovation should start two to three years before the actual renovation takes place. Major renovations should appear in long-term budgeting and planning seven to ten years prior to the project start date. The topic of capital expenditure, or CapEx, planning was discussed earlier in this book.

Building renovations are usually more difficult to manage than new construction because the work must be performed within the constraints of the existing structure, rather than in a wide-open space. They are also difficult because hospitality buildings are usually at least partially occupied during the time of the renovation. Guests staying in hotels or eating at restaurants under construction often complain about a bad view, noise, dust, vibration, and closed amenities during their stay. Renovations are disruptive to the business because a portion of the property that produces revenue is shut down.

FREQUENCY The frequency of renovations depends on the type of space or equipment and the usage the equipment has received. A typical guestroom should be renovated every five to seven years to ensure that the interior finishes are fresh and up-to-date with guest expectations. If the hotel experiences very high occupancy for extended periods of time, however, the guestrooms should be renovated more frequently. The major mechanicals in a guestroom, such as heating and air-conditioning equipment, need to be changed less frequently, ranging between ten and twenty years.

Some larger lodging properties have continuous renovation. For example, a 50-story hotel may renovate the top five floors of guestrooms. Once those rooms are finished, the project moves to the next five floors, and so on. Once all floors are renovated, the process begins at the top again.

Renovations occasionally occur earlier than expected. Activities that trigger early renovation include:

- *Repositioning the property* When a hotel or restaurant is sold or re-flagged under a new franchise or management agreement, the building may need to be renovated to present the correct product image.
- *Legal and regulatory changes* The Americans with Disabilities Act instituted sweeping change for building design, which resulted in significant renovation of many hospitality properties, particularly in restroom design, vertical transportation, and entrance/exit access.
- *Physical damage to the property* A major fire or flood will often require substantial enough repairs that a renovation of at least part of the building is warranted.
- *Changing space usage* A hotel may close down a restaurant and renovate the space as retail space or a nightclub.

The building's major mechanical systems, such as large air handling systems and elevators, generally need to be renovated every 15 to 25 years. These renovations are prompted by a combination of legal and regulatory changes, wear and tear, and efficiency. For example, a renovated elevator controller provides elevator operation that complies with updated codes and reduces the amount of time that employees wait for the elevator. Most major mechanical system renovations involve replacing control equipment and motors, which wear out over time due to operating loads.

As previously discussed, building exteriors require ongoing maintenance. Eventually, they too need to be renovated. The knowledgeable building manager will take this opportunity to choose exterior components and finishes that improve the energy-efficiency of the building and reduce the maintenance requirements, as well as provide a pleasant appearance. If a manager wishes to renovate the building but needs to convince the building's owner or upper management, a simple analysis of existing energy consumption and maintenance expenditures and the savings that the new components would offer may provide the financial ballast for obtaining funding for the project.

Summary

This chapter skimmed the surface of the building's structure and exterior finishes. Foundations play an important role in transferring the building's weight down into the ground. A faulty foundation can be a disaster for a building owner and very expensive to correct. The building's structure is created by the framing, which transfers weight to the foundation. The framing is covered with a skin, or cladding, and protects the interior from the outdoor elements. The cladding also provides the outside appearance of the building. Exterior finishes come in a wide range of materials, with a wide range of costs. There will always be trade-offs, between appearance, installation costs, and maintenance costs.

Insulation helps manage energy costs by inhibiting heat transfer. If you work in an older building that needs to undergo a renovation, you may be surprised to find little or no insulation in the walls. Modern buildings and renovations usually include installing insulation. Other elements include windows, which can be made more energy-efficient with additional panes of glass, roofs, and other exterior areas.

Buildings need to be renovated periodically. The frequency depends on wear and tear, the type of usage, changes in style and taste, legal and regulatory requirements, and catastrophic damage caused by events like fires or floods. Hotels and restaurants tend to be renovated more frequently than other types of commercial buildings. In hotels, cosmetic upgrades are typically performed every seven years (depending on the individual property's needs). More robust building systems, such as elevators, HVAC, and lighting, last longer and are typically renovated every 20–25 years. This work needs to be forecasted and budgeted through a good capital expense (CapEx) planning system.

Key Terms and Concepts

built-up roofs *320*
concrete *308*
concrete masonry unit (CMU) *309*
dead load *306*
deep systems *305*
exterior insulation and finish system (EIFS) *314*

fenestration *316*
fiber-cement board *311*
flat roofs *320*
footing *305*
foundation *304*
glazing *317*
gutters *322*
live load *306*
load-bearing walls *305*

masonry *311*
mat foundation *305*
non-load bearing walls *305*
panic bars *319*
piling *305*
pre-cast concrete *309*
raft foundation *305*
roof drains *322*

R-value *315*
seismic load *306*
shear loads *306*
sloped roofs *320*
thermal breaks *317*
tuck-pointing *312*
window guards *318*
xeriscaping *326*

Discussion and Review Questions

1. Describe the four types of building loads that are imposed on a building's structure.
2. Discuss potential problems that can arise from failing gutters on a roof.
3. Research resources for xeriscaping in your hometown. What types of environmental challenges exist there for landscaping? What types of plants are suitable for that environment?
4. Compare and contrast using bricks and vinyl siding as an exterior finish on a building.

Notes

Information on wood siding http://www.wood-siding-info.com/

Information on aluminum siding http://www.aluminum-siding-info.com/

Information on EIFS http://www.dryvit.com/

Information on vinyl siding http://www.vinyl-siding-info.com/

Information on bricks http://www.stewart-homes-inc.com/brick_terms.htm

Oak Ridge National Laboratory http://www.ornl.gov/sci/roofs+walls/insulation/ins_16.html

American Society of Refrigeration, Heating and Air Conditioning Engineers www.ashrae.org

Xeriscaping www.xeriscaping.org

GLOSSARY

Accreditation: as used in this instance, it is when environmental certifying bodies are certified by other standard setting organizations.

Addressable system: a fire detection system that is "smart" because it can pinpoint the exact location of the smoke detector that tripped the alarm. It uses transponders linked to a computer.

Affiliate certification: second-party certification. It is when an industry or trade association certifies its members who support the association for meeting certain prescribed standards. Affiliate certification lacks credibility, because the member who becomes certified funds the operation of the association and may also influence policies and procedures.

Air-conditioning: air that has been conditioned to provide the correct temperature, relative humidity, airflow, and cleanliness.

Air-handling system: a centralized air-conditioning system that circulates hot or cold water to large fan units. The fans blow air across the water pipes to send conditioned air through the ductwork to one or more rooms. It's generally used for larger areas, such as public spaces and ballrooms.

American Hotel & Lodging Association: a trade association representing the lodging industry. The Educational Institute, the educational wing of the association, produces textbooks, videos, and training programs for every area of the industry.

American Society of Heating, Refrigeration, and Air Conditioning Engineers (ASHRAE): an organization that advances technology to serve humanity and promote a sustainable world. The society writes and promotes standards for refrigeration and indoor environments. These standards are often adopted by governments into building codes.

Amortized: the distribution of a single lump-sum cash flow into many smaller cash flow installments, as determined by an amortization schedule. Each installment contains both the principal and the interest (if any).

Amp (ampere): a unit of electrical flow.

Appliance heat load: heat generated by lights, motors, and other components.

Aquifer: a large, underground water deposit.

As time permits: the lowest priority work request. As is stated, when maintenance personnel have the time, this request will be honored.

Automatic door closures: fire doors that will close when a fire alarm is sounded; often found in hallways.

Backdraft: the introduction of oxygen into a room that has been on fire that causes an explosion when the particulates in the air ignite. Opening a door to a room that has been on fire may cause a backdraft. *See also* **ignition temperature** and **flashover**.

Backlogged: a work request that is postponed because the needed parts or repair person is not available. The affected parties should be informed of the postponement.

Balancing (a system): this action involves the adjusting and recalibrating of a system in order to provide the correct amount of activity to the various areas or equipment that the system serves. For example, air balancing ensures proper airflow and pressure to the areas a fan serves.

Balustrade: the vertical element of an escalator; the handrail rides on the balustrade.

Benchmark: a geographical location whose position is known to a high degree of accuracy and is marked in some way. There may be a metal rod, a small stone obelisk with an engraved metal disk, or a concrete marker. Benchmarks are used by surveyors, building contractors, and architects.

Booster heater: a small, supplemental heater on a dish machine or laundry system that elevates the water temperature to high levels for the sanitizing cycles.

Branch line: a pipe that runs in a fire control system that contains the sprinkler heads.

Breathing line: the location approximately five feet above the finished floor; the height where thermostats are usually installed for thermal comfort.

British thermal unit (BTU): the amount of heat required to increase the temperature of one pound of water by one degree Fahrenheit.

Buffer: a device located at the bottom of an elevator hoistway that cushions the elevator if it falls to the bottom of the hoistway. Buffer types are spring buffers or hydraulic buffers.

Building envelope: the outer shell of a building that is between the interior and the exterior walls. It facilitates the control of the interior's climate.

Built-up roof: a roof made of many layers of membranes; usually a flat roof finish.

CADD: computer-aided design and drafting; software that enables a person to complete architectural and technical drawings.

CapEx: capital expenditures. These are costs for remodeling, refurbishments, and renovations. They go far beyond the annual maintenance (POM) costs. A separate budget is prepared every year for CapEx items. *See also* **property operation and maintenance (POM)**.

Car operating panel: the control panel located inside an elevator cab.

Carbon footprint: a measure of the impact human activities have on the environment in terms of the amount of greenhouse gases produced, measured in units of carbon dioxide.

Carbon monoxide (CO): a deadly gas and a byproduct of combustion.

Case goods: hard furniture as opposed to upholstered furniture (soft goods); for example, credenzas, armoires, tables, etc.

Checklists/punchlists: memory aids. These forms are often used when maintenance personnel are inspecting guestrooms to ensure items are not overlooked.

Chiller: a system that cools water to be circulated throughout the building to air handling units and fan coil units.

Circuit breaker: an overcurrent device in a circuit breaker panel. If too much amperage is drawn by appliances on a circuit, the circuit breaker will disconnect and "blow the circuit" to prevent fires and electrocution.

Cold: the absence of heat.

Color rendering index (CRI): a measure of how closely a light source's ability to show color matches that of the sun.

Commissioning/Recommissioning (of a building): Commissioning is the systematic process of ensuring that a building's complex array of systems is designed, installed, and tested to perform according to the design intent and the building owner's operational needs. It is done before the building is open for service. Recommissioning has the same intent, but it is done after the building has been in operation for an extended period of time. Major systems are retested.

Compactor: a device that shrinks the volume of waste by pressing it into a smaller volume and thus reduces disposal costs.

Composting: the breaking down of organic matter, such as food, down into its elements that can then be used as a soil amendment.

Compressor: in refrigeration, a device used to compress refrigerant gas into a hot, high-pressure gas.

Computerized maintenance management system (CMMS): software dedicated to the administration and management of the maintenance function at a property; typically, a *stand-alone* system not linked to the hotel's property management system (PMS).

CMU: concrete masonry unit; also called cinder block.

Concrete: an artificial stone composed of water, aggregate materials, and Portland cement.

Condenser (coils): the part of a refrigeration system that uses air or condenser water to remove heat from the refrigerant.

Condition-based maintenance: *See* **predictive maintenance**.

Constant pressure system: a type of water supply system that uses pressure constantly applied by pumps to send water throughout a building; suitable for low-rise and/or low-volume applications.

Consumption meter: an electric meter that measures actual energy consumed over time; measures consumption in terms of kWh.

Contour lines: lines that show the slope of a property. *See also* **plot**.

Convection: a process in which a fluid or gas establishes a circular flow pattern based on the fact that warmer substances rise and cool substances sink. Forced convection uses a fan to accelerate the circular flow.

Cooling ton: 12,000 BTUs.

Cooling tower: a part of a centralized cooling system; cools the condenser water used to cool the refrigerant in the condenser.

Correlated color temperature (CCT): the color of a light source; ranges from warm to cool; measured in degrees Kelvin.

Critical incident response teams: specially trained employees who respond to specific emergencies. A property may have more than one critical incident response team. For example, there might be one team trained to respond to fires and another trained to respond to a choking or heart attack.

Cross main: a pipe that extends from a riser to the branch line that contains the sprinkler heads in a fire control system.

Damper: a device that is present in ductwork that permits air to travel through the duct when the damper is in the open position and blocks air travel when it is in the closed position.

Dead load: the weight of the building and the permanent fixtures inside the building; also called static load.

Deferred maintenance: the action of reducing costs by not performing maintenance when it is needed. However, the result is almost always a substantially increased cost when the maintenance is finally performed.

Demand meter: an electric meter, usually found in commercial businesses, that measures the amount of power drawn over a relatively short period of time. The demand is measured in terms of kW. These meters are used in addition to consumption meters in electric service to commercial buildings.

Detail view: an architectural rendering that shows all of the elements of construction of an object in detail. It may be either a plan or elevation view and often shows hidden elements in the construction of the piece. This drawing is essential for the actual construction of the object in question. It is drawn to scale. It serves as a critical source of communication between the architect and the builder.

Dew point: the temperature at which water vapor will condense. The dew point is influenced by the dry-bulb temperature as well as by the relative humidity.

Disinfectants: chemicals, registered with the Environmental Protection Agency, which destroy pathogens.

Door closures: devices that automatically close an open door without human intervention; found on guest room doors.

Downcycling: the making of products of lesser quality out of recycled materials. Some materials, such as many plastics, cannot be recycled indefinitely. In fact many can only be recycled once or twice. When they are recycled, their molecular bonds break down, which in turn creates a weaker product.

Downfeed system: a type of water supply system that pumps water into a holding tank at the top of the building and then uses gravity to distribute water down throughout the building. The tanks may also be staged on intermediate floors in high-rise buildings.

Dry-bulb temperature: the actual temperature of a substance; measured using a thermometer; a method of reporting sensible heat.

Dry pipe: a type of sprinkler system used in cold climates.

Due diligence: a term used for a number of concepts involving either the performance of an investigation of a business or person, or the performance of an act with a certain standard of care.

Dumbwaiter: a lift device that is only intended to move materials only—never people.

DX system: a direct expansion cooling system. Air is drawn over the evaporator coil in this type of system.

Efficacy: a technical term for efficiency. In lighting, efficacy is defined as the lumens/watt.

Effluence: liquid waste. In plumbing systems, this may contain solids and semi-solid materials.

EIFS: exterior insulation and finishing system.

Ejector pump: a type of pump used in sanitary sewer systems. It removes liquid waste from lower levels of the building up to the main sewer outlet.

Electric discharge lamps: a family of lamps that uses a ballast to provide an electric charge to a gas environment.

Electrical plan: a floor plan, to scale, showing the layout of the electrical wiring, outlets, permanent lighting fixtures, junction boxes, circuit breaker panels, and other electrical related permanent fixtures.

Elevation plan: a side view, to scale, of a building or wall.

Elevator capacity: the amount of weight that an elevator is rated to carry.

Elevator rise: the total amount of travel of an elevator, usually measured from the floor of the bottom landing to the floor of the top landing.

Elevator "safeties": equipment that is activated if an elevator is traveling too fast in either the up or down direction. The safeties grip the guiderails, which thus prevents further travel.

Emergency action plan: an OSHA mandated plan for all buildings that are required to have fire extinguishers, including hotels.

Emergency maintenance: *See* **run-to-failure maintenance.**

Emergency maintenance request: the highest priority work request. Usually human safety and financial loss are at issue if the problem is not corrected right away. Maintenance personnel are expected to immediately respond to the problem.

Emergency response plan: an OSHA mandated plan for all businesses that require some or all employees to respond to an emergency.

Energy records: records of monthly energy usage at property (e.g., electrical, gas, etc). Records are used to identify trends and conditions.

Equipment data cards: a form (electronic or hard copy) that contains essential information on each piece of equipment on the property. Essential information might include model numbers, serial numbers, make and model names, electrical information, mechanical information, and maintenance requirements. Some engineering departments place a maintenance log on the opposite side of the equipment data card.

Equipment schematic: a drawing that represents a piece of equipment using abstract, graphic symbols to show elements of the equipment such as wiring, switches, solenoids, fuses, etc., rather than actual pictures of the equipment.

Escalator: a moving stairway that is useful for moving large numbers of passengers a relatively short vertical distance.

Evaporator (coils): the part of a refrigeration system that uses cold refrigerant to remove heat from the air in a room or from chilled water.

Executive committee: the department heads that report directly to the General Manager. For example, Food & Beverage Director, Hotel Manager, Director of Sales and Marketing, Controller, Human Resource Director, Chief of Security, and the Chief Engineer.

Expansion valve: the metering device that controls the flow of refrigerant into a refrigeration system's evaporator.

Fan coil system: a centralized method of heating and cooling a building, where hot or cold water is circulated through the building through units in guest rooms that use a fan to blow air over the hot or cold pipes to provide heating or cooling.

Fenestration: the windows.

Fire rating: the time it will take a fire that is impinging on a surface to burn through that surface.

Fire triangle: the components of a fire: fuel, heat, and oxygen.

Fire-tube boiler: a boiler that heats hot water or generates steam that uses a tank of water, through which fire-filled pipes pass, to transfer heat to the water.

Firefighters' service: a safety feature in elevators that causes the elevator to return to the main egress floor in the event of a fire. Further operation is disabled until the fire danger has passed and an authorized person returns the elevator to service.

Flashover: the near simultaneous ignition of all materials in a room, because all of the materials in the room, including particulates in the air, reach their **ignition temperature**.

Floor plan: an architectural plan to the scale of a bird's-eye view of a single section of a building.

Flowchart: a pictorial representation describing a process being studied; it may even be used to plan stages of a project. Flowcharts tend to provide people with a common language or reference point when dealing with a project or process.

Fluorescent lamp: a type of electric discharge lamp.

Forced convection: the process of using fans to circulate hot air in an oven, which then speeds up the cooking process. There are also forced convection cooling systems where fans are used to circulate air across evaporator coils in freezers and coolers to speed up the cooling process of food contained in these units.

Foundation: the bottom structure of the building that transfers the loads of the building down onto a stable substrate.

Framing: the building's skeleton; carries the building's weight down to the foundation.

Freight elevator: an elevator that is not intended for use by the general public. Freight elevators lack many of the operational devices that are found on passenger elevators.

Frequency: the number of times per second that an alternating current changes polarity; measures in Hertz (Hz).

Full-load safety test: a test performed on elevators every five years to ensure the operation of the elevator's safety equipment; required by law.

Fusible link: a metal that will melt at a rated temperature; used in sprinkler heads and **fire and smoke dampers**.

Garbage disposal: a waste disposal device that grinds food into small pieces that can then pass through the building's sewage system.

Geared elevator: a type of traction elevator that uses a worm-and-gear arrangement to turn the sheave; typically used in medium-rise, medium-speed applications.

Gearless elevator: a type of traction elevator where the elevator's motor directly turns the sheave; typically used in high-rise and/or high-speed applications.

Glazing: the windows.

Global warming: the increase in the temperature of the earth since the mid-twentieth century and its projected continuing upward trend. Global warming leads to global climate change, which leads to disastrous consequences for the earth's people, plants, and animals.

Governor: a safety device in an elevator system that protects the elevator from going into an overspeed condition. If the elevator goes too fast, the governor will trip the elevator's safeties to prevent it from falling down (or up!).

Gravity-fed system: another term for a downfeed system.

Graywater: recycled water taken from sinks, laundry, showers/tubs. The water is filtered and minimally sanitized and is then suitable for use in a variety of non-potable applications.

Greenhouse gases: the gases that prevent heat from being transmitted into space, which then lead to global warming. Man is thought to be the chief culprit in the production of these gases through the burning of fossil fuels. They include water vapor, carbon dioxide, methane, nitrous oxide, ozone, and CFCs.

Greenwashing: a term that merges the concepts of "green" (environmentally sound practices) with "whitewashing" (to conceal or gloss over wrongdoing). Greenwashing is any form of marketing or public relations that links an organization to a positive association with environmental issues for an unsustainable product, service, or practice.

Ground fault circuit interrupter (GFCI): a type of electrical receptacle that provides added protection against electrocution; used in wet areas.

Group relamping: a system where all lamps in a group are changed at the same time to save money through reducing labor costs.

Gutters: channels located at the lower edge of sloped roofs that channel water off the roof and away from the building's foundation.

Hauling charges: the fee for transporting waste to a landfill.

Hazardous waste: waste that is toxic to people, the environment, or both. In the United States, the Environmental Protection Agency stipulates how hazardous waste is to be handled.

Heat energy transfer: the natural flow of heat from a warmer object or environment to a cooler object or environment.

Heat pump: a type of heating system that uses the refrigeration cycle in reverse to provide heat to a space.

Heating load: objects or conditions that lead to a requirement to provide heat.

HEPA filter: High Efficiency Particulate Arrestor (HEPA) filters have very high filtration properties for cleaning air of particulate matter.

High intensity discharge (HID) lamp: a group of lamps in the Electric Discharge family.

Human effluent: liquid and semi-solid waste; a byproduct of digestion. *See also* **effluence.**

HVAC: Heating, Ventilation, & Air Conditioning.

Hydraulic elevator: an elevator that is lifted by hydraulics, using a piston and a cylinder. These are generally used in low-speed and/or low-rise applications.

Ignition temperature: the temperature at which an object will spontaneously ignite. A flame does not need to be present for the object to burst into flame. Every material has its own specific ignition temperature.

Incandescent lamp: a type of lamp that is illuminated by passing an electric current through a filament made of a metal with a high resistance rating.

Incipient stage: the beginning stage of a fire. The only stage where it is appropriate to fight a fire with a handheld extinguisher after the alarm is set off.

Indoor air quality: a broad description of an indoor environment's air movement, speed, relative humidity, and levels of pollutants and odors.

Infectious waste: waste that contains pathogens and is potentially dangerous to anyone who may come in contact with it. It is a type of hazardous waste.

Infiltration: usually describes the process of cold or hot air coming from the outdoors and seeping into the building by a variety of paths, such as through cracks, roofs, and doors.

Infiltration heat load: heat that is transported on air currents through open doors, windows, and gaps in walls, windows, and doors.

Instantaneous heater: a type of water heater that does not store hot water, but instead heats the water instantly as it passes through.

Integrated pest management: the use of multiple methods to curtail insects and vermin at a facility; for example, use of proper cleaning procedures at the property so that pests will not be attracted to the property, use of good bugs (e.g., ladybugs, praying mantises, etc.) to control outside insect pests, using different types of insecticides that are effective, and environmentally benign at the same time. *See also* **integrated resource management.**

Integrated resource management: a management strategy that seeks to produce optimal results by applying the right mix of company resources and approaches to an operational problem. Included in the strategy is the realization that there may not be one best approach to all problems. Sometimes a multiplistic approach may be the best method. *See also* **integrated pest management.**

Inventory records: records of supplies, equipment, fixtures, and furniture stored by the engineering department. When an item is requisitioned, the name of the item, the name of the person who requisitioned it, the reason for the request, the date, time, and other essential information will be noted in the inventory record.

Kilowatt: a measure of power. A kilowatt is equal to 1,000 watts or 1.34 horsepower.

Kilowatt hour: a measure of power consumed over time; 1,000 watts consumed over a one-hour period.

Lamp: the technical term for a light bulb.

Lamp life: the average rated life expectancy for a particular lamp.

Landfill: commonly referred to as a *dump.* It is a site where solid waste is sealed underground. Modern landfills are constructed so that the contents of the landfill do not leach into the soil or aquifers as they slowly decompose.

Latent heat: heat that considers both temperature and relative humidity.

Leachate: liquids that drain or *leach* from a landfill. It typically contains hazardous materials.

LEED®: Leadership in Energy and Environmental Design. It is the environmental building certification program of the U.S. Green Building Council (USGBC).

Life cycle cost analysis: an analysis of the total cost of an object from its purchase to its disposal, or "womb to tomb."

Light emitting diode (LED): a semiconductor chip that efficiently converts electricity to light.

Line: those departments that produce the goods and services that the customer purchases. In a hotel, the food and beverage department and the hotel department are the line departments. Line departments are serviced by staff departments. *See also* **staff.**

Live load: the weight of people and objects moving through a building; also called a dynamic load.

Lock-Out/Tag-Out: a safety program, required by OSHA, to prevent employees from the accidental energizing of a power source.

Lumens: the amount of light emitted by a lamp, as measured at the source; also called "lux."

Luminaire: a technical term for a light fixture.

Maintenance log: a record of maintenance activities at the property.

Maintenance schedule: a list of all equipment and areas in a facility that receive preventive maintenance, and a calendar of when the maintenance is to occur for each item or area. The schedule covers an entire year.

Make-up water: water that is added to a cooling tower to make up for water lost through evaporation.

Manage upwards: positively influence one's superiors.

Matching principal of accounting: the process where revenue is recognized and assigned to the period when it is earned, and expenses are also recognized and assigned to the period when they are incurred. This differs from cash accounting where revenues are recognized when the cash is received and expenses are recognized when cash is disbursed.

Material safety data sheets (MSDSs): informational sheets available from manufacturers of chemicals that describe the toxic effects of these chemicals and the proper procedures to use when handling them. The Occupational Safety and Health Administration (OSHA) requires employers to make these forms available to all employees who may be exposed to these chemicals.

Mechanical plan: a floor plan to scale that shows the details of the heating/air-conditioning, plumbing, or both.

Municipal solid waste: commonly known as trash or garbage; waste generated by residential and commercial sources.

National Fire Protection Association (NFPA): its mission is to reduce the worldwide burden of fire and other hazards on the quality of life by providing and advocating consensus codes and standards, research, training, and education.

Natural draft convection: this process occurs when air currents present transport heat, as in a natural draft oven. There is no fan.

1990 Hotel and Motel Fire Safety Act: an act of Congress intended to increase the fire safety of hotels and motels. It is generally regarded as a largely ineffective piece of legislation.

Off-gassing: the tendency for materials to emit vapors and chemicals. Hotel and restaurant managers are particularly concerned with this issue with regards to Indoor Air Quality and materials that contain high levels of volatile, organic compounds (VOCs).

Ohm: a unit of electrical resistance.

OSHA: the Occupational Safety and Health Administration.

Out-of-order: the status of a room that has a maintenance problem and cannot be rented. A few hotel companies distinguish between out-of-order and out-of-inventory. Out-of-inventory rooms cannot be rented, but an out-of-order room is still inhabitable. The maintenance problem does not make the room uninhabitable. For example, a room with a broken television would be an out-of-order room.

Outside air: fresh air that is introduced into an air handling system's air supply. The percentage of outside air required by law ranges from 10 to 30%.

Outsource (outsourced): the process of subcontracting a function in the enterprise to an outside third party. The purpose of outsourcing is typically based on cost reduction, but it may also be based on other factors, such as the need for expertise not found in the organization.

Overtime callbacks: an option in many maintenance contracts that provides service calls outside normal working hours in the event of an equipment failure at no additional charge to the customer.

Ozone: a gas used to sanitize water in swimming pools and laundry systems. It consists of three oxygen atoms (O_3).

Package terminal air conditioner (PTAC): a stand-alone heating/cooling unit that is often used in guestrooms and offices in the hospitality industry. It is also called a "through-the-wall" unit; a small version of a "package unit."

Package unit: usually a decentralized heating and cooling system that is used to condition the air in larger rooms and public spaces; also referred to as a "split system" or, for cooling, a "DX" system.

Passenger elevator: an elevator that is rated for use by the general public.

Peak-shaving: a method of reducing electrical demand for short periods of time during peak generation hours; used to reduce demand charges in electric bills.

Peel: a large wooden paddle on a long handle used to place and remove pizzas from a pizza oven.

Pendant: a sprinkler head that hangs down from a branch line. The water is emitted in a 360° pattern.

Performance standards: expectations written by management for each duty that is performed by an employee.

Perspective projection: an architectural rendering that represents what is seen by one's eyes. The illusion of depth, height, and width is rendered in the drawing.

PETE: polyethylene terephthalate, a plastic commonly used in food packaging.

Photovoltaic power: electricity generated by the sun.

Piling: an element of a deep foundation system that transfers the building's weight deep into the ground onto stable soil or bedrock.

Piston and cylinder: the devices that raise and lower a hydraulic elevator.

Plenum: metal channels through which air travels; a type of air duct.

Plot: also known as a survey plan. It is a bird's eye view of a building and the land it is on. It is to scale and, in addition to the architecture, it shows landscape features including the slope of the property with the display of contour lines.

Post incident program: a set of planned activities that follow an emergency (e.g., generating press releases, arranging accommodations for guests after a property fire, etc.).

Potable water (potability): water fit for human consumption.

PPM: parts per million.

Pre-cast concrete: concrete mixed, poured, and formed in a factory, as opposed to on-site.

Predictive maintenance: maintenance that uses sensors and computers to determine when maintenance should be conducted on a particular piece of equipment; also known as condition-based maintenance.

Pre-opening budget: a special, one-time budget whose funds are allocated for all of the extraordinary expenses associated with the opening of a property. Pre-opening budgets include the entire costs of employee pre-opening training, china, glass, and silverware in the restaurants, and any costs associated with opening parties and galas. In the engineering department, in addition to training, it would cover all of the tools and equipment needed to maintain the hotel. Pre-opening budgets are usually amortized over three to five years so they don't negatively impact the property's first-year performance.

Pressure drop (in water systems): occurs when water loses pressure over distances or when it needs to travel upwards. The result is a weak flow at the fixture.

Pressure relief valve (PRV): a valve on a hot water or steam boiler that permits the release of excessive pressure, and thus prevents explosions.

Pressurization system: ventilation fans that can be reversed in order to exhaust smoke from a room during a building fire, or they may be used to create a positive air pressure in a room so that smoke cannot migrate into the space.

Preventive maintenance: also known as time-based maintenance; maintenance that is conducted to prevent unnecessary wear and premature failure of equipment, fixtures, and furnishings; usually done on a schedule or after a certain number of hours of operation of a piece of equipment.

Process improvement team: a cross-functional team consisting of employees on all levels of the organization who are working toward a common goal, such as the elimination of problems in the operation of the organization.

Product heat load: heat generated by uncooled food and beverages that must be removed to eliminate spoilage or bacterial growth.

Products of combustion: heat, light, smoke (particulates), and gases. The gases may include carbon monoxide, carbon dioxide, and other gases depending on the substance being burned.

Property management system (PMS): software that performs many different functions in a hotel, such as, payroll and timekeeping, room inventory, yield management, reservations, point of sales systems, and accounting; they may even have a work order preparation package. However, most PMS systems do not contain other engineering-related computerized functions, such as energy management systems.

Property operation and maintenance (POM): the annual maintenance cost of a facility; includes wages, benefits, supplies, and contracted labor (outsourcing) in the daily maintenance of the facility; does not include major remodeling, refurbishment, or renovation costs.

PSI: pounds per square inch. There is psia (pounds per square inch absolute), which is the psig (pounds per square inch gauge pressure which does not take into account the atmospheric pressure) plus the aforementioned atmospheric pressure.

P-Trap: a section of piping immediately below the sink, shower or tub, and toilet drains that provides a liquid seal to block sewer gases.

Pulper: a waste disposal device that shreds primarily food products, cardboard, and paper with water. Then the water is extracted, leaving a dry waste product that takes up less space than the original material. This reduces waste disposal costs.

Ratchet clause: an item found on electric billing tariffs for commercial properties; usually includes a penalty over time for the highest point in electrical demand.

Reactive maintenance: also known as emergency maintenance. *See also* **run-to-failure maintenance**.

Readily achievable: ADA modifications that must be done unless the modifications would cause extreme economic hardship or a great deal of difficulty. The courts decide if a modification is readily achievable for a company.

Reasonable accommodation: An ADA modification that must be done to accommodate a disabled employee unless the modification would cause the business extreme economic hardship. The courts decide if modification is reasonable.

Recycling: the reducing of a product to its elements and then making a new product out of those elements. The purpose is to prevent the wasting of valuable materials, to reduce the need to use new materials, to reduce energy use, and to reduce air, water, and solid waste pollution.

Refrigerant: a man-made chemical that gives off heat when placed under pressure and also evaporates readily when the pressure is reduced; commonly referred to as Freon® which is actually a brand name of a particular refrigerant (i.e., R-22).

Relative humidity: the amount of water vapor the air holds at various temperatures.

Reliability centered maintenance: the determination of the appropriate maintenance strategy (i.e., condition-based, preventive, or emergency) for each piece of equipment in a facility, based on safety and cost concerns.

Remote annunciation systems: an earlier generation of fire detection systems. These systems could not pinpoint the exact location of an alarm. They could only report the approximate location, such as a floor or wing of a building where there was an alarm.

Reserve for replacement: an account into which revenues are placed in the anticipation that the property will need remodeling, refurbishment, and major renovation in the future. The average annual amount that should be placed in the account is 7%.

Retro-commissioning: *See* **commissioning/recommissioning (of a building).**

Return duct: a metal channel through which "used" air in a room travels back to be reconditioned, i.e., heated, cooled, humidified/dehumidified.

Reuse: a waste management strategy that uses an item more than once.

Riser: a large vertical pipe.

Risk manager: in this context, a risk manager is responsible for the mitigation of risk for a property stemming from physical and legal causes (e.g., fire, flood, accidents, etc.) through the use of managerial resources.

Room data cards: a form (electronic or hard copy) that contains essential information on a guestroom. Items that may appear on the form include room furnishings, fixtures, information on the décor, and data on the HVAC system in the room.

Routine maintenance: simple maintenance activities, such as mowing the lawn, oiling squeaky door hinges, cleaning graffiti off a wall, changing a guestroom light bulb, etc.

Routine maintenance request: a mid-level priority work request. Emergency requests and routine requests that have been received prior to this most recent routine maintenance request will be corrected first.

Run-to-failure maintenance: also known as emergency maintenance, reactive maintenance, or breakdown maintenance. This can be the most costly type of maintenance but not in every instance. When the cost or life safety is an issue, however, it is not an appropriate strategy.

R-Value: a material's thermal resistance to heat transfer; a measure of insulating value.

Sanitary sewer system: a system of wastewater piping that carries water out of the building and into the city's sewer system or into a septic tank.

Sanitizer: a chemical that reduces pathogens on a surface to an acceptable level.

Scale: a build-up of minerals on pipes and other equipment.

Scheduled maintenance: maintenance that takes planning, assembling of materials, equipment, and personnel in order to carry out. Examples would include acid washing the hotel swimming pool at the end of the season or the disassembling and cleaning of the boilers. It is a form of preventive maintenance.

Schedules: a procedural plan that indicates the time and sequence of each operation. Examples would be employee work schedules and maintenance schedules.

Section plan: an architectural drawing of a cross-section of a wall or other object. The rendering looks as if a saw neatly sliced through the object.

Seismic load: the movement of the building's weight during an earthquake.

Self-certification: first-party certification; occurs when an organization makes the claim that it has examined its practices and that these practices meet a self-imposed standard. It is a highly suspect practice and the weakest form of certification available.

Sensible heat: the actual temperature; measured using a thermometer; does not consider relative humidity.

Septic system: a type of liquid wastewater management system that removes harmful substances and returns water to the environment; used when the property is not connected to a city sewer system.

Shear load: the force of the wind on a building and the movement it causes.

Sidewall: a sprinkler head that extends out of a wall. Water emerges in a 180° pattern.

Smoke and fire damper: a device found in ventilation ducts to prevent the migration of smoke and fire during a building fire.

Soft goods: upholstered furniture (e.g., mattresses, couches, chairs, etc.).

Source reduction: a waste management strategy that prevents materials from entering into the waste stream by eliminating or minimizing packaging and by buying products in bulk.

Staff: departments that serve the line, such as accounting, marketing, human resources, and engineering.

Standard operating procedures (SOP): written directives that describe how to correctly perform a task to produce a desired result. SOPs are a form of delegation that allows an employee to perform a task correctly with minimal oversight by the management.

Storm sewer system (storm water system): a sewer system that removes environmental water, such as landscaping run-off, snow melt, and rainwater.

Sub-metering: a way that a property that has multiple utility meters can make a determination on how much energy or water is being used by different parts of the property. For example, a property has two electric meters, one on the hotel side and one on the food and beverage side, so that the amount of electricity the kitchen and dining room is using can be determined and monitored. If there is just one meter, it is far more difficult to monitor electrical usage by area or function.

Supply duct: a metal channel through with conditioned air is supplied to a space.

Survey plan: *See* **plot.**

Sustainable: the ability to meet the needs of the current generation without compromising the needs of future generations.

TAB: the testing, adjusting, and balancing of equipment so that it operates as it was designed to operate. *See also* **balancing (a system)** and **commissioning/ recommissioning (of a building).**

Thermal break: a vacuum space between two objects that provides insulation; used in double- and triple-pane windows to increase energy efficiency.

Thermostat: a device that senses the temperature in an area and signals the HVAC system to heat or cool the room.

Third-party certification: the most credible form of certification, because the certification is performed by a disinterested third party who is not controlled or influenced by the organization seeking the certification.

Time-based maintenance: also known as preventive maintenance. *See also* **preventive maintenance.**

Tipping fee: the charge levied for waste delivered to a landfill.

Total quality management: a management approach that focuses on quality, requires the participation of all of the company's employees, and whose goal is the continued improvement of the organization, to the benefit of its customers, employees, and the community in which the organization resides.

Traction elevator: an elevator that is raised and lowered using ropes (cables). They are also called "electric" or "cable" elevators. The two types of traction elevators are geared and gearless.

Transformer: a device that increases or decreases the voltage of an electrical current.

Transmission heat load: heat that passes through walls.

Trend logging: the tracking of changes over time. An example would be the continuous monitoring and recording of temperatures in an area of a building.

Triple bottom line: the accomplishments of a company measured not just in the amount of money the company makes, but also on its impact on the community where it is located and the environment. Profits are important—indeed they are essential for survival—but people and the planet are equally important.

Troubleshoot: a form of problem solving. It is a systematic search for the source of a problem.

Truss: the framework in which an escalator operates.

Unintended throwaways: items of value that enter the waste stream. These items may have to be repurchased by the facility. Examples would include china, glasses, silverware, cleaning products, and towels.

Upright: a sprinkler head that is on top of a branch line. This arrangement is used in storage facilities and other areas, but not in hotel rooms.

UPS system: Uninterruptible Power Supply system; provides continuous, clean power to electronic devices during a power outage or other events with power quality problems.

Utilities: electrical, gas, fuel oil, water, sewer, waste disposal, and in some locales, steam costs; sometimes referred to as energy costs, but that term does not encompass all aspects.

Vertical transportation: a broad category of systems that move people and materials up or down through a building or space.

Volt: a unit of electrical pressure.

Waste: an unwanted or undesirable material; also known as garbage, junk, trash, and rubbish. It is also viewed as a cost. This term can be used as a noun or a verb.

Waste stream: the flow of waste generated by a facility and its inhabitants.

Water feature: a broad category of decorative water systems, such as fountains and ponds.

Water-tube boiler: a type of hot water or steam boiler where a vessel containing fire has pipes full of water passing through it to conduct heat transfer into the water.

Watt: a unit of electrical power. One thousand watts equals one kilowatt.

Wet-bulb temperature: a measure of temperature that accounts for both sensible heat and relative humidity.

Wet pipe: a type of sprinkler system that contains water at the sprinkler head. It is more common in warm climates.

Work order: a formal request for work to be done; also known as a repair order. Those who may initiate a work order may be limited at some properties, but other properties may allow anyone in the organization to submit a work order, including guests. There are standing work orders as well as requested work orders. The standing work orders are for preventive maintenance activities. Work orders often have different degrees of urgency with those items that have safety issues ranked at the top of the hierarchy.

Work schedule: a schedule showing the days and hours an employee is expected to work.

Xeriscaping: a method of landscaping for arid environments; usually uses indigenous plants that have already adapted to local conditions.

Zero-based budgeting: a budgetary process that starts with a *clean slate*. Every budgetary amount must be justified by the budget maker—not just an increase of an item. There are no assumptions made under zero-base budgeting.

Zero-sum game: a game that has both winners and losers. For every winner there must be a loser.

INDEX

(NOTE: "f" indicates a figure)